D0597010

TO APPOMATTOX

★

Nine April Days, 1865

TO APPOMATTOX

Nine April Days, 1865

BURKE DAVIS

★

Rinehart & Company, Inc.

NEW YORK   TORONTO

Published simultaneously in Canada by
Clarke, Irwin & Company, Ltd., Toronto

The Author gratefully acknowledges the following invaluable sources: ALEXANDER C. HASKELL, by Louise Haskell Daly (Plimpton Press, Norwood, Mass., 1934); A. P. HILL: LEE'S FORGOTTEN GENERAL, by W. W. Hassler (Garret and Massie, Richmond, 1957); AUTOBIOGRAPHY OF CHARLES FRANCIS ADAMS (Boston, 1916); *The Confederate Veteran;* IMPRESSIONS OF LINCOLN AND THE CIVIL WAR, by Adolphe de Chambrun (New York, 1952); THE LIFE OF GENERAL ELY S. PARKER, by Arthur C. Parker (Buffalo, N. Y., 1919); MEADE'S HEADQUARTERS, 1863-1865: Letters of Colonel Theodore Lyman, edited by George R. Agassiz (Massachusetts Historical Society, 1922. Atlantic Monthly Press); MEMORIES AND MEMORIALS OF WILLIAM GORDON MCCABE, Vol. 1, by Armistead C. Gordon (Richmond, 1925); MEMORIES OF THE WHITE HOUSE, by W. H. Crook (Boston, 1911); REMINISCENCES OF THE CIVIL WAR, by John B. Gordon (Scribner, 1903); RUSTICS IN REBELLION, by George A. Townsend (Univ. of N. C. Press, 1950); THE SUNSET OF THE CONFEDERACY, by Morris Schaff (Luce, 1912); THREE YEARS WITH GRANT, by Sylvanus Cadwallader (Knopf, 1955); and WAR YEARS WITH JEB STUART, by W. W. Blackford (Scribner, 1945).

The Author further acknowledges with thanks the permission of the following to quote material from their publications:

Thomas Y. Crowell Company, New York, N. Y., for brief excerpts from SOUTH AFTER GETTYSBURG, Copyright © 1937, 1956 by Henrietta Stratton Jaquette.

Duke University Library, for use of the unpublished manuscript, "History of the Battle of Five Forks," by Thomas T. Munford.

Emory University Library, Special Collections Department, Emory University, Georgia, for excerpts from A CONFEDERATE DIARY OF THE RETREAT FROM PETERSBURG, April 3-20, 1865. Edited, with an introduction by Richard Barkesdale Harwell (Emory Sources & Reprints, Series VIII, number 1). Copyright 1953 by the Emory University Library.

Scott Hart, of Washington, D. C., for a brief quotation from an unpublished address on the Appomattox campaign.

Mississippi Department of Archives and History, Jackson, Mississippi, for excerpts from JEFFERSON DAVIS, CONSTITUTIONALIST, Volume VI of the LETTERS, PAPERS AND SPEECHES OF JEFFERSON DAVIS, edited by Dunbar Rowland.

The University of North Carolina, Southern Historical Collection, for the use of the "Diary" of J. A. Albright.

Virginia Historical Society, Richmond, Virginia, for permission to quote from the Southern Historical Society *Papers.*

To Mary Ellen Blackmon, Alan Manchester, Vera Largent,
Algie Newlin and Hugh Lefler, teachers and historians

★ CONTENTS ★

TO APPOMATTOX

★

Nine April Days, 1865

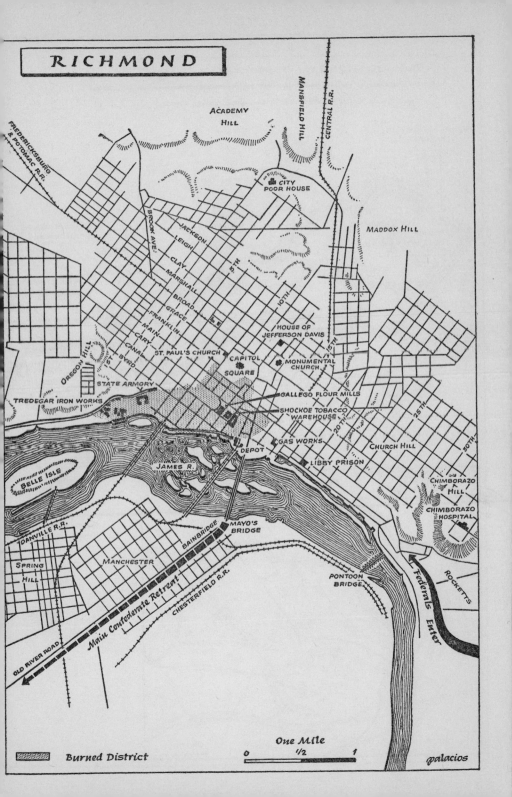

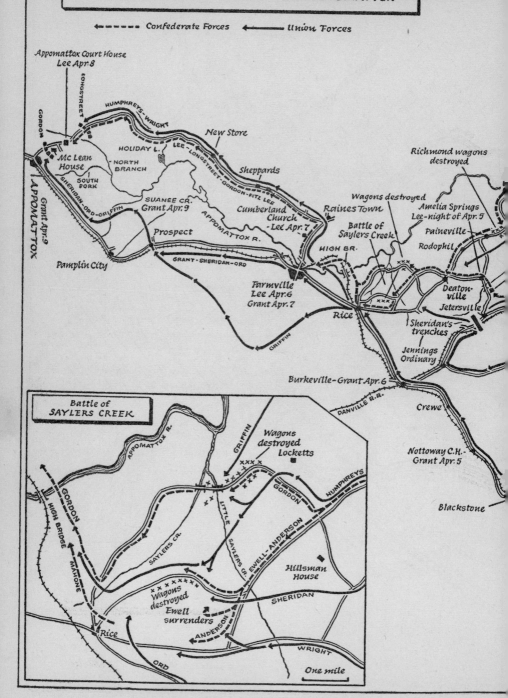

From RICHMOND and PETERSBURG to APPOMATTOX

←----- Confederate Forces ← Union Forces

Appomattox Court House
Lee Apr. 8

LONGSTREET

Richmond wagons
destroyed

HUMPHREYS-WRIGHT

GORDON

New Store

HOLIDAY L.

NORTH
BRANCH

McLean
House

SOUTH
FORK

SHERIDAN-ORD-GRIFFIN

LEE-LONGSTREET

Wagons destroyed

Sheppards

Amelia Springs
Lee-night of Apr. 5

Paineville

APPOMATTOX

Grant Apr. 9

SUANEE CR.
Grant Apr. 9

LEE-LONGSTREET-GORDON-FITZ LEE

Cumberland
Church
Lee Apr. 7

Raines Town

Battle of
Saylers Creek

Rodophil

Prospect

APPOMATTOX R.

HIGH BR.

XX

Deaton-
ville

Jetersville

Pamplin City

GRANT-SHERIDAN-ORD

Farmville
Lee Apr. 6
Grant Apr. 7

XXX

Rice

Sheridan's
trenches

GRIFFIN

Jennings
Ordinary

Burkeville-Grant Apr. 6

Crewe

DANVILLE R.R.

Nottoway C.H.-
Grant Apr. 5

Blackstone

Battle of
SAYLERS CREEK

APPOMATTOX R.

GRIFFIN

Wagons
destroyed
Locketts

XXX

GORDON

HIGH BRIDGE

MAHONE

SAYLERS CR.

LITTLE SAYLERS CR.

GORDON

HUMPHREYS

EWELL-ANDERSON

Hillsman
House

Wagons
destroyed
Ewell
surrenders

SHERIDAN

Rice

ANDERSON

ORD

WRIGHT

One mile

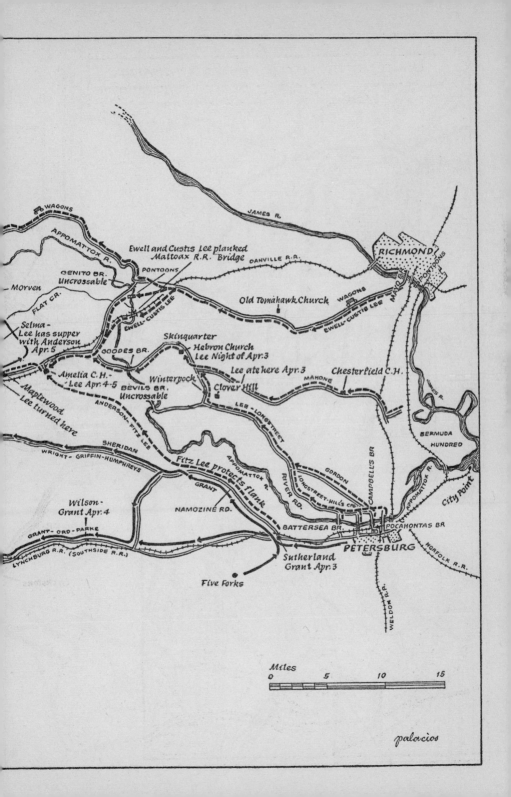

WAGONS

APPOMATTOX R.

JAMES R.

RICHMOND

Ewell and Custis Lee planked
Mattoax R.R. Bridge

DANVILLE R.R.

PONTOONS

PONTOONS

GENITO BR.
Uncrossable

Morven

FLAT CR.

EWELL-CUSTIS LEE

Old Tomahawk Church

WAGONS

MAJOR CR.

EWELL-CUSTIS LEE

JAMES R.

Selma -
Lee has supper
with Anderson
Apr. 5

GOODES BR.

Skinquarter

Hebron Church
Lee Night of Apr. 3

Lee ate here Apr. 3

Chesterfield C.H.

Amelia C.H. -
Lee Apr. 4-5

BEVILS BR.
Uncrossable

Winterpock

Clover Hill

MAHONE

Maplewood
Lee turned here

ANDERSON-FITZ LEE

LEE - LONGSTREET

BERMUDA
HUNDRED

SHERIDAN

WRIGHT - GRIFFIN - HUMPHREYS

Fitz Lee protects flank

APPOMATTOX R.

GORDON

LONGSTREET-HILL'S CR.

CAMPBELL'S BR.

APPOMATTOX R.

City Point

Wilson -
Grant Apr. 4

GRANT

NAMOZINE RD.

RIVER RD.

BATTERSEA BR.

POCAHONTAS BR.

GRANT - ORD - PARKE

LYNCHBURG R.R. (SOUTHSIDE R.R.)

Five Forks

Sutherland
Grant Apr. 3

PETERSBURG

NORFOLK R.R.

WELDON R.R.

Miles

0   5   10   15

palacios

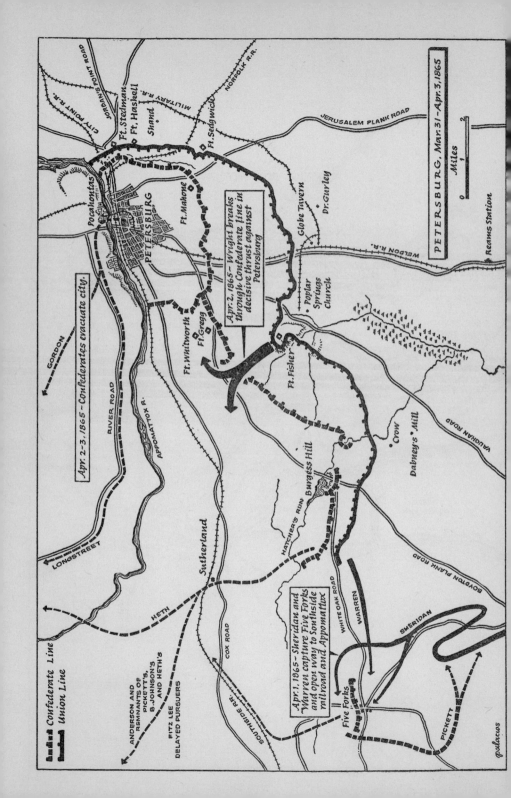

PETERSBURG, Mar. 31 – Apr. 3, 1865

Miles
0   1   2

Confederate Line
Union Line

JERUSALEM PLANK ROAD

NORFOLK R.R.

Ft. Sedgwick

Globe Tavern

Dr. Gurley

Reams Station

WELDON R.R.

Ft. Stedman
Ft. Haskell
Shand

MILITARY R.R.

JORDAN'S POINT ROAD

CITY POINT R.R.

Pocahontas

Ft. Mahone

PETERSBURG

Poplar Springs Church

Apr. 2, 1865 – Wright breaks through Confederate line in decisive thrust against Petersburg

Ft. Whitworth

Ft. Gregg

Ft. Fisher

GORDON

RIVER ROAD

APPOMATTOX R.

Apr. 2-3, 1865 – Confederates evacuate city.

Crow

Dabney's Mill

VAUGHAN ROAD

LONGSTREET

Sutherland

HETH

Hatcher's Run

Burgess Mill

COX ROAD

SOUTHSIDE R.R.

ANDERSON AND
REMNANTS OF
PICKETT'S,
B. JOHNSON'S
AND HETH'S

FITZ LEE
DELAYED PURSUERS

Apr. 1, 1865 – Sheridan and Warren capture Five Forks and open way to Southside railroad and Appomattox

WHITE OAK ROAD

WARREN

Five Forks

SHERIDAN

PICKETT

BOYDTON PLANK ROAD

Pollacus

I

Prologue

★

THE WINDS of late March scuffed the dark James and tore tatters of smoke from factory chimneys. They howled on the barred windows of Libby and Belle Isle, where the prisoners were, and fell upon crowds in Capitol Square, where people stared at drilling Negro troops of the Confederacy—the first.

In moments when the wind died a humid heat came from the river, and there was something more: The pulsing of guns from the south and west, louder today.

A nineteen-year-old midshipman climbed from the Navy landing at the waterside, a gunner on a day's leave from a river Battery. His name was James Morris Morgan.

Morgan had almost a thousand dollars on his back, for he wore a splendid new gray uniform whose cloth he had sought in the shops for weeks. His boots, sickly in color, half-tanned and squeaky, had cost $300. But he had so spruce a look that he had more than once, these last few days, been asked to stand as a groomsman at a wedding.

In store windows as the boy passed were crude signs telling as surely as if they were calendars of Richmond's four years at war:

Bacon, $20 a pound. Live hens, $50 each. Beef, $15 a pound. Fresh shad, $50 a pair. Butter, $20 a pound.

A hundred thousand people now thronged the little city and the markets could not decently feed 70,000—to say nothing of the army in the trenches outside.

Young Morgan walked through Capitol Square beneath tossed branches of budding trees, and into the building where the Confederate Congress was in session.

Even here he heard the guns. Timbers shuddered underfoot and there was a rattling of windowpanes. He went into the Senate chamber for a few minutes and emerged with an expression of youthful outrage. The Senators had to raise their voices to be heard over the guns—yet they were debating the question of just how many newspapers should be left on their desks each morning.

Morgan wandered downhill into one of the hospitals, a converted tobacco warehouse still odorous of its trade, now packed with sick and wounded; women of the city passed among the cots.

Near the doorway Morgan found the friend for whom he sought, Captain F. W. Dawson, a wounded cavalryman who had ridden with Jeb Stuart in the war's good old days.

Dawson lay in the cooling breezes from the door, his pale face flat on his cot. He whispered, "For God's sake, Jimmy, make 'em move me to the back."

"You'll get no air back there," Morgan said. "This is the best spot you could find."

Dawson shook his head. "Every damned woman that comes in that door scrubs my face and pokes me full of homemade jelly. My face is sore and I'm ready to pop."

Morgan laughed, but he sent a note to the head surgeon and did not leave until he had seen an order fixed to Dawson's cot:

This man must be washed and fed only by regular nurses.

Young Morgan left him at last and went back to his guns by the river.

Fannie Walker was a copying clerk in the Bureau of War, an earnest young woman who shared the optimism of the city's youth.

Late in the afternoon as she was on the point of leaving her office amid a swarm of girls, Dr. Cooke, her chief clerk, entered with a final packet of letters for copying. Fannie began work anew with a sigh. As she opened the pack she glanced at the signature: ". . . R. E. Lee."

Her pen scratched a few lines and halted. She turned to Cooke. "Oh, Doctor! If this is true we are lost!"

Cooke glanced at the dispatch. General Lee made an urgent request for more troops and provisions. Without them, the message said, "we cannot hold Petersburg." Not even Richmond pretended that there were more troops or provisions.

Cooke shook his head. "Remember," he said, "mum's the word."

Fannie went home with a burden of dread she dared not reveal; she thought that she must be one of the few people in Richmond who knew that the city was doomed.

Only the heedless could not sense catastrophe at hand. One of those who had expected it daily was Captain Micajah H. Clark, a confidential secretary to President Jefferson Davis who had once been in the Treasury Department. Clark now watched gloomily the long queues of civilians and warworn soldiers who crowded about the doors of the Treasury.

For almost a month, "for the relief of the people," the Treasury had passed out silver coin—at the rate of $1 for each $60 in paper. Most of the city's people had not seen such coins since the beginning of the war. Clark knew that the silver could have but one purpose: It could be spent outside the Confederate lines when the Yankees broke through. The ratio of paper to silver was rising; it would soon reach 70 to 1.

In one large house, as in dozens of others this night, a "Starvation Party" was in progress. The music and laughter, as noted by a young diarist, T. C. DeLeon, matched that of the brilliant balls of other days. More than a hundred young women and their escorts thronged the party. Most of the men had come from the trenches since nightfall.

DeLeon thought the young men "worn and tired from camp and famished for society and gayety of some sort." An old Negro fiddler provided the music and, when the growing dance drowned out his tunes, a girl in a rather frowsy dress joined the Negro, playing a piano.

Refreshments were forbidden, and on tables were ranged ornate bowls, relics of the gay old life, now filled with water. Nothing stifled the high spirits of the dancers.

"Never, amid the blare of the best-trained bands," DeLeon said, "the popping of champagne, and the clatter of forks over *pâté de foie gras,* was there more genuine enjoyment and more courtly chivalry than at these primitive soirees."

The party went through the dances of the "graceless, God-less German cotillion" in defiance of the city's pious elder citizens who had proclaimed them sinful. From his corner DeLeon watched admiringly:

"Despite the denunciations, the ridicule, and even the active intervention of one or two ministers, the young soldiers and their partners whirled away as though they had never heard a slander or a sermon."

DeLeon wrote as if he could hear, above the tinny music, Richmond's struggle to preserve the old social amenities as she neared ruin. He spoke for the young men in the room:

" 'But,' said the dancers, 'we do the fighting—we are the ones who are killed—and if we don't object, why in the deuce should you? Cooped up in camp, with mud and musty bacon for living, and the whistling of miniés and whooshing of shells for episode, we long for some pleasure when we can get off. This is the sole enjoyment we have, and we go back better men in every way for it.' "

The dance went on.

DeLeon seemed to haunt every entertainment in the city, lured by music and laughter as they drowned "rumble of dead cart and ambulance."

DeLeon saw that the gaiety was a feverish symptom of Confederate weakness, "only a spasm." In the streets he saw what was happening: "Desertions from the army were assuming fearful proportions that no legislation or executive rigor could diminish. Every day saw brigades double-quicking back and forth through the suburbs; the continuous scream of steam whistles told of movements here and there, and every indication showed that the numbers of men were inadequate to man the vast extent of the lines."

Day after day in late March he saw covert moves of the government: First the archives and papers of the departments; then heavier stores, guns and supplies not in daily use; then the few reserve medical supplies rattled off in the infrequent trains from the Danville depot; last of all, the young women of the clerical offices, sent to safety in Columbia, South Carolina.

A. R. Tomlinson, a wounded soldier, was now a sergeant of guards at Winder Hospital. He was always hungry, and could hardly stand his post between the meals of gruel and small bits of bread. He watched others eating but could not bring himself to join them.

He wrote: "The surgeons and matrons ate rats and said they were as good as squirrels, but, having seen the rats in the morgue running over the bodies of the dead soldiers, I had no relish for them."

Colonel Walter Taylor often came into the city from Petersburg in these days. He usually went first to his fiancée, Elizabeth Selden Saunders, the daughter of a prewar Federal Navy captain. Taylor was a romantic figure, a slight, handsome, still well-dressed boy in his mid-twenties who had spent the war as General Lee's most intimate staff officer. His coat was perhaps a bit large, but the cloth was fine and the sleeves were looped with gold. Taylor wore a tiny mustache and a struggling Vandyke.

Near the end of March he visited other women friends in their fallen estate at a rooming house called The Arlington. They were three women, a mother, daughter and a stranger taken in, out of necessity, to share their small room. In other days they had lived like empresses in the city, with a great house, several carriages and servants they hardly troubled to count. Taylor gallantly concealed the name of the proud family in his memoirs.

Now, as he climbed steep stairs to their room, he had no need to be told their story. Sights, sounds and smells were enough. There were a few pieces of furniture, including a lumpy bed. A crude coalbin occupied one corner. Sticks of stovewood were piled under the bed. Taylor laughed:

"I fully expect to come here some day and find a pig tied to the bed, and a brood or two of poultry."

He was not far wrong. Until a day or so earlier the women

had had a hen tethered to the bed, stuffing her with dried peas in a vain attempt to fatten her for the pot. They cooked on a fireplace grate—though when there was a miracle and they found a stringy roast or a pound of flour, they might command the services of a Negro cook who lived in the rear of the house.

Rent for the room was $25 a month, the price of a large house in prewar days.

These women were friends of Taylor's fiancée, Betsy Saunders, and they had a gay hour together, as a climax descending to the landlady's rooms to play the piano and sing. When Taylor had gone, gaiety disappeared and the women returned to work. They huddled near the failing source of light at the windows and went back to their sewing. From odd bits of silk they knitted ties and socks and sold them in the streets. Profits went into sorghum and tea and other delicacies, for the staples of their diet were inevitable: boiled rice, dried apples, beans, and field peas, day after day.

John Beauchamp Jones was a leader of Richmond culture. He had been editor of *The Saturday Visitor* and *The Southern Monitor*, in Baltimore, had been praised by Poe, and was author of the novel, *Wild Western Scenes*, which had sold more than 100,000 copies before the war. He had married a Virginian and come to Richmond as a War Department clerk to see the conflict at first hand.

Now, as spring came on, Jones recovered from an illness and his only work was the daily entry in his diary. On March twenty-ninth he had a little smoked herring and a cup of tea, all that his house afforded. He felt better, reduced his medicine to ten grains of blue mass and told himself that he must avoid overexertion. He had a visit from General Lee's son Custis, who had spent most of the war in Richmond offices. Jones did not neglect the diary, and he seemed to see or hear everything:

> The papers give forth an uncertain sound of what is going on in the field, or of what is likely to occur. The Negro experiment will soon be tested. Custis says letters are pouring in at the Department from all quarters, asking

authority to raise and command Negro troops. One hundred
thousand recruits from this source might do wonders.

He recorded a dispatch from General Lee in the field, reporting that the Federal cavalryman, Sheridan, had swept around
Confederate lines below Petersburg, crossing Hatcher's Run and
marching for Dinwiddie Court House. The enemy aim was to
cut the Southside Railroad. Jones thought they might succeed,
and cited the ominous words of General Lee:

> We have here no adequate force of cavalry to oppose
> Sheridan, and it may be possible, if Sheridan turns his head
> this way, that shell may be thrown into the city.

Jones noted an even more insistent sign that all was not well:

> Mrs. President Davis has left the city with her children
> for the South. . . . Some of their furniture has been sent to
> auction.

Inflation had not spared Jefferson Davis. The distant Mississippi cotton empire was no longer able to sustain his family in
the capital.

He had already sold his own horses, except for one he
rode daily, and he was now forced to sell at auction even the
matched team of carriage horses used by his wife. A band of
patriots rescued the animals from the auctioneer and sent them
back to the Confederate White House with compliments. The
eminent man of business, James Lyons, signed their note. The
horses had cost the Samaritans $12,000—but today that was, after
all, only $240 in hard money.

No sooner had Varina Davis got back her carriage horses
than a provost marshal's guard halted her on the street and seized
them once more, leading them away for government use. The
President would not lift a hand to save them, but again wealthy
friends returned the animals to the household.

They were still in want at the Presidential mansion. The
public began to note in store windows items which had become
familiar during the four-year reign of the Mississippi Rose as
First Lady of the Confederacy: an old green silk gown, laces,

silks, gloves, feathers, artificial flowers; and from the rooms of the mansion, imported works of art, furniture, china, glass and silver. Gossiping women knew more certainly than from an official pronouncement that the end was at hand.

Varina Howell Davis was almost thirty-nine years old, a dark-eyed, striking woman of no real beauty. She had already merged into Southern legend, though leaders of Richmond society had greeted her coolly. She was a bona fide patrician, if any were, though the roots of her lineage spread beyond the Mason-Dixon Line. Her paternal grandfather, William Burr Howell, had been Governor of New Jersey and a naval officer in the War of 1812. Her mother was a Virginian, Margaret Louise Kemp, who was born on farmlands over which the battles of Bull Run were to be fought. Grandfather Kemp, a man of means and a graduate of Trinity College, Cambridge, had been a refugee from Ireland to Virginia, fleeing a charge of treason; in turn, he had fled to Mississippi after killing a Virginian in a duel.

Varina was the second Mrs. Jefferson Davis. She had lost one son in infancy, and another, little Joe, had fallen to his death from a porch of the Confederate White House during the war. Now, in this March of 1865, there were four Davis children: Maggie, nine; Jefferson, Junior, seven; Willie, four; and the baby, Varina Anne, a fat, red, teething infant of nine months.

One morning in the last week of the month Davis faced his wife with an expression of finality on his grim lips. She had expected the crisis for months, and saw that he had been postponing it with dread. She thought his air "gentle, but decided."

"My headquarters must soon be in the field, Winnie," he said.

She stared at the firelight on the Carrara marbles of the hearth with a feeling she would not see it again.

"Yes, Banny, but——"

"You and the children would only grieve and embarrass me. You know there will be no place for you."

"I can't leave you."

The hollow-cheeked President brought it to an end:

"I have confidence that you can care for the babies, and I know you want to help me. The only way is to take them to a safe place."

She thought she had never seen him so sad as when he said at last:

"If I live you can come to me when it's over. But I don't expect to . . . survive the destruction of constitutional liberty."

There was a touch of his old fire in the final words, but he reached into a pocket and poured in her hand a small mound of gold coins; he kept for himself one five-dollar piece. He also gave her a bundle of Confederate bills; his engraved image stared up at her from one of them with a hawklike defiance.

He had few further instructions.

"I hope you will not ask any of our Richmond friends to keep our silver plate," he said. "It might bring some outrage upon them, if the enemy found them out."

"I can take the flour with me, I suppose, Ban."

"No," he said, "you must not take away anything in the shape of food. The people need it so badly. You must leave it here."

She turned to the house servants, giving orders to take furnishings to the auction houses and to begin the packing.

A few hours later Davis came into her room with a small pistol, twirling its chamber and showing her how to load, aim and fire it. He was like a solemn schoolmaster before a child who did not fathom the hidden meaning of his words.

"If you fall into . . . the wrong hands," he said, "you can at least force them to kill you. But you must do as I say. When you hear the enemy approaching, wherever you are, you must go. If they will not leave you undisturbed in our country, make for the Florida coast and take a ship."

There were few last-minute details. Varina asked her Irish housekeeper, Mrs. Omelia, to see that the remaining treasures went into safe places, but she did not trust the woman, and feared that all would be lost.

Good news came from the auction house—a draft for $28,400, for goods gobbled up by eager shoppers. By telegraph Mr. Davis rented a house for Varina and her party in distant Charlotte, North Carolina. She made ready for her trip by packing only a few pieces of clothing, but as they left the mansion her carriage horses were in the little procession.

They left in the rainy evening of March thirty-first with red auction flags still flapping along Clay Street. There was a chill in the air, but fruit trees were already in bloom. The party rattled toward the depot.

Midshipman James Morris Morgan had spent a memorable day at Battery Semmes, whose guns faced the enemy at close range. In the morning a cannon had exploded, with heavy casualties, and soon afterward a well-aimed Yankee shot disabled an eight-inch gun. At noon, more unexpected than the remarkable shot from the enemy, came a summons for Morgan from the office of the Secretary of the Navy in Richmond.

The boy went as he was bidden, his belongings in a sea bag, apprehensive until the smiling Stephen Mallory himself shook his hand and put him at ease.

"Mrs. Davis is leaving for the South," Mallory said, "and I want you to act as a guard for her." He smiled more broadly. "It may involve a dangerous duty. The daughters of Secretary Trenholm will go along."

Morgan's mind was not on the coming tragedy of Richmond's fall as he hurried from the room. Betty Trenholm, daughter of the Secretary of the Treasury, was his fiancée.

The boy was puzzled by inactivity at the White House when he called; Mr. and Mrs. Davis gave no sign of an impending journey or separation. At the Trenholm home there was a similar air of unreality. The family chattered and lingered over dinner as if nothing were awry, and when a messenger came, directing the girls to meet Mrs. Davis at the depot, they rose leisurely from the table as if they were off for a stroll.

They went through deserted streets to the station, where Morgan led the young women to a passenger car, looking about him in dismay. The paint had long since weathered away, and the interior, lit by smoking lamps, was a ruin of scarred and peeling varnish, the plush seats soiled and torn. He thought that there must be fleas.

The Davises arrived, tumbling from the crowded carriage, which Morgan thought must be almost the last private vehicle left in Richmond: Mrs. Davis, her younger sister, Maggie Howell, the four children, two mulatto servants, the maid, Ellen, and the coachman, James Jones. There was also President Davis, come to see them off, and his private secretary, the immaculate Burton Harrison, who was leaving with Mrs. Davis.

The little train had three cars. Into one of them James Jones led the carriage horses. The refugees followed Mrs. Davis into another, where Morgan and the Trenholm girls greeted them. There were no other passengers.

The sleepy children stretched on the dirty brown plush of the lumpy seats, but stirred when the President entered and began talking with his wife. Davis soon went outside and gave Harrison final instructions.

"Latest word from General Lee is that Sheridan is moving around our right flank with cavalry to tear up the railroad. He may remain there, return to Grant, or join Sherman in the South.

"When you have seen my family safe in North Carolina, come back to me here as soon as you can."

Despite several calls from trainmen that they would soon depart, it was ten o'clock before the train creaked into motion. Davis said his farewells and hurried to the platform. Harrison waved to him from the steps as the cars jerked from sight.

Morgan helped the women to settle for the journey and tried to make himself comfortable on a forward seat. He discovered that his suspicions about the fleas were well founded.

The train rattled along, but within a few moments halted on a slight grade and refused to budge. Rain began to drip from the ceiling of the car and bedding was soaked. Children cried and the women crouched miserably. The train sat on the outskirts of Richmond until dawn before it crept away to the southwest.

One of those left behind in the capital was Mrs. Judith Brockenbrough McGuire, one of the most loyal patriots left to the Confederacy. While Mrs. Davis fretted in her leaky railroad car during the early morning of April first, Mrs. McGuire wrote in her diary:

> The croakers croak about Richmond being evacuated, but I can't and won't believe it.

★ THE TRENCHES ★

FOUR YEARS at war had made Robert Lee an old man. Even the most devoted of his intimates noted it. Colonel Armistead Long of his staff wrote:

"He had aged somewhat in appearance . . . but had rather gained than lost in physical vigor, from the severe life he had led. His hair had grown gray, but his face had the ruddy hue of health, and his eyes were as clear and bright as ever. . . . Though always abstemious in diet, he seemed able to bear any amount of fatigue."

Lee rode the crooked crescent of his lines almost daily even now, peering over the bristling forts and ditches to the enemy. He still wore a uniform of plain gray, without the buff facings and gold lace affected by general officers, so that many men took him for a colonel. A North Carolina captain looked at him in wonder: "There is a fearless look of self-possession without a trace of arrogance."

His troops, however, did not stand in awe of him. On a recent day when he was trotting behind the lines, men stepped into the path of gray Traveller, demanding his attention. One of them stuck out a bare foot for Lee to see.

"I've got no shoes, Ginral."

Another shouted, "I'm hungry, sir. We've got nothing to eat."

Lee hid his despair from the men but could not keep it from the reports to Richmond.

He called for more Negro laborers; he had only 1200 of the 5000 he needed, and many had deserted. His soldiers could not leave the trenches to work.

"There is a great suffering in the army for want of soap," he wrote. Skin diseases were rampant, and Lee could not understand why quartermasters did not supply the plentiful commodity, lye soap.

The cavalry was dispersed for lack of forage.

For three days his commissary had "not a pound of meat."

"You must not be surprised if calamity befalls us," he had warned as early as February.

A single stick of firewood now fetched the price of $5 in the trenches.

Even a child could guess from Lee's manner that hope was gone. One day the commander rode beside a mule-drawn army ambulance as escort to a little girl from Petersburg, Anne Banister, whose father had died in defense of the town. The child sat beside the driver, now and then slapping the mules with a whip. Lee halted her, but the girl persisted.

"Anne, you must not do that again," Lee said sternly. "These animals are on half feed, as we all are, and I don't feel entirely at ease about using them like this."

The girl was silent for the rest of the ride, but went in tears to her mother. "I don't believe General Lee thinks we are going to win the war."

"Of course we can't win," the woman said. "We are all starving."

Yet Lee's good humor did not desert him. He entertained a visiting dignitary, B. H. Hill, and said quietly, "Mr. Hill, we made a great mistake in the beginning, and I fear it will be fatal."

"What is that, General?"

"Why, we appointed all our worst generals to command the armies, and all our best generals to edit the newspapers. I have given the work all the care and thought I could, and sometimes, when I was through, my plans seemed to me to be perfect. But when I have fought the campaigns I have discovered defects.

"When it was all over, I found by reading a newspaper that these editor-generals saw all the defects plainly from the start . . . but they did not tell me until it was too late."

Hill smiled uncertainly as Lee paused.

"I have done my best," Lee said, "but I haven't succeeded as I would like. I'm willing to yield my place to these best generals, and I will do my best for the cause by editing a newspaper."

Lee once became so desperate as to ride up to Richmond
to talk with the politicians, and afterward gave a rare display of
temper to his son Custis and others of his family: "The Congress
don't seem to be able to do anything except eat peanuts and
chew tobacco, while my army is starving."

On March twenty-eighth, when the sky cleared after weeks
of rain, Lee saw the enemy in motion; great columns crawled
southward behind the Federal lines, and outposts reported a major movement of cavalry. Lee saw what he had long feared, a
general turning movement against his flank, toward the last feeble link with the South, Southside Railroad. He was not strong
enough to prevent it.

He wrote a homely note to his wife, Mary, in Richmond:

> I have received your note with a bag of socks. I return
> the bag and receipt. The count is all right this time. I have
> put in the bag General Scott's autobiography, which I
> thought you might like to read. The General, of course,
> stands out very prominently, and does not hide his light
> under a bushel, but he appears the bold, sagacious truthful
> man that he is. I enclose a note for little Agnes. I shall be
> very glad to see her tomorrow, but can not recommend
> pleasure trips now.

He did not repeat the words of warning he had written her
so recently:

> Should it be necessary to abandon our position to pre-
> vent being surrounded, what will you do? Will you remain,
> or leave the city? You must consider the question and make
> up your mind.

At ten o'clock on the morning of March thirtieth Lee came
to the far right of his line, where he had pushed George Pickett's
three little brigades during the rainy night; for all his care in
pulling the men from trenches yesterday, they had been seen by
Federal lookouts. The men marched along the Southside Railroad to Sutherland's Tavern, ten miles from Petersburg, then behind Fitz Lee's cavalry to the very end of the gray line.

Walter Harrison, the adjutant general to Pickett, watched Lee as he talked with his commanders. The generals had few suggestions, except for Harry Heth, who was still full of fight. "I'll attack in my front, and let Pickett support from the flank."

Lee shook his head, and at last sent Pickett beyond the protection of his trenches to the right, toward Dinwiddie Court House. He added to his little force two riddled brigades of infantry and six cannon under Colonel Willie Pegram. For the guns, at least, the army could afford no more spirited commander.

Lee hung about, waiting. His reward was a dispatch from Fitz Lee:

> Enemy cavalry in force at Five Forks, driving in my pickets.

With the dispatch came a prisoner, a smiling young Federal captain of cavalry who seemed to have no fear of Lee. He spoke up under questioning:

"What were you doing at Five Forks?"

"We're turning you, sir. The whole line."

"Sheridan's command?"

"Yes."

"In what force?"

"All of it, about fifteen thousand."

A staff officer nearby gave a low whistle. Lee gave the boy a quick look of speculation.

"He does not believe him," Walter Harrison thought.

"Is there more?" Lee asked.

"A big infantry force with Sheridan at Dinwiddie," the captain said.

Lee hesitated a moment and then, as if he had no alternative, passed his orders: Fitz Lee would lead the cavalry to Five Forks, with Pickett's men behind. Pickett would take command.

Before he left the spot there was the faint crackling of rifle fire from the southwest, where the cavalry had met bluecoats. Such of the great men as were left to the cavalry corps were taking the tired brigades into position: Fitzhugh Lee, Rooney Lee, Thomas Munford, Thomas Rosser.

General Lee turned back toward Petersburg, going slowly behind the entrenched line; men were twenty feet apart in the earthworks.

Near the tag end of the trenches lay a handful of elite troops, such as they were—the Sharpshooters of McGowan's Brigade of South Carolinians. In the months of siege these men had been trained as marksmen; they were armed with Enfield rifles, and many of them were deadly accurate to a range of 900 yards.

Brevet Captain William H. Brunson, who commanded a company of them, was led by a guide to a dangerous spot: "Yanks in that skirmish line over there. Been there since Wise's brigade pulled out. Hold this line."

The line was three quarters of a mile long and the company was weak. Nonetheless it survived the adventure. Brunson remembered it:

"A company of Federal cavalry, mistaking us for their own men, rode up within twenty yards of where we stood. A single volley from my line unhorsed nearly the last man of them, and in a few minutes my barefooted crowd were up to their knees in cavalry boots."

But it was the beginning of retreat, and Brunson was sent to a bridge in the rear, on Hatcher's Run, to screen a demoralized brigade. The Sharpshooters startled a big enemy force by springing from thickets in a screaming charge and, while the bluecoats fled, trailed rearward, beyond the hospital of Pickett's division, into an apple orchard where they would not draw fire on the wounded. They skirmished most of the day.

★ THE ENEMY ★

MR. LINCOLN had come down from Washington on the paddle wheeler *River Queen* to visit the army. He disembarked in the teeming new harbor at City Point, where the Appomattox flowed into the James, amid a swarm of tugs, sailing ships, barges, troopships, steamers, all crowding toward the wharves and warehouses which lined the banks as far as the President could see. Beyond, the army's traffic simply filled the landscape. Wagons, ambulances and soldiers threaded the bluffs to the riverside and there was a din of wheels, ship's boilers, screaming anchor chains, and boat whistles. Coffins by the thousand were carried on homeward-bound ships. When night fell, the burning lights of vessels gleamed red, blue, and yellow on the water, and sounds fell away to the occasional chuffing of a tug and the bells on men-of-war striking the hours.

The President settled on the *Malvern,* a captured blockade-runner now serving as flagship for Admiral David Porter, and chose a miniature stateroom in which, Porter complained, "I couldn't swing a cat." Lincoln slept in a space little larger than a closet.

The President placed his boots and socks outside his door the first night. Porter found holes in the socks; he had them washed and darned, and the boots shined.

Lincoln beamed at breakfast. "A miracle happened to me last night. When I went to bed I had two large holes in my socks, and this morning they are gone. That never happened to me before. It must be a mistake."

"How did you sleep?"

"Well enough, but you can't put a long blade in a short scabbard. I was too long for that berth."

While Lincoln visited the army that day, carpenters swarmed on the *Malvern* to dismantle, enlarge and reassemble his state-room. New bedding was installed. The changes were not mentioned to the President.

Lincoln emerged smiling the next morning.

"A greater miracle than ever happened last night," he said. "I shrank six inches in length and about a foot sideways. I got somebody else's big pillow and slept in a better bed than I did on the *River Queen.*"

The President seemed happy to be marooned from advisers and office seekers, especially those of his Cabinet who were for-ever quoting from German military experts to him. Porter handed him a telegram from William S. Seward, his Secretary of State:

Shall I come down and join you?

Lincoln grimaced at Porter. "No," he said. "I don't want him. Telegraph him that the berths are too small, and there's not room for another passenger."

"But I can provide for him if you wish."

"Tell him, then, that I don't want him. He'd talk to me all day about Vattel and Puffendorf. The war will be over in a week, and I don't want to hear any more of that."

The army watched with unconcealed curiosity as Lincoln stalked among the commands. On March twenty-sixth he rode with General Grant and a little escort to the headquarters of General George Meade. They passed a body of some 1500 Confederates, prisoners of the 9th Corps.

Colonel Theodore Lyman of Meade's staff thought the prisoners the most disheveled he ever saw: "They grew rougher and rougher. These looked brown and athletic, but had the most matted hair, tangled beards, and slouched hats, and the most astounding carpets, horse-sheets and transmogrified shelter-tents for blankets."

Meade turned to Lincoln. "I have just now a dispatch from General Parke to show you."

"Ah," said Lincoln, pointing to the prisoners, "there is the best dispatch you can show me from General Parke."

The officers laughed, but young Lyman stared at Lincoln in fascination.

"The President is, I think, the ugliest man I ever put my eyes on. On the other hand, he has the look of sense and wonderful shrewdness, while the heavy eyelids give him a mark almost of genius. He strikes me, too, as a very honest and kindly man; and, with all his vulgarity, I see no trace of low passions in his face. On the whole, he is such a mixture of all sorts, as only America brings forth. He is as much like a highly intellectual and benevolent satyr as anything I can think of. I never wish to see him again, but, as humanity runs, I am well content to have him at the head of affairs."

Two days later, on the morning of March twenty-eighth, Lincoln came under the eye of an attentive reporter, Charles C. Coffin of the Boston *Journal*. Lincoln entered Grant's headquarters cabin on the bluff over the James for a conference with his commander and General William T. Sherman, who had come up from North Carolina for final instructions. The President doffed his tall hat and ducked into the door, round-shouldered and loose-jointed, in comic contrast to the low, stout Grant, who puffed a cigar in silence, his face impassive under the stiff brim of a new hat. Sherman impressed Coffin more strongly than either: "Tall, commanding forehead, almost as loosely built as the President. His sandy whiskers were closely cropped. His coat was shabby with constant wear. His trousers were tucked into his military boots. His felt hat was splashed with mud."

George Meade hung about them, tall, thin, with straggling gray beard and stooped posture. There was Sheridan, too, shorter even than Grant, and full of hurried talk and enthusiasm.

It was Lincoln who turned to the table in the cabin, where a huge map lay open.

Grant ran a thick finger down the tracing of his forty-mile entrenched line and stabbed a point at the junction of roads to the west and south.

"Five Forks," he said. "I'll try to take it. That would pull Lee out of the trenches to fight."

He explained how Sheridan's horsemen would move during the afternoon, leading the sweep against the Confederate flank. Coffin went out to stare at the country where the assault would be made, making notes of it before darkness fell.

Hatcher's Run wandered southeastward through the eroded clay hills; three roads leading southwest from distant Petersburg crossed the stream: Vaughan Road to the east, then Squirrel Level Road, and, nearest of all, Boydton Plank Road. Within sight was the bridge of the Plank Road, held by the Confederates.

The country beyond the trenches was densely wooded, chiefly with pine, with rare clearings marking sites of old sawmills. The Plank Road led through the pines, fifteen miles from Petersburg, to Dinwiddie Court House. Some four miles away lay the road junction known as Five Forks, the key to the Confederate position.

If Grant could move the army in the swimming roads, Coffin reflected, the movement would be like that of fishermen stretching a seine. One end would be fastened to the bank of the

Appomattox, and Sheridan would draw the other past Dinwiddie to Five Forks, and beyond to the railroad, perhaps, to snare Lee's whole army.

Sheridan's regiments moved through the gray afternoon. The Rebels were restive the next day, and firing increased. Nightfall of March twenty-ninth brought an artillery duel. Coffin described it for his eager New England readers: "I stood upon the hill in rear of the Ninth Corps, and witnessed the display. Thirty shells were in the air at the same instant. The horizon was bright with fiery arches, crossing each other at all angles, cut horizontally by streams of fire from rifled cannon. Beneath the arches thousands of muskets were flashing. It surpassed in sublimity anything I had witnessed during the war."

The night was very dark, and there was a wind from the south, bringing more rain. Tomorrow, surely, the army would bog down once more and the offensive must be postponed. On this day Sheridan made headquarters at Dinwiddie. Grant moved to follow him.

Mr. Lincoln came ashore from the *Malvern*, rowed through the harbor by sailors in a drizzling rain. Before eight-thirty he was at Grant's headquarters to say good-bye. The field commander was in a joking mood, telling the President of the ingenious suggestions for winning the war which were poured upon him daily.

"The latest one was to supply the men with bayonets exactly a foot longer than the enemy's, and then charge. When they met, our bayonets would go through them, they couldn't reach us, and the war would be over."

Lincoln laughed. "Well, there's a good deal of terror in cold steel. I got a chance to test it myself once. When I was a young man, walking on a back street in Louisville one night about midnight . . . a very tough-looking citizen sprang out, reached back of his neck and pulled out a bowie knife that looked to me about three feet long. He flourished that thing before my face to see how close he could come to cutting off my nose without touching it. He held his knife close to my throat and said, 'Stranger, will you lend me five dollars on that?' I never reached in my pocket and got out money so fast in my life. I handed him a bank-note and said, 'There's ten, neighbor, now put up your scythe.'"

Grant turned away to his cabin door, where he kissed his wife; she stared after them with her long, plain face pale but composed, as the officers walked toward a little military train.

In the party was General Horace Porter of Grant's staff, who noted that Lincoln looked older, with deeper lines in his face and darker circles under his eyes. Lincoln stood at the rear as the officers climbed to the platform and raised their hats. His voice almost broke as he called to them, "Good-bye, gentlemen. God bless you all. Remember, your success is my success."

The train moved away. It went like a fly over a corrugated washboard, Horace Porter thought, over the new tracks laid by engineers to the rough contour of the land. Within the train, headquarters quickly assembled.

Grant took a seat at the end of the car, went through his familiar routine of striking his flint and slow match, and was soon half-hidden in blue cigar smoke. Porter and several others sat near the commander, who began to talk of his plan of campaign. He halted as if his attention had been diverted.

"The President is one of the few visitors I ever had who never tried to squeeze out of me every one of my plans—though he's the only one with a right to know them."

Grant looked through the dirty window at snaking lines of infantry on the move.

"He will stay at City Point," he said, "and he'll be the most anxious man in the country to hear from us, his heart is so wrapped up in it. I think we can send him some good news in a day or two."

Older officers exchanged glances. They had never known Grant to express such optimism at the opening of an offensive.

The train rattled through light rain to the end of the thirteen-mile track, where they followed Grant out. They mounted horses led from the baggage car, rode slowly along the Vaughan Road and in midafternoon camped in a cornfield. At night rain fell in torrents, rose from nearby swamps and made fields into shallow lakes.

Behind, along the abandoned line, were thousands of chimneys, desolate in the rain, tents stripped from them; roofless huts marked the old camp of an army corps. Columns struggled in the roads which were like porridge as the miserable troops were driven westward. The chief quartermaster complained to Colonel Lyman that it was the worst moving day of his memory. A train of 600 wagons, though aided by 1000 engineer troops, spent fifty-six hours in moving five miles.

But, like Lyman, the men could raise their heads and look across the landscape: "One pretty sight was a deserted farmhouse quite surrounded by peach trees, loaded with blossoms. In the distance it seemed covered with pink clouds."

Horses inched along with water up to their bellies and wagons almost disappeared in the sloughs. Men made jokes in the ranks:

"If ever anybody was to ask us if we'd ever been through Virginia we could say, 'Yes, sir! In a number of places.' "

Soldiers shouted to passing officers on horseback:

"When the gunboats coming up?"

Phil Sheridan was in a hurry, and the cavalry suffered. There were no tents, and the mess wagons were stuck in the mud somewhere in rear of the driving columns. Sheridan himself was among the first men to ride into the country crossroad hamlet called Dinwiddie Court House, where four roads intersected, the most vital leading through Five Forks to the Confederate flank. There was little else.

Sheridan's bright black gaze found a headquarters site:

"A half-dozen unsightly houses, a ramshackle tavern propped up on two sides with pine poles, and the weather-beaten building that gave official name to the crossroads."

The staff had no more than peeked into the primitive tavern when a rainstorm broke upon them. There was promise of a bleak night, but soon there was laughter and the tinkling of a piano; officers found two women in the place, refugees from Savannah to Petersburg to Dinwiddie, they said, and in gay spirits despite all. They exacted promises from the cavalrymen:

"You gentlemen won't fight right here at the Cote House? We know you won't. Our gentlemen were on picket right about here, until you came up, and they told us they'd not allow bloodshed. Can't we expect the same of you Northern gentlemen?"

The staff found coffee in an officer's haversack and the women brewed a pot for the staff. There was late singing at headquarters.

Dispatch riders soon found the place, and messages came in from Grant: This was no longer intended to be a cavalry raid backed by infantry. The entire army would join the offensive. Sheridan slept contentedly in a fat Virginia feather bed, despite warnings from his staff that Confederate agents might attack him there. In the morning there was more rain.

Sheridan moved the troops into position in a downpour, covering the roads, with a wary eye toward Five Forks; the Confederates were beginning to stir.

The two women at headquarters were still thumping the tinny piano when there was a glum note from Grant. Sheridan read it with impatience:

> The heavy rain of today will make it impossible for us to do much until it dries up a little, or we get roads around our rear repaired. You may, therefore, leave what cavalry you deem necessary to protect the left, and send the remainder back. . . .

Sheridan quickly mounted the big Confederate gray pacer he called Breckinridge, captured from the enemy, and with an officer and about a dozen cavalrymen he rode to the cornfield camp of Grant near Gravelly Run. Sheridan's party and the headquarters throng regarded each other with amusement. The little cavalry chief's horse plunged in mud to the knees at each mincing step, and the riders were splattered almost beyond recognition. The infantry officers stood about Grant's tents like roosting chickens, perched on boards and logs to prevent their sinking into the mire.

Sheridan bantered with Grant's staff:

"I can drive in the Rebel cavalry with one hand, and if they give me infantry, I'll strike Lee's right so hard they can break the lines and march to Petersburg." He became so excited that he ended by shouting.

"How will you get forage in this weather?" someone asked.

"I'll get all I want. I'll haul it out if I have to set every man in the command to corduroying roads. I tell you I'm ready to strike out tomorrow and go to smashing things."

The little horseman paced back and forth in the slush, splashing his boots to the hips.

"That's the kind of talk we need at headquarters," an officer said. "You go in and tell Grant that."

"I don't want to break in there. He's with Rawlins, you say."

An officer went in to Grant. "Sir, General Sheridan's here with some mighty interesting matters. He'd like to come in and talk with you."

Grant was engaged in a slow argument with John Aaron Rawlins, his chief of staff and closest friend; Rawlins urged that the attack be continued.

"Bring him in," Grant told the intruding officer, and as Sheridan entered Grant was chiding the chief of staff, "Well, Rawlins, I think you'd better take command."

Sheridan excused himself. "I'm cold and wet," he said. "I'll go to the fire." He went out, and soon disappeared into the tent of General Ingalls. Within a few moments, Grant sought him there.

"I'm afraid we can't move," Grant said. "If we have no roads, we'd best pull back."

"Please let me go on," Sheridan said. "The men are already moving, and we're covering the roads on the flank. We may have a chance later, but you know what they'll say if we turn back now. Burnside's Mud March of 'sixty three all over again."

"It's my better judgment to go on," Grant said, "but they all find reasons to stop. They lose wagons, they say, and wear out the men, and wet the ammunition, and say they'll have no artillery left. I want to go ahead if it can be done."

"We can do it without trains," Sheridan said. "We have them just where you want 'em." He saw that Grant needed little persuasion, and fell silent.

Grant soon rose. "We'll go on," he said. Sheridan recognized the determination in the quiet voice.

Late the next morning Sheridan's exposed men were struck by Confederate cavalry, and when fighting slowed, gray infantry howled through pine woods after them. Bluecoats fell back in stubborn lines from Five Forks toward their camp at Dinwiddie, and skirmishing became heavy.

Horace Porter, riding from Grant with important dispatches, came near the firing and noted a cheering sign: Along the road, within rifle shot of skirmishers, was one of Sheridan's big regimental bands, mounted on fine gray horses. They blared away at "Nellie Bly" and the music carried down into the wet thickets, even over the thundering of the new repeating rifles of General George Custer's men. Porter could no longer hear the minor shriek of the Rebel Yell.

II

Saturday, April 1

★

★ RICHMOND ★

THE WAR CLERK, John Beauchamp Jones, felt better in the clear, pleasant weather of this Saturday. He walked to the War Department offices through Richmond crowds that were vaguely uneasy, speaking to acquaintances, and when he had reached his office made one of his meticulous diary entries:

> Vague and incoherent accounts from excited couriers
> of fighting, without result, in Dinwiddie County. . . .

Jones peered curiously into the record books of the conscript office and was stunned by what he saw: more than 60,000 troops were absent without leave—deserters. All Virginians, he noted.

John M. Daniel, the fiery editor of the Richmond *Examiner* who had poured vituperative scorn on the heads of President Davis and General Lee and officers and politicians without number, was dead today. Jones noted no signs of mourning.

A rumor was adrift in the streets that the Confederacy had signed a treaty with the Mexican government of Maximilian.

Early in the morning Captain William H. Parker, of the Navy's school ship, *Patrick Henry*, went up from the James to Secretary Mallory's house, seeking news.

Parker was a thirty-four-year-old veteran of the Mexican War and an old U.S. Navy hand. When he came near Mallory's home he gave no sign of surprise at the strange sight:

Stephen Mallory paced up and down on the peaceful walk with a big pistol in his hand. His manner was so calm that Parker assumed he had been out target shooting.

Mallory was a smiling, urbane man who had brought much to the Confederacy. The son of a New England engineer, born in Trinidad, he had grown up in Key West, fought the Seminoles, practiced law, been collector of customs and served in the U.S.

37

Senate, where he had fought for naval reforms. He had literally given the Confederacy its little ironclad Navy. Parker admired him greatly.

"Any news from the army, sir?" Parker asked.

Mallory seemed distracted. "The word from General Lee is good. Affairs about Petersburg are promising, they say. Promising."

"I'll spend the night in the city," Parker said, "if nothing is likely to happen that would call for me aboard ship."

"No, no," Mallory said. "I know of nothing to keep you there. Do as you wish. I'll call if I need you."

Parker went out with friends for the evening, but he noticed in the streets some of the home guard, marching out the Brook Turnpike. Bystanders spoke vaguely of a threatened raid on the city. The night passed in quiet.

The camp of the 7th South Carolina Cavalry was east of the city and north of the James, within sight of the enemy. Saturday morning was peaceful and almost soundless, but Edward M. Boykin, who was at headquarters when orders came, thought this must be the day they had long dreaded.

The orders were simple enough: Send the dismounted men of the regiment to Lieutenant Colonel Barham of the 24th Virginia Cavalry, for duty on the lines.

Cavalrymen to stand in the trenches. It gave him a feeling of what was to come, Boykin said, but he added, "It was difficult to say what was expected."

A party of the regiment trailed off toward the bluecoat lines, leaving behind a row of bony horses.

Not far away from the South Carolinians, near Chaffin's Bluff, was the remarkable force commanded by Custis Lee, a patched-up emergency brigade of 1300 local guards from Richmond, chiefly clerks and an artillery group of six battalions.

The artillerymen, except for a Georgia crew, had seen no field service; the others had been posted at guns in Richmond for months. And though enlistment cards read "heavy artillery," many were light artillerymen, and one company was, in truth, of cavalry.

The gunners, however, had a talented leader, Colonel Stapleton Crutchfield, once chief gunner to Stonewall Jackson; he was only now recovering from a wound suffered almost two years ago, when Jackson had fallen.

The dress of the gunners set them apart from any other Confederate troops—scarlet caps and trim.

Custis Lee's sector was near Fort Harrison, the scene of bitter fighting in the past few months, where the pickets were almost face to face. At one spot the hostile lines were divided by logs thrown across a path a few feet apart as the limits of sentry beats.

Between 10 and 11 P.M. of this night Captain McHenry Howard of Baltimore, of Custis Lee's staff, was falling asleep in his tent when a red glare lighted it, and distant gunfire aroused him:

"The night was very dark and cloudy, the atmosphere damp and heavy. . . . Dressing ourselves and mounting the works, we watched and listened for half an hour, but the battle was across the James, and all remained quiet on our part of the lines; and the 'Richmond defenses' came to the conclusion that so far it was no affair of theirs, and like true soldiers went to sleep as fast as they could."

Lieutenant General Richard S. Ewell, commander of the city's defenses, had lost none of his vitality, for all that he had lost a leg and wore a gray fringe on his domed bald head. He was up through the night, driving his staff, tagged at every step by his Apache boy, "Friday," a relic of his days on the plains.

Ewell piped in his thin voice and gave orders with the quaint gestures that had won him the sobriquet "The Woodcock." In his convalescence two years before, Ewell had married his widowed cousin, Lizinka Campbell Brown, whom he still introduced to friends as "Mrs. Brown." Ewell had done his best to organize the city's defenses.

He had laid careful plans for this night; months ago he had given orders as to how tobacco warehouses should be burned, at the threat of enemy occupation.

Ewell had foreseen that the city might be looted by its own people: "I begged them to organize a volunteer guard force for an emergency, promising the necessary arms. I regret to say but one man volunteered."

Not long after dark, Ewell had a sobering message from General Longstreet: Old Pete had been called south of the James with his divisions. He would leave General Kershaw on the Richmond front line. Ewell was to assemble all troops he could find, send them down the Darbytown Road and report to Longstreet's head-quarters.

Ewell sent his staff to collect convalescent soldiers and militia, and mounted for the ride. This was not a simple process, for he must be strapped into the saddle by his wooden leg while the patient old gray, "Rifle," waited for the Indian boy to be done.

Longstreet ordered Ewell to relieve two brigades left on picket duty, using his home guard, and send the regulars to the relief of Petersburg.

★ **THE ARMY** ★

AFTER DARK the rain had stopped, though it was little enough comfort to George Pickett's troops, waiting in the pines. The roads were still liquid, and the men were cold and hungry.

General Pickett had reassured himself yesterday, pushing the enemy from Five Forks to within half a mile of Dinwiddie Court House, where he now camped.

At 9 P.M. cavalry scouts brought in two prisoners, and at sight of their corps insignia Pickett's confidence began to seep away. The Federals were infantrymen. Not only had Sheridan 12,000 troopers in his path, but a big force of Grant's real power was at hand, perhaps more than one corps.

Pickett hesitated until well after midnight, and then got off a dispatch to Robert Lee: The day had brought victory to the isolated right wing, but now he was seriously outnumbered. He would fall back nearer the comforting flank of the entrenched Confederate line.

In short, Pickett would give up the ground won the previous day, and await the enemy attack nearer Lee's entrenched line. His courier left with the message at 2 A.M.

Lee did not conceal his surprise at this dispatch. He replied immediately with a warning that Five Forks must be held at all costs, as the shield to the Southside Railroad and key to the entire position. He gave reluctant blessing to Pickett's retreat.

It was not quite two years since Gettysburg, when Pickett had led a fateful charge of which Lee had written him:

You and your men have covered yourselves with glory.

Pickett's name had been heard less often in the days since, and the commander had at least once chided him for bickering and controversy with other officers. It was months ago that the ordnance chief, General Josiah Gorgas, entering in his diary a rumor that Pickett had been relieved of his command, wrote: "Pickett is very dissipated, it is said."

Pickett could not be criticized for lack of promptness tonight, at any rate. His men were moving back toward Five Forks at the moment the dispatch went out to General Lee. It was slow work, for the route was as nearly a stream as a roadway, and pine torches gave scant light to the troops. They came, exhausted, to Five Forks at dawn. There was no sign of Federal pursuit.

Pickett left the choice of a defensive battle line to no one else. He rode in the gray morning along the White Oak Road, at right angles to the Ford Road. The Southside Railroad was some two miles in his rear. Pickett had the men entrench, but took little time in selection of the ground, which was in places low and difficult to defend. Crews felled trees in front of the line until in some places the logs were piled chest-high, at the edge of a woodland. Men sensed no anxiety in the general; the worst to be expected was a sharp attack by Sheridan's cavalry, which could surely be driven off. If blue infantry came in, they had only to call up help from the end of the entrenched line. No one on the isolated flank yet knew that the anchor regiments of Lee's thin line had already attacked on their front and been so roughly handled that they now huddled in the trenches, ready for retreat.

By late morning Pickett was satisfied with his line at Five Forks. From left to right he had placed his infantry:

The brigades of Matt Ransom and William Wallace, acting as one command, since they were under 1000 strong; George Steuart's brigade of about 1000; Corse's, about 1100; and William Terry's, no more than 800.

Beyond these there was only cavalry. To the left, hardly more than a picket line stretching toward the Petersburg trenches, was a regiment of T. T. Munford's horsemen and the decimated brigade of twenty-four-year-old General William Roberts. To the right of the line was Robert Lee's son Rooney, with some 2500 troopers.

Pickett sent his wagons back, to the north of Hatcher's Run, with his meager reserve strength to guard them—two brigades of cavalry under Thomas Rosser.

Fitz Lee, the senior cavalry commander, came up after noon with about half his men, some 900 of them. Soldiers cooked their meals, but few of them had more than parched corn. The morning passed with nothing more serious than brief distant crackling of skirmishes with the enemy, which came on slowly.

Pickett had chosen the gun positions as well as the infantry line, though Colonel William Johnson Pegram, the twenty-two-year-old genius of artillery, was there. He had six guns, three of them in the center of the line, commanded by two of Pegram's boy lieutenants. Farther to the right, where they swept an open field before a farmhouse, were the other guns, under a skilled veteran, Captain Thomas Ellett.

William Pegram was a handsome boy who had fought his guns since his enlistment as a private in 1861. Only his youth had cost him a general's stars; he had been often praised by Lee, A. P. Hill and Stonewall Jackson, and, since the death of the legendary John Pelham, had been the army's favorite gunner.

Today he was worn from two days of fighting, in the saddle night and day, wet to the skin most of those hours as he drove the guns through muddy roads to this front, fighting off cavalry patrols of the enemy. For breakfast this morning he had taken a handful of corn from his horse's ration and parched it over a fire, sharing even that with an officer of his command.

Pegram did not protest Pickett's gunsites, though they were far from ideal; the center position in particular seemed vulnerable. Pegram watched in the quiet until noon, and while axes still rang and the little line grew, he fell asleep on the wet ground near Ellett's guns on the right. He had no blanket.

General Thomas Rosser had about him the aura of the cavalry's great days—an immense young man, high-shouldered, black-eyed, quick-tempered, with a weakness for alcohol which he fought manfully. Drinking had not affected him as a field commander, and before Jeb Stuart's death last spring, Rosser had been at the head of many reckless charges which had saved the army from disaster.

There was smoldering enmity between Rosser and Thomas Munford, for a recent quarrel had led to a court-martial. Munford had won acquittal and now had his own division of cavalry, but no one had forgotten.

Rosser was fresh from triumphs in the Shenandoah Valley, in a hard campaign which had left his horses jaded and sore-backed. But yesterday, as he crossed the Nottoway River riding down to this flank, Rosser had succumbed to his weakness for good food. He borrowed a seine and waded the cold water with a Negro servant and aides, and caught a number of big shad. He had carried the fish in a headquarters wagon through a sharp skirmish yesterday, when he got a painful flesh wound in an arm. Rosser was not ready for action this morning.

He explained to Pickett that he must rest the mounts of his command.

"I've got to go back and unsaddle and feed," he said. "I won't be able to fight from horseback much longer, if I don't cure those saddlesores."

Pickett agreed. Rosser turned for a last word:

"I want you to come back and have lunch with me. A shad bake, I might say. We've got some nice ones."

Pickett accepted immediately. "Fine, fine. I'll be with you in an hour."

Rosser rode off, but paused on his way to invite Fitz Lee to the feast.

There was quiet on the line at Five Forks; from the distant left, toward the lines of the main army, there was a rattle of fighting, but it had a scattered sound and was not thought to be serious. Far in the rear, at Rosser's camp, the tantalizing aromas of hickory smoke and broiling shad began to rise.

Fitz Lee was in the saddle at Five Forks, ready for the two-mile ride back to Rosser's camp, when Tom Munford rode into sight. Munford was excited. He passed Lee a dispatch from one of his troopers on the left flank.

A tide of Federal cavalry had poured over White Oak Road, scattering the brigade of Bill Roberts. Pickett's force appeared to be cut off from the main army.

Fitz read the message, too hurriedly, Munford thought, and gave no sign of concern.

"Well, Munford," he said, "I wish you would go over in person at once and see what this means. If necessary, draw up your division and let me hear from you."

The message did not go to Pickett, though it was about this time that Munford watched Fitz Lee and Pickett ride to the rear. The troops lying in line paid no attention to the departing generals, and big Rooney Lee, at the far right with his troopers, was not told of the shad bake, nor that his superiors had left the field, leaving him the senior officer.

The shad bake on the banks of Hatcher's Run was a great success. Rosser's headquarters cook served the big fish, brown and succulent from the glowing mounds of coals. It was a familiar rite to Tidewater Virginians, with the shad split and spread flat across green withes cut from the woods, a crude method of planking. The networks of spiny bones did not mar the contentment of the generals. None of those who watched the feast in the lee

of Rosser's wagon recorded that there were drinks, possibly because so familiar a custom was beneath special notice. In any
event, the officers were around the fire for two or three hours.

Two couriers from the front rode up swiftly.

"The enemy's coming in on White Oak Road, General," one
of the men said.

Rosser, Pickett and Fitz Lee listened, but heard no firing
from the front. A dense pine forest lay between them and Five
Forks, but it did not occur to the hungry officers that it could
muffle the rolling of musketry. They lingered, and Rosser continued to listen. He recorded: "Some time was spent over the
lunch, during which no firing was heard, and we concluded that
the enemy was not in much of a hurry to find us at Five Forks."

About 4 P.M. Pickett asked Rosser for a rider to carry a message to Five Forks, though he was not visibly alarmed. Rosser
called up two men, and took his usual precaution of sending one
a few hundred yards in front of the other, for the safety of the
message. The two riders galloped off, but a moment later gunfire
rolled through the woods.

The generals saw a line of bluecoats seize the leading courier.
The other trooper galloped back to Rosser.

"Woods full of 'em, sir. They've got behind the men at Five
Forks, too."

Pickett rode quickly toward the front. Within a moment he
was back, calling for the Dinwiddie Troop to guide him; he
seemed to be cut off from the command.

During the hours of the shad bake, Tom Munford rode to
the left to carry out Fitz Lee's orders. He carried with him three
or four couriers and a favorite staff officer, Fitz's brother, Captain Henry Lee.

He reached the far end of the line and saw Federals on
White Oak Road. An officer told Munford the enemy riders
were MacKenzie's cavalry. Munford soon saw more: In a field
near White Oak Road, columns of blue infantry had formed;
through his glasses he made out their insignia: 5th Corps. Munford sent a rider to Fitz Lee and Pickett with this information
and ordered his division to him by way of a narrow woods road.

Munford was impatient and, as the Federals continued to

gather in his front, sent Henry Lee to hurry the troops and then carry word to Fitz Lee and Pickett. "Tell them personally what you've seen," Munford said.

For some time Munford had no reply, and sent more couriers after Henry Lee. He had little time for more; his division was under brisk attack and being forced back through the woods. Munford left the field to call for help.

He and a few men were pursued by Federal riders into the Ford Road, where he met Pickett.

Pickett's dark curls were tousled around his flushed face. He shouted to Munford, pointing to the front.

"What troops are those?" he called, but did not pause for an answer. "I've got to get in to Five Forks. For God's sake do something to hold them off while I get by."

Captain James Breckinridge, commanding the sharpshooters of the 3rd Virginia Cavalry, was beside Munford, and without waiting for a command, rode at the oncoming Federals with his handful of riders, firing rapidly. Breckinridge fell dead from his saddle, but Pickett, racing past in Indian fashion, his head low on the neck of his horse, escaped a volley from the bluecoats and was soon out of sight. Fitz Lee, who tried to follow, was driven rearward. Up ahead, furious firing shook the woodlands.

Tom Munford noted that the shadows were already growing long.

The first volley of musketry brought Willie Pegram to his feet among Ellett's guns, and he was soon galloping on his white horse toward the vulnerable center. A witness, W. Gordon McCabe, recalled the spot at this moment: "The little salient was literally ringed with flame. The guns were using double canister at short range and their cannoneers were serving their pieces with a coolness and rapidity beyond all praise. Within thirty yards or less of the guns the dense columns of the enemy were staggering under a rapid fire."

Pegram rode to this battery shouting encouragement to his men. McCabe saw "a sweet serenity" on his face as the boy colonel studied the effects of his gunfire.

"Fire your canister low, men!" Pegram shouted. It was his last order. He tumbled from his saddle and into McCabe's arms. "Oh, Gordon," Pegram said, "I'm mortally wounded. Take me off."

The gun's lieutenant fell across the barrel a moment later, shot through the head. The battery continued to fight, ripping the blue lines until it was overrun. Federals came from both flanks. A gunner felled the first man with a sponge staff, but the graycoats were borne under and the guns fell quiet. Thousands of men overran the position and swept into the woods behind.

On the left of the line Matt Ransom's men were hurled back by the attack. The outside regiment was the 24th North Carolina, rolled in on its neighbors in a melee of flight and carrying the adjoining four regiments from the line. Ransom lost his hat, and one of his soldiers, W. N. Rose, Jr., saw him floundering in the thick pines on horseback, rallying his men. Rose wrote of the swift Yankee victory: "They were a sublime sight in their long lines of blue. We prepared to receive them as they came, but soon yelling commenced on the right of Ransom's brigade, and they came in both front and rear and poured into us a heavy enfilading fire. . . . We were now powerless to help ourselves, as the Yankees were closing in upon us from every quarter, and the order was given to fall back by companies, beginning on the left of the regiment; but before the right companies received the order the enemy had cut off all chances of retreat."

The 24th North Carolina was gone, except for a handful who escaped the woods. Even then, Major Thaddeus Love did not surrender. He twisted the U.S. flag from the hands of a color-bearer who charged by him, and went down, flailing about him with the staff.

General Ransom made a last effort to hold the flank after one mount had been killed under him. He led a thin line of survivors from the woods, but went down with his horse in a volley. Rumors went through both armies that Ransom was dead, but two captains ran to him, found him pinioned under his thrashing horse, and freed the general; he escaped on foot.

Tom Munford pointed out to Ransom a good gun position, but the infantryman refused to send artillerymen there. Munford himself had no orders.

When Pickett reached the men of his front line, he found they had been pushed back half a mile or more from the original position. He flung himself into the work of rallying the men as if he would atone for his absence.

Lieutenant Colonel Walter Harrison, his adjutant general, was near the lank-haired commander:

> Pickett got a sergeant and men enough to put one piece in position on the left and fired eight rounds into the head of the enemy column, when the axle broke and the piece was disabled. . . . He had also pulled out Terry's brigade from their position and threw them on the left flank, charging over Wallace's men and forcing them back to their position.
>
> Even then, with all the odds against us, we might have held until night, which was fast approaching, but the ammunition was fast giving out. Colonel Flowers' regiment fought hand to hand after the cartridges were gone, but to no avail, though the enemy lay in heaps. The left was completely turned.

The staff tried to stem the ensuing panic, but it was too late.

Corse's brigade was standing firm, and some men from broken regiments rallied on it; it was a momentary pause.

Pickett was still with the broken battery when he was startled by a bluecoat trooper jumping the breastwork on a mule, crying to him to surrender.

"Damn you," Pickett shouted, and galloped from the enemy ring just before it closed. He fled with his men toward White Oak Road, but was forced to turn; the blue regiments of Crawford and MacKenzie were sweeping up survivors there. Elsewhere, the men of Custer and Devin were scattering the last organized Confederate troops through the woodland.

At last only Rooney Lee's troopers withdrew in good order, having beaten off savage attacks. Even they paid dearly. Walter Harrison thought their clash with the enemy on the cleared field near the Gilliam farmhouse "one of the most brilliant cavalry engagements of the war," a series of charges and head-on collisions with ringing sabers and banging pistols.

A staff officer who had seen every battle, from the first of Jeb Stuart's clashes, said he never saw such desperate fighting as the last charge provided, when nine colonels went down within his view. Mrs. Gilliam later reported that her lawn and garden, a space of not more than a dozen acres, was so littered with the bodies of horses that it took many days to drag them away and end the overpowering stench of the field.

When the troopers made camp that night they lacked even the spirit to sing the grim song which had become the favorite in the shrinking ranks of late:

> Stand to your glasses steady,
> 'Tis all we've left to prize;
> Here's to the dead already,
> Hurrah for the next man who dies!

After dark, when the field had cleared, Gordon MoCabe had Willie Pegram's stretcher loaded into an ambulance and rode with him through the confusion of Pickett's retreat. The jolting wagon, driven rapidly toward Ford's Station on the Southside Railroad, wrung groans of agony from the colonel.

McCabe held Pegram in his arms, and now and then prayed aloud for him. He kissed the white face several times. Pegram stirred.

"If it is God's will to take me, I'm perfectly resigned. I only want to live for the sake of my mother and sisters."

A few minutes later Pegram muttered, "Take my love to Mother and the girls, and tell them I thought of them at the last."

McCabe groaned. "My God, my God, why hast Thou forsaken me?"

"Don't say that, Gordon," Pegram said. "It isn't right."

McCabe kissed Pegram once more. "I never knew how much I loved you until now, Willie." It was the first time he had called the colonel by that name.

Pegram squeezed McCabe's hand. "But I did," he said.

The ambulance rocked on in the darkness, with the sound of McCabe's prayers so loud that the driver heard it over the creaking of the wagon and the hoofs of the mules.

It was after 10 P.M. when they halted at Ford's Station. Mc-Cabe found a bed for Pegram there, gave him morphine until his pain was eased, and sat beside his cot for hours, despite a midnight alarm that the enemy was coming. McCabe sent off an orderly with their horses, pistols, sabers, and spurs, expecting to be captured, but they were not disturbed. McCabe wrote:

"I shall never forget that night of waiting. I could only pray. He breathed heavily through the night, and passed into a stupor. I bound his wounds as well as I knew how and moistened his lips with water. Sunday morning he died as gently as possible."

McCabe had Pegram wrapped in a blanket, saw him buried in a trench which he helped to dig, and read the Episcopal funeral service over him.

The day passed slowly at Lee's headquarters in the Turnbull house. There were discouraging reports from Anderson's fight at the end of the trenches, but for hours there was nothing from Pickett. Rumors flew.

In the afternoon there was a long message from President Davis in Richmond, a rather querulous dispatch about assigning officers to raise Negro troops. The President complained:

> I called for the recommendations made by you, and so few names were presented that I infer you do not find it desirable to rely on officers sent to recruit for their own commands.
>
> I have asked often but without satisfactory reply how many of the exchanged prisoners have joined the army. Your force should have been increased from that source 8,000 or 10,000 men.
>
> Last night we had rumors of a general engagement on your right. Your silence in regard to it leads to the conclusion that it was unwarranted. . . .

Near the end the President came dangerously close to revelation of his secret desperation:

The question is often asked of me, "Will we hold Richmond?" To which my only answer is, "If we can, it is purely
a question of military power." The distrust is increasing, and
embarrasses in many ways.

Long before he heard from Pickett, Lee telegraphed Davis
of his concern. He left little to the imagination:

> The movement of General Grant to Dinwiddie C. H.
> seriously threatens our position, and diminishes our ability
> to maintain our present lines in front of Richmond and
> Petersburg. . . . It also renders it more difficult to with-
> draw from our position . . . and gives the enemy an advan-
> tageous position in our rear. . . . I fear he can readily cut
> both the Southside and the Danville Railroads, being far
> superior to us in cavalry.
> This in my opinion obliged us to prepare for the neces-
> sity of evacuating our position on James River at once, and
> also to consider the best means of accomplishing it, and our
> future course. I should like very much to have the views of
> your Excellency upon this matter as well as counsel, and
> would repair to Richmond for the purpose, did I not feel
> that my presence here is necessary. Should I find it prac-
> ticable I will do so, but should it be convenient for your
> Excellency or the Secretary of War to visit headquarters, I
> should be glad to see you. . . .

When Lee at last heard of the disaster to Pickett, he took
emergency measures left to him. He called Longstreet down from
the north side of the James, removing most of Richmond's protection in an effort to bolster for a few hours the doomed lower
reaches of his line.

General Ambrose Powell Hill's sector of the line lay south
of Petersburg, near the city, facing the massed strength of the
enemy. Danger seemed greater than ever today, and the general
was out at daybreak with his staff and a handful of couriers.
Though Hill looked frail, and had been called from sick leave,
he was in the saddle all day. Men in his ranks seemed to take
heart at sight of his long pale face; they could remember his red
battle shirt at Sharpsburg, so long ago, when The Light Division

had saved the army. General Hill's decline had matched that
of the Confederacy.

A vague illness had plagued him through the winter—perhaps psychosomatic, perhaps only the vestige of a case of malaria
from his early manhood. Officers recalled that Hill had often
been sickly, sluggish and eaten by anxieties in moments when
battle action was pending, as at Gettysburg and The Wilderness.
Now, in any event, emergency had called Hill from his wife and
two baby girls. It was perhaps as well, even for his health, for
in Richmond when citizens asked him if the city might fall, Hill
was visibly shaken, and was given to shouting, "I don't want to
survive the fall of the city!"

Sergeant G. W. Tucker, who was Hill's favorite courier, rode
with him today. They did not shirk. The general led them, riding his big horse, "Champ," the route from Burgess' Mill to the
log and mud work which was the anchor of his line, Fort Gregg.
There was now little more than a skirmish line in the trenches:
General Cadmus Wilcox commanded the left, and General Harry
Heth the right.

In late afternoon when Hill heard of Pickett's disaster at
Five Forks, he took the staff slowly along the lines to Fort
Gregg, where he sat for a long time. Tucker found him strangely
withdrawn:

"He passed only a few words with his staff party, or those
very, very few in the trenches there. He seemed lost in con-
templation of the immediate position, at which the Confederate
line had become so terribly stretched."

Hill gazed solemnly at the landscape, with one last look at
the unfinished line of rifle pits trailing off from one flank of Fort
Gregg. It was 9 P.M. when he left the place.

The general returned to his headquarters at the plantation
house Indiana on the outskirts of Petersburg, and soon crossed
the road to the cottage of the Venable family, where he lived
with his wife and children.

After nightfall men in the lines passed rumors of the collapse on the far right; there were mysterious movements through
the night.

Percy G. Hawes, a child courier bivouacked in the farmyard of the Whitworth family within half a mile of Robert Lee's headquarters, wrote:

> All during the day there was a feeling of unrest and apprehension, even among the animals. We could hear the distant firing . . . see the moving troops and the hurrying to and fro of couriers about the quarters of General Lee . . . a thoroughly disagreeable day, with nothing to do but look on and be miserable.
>
> As night came on the enemy began shelling our line at every point. The greater part of the night I lay in my tent awake, watching the pyrotechnic display of the shells.

Some miles to the right, quite near the scene of Pickett's defeat, lay the South Carolina brigade of General Samuel McGowan, just pulled from the line near Petersburg. It had marched and countermarched without obvious purpose during the day, and at noon had crept back into the trenches at the very end of the gray line. It had driven off occasional sharpshooters.

As the bright, warm day faded, Captain J. F. J. Caldwell of this brigade was prodded into alertness:

"As night approached the enemy showed a disposition to push upon our picket, and the discharges between the lines became far more rapid and continuous. By dark, it was an almost incessant rattle. . . .

"Not long after dark there was a great stir among Johnson's division, which was next to us on the right. . . . We heard that they had been ordered to move to the rear in the direction of the Southside Railroad. Their pickets, withdrawn at the same time, left not only the flank of our line open, but at least a third of the brigade entirely open."

One of General Bushrod Johnson's staff officers passed a rumor to Caldwell, "They say the Yanks whipped hell out of Pickett over there today. Nobody knows how big a loss. Johnson's been called to save the railroad."

★ THE ENEMY ★

PHIL SHERIDAN was in and out of the fat feather bed in Dinwiddie
Tavern during the night. Before midnight an exchange of dispatches made it clear that the Confederates had left an invit-
ing gap between George Pickett and the old entrenched line. The
messages between Sheridan and Grant were almost exultant.

At 3 A.M. Sheridan wrote in this vein to General Gouverneur
K. Warren, of the 5th Corps, whose infantry he must use today:

> I am holding in front of Dinwiddie Courthouse, on the
> road leading to Five Forks, for three quarters of a mile with
> General Custer's division. The enemy are in his immediate
> front. . . . I understand you have a division at Boisseau's;
> if so, you are in rear of the enemy's line and almost on his
> flank. Possibly they may attack at daylight; if so, attack
> instantly and in full force. Attack at daylight anyhow. . . .
> Do not fear my leaving here. If the enemy remains, I shall
> fight at daylight.

Dawn was foggy, but as Sheridan emerged from the tavern, mists were rising. The woods in his front were quiet, and he
could learn nothing from Warren; his orders, in any event, had
not been obeyed. He spent an hour puzzling out the situation in
his front, growling profanely to his staff, wishing that he had got
the 6th Corps, as he had requested of headquarters.

The cavalry left the barricades of the night before and
went slowly after the retreating Confederates toward Five Forks.
In advance were the dismounted men of Custer in tight breeches
and short jackets, looking, one officer said, "as if they had been
especially equipped for crawling through knotholes." They pushed
for a mile or more, and still no sound from the distant infantry
signaled the closing of Sheridan's trap.

At 10 A.M. Sheridan was joined in the Five Forks road by
Horace Porter, who had ridden with a few couriers the fifteen

miles from Grant's headquarters with the commander's emphatic orders:

"I want you to spend the day with Sheridan, and send me bulletins every half hour or so. Tell me all his progress. You know my views, and I want you to give them fully to Sheridan. Tell him this movement is in his hands, and he must be responsible for its execution. I have every confidence in him."

Sheridan explained to Porter, "The enemy's falling back steadily. We've had several brushes. I'm damned tired of the delays in getting the infantry up against them. I'm going to strike him with all we have, as soon as I get Warren into line. I think Pickett will stand behind some works he's building at Five Forks."

In less than an hour Warren arrived, his mustache twitching with vexation. He had a division behind him—Crawford's—and reported it ready to go into line, when others were upon the flanks. Sheridan had little to say to him.

Before noon, Colonel Orville Babcock of Grant's staff came from headquarters with a message for Sheridan: "General Grant says that, if in your judgment the Fifth Corps would do better under its division commanders, you are authorized to relieve General Warren and order him to report to General Grant at headquarters."

"I hope it won't be necessary," Sheridan said. He began to talk of his plan of attack.

Babcock left him as Sheridan passed orders: The 5th Corps was to move to a nearby church, form lines and wheel left, to attack the enemy flank; Pickett's log breastworks were turned at an angle near that spot. While the infantry charged, the cavalry, dismounted, would hit the front of the line.

An hour passed, with no firing from Warren. Sheridan's impatience was sketched by Porter: "He fretted, restive, and made appeals for haste. He dismounted from his horse and paced up and down, struck the clenched fist of his hand into his palm, and fretted like a caged tiger. He said at one time, 'This battle must be fought before the sun goes down. All conditions may be changed in the morning. We have but a few hours of daylight. The cavalry is shooting up the ammunition.'"

A covey of staff officers galloped toward the infantry to prod the attack. Warren came, and Sheridan explained the situation to him once more. "He seemed to understand," Sheridan wrote.

It was 4 P.M. before the attack was called, and firing tore the woodland about Five Forks. Sheridan rode to Gravelly Run Church, where the infantry was coming out, and saw Warren sitting under a tree, sketching the terrain for his officers. Sheridan exploded, repeating his fears that night would come before the fight opened. The little cavalry chief recalled:

"Warren did not seem to be at all solicitous. His manner exhibited decided apathy, and he remarked with indifference that 'Bobby Lee was always getting people into trouble.'"

Sheridan reflected that it was no wonder that, with such an attitude, Warren had taken three hours to march two miles. He said of Warren: "His manner gave me the impression that he wished the sun would go down before the attack could be completed." He was near the limit of his patience when Warren's infantry charged, led by the division of General Ayres. Porter was there:

"Ayres threw out a skirmish line and advanced across an open field which sloped down toward the dense woods, just north of White Oak Road. We soon met with a fire from the edge of the woods, a number of men fell and the skirmish line halted and seemed to waver."

Sheridan, spurring his big black Rienzi, was among them, yelling, "Come on, men. Move at 'em on the jump, or you'll not catch a one. They're ready to run now! Go for 'em!"

A man beside him was struck in the neck by a bullet; blood pumped from his throat.

"I'm killed," he yelled, and dropped to his knees.

Sheridan leaned over him. "You're not hurt a bit! Pick up your gun, man, and move on!"

The man lurched to his feet, charged forward and fell dead. The line plunged down the slope toward the Confederates.

The first men into the woods were staggered by fire from the hidden breastworks, and there was confusion. Sheridan was among them.

"Where's my battle flag?" he shouted.

A color sergeant handed it to him, and the general waved it overhead like a boy, yelling. Porter watched in amazement:

"Bullets were like a bee swarm. One hit the flag, one wounded Captain A. J. McGonigle by his side, and others hit two or three staff horses. All this time, Sheridan dashed about from one part of the line to the other, shaking his fist, waving the flag, yelling, swearing, praying."

General Ayres led infantrymen into the breastworks and Sheridan spurred Rienzi over the logs at the angle, and landed in a line of graycoat prisoners who had dropped their guns.

"Right over there, Johnnies. Get along now, and leave your guns. You'll never need 'em again. Are there any more of you? We need you all."

Near the end, when the firing dwindled, Sheridan was told that Crawford's division was moving straight north, leaving a gap in the line into which the enemy was driving.

"Where's Warren?" Sheridan bellowed. He reined from the line to seek the perplexed general, but Warren was nowhere to be found. Sheridan had the line closed and was sending out orders when one of Warren's officers found him, reporting the rounding up of prisoners.

"By God, sir, tell General Warren he wasn't in that fight!"

The officer stammered. "I can't deliver it verbally, sir. Can I take it down in writing?"

"Take it down, sir! Tell him by God he was not at the front."

General Griffin, one of Warren's division commanders, soon rode up and Sheridan astonished him: "Griffin, take command of the Fifth Corps. I've relieved Warren."

He sent a written order to Warren and turned into a nearby grove, where he found loitering soldiers. He rose in his stirrups and waved his hat.

"I want you men to know we've got a record to make before sundown that will make Hell tremble!" He pointed to the South-side Railroad tracks. "I want you there!"

He was driving men toward the railroad when Warren came up with the order in his hand.

"Won't you reconsider this, General?"

"Reconsider, hell! I don't reconsider my decisions. Obey the order!"

Warren turned away, Porter sent Grant a report of the

change in command, and Sheridan sat watching squads of his men throwing down hundreds of captured Rebel muskets to fill in the ruts of a road.

The famed reporter of the New York *World*, George Alfred Townsend, was late for the battle at Five Forks, and at dusk, after a ride of twenty-five miles, he rode into Sheridan's lines, where he was forced off the road by a file of captured Confederates so long that they trailed by for half an hour. He passed a huge pen where thousands more were under guard, and after dark came upon the Methodist church at Gravelly Run, a tiny white frame building in pine woods, its pews standing outside, covered with soldiers. Inside were the more fortunate casualties of Five Forks:

> I found on its bare floors the screaming wounded. Blood ran in little rills across the planks, and human feet . . . had made indelible prints in every direction. . . . Federal and Confederate lay together . . . and all the while came in the dripping stretchers.

Townsend rode a mile away to the intersection of the five roads and entered a circle of men lying under trees. Custer was among them, trying to sleep, his face covered with yellow curls. Townsend saw General Joshua Chamberlain of the Maine men, whom he had met the day before.

"News enough today, Townsend," the officer said. "Sheridan fought his big battle here this afternoon. Cut up a whole division. Warren's removed from command. Griffin's in, and I've taken Griffin's division."

"Where is Sheridan?"

Chamberlain pointed. The cavalryman lay beside a leaping fire, red-faced and beaming, chewing a piece of cheese. Townsend was introduced to him.

"General, you've done a great day's work here," the young reporter said. "If you'll help me for a minute or two to get some idea of what it was like, I'll leave tonight and take it to New York for the papers."

Sheridan drew out his field map and for twenty minutes explained the fighting and its significance for Townsend. He named the commanders of divisions, brigades and regiments, and the numbers of troops.

"Most generals would have made a great secret of these numbers," Townsend said, "or lectured me at the expense of interesting details about the enormity of printing army news."

Townsend asked point-blank, "How many men were in the Fifth Corps?"

"I'll tell you for your own information," Sheridan said, "but don't print it. There were about ten thousand."

Townsend made some notes on an envelope, shook hands with Sheridan and walked a few feet away, where he made fuller notes. He worked through the crowd of officers, asking for details of the moves Sheridan had explained, and was soon satisfied that he had a clear picture of Five Forks. At midnight he left on the long road to New York.

Horace Porter had left Sheridan at 7:30 P.M. to ride through the victorious wing of the army back to headquarters. He had never seen the army in such a mood:

"Coffeeboilers had kindled fires, and there were cheers on all sides. A horseman had to pick his way through this jubilant condition of things as best he could. . . . As I galloped past a group of men on the Boydton Plank Road, my orderly called out to them news of the victory. The only response was from one of them who raised his open hand with thumb to his nose, and yelled, 'No you don't—April Fool!' I then realized it was the First of April."

Porter had ridden so fast that he reached Grant before couriers he had sent ahead. He threw headquarters into turmoil:

"General Grant was sitting with most of his staff about him before a blazing fire. He wore a blue army overcoat, with a cigar in his mouth. I began shouting the good news as soon as I got in sight and in a moment all but the imperturbable commander-in-chief were on their feet giving vent to wild demonstrations of joy . . . grasping of hands, tossing up hats, slapping backs."

Grant asked quietly, "How many prisoners?"

"Over five thousand."

Only now did Grant's expression change. He scrawled an order on his manifold pad and passed it to an orderly. "Put it on the field wires," he said, and turned to Porter, who thought the commander's voice as calm as if he had commented on the weather. "I have ordered an immediate assault along the lines."

It was about 9 P.M. Half an hour later, General Meade had convinced Grant that attack should be postponed. The army was now ordered to delay attack until 4 A.M.

Grant wired President Lincoln, far to the rear on the James:

> I have just heard from Sheridan. He has carried every-
> thing before him. He has captured three brigades of infantry
> and a train of wagons and is now pushing his success.

Not long after midnight Grant went to sleep, as if, Porter wrote, "the next day would bring a picnic instead of a decisive battle."

In the afternoon Grant had got early trophies from Sheridan, half-a-dozen Confederate battle flags taken at Five Forks. He had hurried them off to Lincoln by Sylvanus Cadwallader, the New York *Herald* reporter who had been the commander's friend and companion since the campaigns in the west.

Cadwallader rode through roads deep in mud until at dark he reached the docks at City Point, where Lincoln, advised by telegraph, had a tug waiting for him. The President reached for the reporter from the hatchway of his boat as if he could not wait to put his hands on the captured flags. He shook them out.

"Here is something material—something I can see, feel and understand. This means victory. This is victory."

Lincoln led Cadwallader into a cabin and had him repeat the message from Grant. He questioned him sharply about things at the front, and did not rest until the reporter had described everything he had seen. Lincoln then went to maps on a table, where Union troops were marked with redheaded pins, and Confederates by black ones. He made rapid movements at Cadwallader's direction. The reporter was aboard for almost two hours.

III

Sunday, April 2

★

Fort Mahone, aptly enough, was called by the Yankees Fort Damnation. It lay among ravines and stump-covered slopes near Battery 30, a massive pile of red clay and pine logs. Big guns and fieldpieces were sown thickly here, a wicked salient outthrust from Lee's lines. Its gunners had made its reputation; it was thought to be invincible.

In the ditches adjoining Mahone lay the 53rd North Carolina, which had come down from the Shenandoah Valley fighting in October. Some 300 yards behind them was the chief landmark of the salient, a large white-painted box of a place, the Wilcox-Browne House. War had demolished its outbuildings.

The regiment's sergeant major, Hampden Osborne, watched the front uneasily in the first dark hours of morning. Just before midnight as he had been comfortably crouched over the table in his tent—a canvas-topped pit dug five feet into the clay—a fury of mortar fire broke out. He had been playing checkers with his friend Alex Trotter when he saw through the tent flap the first angry smear of a fuse in the sky. It was followed by a peppering from Yankee fieldpieces, flinging the deadly three-inch percussion shells. The gray infantry had been put into line to meet an attack.

Pickets soon tumbled in from the darkness. Yankees had overrun the outermost rifle pits. Osborne knew that an offensive was coming, and he called for volunteers:

"All right, men, who's falling in? We've got to clear 'em out of picket, or we'll not be here by morning!"

He got a few men, and watched them stumble away down the trench behind Colonel John R. Winston, of the 45th North Carolina, who had volunteered to lead them. Ten minutes later there was a rattling of muskets and yells drifted up the ravine; they sounded suspiciously like enemy shouts of triumph. Osborne was convinced when some of the man came back, two of them bearing Colonel Winston, who was bleeding from a wound.

A bit later, about 2 A.M., the enemy came on again, and the rifle pits were overwhelmed; another wave of the tattered gray-coats clambered out to fight for them. Shells began to fall again, and the ranks in the trench about Osborne were becoming thin. Just as daybreak tinged the sky, a line of dark figures appeared over the parapet, cheering: the enemy.

When the first enemy line was a hundred yards into the open another wave followed, then another. Battery 30 opened guns on them, and soon smoke drifted so heavily in the ravine that Osborne could not see. He heard men running behind him. "Yanks in Fort Mahone," one of them yelled. Osborne knew that his trench could be flanked with Mahone lost, and almost before he thought of it bullets were spattering in the clay beside him. He ran for his tent a few yards to the rear and in the two or three minutes that he scrambled for his regimental papers in the shelter, fifty or more bullets cut the canvas overhead. He made his way to Battery 30, where the guns were firing double canister at top speed. Blue bodies were scattered on the slope below them. The Federal charge had slowed.

Osborne now saw 2000 or more bluecoats crowded between Fort Mahone and a trench, held there by fire from the cannon. There were no grenades, and the huddled enemy troops were safe until the Confederates stormed back into Fort Mahone and someone turned a battery to the rear. Grapeshot butchered hundreds of the helpless men at point-blank range, until those who could move scrambled downhill and back to their lines. Osborne thought he had never seen such slaughter.

For an hour he worked, running cartridges from the rear in blankets with Alex Trotter and a commissary sergeant, a thousand each at every trip. When the line had plentiful ammunition he organized a canteen squad, passing water for the rest of the morning. He ate nothing until afternoon, when he chewed a piece of corn pone and fell asleep in a trench. He woke up about five o'clock to find his sector quiet; there was a roar to their left, on A. P. Hill's lines. Osborne thought that they had weathered the day, and that the enemy had once more failed.

Soon after dark the order came to march his forty survivors across the Appomattox to the railroad, and to have three days' rations cooked for the brigade.

They walked through Petersburg and saw tearful women in doorways; some of them offered food, and one, sobbing, touched Osborne's sleeve and said, "God bless you."

Along A. P. Hill's line, running from Fort Gregg near the outskirts of Petersburg south and west to Burgess' Mill, on Hatcher's Run, the midnight flashing of enemy artillery leapt from battery to battery and the roar was endless, increasing by the hour.

The corps chief of staff, Colonel William Palmer, shook awake Major Starke, the adjutant, and sent him to find out what was happening on the front. Starke was back long before daylight. He went in to Hill.

"The enemy's got into part of our line near the Rives Salient," he said. "And it looks bad in the trenches in front of the city."

A few moments later Colonel Palmer saw the General's slave, Charles, leading Hill's dappled gray horse. Palmer ran to Hill, who was mounting.

"I want to go with you, General."

"No," Hill said. "I'm going to see General Lee. Please get the staff up, and have the wagons hitched and ready to move. I'll be back."

He went off through the fog toward army headquarters at the Turnbull house a mile and a half to the west. He rode past the couriers' quarters, where Sergeant Tucker was grooming a horse.

"Follow me to General Lee's with two couriers," Hill called. He trotted from sight. Tucker hurried off the couriers, Kirkpatrick and Jenkins, and followed them when he had saddled.

Hill strode into General Lee's room without being announced. The generals were talking about the darkening situation when Colonel Charles Venable of Lee's staff flung open the door. He shouted, "Wagons are flying down the road toward Petersburg and Union skirmishers are behind Hill's right."

Hill tore from the house like an excited boy and vaulted into his saddle so recklessly that Lee sent Venable after him to urge caution. When he had been halted, Hill told Venable patiently that his lines were cut in two, and that he must save them. He promised that he would be careful and spurred away, followed by Venable, Tucker and Jenkins.

Hill rode down a ravine toward a branch of Old Town Creek, and hardly a quarter of a mile from Lee's headquarters stumbled upon two enemy infantrymen. Tucker and Jenkins rode them down, and the bluecoats dropped their rifles.

Hill sent the courier Jenkins rearward with the prisoners.

Tucker drew his Colt Navy pistol and rode on in advance of Hill and Venable, the weapon lying ready on his saddle. They rode into cover of bushes by a small stream and, while their horses drank, Hill peered through the mist. Tucker looked up the hill with concern; hundreds of men swarmed around the log huts Mahone's men had abandoned in mid-March.

"What troops are those, sir?" he asked.

"The enemy's."

Bullets spattered about them. Hill saw across the Boydton Plank Road half-a-dozen Confederates, falling back before the enemy, and sent Venable to rally them. After watching for a few minutes as Venable tried in vain to halt running troops, Hill recalled him and they rode across a hillside where they met men of Colonel William Poague's artillery battery. Hill left Venable behind to direct these guns against the enemy.

Hill and Tucker trotted into a thin pine forest. It was becoming full daylight.

"Excuse me, sir," Tucker said, "but where are you going?"

"Sergeant, I'm obliged to go to the right of the line as soon as I can." He pointed toward the southwest. "We'll go up this side of the branch and that will cover us until we're in the field behind General Heth's headquarters. I hope the road will be clear there."

Their horses clattered over the plank road and for more than a mile they rode in lonely silence. As they emerged from the woods, Hill seemed startled by a sudden realization of their predicament. He turned to Tucker:

"Sergeant, if anything happens to me, you must go back to General Lee and report it."

They rode into the field near Heth's headquarters, about two miles from the Turnbull house. Tucker saw that the road nearby was full of troops. Hill turned his glasses on them.

"There they are," he said.

Tucker did not need to be told that they were Federals.

"Which way now, General?"

Hill pointed to the woods parallel to the road, and Tucker galloped ahead of him. As they neared the forest Tucker saw a squad of bluecoats, two of whom were in advance. The leading pair took cover behind a huge oak, and one above the other leveled their rifles beside the trunk. Tucker looked quickly to Hill.

"We must take them," the general said. He drew his pistol for the first time.

"Stay where you are," Tucker said. "I'll take 'em."

He was within twenty yards of the waiting marksmen. Tucker shouted.

"If you fire you'll be swept to hell. Our men are here. Surrender!"

Hill was beside him, yelling, "Surrender, you!"

They were almost on the enemy when one of the bluecoats began lowering his gun; he snapped it back to firing position as his companion spoke.

Both bluecoats fired at the general. Tucker caught the bridle of the gray and wheeled. Hill lay on the ground, outstretched and still. Tucker rode off quickly the way they had come. He changed to Hill's horse and galloped for headquarters, circling parties of enemy skirmishers, but driving straight through the narrow streets of Mahone's old hut city, under sporadic fire.

The boy courier, Percy Hawes, stationed half a mile from General Lee's headquarters at 2nd Corps Artillery, lay in his tent shelter most of the night watching mortar shells over the lines. They fell at a distance, but the older couriers watched them apprehensively. The distant firing toward Five Forks in the afternoon seemed to upset them, and when they saw messengers moving so swiftly in and out of Lee's quarters, they began to pack their knapsacks.

Hawes had dozed when, about 3 A.M., he was aroused by a man running past, and shouting, "Bill, if you want them old cows you better hurry up. The Yanks have broke the line."

A wagon driver leapt from his tent and shouted until Negro

servants were up and harnessing the teams. Within five minutes wagons were loaded, tents were going down and the post had disappeared. The wagons went toward the headquarters of General W. N. Pendleton, the artillery commander. Hawes remained.

He took his mare behind a shed to feed her, and between the slats of the building saw a line of enemy skirmishers. They came carefully, as if expecting trouble. He rode from the shed, but as he left was exposed on a slope, and came under fire. He galloped to General Lee's headquarters.

Heavy fighting erupted on General John B. Gordon's front at three-thirty, preceded by mortar fire so heavy that men were jarred from their feet in the clay pits. Fogs of sulphurous smoke lay everywhere. Near the Appomattox, enemy infantry tore away part of the front line, and that was only the beginning. The mud-covered Confederates slithered a few yards rearward into mazes of pits and runways, and fired on the enemy from new angles. Combat became individual and raged between isolated posts in trenches which led nowhere.

On other reaches of Gordon's lines, the enemy was beaten off, and for hours there was a lull, with occasional bursts of firing from the Federal siege guns. Blue troops massed opposite the thinnest spot in Gordon's front, where McGowan's brigade had been pulled out to meet the flanking blow on the south.

Captain John Gorman, of a North Carolina regiment, watched the enemy in admiration: "I saw them when they first came in sight, marching in line of battle, their columns deep, apparently by divisions, their guns sparkling in the sun, and their blue uniforms seemingly black in the distance. They drove the Confederate skirmishers before them with impunity, and when they reached point blank range received the fire of the batteries without staggering . . . the Confederate batteries were carried in a moment, and the long line of breastworks was theirs."

Federal cheers drowned the sound of adjoining battles as the skirmishers drove Confederates from the field. One wing of the oncoming enemy lapped over Fort Mahone and halted before Fort Gregg, an outpost to which a few graycoats ran. Only this fort now stood between the Federals and complete victory; if they swept past it they would drive to the banks of the Appomattox and cut the right wing, the men of A. P. Hill and Longstreet, from the main body of the army.

Trickles of reinforcements into the fort had an oddly irrelevant look. The blue mass paused before rushing forward against the tiny mound.

John B. Gordon watched the carnage from his line, constantly moving. He was a favorite with the troops, a lean man of erect bearing and jet-black hair, a deeply scarred cheek and striking eyes; his men found them sparkling with defiance, but an enemy reporter thought them "as fierce and nearly cruel blue eyes as ever I looked into." The army was fond of repeating an observation made of Gordon: "It'd put fight into a whipped chicken, just to look at him."

Today Gordon looked admiringly as his men fought: "With barely 6,000 men I was holding six miles of line. Just about 1,000 men to the mile, or about one to every two yards. . . . Some part of this thin line was being forced continually . . . our line would bend and twist and swell and break and close only to be battered again once more. . . . Men weak and hungry never complained . . . fought grimly, as men who had made up their minds to die . . . the men, dropping in the trenches, would eat their scanty rations, try to forget their hunger, and snatch an hour or two of sleep."

Gordon pushed the enemy from much of his line and held on, despite the offensive, still a shield of sorts for Lee.

Even in these moments Gordon's scarred face wore a distracted look. Yesterday, in Petersburg, his wife had borne him a son.

William Miller Owen served with the Washington Artillery of New Orleans; his first sight of the action had been at dawn, when a solid shot fell near him, showering him with dirt. Infantrymen left the trenches and ran across the fields.

"A retreat," Owen said.

"Nah," said a companion. "Those boys are chasing rabbits, Owen."

Within five minutes more guns had joined, and musket fire was general; retreating Confederates swept past the gunners in their covered pits. "The lines are broken," Owen thought, "and the army is cut in two."

When the light grew stronger he saw Lieutenant Battles of his command hitch horses, so that he might take his guns back to Fort Gregg. Before the horses appeared, Federal infantrymen swarmed over the works and took Battles and all his gunners.

Lieutenant Frank McElroy led a charge of his cannoneers and rescued Battles and the guns, and the battery rumbled down the Boydton Plank Road, where it halted behind the Mississippi Brigade of General Nat Harris and fired on the enemy. There were few targets, and McElroy at last moved, driving the men toward Fort Gregg. The Mississippi Brigade fell back when the big guns had gone, but from it a few men were sent to make a stand at Gregg.

Robert Lee could not have slept, even without the disaster at Five Forks and the collapse of the right. His rheumatism had never been worse, and the shooting pains were so persistent that he broke his stoical silence to complain of them to the staff. A light burned all night in his room at Edge Hill, the William Turnbull home where they had lived in the winter. The house was two and a half miles southwest of Petersburg on Cox Road.

The right flank of the army was gone, but orders went out through the night. Lee hourly expected Longstreet; he was late.

Before dawn, not long after A. P. Hill had left, Longstreet came in—he had got the order only at seven o'clock last night, and had promptly put Field's division on trains. Old Pete himself had come south by horseback with his staff, to save room on the cars.

He found Lee still in bed. The commander motioned Longstreet to sit beside him and asked him to put Field's troops on the right flank as soon as they came in. He spoke of Pickett's loss without bitterness, and then seemed to wander a bit, talking about the repeating rifles of the enemy and their overpowering numbers in the fight of yesterday.

Lee had not finished his instructions when a staff officer came to the door. "General, the lines have broken out front. You'll have to go."

Longstreet saw the astonishing calm of the commander even at this moment. "Drawing his wrapper about him, he walked with me to the front door and saw, as far as the eye could cover the field, a line of skirmishers in quiet march toward us."

Wagons and men hurried from the place. Lee dressed quickly and within moments was on Traveller, riding with the staff. Walter Taylor was even now in the house, standing over the telegraph operator in an effort to get off Lee's messages to Richmond. One of them was vital:

> It is absolutely necessary that we should abandon our position tonight, or run the risk of being cut off in the morning. I have given all the orders to officers on both sides of the river, and have taken every precaution that I can to make the movement successful. It will be a difficult operation. Please give all orders that you find necessary in and about Richmond. . . .

Taylor was almost casual as he dodged enemy fire in the exposed place:

"I held on as long as I could, until the shells of the enemy began to crash through the house. The operator informed me that he could no longer work his instrument."

"Detach it, and take it with you," Taylor ordered the telegrapher. The man hurried from the house, mounted a waiting horse, and joined the retreat.

An enemy shell fell beneath the telegrapher's horse, tore off all the animal's legs, and sent the rider sprawling. "He quickly gathered his instrument together and the last I saw of him he was making very good time for the city," Taylor wrote.

Behind them shells had ignited the Turnbull house, and flames lapped from the windows. Lee took the blame for the destruction. "I'm afraid it was burned because they knew I had been there," he said. "I should not occupy a private house."

Lee turned to Armistead Long of his staff: "This is a bad business, Colonel. Well, it has happened as I told them at Richmond it would. The line has been stretched and it has broken."

The party met Sergeant Tucker leading General Hill's gray horse. The artillery courier, Percy Hawes, stood nearby. "I will never forget the expression on General Lee's face," he wrote.

Lee asked Tucker for details of the general's death, and heard them somberly. His voice was almost drowned by gunfire, "Those of us who are left behind are the ones to suffer."

He sent Colonel Palmer and Tucker to tell the widow of their loss: "Colonel, break the news to her as gently as you can."

Palmer and Tucker evaded Federals pouring through the lines and were soon at the Venable house. As they dismounted they heard Mrs. Hill inside, singing loudly at her work. Palmer hesitated, and did not knock on the door. He walked quietly into the hall, but the sound of his boots stopped Mrs. Hill's singing. Tucker heard her voice from where he stood on the porch:

"The General's dead. You wouldn't be here unless he was dead."

Robert Lee rode toward Petersburg, determined to find a way to hold his lines until night. He was interrupted by a reply from Jefferson Davis to an early dispatch of warning, complaining that such short notice would mean "the loss of many valuables, both for want of time to pack and of transportation."

Lee's calm was unbroken. As late as 3 P.M. he dictated a lengthy message to Davis full of plans for raising Negro troops to save the South. He was, however, insistent that he must abandon Petersburg in the night.

The orders for marching west had reached all commands:

> General Longstreet's Corps and General Hill's Corps will cross the pontoon bridge at Battersea Factory and take the river road on the north side of the Appomattox at Bevils Bridge tonight.

> General Gordon's Corps will cross at Pocahontas and Railroad bridges, his troops taking the Hickory Road, following General Longstreet to Bevils Bridge, and his wagons

taking the Woodpecker Road to Old Colville, endeavoring not to interfere with Mahone's troops from Chesterfield Courthouse, who will take the same road.

General Mahone's Division will take the road to Chesterfield Courthouse thence by Old Colville to Goodes Bridge. . . .

General Ewell's command will cross the James River at and below Richmond, taking the road to Branch Church, via Gregory's, to Genito Road, via Genito Bridge to Amelia Courthouse. . . .

The movement of all troops will commence at 8 P.M., the artillery moving out quietly first, infantry following except the pickets, who will be withdrawn at 3 A.M. . . . Every officer is expected to give his unremittent attention to cause these movements to be made successfully.

After all the infantry and artillery has crossed, Pocahontas and Campbell bridges will be destroyed by the engineers. The pontoon bridge at Battersea Factory and the Railroad bridges will be reserved for the pickets.

First, he must save the army. He rode Traveller near the front, as if by instinct, to a point near Fort Gregg, where ruin faced him at this moment. It was near 9 A.M.

The enemy had poured through the gap in Gordon's line and now gathered strongly at the head of the valley between the Boydton Plank Road and Old Town Creek. If they stormed down the valley in force, they would reach the Appomattox and take Gordon's entire line in rear. There could then be no retreat.

Fort Gregg was a plump semicircle of packed earth lying on the muddy plain, protected by a trench fourteen feet wide and six feet deep, its earthen walls eight feet thick, topped with a palisade of logs. There were embrasures for six guns, and inside, a firing step so that riflemen could man loopholes. There was one weak spot. On the right flank, leading out toward smaller Fort

Whitworth, was an unfinished trench with a parapet. Attackers reaching that parapet might climb into Fort Gregg.

Whitworth was some 200 yards away, little more than an unfinished three-gun battery, with no ditch to break an infantry charge.

Until the dozen or more men of the Washington Artillery struggled into Gregg with their three guns, these works were undefended, but Gregg was stacked with ammunition in pyramids: solid shot, canister, grape and bomb.

Under orders from General Cadmus Wilcox, the senior on this sector, General Nat Harris of the Mississippi Brigade poured men into the two works. The 12th and 16th regiments, now no more than 200 men, trotted into Gregg, Lieutenant Colonel James H. Duncan in command and Captain A. K. Jones second. Harris himself took the remaining 200 into Whitworth.

A party ran from Whitworth under enemy guns and set fire to rows of abandoned army huts in front, to remove them as cover for the attackers. The flaming buildings halted the Federals in that area, but lines advanced on Gregg without a pause.

When the Mississippians ran into Gregg they found about a hundred men hiding there, refugees from broken regiments who begged to be allowed to go to the rear. Duncan saw that they were demoralized and sent them out running. He ordered them to leave their muskets behind; they did so gladly. A few other men straggled in, chiefly North Carolinians from General James Lane's brigade.

Captain Jones was called to the rear entrance, where he saw General Wilcox.

"Are you the commanding officer?" the general asked.

"Colonel Duncan is."

"Send for him."

Wilcox was nervous. He did not wait for Duncan to come, but shouted into the rear doorway, "Men, the salvation of the army is in your keep. Don't surrender this fort. If you can hold for two hours, Longstreet will be up."

Crashing shells drowned his voice, and for a moment the general shouted to the startled men with silent openmouthed grimaces. Someone yelled, "Tell 'em we'll not give up."

Wilcox walked to the Petersburg side of the fort and lay against the logwork, talking with General Lane of the North Carolinians, with whom he had been carrying on a debate since the enemy break-through.

"You know I didn't want to come in here," Lane said. "It was against my judgment."

He pointed down the valley, where the bulk of his command lay, a thin bulwark in the Federal path in case the forts fell.

"I don't want to be captured or killed here," Lane said. "You know that's what's going to happen. Let me go down there and take command, where we can dam up this gap."

"All right," Wilcox said quickly. "I suppose you should. Go ahead." He clambered out of sight and rode to the rear with his staff.

Lane sent a captain inside to count the men of his command. The officer soon returned. "I can't do it, sir. They're so mixed up with all the different commands they can't be counted, unless we call them down, and they'd be under fire."

Inside, shells tore great splinters from the logs and drove them into the bodies of men crowded below.

General Lane left a lieutenant in command of his troops in Gregg and went rearward. He saw artillery being pulled out of Whitworth, and assumed that fort had fallen. He remembered of his escape: "I started at a dignified quick-step, but the enemy's fire soon made us double-quick, and then forced us to run." He was soon driven to the inner line of defenses.

The men of Fort Gregg faced the enemy alone. At least one of them thought of the Alamo in this moment. They had been under heavy artillery fire for half an hour when the first serious Federal charge came. By now six or eight men had been shot while manning Gregg's big guns and the cannon had fired only a few shots before they were disabled. It was left to the riflemen.

The bluecoats came into the open.

Captain Jones saw it as if it were a game:

"When the cannonading ceased, the infantry advanced in beautiful order until they got in range of our rifles, when we pelted them right merrily, and so effectively that they retired out of range; but soon their lines were reformed, and then they came in a run. Their battle lines were three fourths of a mile long, but before getting to the fort they were solid masses of men.

"In these charges there was no shooting but by us, and we did cruel and savage work with them. When they got within 25 or 30 yards of the fort they were safe, for we could not see them again until they appeared upon the parapet."

A moment of silence on the field was broken by faint cheering for the defenders of Gregg from the main Confederate line in the rear. The work was almost surrounded, however, and men at the loopholes saw that they could get no help from Whitworth.

A fresh Federal line came out; onlookers from the fort estimated its strength at 9000, and far behind it, from the dark columns still waiting, reserves seemed to be without limit. It was nearing noon.

Surgeon George Richards of the 2nd Corps, the only doctor in the fort, squatted by Captain W. S. Chew and Lieutenant McElroy, the gunners. "Surrender the place, Captain," he said. "The army's had time enough to get in line now. They'll come in on us next time."

"Let it go as it will," Chew said. "We'll not give up."

It was pride in the guns as much as anything else; they had been taken from the enemy long ago in the army's heyday, at Winchester, on the way to Gettysburg.

Colonel Duncan watched the blue lines come on, and called to his men, "Wait. Wait. Steady. Hold fire." It became so quiet that the scuffing of Federal boots sounded in Gregg. The enemy was very close before Duncan yelled, "Fire!" Dozens of bluecoats fell, but the line did not falter. The charging troops scrambled among the 2000 or more crouching survivors of the first attacks and bobbed over the parapet, fighting for footholds, tossing rifles ahead of them. They fell in heaps. Other Federals came on the unfinished parapet and two of them leapt into Gregg. Bayonets were driven through their bodies before they reached the ground. A rush of the enemy came over the wall, and there was no longer time to reload. The graycoats fought with musket butts.

Buxton Conerly, who was barely eighteen, was among the privates of Company E, 16th Mississippi, one of twenty-five men defending the rear gate of Gregg. He found himself in a weird struggle:

"Now the solid shot and bombshells found in the fort came into use. Our men hurled them on the heads of the enemy in the ditch. The fuses of the bombshells were fired and rolled on them. This work did not stop until all, or nearly all, of the solid cannon balls and shells were gone. Brick chimneys built to tents for artillerymen were torn down and the bricks thrown at the enemy. Numbers of efforts to scale the wall were made, but the Federal soldiers would not act together, and the most daring ones were shot down on the walls and fell on their comrades below. A color bearer fell on the fort, with his flag falling over on our side."

A straggler who found himself in Gregg was A. A. Garrison of the 37th North Carolina, eighteen. He worked rapidly as long as Gregg held out:

"A man of Company D, our regiment, volunteered to shoot while three of us loaded, and we did the best that was possible. I had about eighty rounds of new cartridges; and when I surrendered my cartridge box was nearly empty. This soldier took good aim, and I think he must have killed and wounded scores of the enemy. Near the close he was shot through the jugular vein."

Garrison left the work as a prisoner.

General Lee watched the scene through glasses. A courier, William Callerton, carried his order to a knoll nearby and Colonel William Poague's field guns opened on the fort. The first shell killed half-a-dozen Federals near the front wall. Others burst rapidly and drove the bluecoats to the far side of the work.

Surgeon Richards thought that only this fire prevented the slaughter of all survivors. The doctor counted twenty-seven Confederates when quiet fell.

Captain Jones saw the final moments: "The battle flags of the enemy made almost a solid line of bunting around the fort. The noise was fearful, frightful and indescribable. The curses and groaning of frenzied men could be heard over the din of our musketry. Savage men, ravenous beasts! We felt that there was no hope for us unless we could keep them at bay. We were prepared for the worst, and expected no quarter.

"We lost about forty men killed in the fort after its capture, and fully that many Federals were killed by their own men. It was ten minutes before the shooting could be suppressed."

Jones thought the Federal dead piled before Gregg were thicker than those of Fredericksburg or the Bloody Angle at Spotsylvania; he estimated the enemy dead at 1200. The prisoners trailed away from Fort Gregg to the Federal rear; Colonel Duncan was left behind, unconscious with a head wound.

General Longstreet, studying the enemy with his glasses, saw General Gibbon near the enemy front: "I raised my hat, but he was busy, and did not see me." Old Pete also recognized General Grant, whose wedding he had attended so long ago.

The enemy now mystified the Confederate command; Federal signalmen were in action, wigwagging and bringing more troops into action in the valley leading to Petersburg. But the new columns did not drive into the vulnerable gap between the wings of Lee's army. They went, instead, after a body of cavalry, down their lines toward the Appomattox.

From the neighborhood of fallen Gregg the observant Captain Gorman saw smoke on the enemy's trail toward the river. Field's division, led by a Texas brigade, was now on the right flank, a thin shield for the army to the banks of the Appomattox. But though the enemy had overwhelming numbers, with only a narrow creek between them and the men of Field, they did not attack.

General Field, who had arrived a few hours earlier, did not understand the reluctance of the enemy. He watched a brief skirmish ended by the men of the Rock Brigade of his General Henry Benning, and then:

"The enemy, not finding us inclined to give way for him,

contented himself with forming line in front of us, but out of range. We stood thus in plain view of each other till night, when our army began its retreat."

The defenders of Fort Gregg had won a breathing spell and perhaps saved the army from massacre on the rutted plain outside Petersburg.

To the southwest of this spot, where Lieutenant J. F. J. Caldwell lay in the ranks of McGowan's South Carolinians, disaster struck anew. Caldwell had been awake all night during the attacks near Petersburg: "So the night passed in watching, in closing to the right or left, in listening to the great roll of musketry sweep for miles along the line. . . . When day dawned, we were exhausted by waking and anxiety."

Caldwell fell asleep in the morning. He heard men packing knapsacks and running, but did not stir. An officer called him, but Caldwell thought sleepily that he could catch a few more winks, and overtake them on horseback. He was startled awake by sudden silence:

"I rose and looked to the right. The line was more than a hundred yards from me. I looked to the left, and not a man was in sight. I knew the fate of Petersburg was sealed."

Caldwell spurred after his brigade, which was marching northwest. The column joined other troops, crossed Hatcher's Run, and hurried to the Southside Railroad. The infantry moved so fast that wagon drivers and gunners could whip their teams to full speed in the rear. Caldwell thought it a noisy retreat, indeed.

Four shrunken brigades came to Sutherland's Station: McGowan's and Scales' of Wilcox's division, and Cook's and McCrae's of Heth's—in all, fewer than 4000 men from A. P. Hill's line.

Cadmus Wilcox put them in line parallel to the railroad on a ridge between a farmhouse and a church.

The Federals charged. General Wilcox watched it: "They lost no time, but rushed forward in a disjointed manner, yelling furiously. Our artillery opened fire on them, but without effect. They came up against the right, still yelling. When at a convenient distance they received a cool, well-directed and destructive fire that . . . sent them to the rear in great disorder."

Another witness was Major Dunlop, commander of the McGowan Sharpshooters: "I stood upon a stump on the hill . . . where the sharpshooters were contending with the Federal right, and great tears of overwhelming admiration flowed down my cheeks as I contemplated the grand courage of that glorious little band of heroes. . . . I could hardly stand it."

The Federals fell back to form again. Men of Caldwell's line ran to a wounded bluecoat in their front who was in agony with a broken thigh.

"God damn you Johnnies!" he yelled. "Get away from me. I'll not be taken."

The writhing boy begged the Confederates to shoot him and when they refused, he slashed his throat with a pocketknife. He died as a second Federal charge was launched.

The bluecoats were more orderly now, and reached the Confederate line on the left, driving in skirmishers, still cheering. They were pushed back through the trees once more and there was a wait of an hour before they stormed for the last time. The Confederate line, Major Dunlop saw, was "enveloped in one living cloud of bluecoats." After one volley the line broke into flight.

Caldwell said: "Now was the most disorderly movement I ever saw among Confederate troops. We had to pass from 200 to 300 yards through a clear field under the fire of infantry from flank and rear, and under artillery. The whole air shrieked with missiles, the whole earth trembled. We fled for the cover of woods and distance."

Major Dunlop saw it as "a perfect bedlam. Officers and men, mixed together in the wildest confusion, fled before the withering fire until the point of danger was passed, when they came together, were assorted out and formed into some sort of organization and continued the retreat."

Captain Brunson's sharpshooters were the last to break. Brunson said: "We gave them a blizzard, and, feeling lonesome, departed."

The enemy captured 600 men, two guns and a regimental flag; they took three of the five regimental commanders of Mc-

Gowan's Brigade and drove the remnants to the banks of the Appomattox.

Caldwell rode amid the retreat:

"A weary, mortified, angry stream of men poured through the fields and roads, some pushing toward Amelia Courthouse, some making direct for the river."

Commands were mingled, many officers were gone, and lost men strayed off, but most of them thought only of crossing the river and putting the enemy behind. Some struck the river too low down, could not cross, and were swept up by Federal cavalrymen. A few found a ferry and escaped. The majority went up the river bank with Caldwell:

"I regret to relate that a good many men threw away their arms . . . so we wandered, strung along the river bank for miles, floundering in the beds of small streams or in mudholes filled by the recent heavy rains, pressing forward to some point undetermined in our own minds.

"Night fell upon us, but even that brought no repose until, at a late hour, we collected a little band and lay down by the roadside in utter exhaustion and almost despair. Some of us were so worn that we slept like the dead; others so anxious that we could not sleep at all. I never saw more haggard countenances in my life. I, for one, felt years older than I had that morning. I was seized with a burning fever and a hunger equally consuming. I had had no food since the evening before, and no sleep since Thursday night."

The few men who had fled with Major Dunlop were even less fortunate. They struck the stream farther to the east, and found it too strong for swimming. One man, Frank Sheely, drowned as the party watched, helpless to save him.

Dunlop put a picket line on a hill by the stream and set to work on a raft. He impressed a party of Negro laborers who were cutting wood for the town of Petersburg, and they had the raft well begun when pickets yelled that Yankees were coming.

The little command scattered. Dunlop recalled of it:

"We dispersed in amusing haste and concealed ourselves in a dense thicket of switch cane and underbrush along the river bank, where, once hidden, we were afraid to show our heads above the cane, lest our hiding place be discovered. . . . We remained in the thicket, as quiet as mice, until after dark."

The men came out and looked up and down the river, in every cove and under every bit of brush, in search of a boat to cross the river. There was nothing. They turned then in the other direction, and scouted carefully along the Federal lines. The fires of the enemy ringed them in completely. There seemed to be no escape.

General Lee had moved steadily nearer Petersburg, and was for a time at the home of the Dupuy family at the outskirts, where messengers besieged him. At dusk, when quiet had fallen, Colonel Walter Taylor found him alone.

"If you can spare me tonight, General, I want to go into Richmond," Taylor said. "I can join you in the morning."

He saw hesitation in Lee's manner. "My mother and sister are there, sir, and I want to tell them good-bye. And Betsy, Miss Saunders, my fiancée. We want to get married tonight."

Lee stared. "Married. Not tonight?"

"Her home's behind the enemy lines, and she's alone in Richmond. If we hold a line somewhere south, then she could come to us."

Lee smiled. "Go on," he said.

Taylor and a courier galloped from Petersburg to Dunlop's Station, north of the Appomattox. A little train with steam up was on the track, but the railroad agent would not let the colonel take it.

"Last ambulance train for the wounded," he said. "I got orders to hold it right here."

"I must get to Richmond. Isn't there another engine?"

The agent pointed to a locomotive in the distance, its course marked by a tortured column of smoke. "Yonder goes the last one," he said.

Taylor tossed his reins to the courier. "Join me in Richmond as soon as you can," he said. The colonel leapt into the engine of the ambulance train and shouted to the engineer, "Detach it and catch that engine. Fast. It's life or death."

They roared along the track at high speed, but caught the locomotive only as it reached Falling Creek, about three-fourths of the way into Richmond. Taylor jumped aboard and sent the ambulance engine back to Petersburg.

Dr. John Herbert Claiborne was in charge of the two over-flowing army hospitals in Petersburg and, when he had finished his day there, had worked in his office on Washington Street. The wounded arrived constantly.

Claiborne learned of the army's plight at 11 A.M. when Colonel Henry Peyton of Lee's headquarters came with news of the broken lines and the death of A. P. Hill.

There was also bad news from west of the city. An assistant surgeon who had explored out Cox Road came back in haste. The Yankees were already closing in, he said, and were at the Whitworth house, not a mile away; they were swinging around and might soon encircle the town. From another direction, the Fair Grounds Hospital, news was even worse. A frightened messenger told Claiborne, "They've got the surgeons hiding behind trees, dodging fire. Lots of them wounded ain't nearly as bad as they thought. They're running out of there, and don't stand on the order of going, neither, Doc."

At 2 P.M. Claiborne got orders to leave the city as soon as he could assemble a train, taking every available surgeon, servant and hospital attaché. They would pack medicines in wagons, cross the river at Campbell's Bridge, and move along the Chesterfield Courthouse road.

Claiborne found that he could take but few from the medical corps, since the staffs of the crowded hospitals could not be spared.

"When I mustered my little force at sunset," he said, "I found I had four surgeons and as many attachés, one ambulance and driver, one buggy, and four colored servants."

He also had, though he did not realize it, a wounded soldier in the wagon, a Captain Riddick. With the officer rode his sister, a pretty girl of about seventeen who refused to leave his side. Another who trailed along in the walking party was a stout Confederate chaplain, a stranger to Dr. Claiborne.

As they left, the mother of the doctor's youngest slave entertained the company with an admonition to her grinning sixteen-year-old son, "Don't you dare come back. You follow him to
the end of the earth."

Claiborne was ready to follow the procession to the west
when soldiers dropped stretchers of more wounded in the yard
before his office; a crowd of women had gathered, some of them
sobbing. Claiborne pulled back the blanket from one stretcher
and recognized the soldier as a boy he had known from child-
hood. His arm was torn off at the shoulder and the wound was
covered with dirt and powder grains. The dying boy stared at
the doctor without recognition.

"As I turned away," Claiborne wrote, "a poor woman caught
me by the hands. 'Doctor, won't you have somebody help me
carry my poor husband home? I can nurse him better than anybody else.'"

The woman pointed to a stretcher where a middle-aged
Petersburg militiaman lay, a fourth of his skull shot away, the
veined gray mass of his brain exposed.

"Madam," Claiborne said slowly, "I can't help you now.
An army of surgeons couldn't save him."

The woman's scream was the last of the Petersburg sounds
he heard, above the guns, as he spurred his horse after the little
hospital caravan.

The ordnance reserve train of the army stood between the
Richmond-Petersburg Pike and the Woodpecker Road, not far
from Swift Creek—forty-four wagons under the command of
Lieutenant Joseph Packard. A storehouse at the spot was
crammed with artillery ammunition, piles of mortar shells and
more than 1300 pounds of gunpowder in boxes.

In the late afternoon an order reached the train: Captain
Fred Colston, the assistant ordnance chief, was to see to the
destruction of the supplies, except those that the wagons could
carry, and join the retreat at nightfall.

Packard and Colston directed their men for an hour or more
as they tossed mortar shells into Swift Creek above Dunlop's
Station. Others carried ammunition to the Pocahontas and the

upper pontoon bridges for the use of engineers. The wagons moved at dark, but Packard and Colston were forced to wait. A companion, Sergeant Robert S. Burwell, was in Petersburg passing good-bye kisses to the lady friends of a wide acquaintance.

About midnight they went to Dunlop's Station to blow up stored ammunition. A quartermaster officer arrived at the same time with orders to burn surplus food. Packard remembered of his last moments in the Petersburg campaign:

"I took a ham from the pile, which I strapped behind my saddle. . . . About one o'clock we rode on to overtake the train, and about an hour later we heard a tremendous report; the quartermaster had carried out his instructions. At intervals during the night as we rode along we heard the explosions which followed the destruction of our fleet in the James River. Many times during the night the sky was lit up from these explosions, and the earth seemed to tremble beneath our feet."

In General Gordon's old brigade, now commanded by General Clem Evans, was Private I. G. Bradwell, a picket in the outermost line, quite near the enemy. Bradwell looked back from his post about 10 P.M. to see his companions retreating. The regimental flag trailed off with them in the moonlight. He did not expect to see it again.

An officer crawled behind the picket line, whispering an order, "I'll send relief at midnight." The hissing died away to the left as word was passed to other sentries.

It was still, with a rare shot echoing from the field. Houses burned far away, beyond Petersburg. As the moon rose it became brighter and Bradwell grew nervous. He crawled to his left and found the next picket, one Haynes.

"You seen an officer with orders?"

Haynes cursed. "Officer! You know I ain't seen no damned officer out here."

The two of them crawled farther to the left, a hundred yards or more, and met a third sentinel by the name of Williams, who had seen no one since the regiment had pulled out.

"Let's leave," Bradwell said. "Far as I know, there ain't a soul on the whole line but us."

They were soon stumbling across the burrows in which the army had lived and fought for nine months. Bradwell wrote: "Confederate commissary stores were afire in Petersburg, with flames leaping high as we entered the zigzag way leading out into the open field in the rear. As we appeared in the moonshine, rising the hill beyond, in plain sight, the enemy opened with cannon. We tried at first to run to get out of range, but we were so weak from hunger that we had to go slow and stand it. The shells passed over, and we were soon in Petersburg."

Bradwell thought they were the last to leave the lines before the city. The forty miles of entrenchments were empty.

In the half-darkness, as columns poured over the bridges and wound westward along the Appomattox, the 44th North Carolina moved across its bridge.

The regiment was old, but had flown a new flag since January; the original was so tattered and soiled that other regiments could no longer identify it at brigade drills, and the proud 44th discarded it at last.

Tonight, in G Company, Color Sergeant George Barbee ripped the new flag from its staff just before they moved over the river, and picked up a stone from the roadside. When he reached the middle of the bridge he wrapped the flag around the stone and flung it far downstream. It fell into the dark river with a silvery splash.

★ THE ENEMY ★

THE TWO Federal infantrymen who had fired on General A. P. Hill would not forget the foggy early morning, though at first they thought their victim was only another Confederate.

Corporal John W. Mauk and Private Daniel Wolford, of Company F, 138th Pennsylvania Infantry, who were hardly more than boys, went over the Rebel works in the first attack, and with a segment of the 2nd Brigade, 3rd Division, 6th Corps, became separated from the main body in the mist. They crossed a railroad and wagon road, seeking the enemy.

Mauk and Wolford joined a halfhearted attack on a Rebel wagon train, and were looking for entertainment when they noticed a group of Union stragglers at breakfast in a swamp. As they approached these laggards, Mauk and Wolford saw two officers riding toward them. The boys went forward until they saw that the horsemen were Confederates with cocked revolvers in their hands. The Federals dived for a tree and held their rifles ready.

One of the Rebels urged his horse ahead and called, "Surrender, or I'll shoot you! Troops are coming in from our left!"

"Let's shoot 'em," Mauk said.

They fired, and Mauk's man tumbled from his saddle. The other galloped away leading a gray riderless horse. Mauk remembered: "Not knowing what was on our flank, and not being able to see in that direction, we backed out and went farther down the swamp and crossed."

Mauk was curious, however, and a few minutes later he said, "Wolford, I'm going to see what that officer had on him." He ran back up the hill, but saw a Rebel skirmish line coming. Mauk put the dozen or so stragglers in the swamp into line, and when the skirmishers came near, Mauk yelled to them, "Throw up your hands, advance and give an account of yourselves." The newcomers obeyed.

Mauk listened skeptically to the story one of them told, "We captured these Rebs, here, and we're taking 'em to the rear." Six or eight of these men carried guns and were in Federal uniform.

Mauk hesitated, but told them to go about their business. As they left one of them called, "Wasn't there a man killed in here somewhere? A Reb officer?"

Mauk pointed in the direction of the body, and the party marched off. It was an hour or so later before it occurred to him that this might have been a Confederate ruse to recover the body. A call to brigade headquarters enlightened him. General Horatio Wright listened to his account of the incident and at the end asked, "Do you know who you killed, Mauk?"

"No, sir."

"You've killed General A. P. Hill, of the Confederate army."

At three o'clock in the morning Colonel F. C. Newhall came to Grant's headquarters from Sheridan, his uniform spattered with mud. Grant woke up to hear the news, listened briefly without a change of expression and said, "I'm going to move the Army of the Potomac. Tell Sheridan he must look out for Lee to push in his direction."

The commander turned back on his cot and was asleep again before Newhall left on his fifteen-mile return journey to Sheridan's camp.

Grant was up at four, expecting to hear the opening of the attack, but word came from many posts that it was too dark for the men to see. The headquarters telegraphers received a dozen complaints of confusion in the darkness; troops could not see well enough to tear away obstructions before the enemy trenches. Grant agreed that the offensive should be postponed once more.

At four forty-five the first gray streaks appeared in the sky, and in a roll of artillery that shook the ground for a mile in rear, the infantry advanced.

At five fifteen Grant had the first message of progress. General Wright's corps had carried the line in front and was pushing on. Parke was next. He had taken the works before him, and had two pieces of artillery and 800 prisoners.

At six forty, Grant telegraphed Lincoln:

Both Wright and Parke got through the enemy's line. The battle now rages furiously. Sheridan with his cavalry, the 5th Corps, and Miles' division of the 2nd I sent to him since 1 this morning, is sweeping down from the west. All now looks highly favorable. Ord is engaged, but I have not yet heard the result on his part.

He also sent a cheerful dispatch to Sheridan, and had begun another to Lincoln when Ord reported that he was clearing his front, taking trenches and captives—some of the earthworks were along an important sector at Hatcher's Run. Grant added this to his telegram to the President.

He then rode to the front. Nearby troops were astonished to see the commander riding over a steep hill of the captured works. Grant passed a herd of some 3000 prisoners. Horace Porter, who rode with him, thought it must have been a memorable moment for the general as the prisoners swarmed by: "His whole attention was for some time riveted upon them. We knew he was enjoying his usual satisfaction."

A guard yelled to the straggling Confederates, "There's General Grant!" The men were instantly "wild with curiosity" to see the Union commander.

Grant rode by a division of the 6th Corps, and the men broke into cheers. Grant met Meade at about 9 A.M. The generals consulted briefly, and Meade went down his line of battle with Colonel Theodore Lyman, who found himself taking orders on his manifold pad so rapidly that he thought three men could not have kept pace with the gruff old voice.

Grant had ordered Meade and Ord to press the inner lines around Petersburg; he could see nothing to prevent their sweeping to the Appomattox. He used his glasses now, watching Lee's army stubbornly blocking attacks from Parke's divisions; he suspected that Longstreet's corps was arriving.

Grant dismounted near a farmhouse on a knoll within a mile of the enemy line; he sat at the foot of a tree, receiving dispatches, dictating and writing orders, smoking his cigar, and using the big field glasses. Staff officers swarmed about him, and the Rebel gunners soon took notice. Shells burst near the tree and the group scattered, but Grant remained at his seat against the tree trunk, writing and chewing on the cigar. Officers urged him to move, but he remained for fifteen minutes after the staff had retreated, until in an even hotter Confederate fire, he stood, brushed idly at his coat and turned toward the rear of the farmhouse.

"Well," he said, "they do seem to have the range on us."

Meade and Lyman galloped toward Petersburg during these moments, over newly won ground that gave Lyman strange sensations, for they passed a huge oak where he had been under heavy shelling months before, at the first fight along Hatcher's

Run; there was an earthwork from which Rebels had killed his friend, Charlie Mills; then beyond Hatcher's Run itself, over the frowning line of forts to a rise commanding a view of Petersburg, where they came upon heavy columns of Union troops. These men cheered Meade, the chorus of cheers passing from regiment to regiment. Meade's party met Grant again as he waited at the farmhouse.

Lyman pawed among piles of papers in the deserted house and saw that this had been the post of a Rebel ordnance sergeant; his returns lay on the floor. He had also left a diary, in which he protested the profanity and other vices of Confederates.

A little after noon Grant's officers watched the gathering force before Fort Gregg and Fort Whitworth; from their distance the earthworks did not look formidable. Morris Schaff, who was in the headquarters group, sketched it:

> These works rose from a sluggish, difficult slough. Gibbon moved up Foster's division to charging distance, some 400 or 500 yards from Gregg, Osborn's brigade on the right, Dandy's and Fairchild's on the left. Turner marshalled two of his brigades, Potter's and Curtis' in close support, and at 1 P.M. the trumpet sounded charge, and off with determined faces and rippling colors. . . .

> Osborn's 39th Illinois, moving straight forward, struck the front of Gregg; the 67th Ohio the salient to the right; the 62nd Ohio and the 199th Pennsylvania that on the left. Dandy led on the 100th New York, the 10th Connecticut and the 11th Maine.

> No sooner had they cleared the hampering slough with its sluggish pools and mane of willows than the little garrison opened. . . . By the time our men reached the moat, the slope was strewn with bodies . . . the moat soon filled with men struggling frantically to clamber up the high parapet, where they met with pistol and bayonet, and only after 25 or 30 minutes of awful slaughter was that heroic garrison conquered. Dandy said: "I forebear to describe the scene

inside that work after the surrender, but I think at least half
the entire garrison was killed."

Charles Carleton Coffin, the Boston *Journal* man, had walked
quite close to the lines at Gregg, and when he saw the U.S. flag
rise over the work, was seized by emotion:

> It was inspiriting to watch the tide of victory rolling
> up the hill. With that Sunday's sun the hopes of the Rebels
> set, never to rise again. The C.S.A.—The Confederate Slave
> Argosy—freighted with blood and groans and tears, the
> death-heads and cross-bones at her masthead, furnished
> with guns, ammunition and all needful supplies by sympa-
> thetic England, was a shattered, lifeless wreck.

When it was over, the cavalry column turned for the river,
but the infantry stalled; the blue lines curled and broke against
Field's division, and Gordon's line fought with fury. Commanders halted the troops, and Grant sent no orders to renew the
assault.

At about this hour, on the extreme right of the Confederate
line, General Miles's division had struck the enemy and after a
sharp encounter had cleared the field, taking two guns and almost 1000 prisoners.

When he got this news, at 4:40 P.M., Grant telegraphed
Lincoln, asking him to visit the front the next day. There was a
quick reply:

> Allow me to tender you and all with you the nation's
> grateful thanks for the additional and magnificent successes.
> At your kind suggestion, I think I will meet you tomorrow.

Phil Sheridan had pushed cautiously north and west during
the day, toward the Appomattox, made less aggressive by Grant's
warning that Lee might turn his whole army upon him.

By 10 A.M. he had reached Ford's Station on the railroad
and found warm tracks of the enemy.

"They done took out of here about two hours ago," a Negro
told him.

Sheridan's horsemen found only a small train with some

medical supplies and a dozen wounded—but before the command left the station a few Confederates came uncertainly from the upper floor and gave themselves up. Sheridan rode toward Sutherland's Station and, after the infantry fighting there in the afternoon, he settled down for the night.

Night fell before Lincoln left his seat beside the telegrapher at the rear headquarters of the army. He went aboard the *Malvern*, where he had no need of dispatches to see that the fighting went well. Above the din of musketry and artillery occasional explosions flared; the dark water ran red with their light. Lincoln would not leave the deck.

He spoke to Admiral Porter with a trace of impatience, "Can't the Navy do something at this particular moment to make history?"

"The Navy's doing its best," Porter said, "holding the enemy's four ironclads in uselessness up there in the river. If those boats could reach City Point they would cause havoc. They came near it once."

Porter explained that the channel had been filled with stones to prevent the Rebel vessels from descending.

Lincoln persisted, "Can't we make a noise, then?"

"Yes, and if you desire it, we will commence."

Porter telegraphed Lieutenant Commander K. R. Breese, the fleet commander up the river, to load the big guns with shrapnel and fire on the enemy forts until ordered to stop. The firing began at 11 P.M., and rolling echoes seemed to redouble the torrent of sound.

In less than half an hour the greatest explosion of the night jarred the deck of the *Malvern*. Lincoln was anxious. "I hope to heaven one of our vessels hasn't blown up."

"No," Porter said. "It's farther upstream. Doubtless the Rebels, blowing up the ironclads." Two more explosions followed, and Porter said with a satisfied air, "That's all of them. No doubt the forts have fallen. Tomorrow you can go up to Richmond."

When the explosions died away, and firing almost ceased, the President heard frogs piping in the marshes, and smelled spring in the warm wind off the river.

★ RICHMOND ★

AT 1 A.M. General Dick Ewell sent a staff officer to Chimborazo Hospital—a maze of wooden buildings housing convalescent soldiers. A shout rang down a corridor and Captain H. E. Wood, commander of the hospital's emergency corps, tumbled from bed. He was ordered to report to Ewell with his men, and the cripples and clerks and half-sick men were soon in the road, some 1200 in all, straggling along with a motley of arms. They marched into Capitol Square, where Wood reported. Ewell did not recognize him. "If you have anything to say to me, say it quickly," the General said.

His memory refreshed by a copy of the order, Ewell sent Wood's force to relieve General Field's division, which was moving to the aid of General Lee. On the route the hospital brigade was joined by a few cadets from Virginia Military Institute. Wood spread the men thinly in the dark trenches, so far apart that they were barely within calling distance of each other. They waited.

The literary clerk of the War Department, J. B. Jones, watched the hospital militia passing as he prepared his morning entry for his inevitable diary:

> Bright and beautiful. The tocsin was sounded at daybreak, and the militia was ordered to the fortifications. . . . A street rumor says there was bloody fighting yesterday a little beyond Petersburg.

John H. Reagan, the old Indian fighter from Texas who was Postmaster General of the Confederacy, had spent most of the night in the War Department and returned there early this morning. He was there when two dispatches came in from General Lee, making it clear that the army must fall back in the evening.

Not in so many words was Richmond ordered evacuated—but there was a warning to carry off public archives.

Reagan found President Davis on the way to church and told him the news from the front, but Davis did not take it as final. The President went toward St. Pauls.

Captain Parker of the Navy was up early, and after his night in Richmond went back to the school ship *Patrick Henry* and mustered his young men as usual. As he was piped aboard he saw a company of home guards marching nearby. He was puzzling over this ominous sign when he had an order from Secretary Mallory to have the corps of midshipmen at the Danville depot at 6 P.M. Parker was not alarmed, and gave orders to cook three days' rations, expecting to remain aboard himself and send the men off with a subordinate.

Something led Parker to go ashore once more, however. As he came to the dock, a horde of Union soldiers, prisoners, passed him on their way downriver, to be exchanged. "That's strange," he thought. "Prisoners always go off at dawn."

On Main Street he met a man who was almost frantic with excitement. "How do you get to Drewry's Bluff?" the man yelled.

"Is there some news?" Parker asked.

"You don't know? They're evacuating town tonight!"

Parker hurried back to his ship and ordered off all but ten men, who were detailed to burn the vessel before leaving. Parker then reported to Secretary of the Navy Mallory.

"You will go with the President and Cabinet to guard the gold treasure and archives," Mallory said.

When he went into the streets afterward, Parker was struck by the city's calm: "A peculiar quiet, a solemnity . . . the pale, sad faces of ladies."

Down the river, below the city, was old Fort Harrison, battered by months of shelling. In the morning sunshine the 1st Engineer Regiment was digging like so many gophers, mining the earthworks. Aside from the thumping of picks, Corporal

M. W. Venable of Company H heard only the roll of guns from the direction of Petersburg and the clang of church bells. He and a companion were interrupted as they dug holes for the explosives, and sent to a wharf.

They met the "flag of truce" boat, riding low in the water and swarming with Federal prisoners moving down to be exchanged. Venable talked with some of them as workmen opened a section of the pontoon bridge for the prison boat. They had news:

"You got whipped over at Five Forks, and the army is pulling back," they said. "Richmond is to be cleared out tonight. We'll capture you before the week is out, Johnny."

Venable and his friend laughed at the pale, bony, long-haired men from the prison pens. "You'll do well if you can catch what's in your shirts," Venable said.

But when Venable got back to Fort Harrison, his company was falling into line, and a drum rolled without ceasing.

St. Pauls Church stood on the corner of Grace and Ninth Streets, its tower thrusting more than 225 feet into the warm April air. Worshipers thronged up its low, wide stone steps and between the columns, through the façade which had been copied from the Athenian temple known as the Lanthorn of Demosthenes. Inside, settling into quiet, the crowd sat in a spacious room with French gray walls, on pews painted to resemble white oak, capped with rosewood. The seats were none too comfortable, for the fine cushions had been given to the hospitals more than two years earlier. The church was fifteen years old.

It was communion Sunday, and in the congregation, as usual, were many of the leaders of the Confederacy. President Davis was in his pew, Number 63, with one of his aides, Governor Frank Lubbock of Texas. Behind the President sat General Josiah Gorgas, the Chief of Ordnance. The service opened with prayers.

The stout, aging sexton of the church was William Irving, an Englishman who had served it from the beginning, dressed today in a faded blue suit, with polished brass buttons and ruffles at his wrist and neck. Near noon a young man in civilian clothes entered the vestibule and approached Irving.

"I must see President Davis," he whispered.

"I'll call him when the prayer's done."

The boy waited impatiently for a moment. "I can't wait longer," he said. He pulled paper and pencil from his pocket and wrote a note:

> General Lee telegraphs that he can hold his position
> no longer. Come to the office immediately. Breckinridge.

Irving read the note and took it down the aisle on tiptoes to the President. Davis glanced at the paper and rose. His face was calm, but many people raised heads to watch him leave, and there were expressions of alarm.

An officer of the Ordnance Department, Lieutenant Colonel William L. Broun, was in a pew some distance behind the President's; while Broun wondered about the departure of Davis, he saw Irving return and tap General Gorgas on the shoulder; Gorgas also left the church. A moment later the sexton called Broun, and then went to the far side of the church and asked General Joseph Anderson, the head of the Tredegar Iron Works, to follow him.

The rector was Dr. Charles Minnigerode, a tiny German immigrant whose fervid manner of speech betrayed his native accent after many years in Richmond.

Minnigerode saw Davis leave, followed by others, and when the prayer was ended, the minister went into the chancel to deliver his usual brief Communion Service talk. Irving called out half-a-dozen other men while he spoke. The congregation, he saw, was restless, and Minnigerode hurried to the end as quickly as he could without giving signs of alarm. At last, when the sexton came into the front of the church and called Minnigerode's assistant, The Rev. Mr. Kepler, people began leaving the pews. Minnigerode ceased speaking. The rector found the city's Provost Marshal, Major Isaac Carrington, in the vestry room, and was told that Lee's lines were broken and that Richmond was lost.

In the vestibule Mrs. Edwin Hobson, who was General

Joseph Anderson's daughter, met a Confederate officer. He told her the news from the front. She laughed. "I don't believe a word of it. You're April Fooling me, like I did you yesterday."

Constance Cary, the beautiful young woman who had been a celebrated belle of the city, was in the church and had known at once that disaster had struck. She saw Davis take the message in the pew just in front of her and the color drain from his already pale and sunken cheeks. She forced herself to remain behind as others left the place, but when the shortened service was over Connie joined friends on the steps. She saw strange new signs:

"There was little discussion of events. People meeting each other on the streets would exchange silent hand grasps and pass on. I saw many pale faces and trembling lips, but I heard no expression of fear. Movement was everywhere, nowhere panic."

As she walked home Connie breathed deeply of the garden smells along "begarlanded Franklin Street," as if for the last time. She passed knots of friends who spoke rapidly with an air of departure. When she reached home, her brother left for the railway station; his parting gift was an astonishing treasure, a ham given him by a Negro that morning.

Not far away, in St. James Church, the shrewd diarist Judith Brockenbrough McGuire saw General Samuel Cooper, the Confederate Adjutant General, as he was called from the building. There was no excitement until afterward, when the congregations of the two churches mingled, and people from St. Pauls brought the news.

"Not until then," Mrs. McGuire said, "did I observe that every countenance was wild with excitement. The inquiry, 'What's the matter?' ran from lip to lip, no one seemed to hear or answer." She had a "strange, unrealized feeling," even when she heard that her son, a teacher of mathematics for the naval cadets, had been ordered south with Captain Parker, to help guard the President and the Confederate gold.

In the evening, she remembered: "We collected in one room and tried to comfort one another. We made large pockets and filled them with as many of our valuables as we could suspend from our waists. . . . Baggage wagons, drays, carts, and ambulances were driving about the streets."

She had a final blow to convince her that the Confederacy was gone—when she tried to hire a servant to run an errand her money was scorned as worthless. "We are in fact penniless," Mrs. McGuire mourned.

A mile in the rear of the outermost defense line of Richmond, north of the James, the 3rd Artillery Battalion had been relieved for church services. The Rev. Henry M. White preached in an open field, and afterward many of the soldiers went in to Richmond. While they were absent an order came to be ready to move, but this was thought to be only a precaution.

Private W. S. White, of the 3rd Company, Richmond Howitzers, was one who gave little attention to rumors of unrest in the city. Most of the command's horses were long since gone, and he helped the officers salvage the big guns. The 3rd Company was forced to leave all but two caissons, and even so the huge brass Napoleons were reduced to four horses each, rather than the usual six. There would be trouble on the road wherever they went. At the day's end the Rockbridge Artillery was reduced to four guns, the Salem Artillery to four, the Powhatan Artillery to three, and the 3rd Howitzers three—a total of fifteen for the battalion.

There were no wagons for fodder or food, and rations were issued on the spot, each man taking as much as he could carry. At last, when orders came to move, there was a rush, and drivers looted the last supplies of meat, molasses, meal and flour. They marched for the city. Private White was conscientious, but soon discouraged:

"I started with about twenty cannoneers to my gun, but when we had nearly reached the city only two of them could be found, one of whom was quite lame and the other one so lazy that if he ran away he would be too lazy to stop."

White thought these men had gone to bid farewell to friends and relatives in Richmond, and since he also had friends there, he turned over command of his gun to the lame cannoneer and left the line of march himself.

Major Robert Stiles, a young veteran of the war's bloodiest fighting, commanded an artillery battalion east of the city, on the banks of the James. Tonight he read to his men by torch-light, from the 91st Psalm, which he called The Soldier Psalm:

"Thou shalt not be afraid for the terror by night, nor for the arrow that flieth by day.

"Nor for the pestilence that walketh in darkness, nor for the destruction that wasteth at noonday.

"A thousand shall fall at thy side, and ten thousand at thy right hand; but it shall not come nigh thee."

Stiles saw that one of his younger men, a handsome boy in his teens, by name Blount, was staring with tear-filled eyes, strongly moved by the reading. He was fumbling for words to reassure the frightened boy when the company adjutant came up with a dispatch in his hand.

"Wait," Stiles said. "I'm satisfied I know what that paper says. We've come to the end here. Let us pray."

Afterward Stiles read an order to join the retreating army and the gunners, who had known only garrison duty in river forts, were armed as infantrymen and moved toward Richmond. Stiles wrote:

"They had more baggage piled upon their backs than any one brigade, perhaps I might say division, in Lee's army was bearing at the moment."

But by morning, he saw, the men had learned, and walked lightly, with the road behind them strewn with dis-carded clothing, blankets and canteens.

Dick Ewell had been back in the city since 10 A.M., recalled by an order from Longstreet's headquarters. He had galloped most of the way, strapped to the flea-bitten gray, Rifle, with the inevitable Apache boy at his side.

He found orders for the evacuation in his office at the corner of Seventh and Franklin Streets and sent men to prepare for the destruction of stores when night came. There was too little time for the matters now pressing upon the crippled general.

Men from Custis Lee's patchwork battalion begged him for

wagons or carts to haul the big guns, since they had no transport. Ewell sent his staff to comb the city.

There were no guards left for Richmond, and Ewell fumed: "The militia had dispersed—being mostly foreigners."

He had sent the few local troops left to him to take prisoners from Libby and Castle Thunder and guard them on the westward march.

By 2 P.M. crowds gathered around Ewell's headquarters and the Spotswood Hotel, blocking the streets and walks, gossiping about the rumors. Among them was Captain McHenry Howard of Custis Lee's command. Howard had come in to church, but was so startled by the commotion that he wandered the streets. He saw one of Pickett's officers push through the mob into headquarters; men who had spoken with him at the door passed the rumor: "He had to come in by train all the way around by Burkeville. Pickett is cut off."

Howard rode through the streets to rejoin his command, watching the people:

"Bundles, trunks and boxes were brought out of houses. . . . Vehicles of every sort and description, and a stream of pedestrians with knapsacks or bundles filled the streets which led out from the western side . . . a few wounded officers were borne along on litters, their calm, pallid faces in strange contrast with the busy ones around.

"Ladies stood in doorways or wandered restlessly about the streets, asking every passerby for the latest news. All formality was laid aside . . . all felt the more closely drawn together."

Joseph R. Haw was a young clerk in the Ordnance Department. He went to a Presbyterian Church on this Sunday morning and heard the Rev. Moses Hoge announce the breaking of Confederate lines at Petersburg. When he went outside and passed the capitol, Haw saw a man building a bonfire of new, unsigned Confederate money in a street.

When the crowds from church had dispersed the city changed, almost in the wink of an eye. The Richmond *Whig* sketched the moment:

Suddenly, as if by magic, the streets became filled with men, walking as though for a wager, and behind them excited Negroes with trunks, bundles and luggage of every description. All over the city it was the same—wagons, trunks, bandboxes and their owners, a mass of hurrying fugitives, filling the streets.

President Davis held a Cabinet meeting shortly after noon, with former Governor John Letcher and Mayor Joseph Mayo attending. For once there was no bitter clashing; plans of evacuation were discussed. Most of the important papers of the Post Office Department were already gone, Reagan reported; other archives would be moved or burned. The increasing roar of cannon shortened the session and the executives scattered to finish their packing. They agreed to meet in the evening at the railroad station for the journey to Danville, and to the south, if need be.

General Gorgas, the ordnance expert, lived in the Armory, and he hurried there and began tossing clothes into bags while his wife, Amelia, tried to help him. He was too busy for more than a few words:

"You must not stay in the Armory when the enemy comes. They will want it for barracks."

There was little discussion of the decision of Mrs. Gorgas to stay behind while her husband fled. She knew that other Cabinet wives would share her fate. In the late afternoon the Gorgas family moved its effects to the home of a relative so that Amelia would be safer, but the work of moving furniture was far from complete. Gorgas left his wife a horse and wagon.

War Clerk J. B. Jones, wandering by the depot in the afternoon, met General James L. Kemper, who was looking for General Ewell. "I can't find anybody to give me orders," Kemper said.

Jones thought that had an alarming sound, and grew more concerned when he found that eight trains would leave for Danville during the night. He was told sternly at the railroad office,

"No provision for civil employees or their families. Absolutely not."

Jones talked with James Lyons, the friend of the Jefferson Davis family who had been a power in Confederate councils.

"My friends advised me to leave," Lyons said, "but my family is sick, and I think I should stay. But, being an original Secessionist, they tell me the enemy will make me one of the first arrests, and string me up."

"I don't agree," Jones said. "I think your presence here might help us all."

Jones walked down the street and saw officers hurrying with trunks after they had been turned away at the depot.

On Ninth Street he met Judge John A. Campbell, the dignified Alabaman who had been a justice of the United States Supreme Court before the war, and in his youth had been appointed to West Point by John C. Calhoun.

Campbell, the assistant Secretary of War, had great influence in the government, though it had diminished in recent weeks since the failure of the peace conference with President Lincoln, to which Campbell had been a Southern delegate. The Judge was talking to himself as he hurried along with two books under his arm.

Jones tried once more to find a way out of the city, but Campbell could not help. "They've left it to the chiefs of bureau to decide which clerks to take," he said. "And they will be small in number, I'm afraid."

He walked on, and Jones went toward the War Department. He passed squads of local troops impressing horses. Others, Jones thought, were on their way to burn public stores. Jones had an eye for the slaves:

> The Negroes stand about mostly silent, as if wondering what their fate will be. They make no demonstrations of joy.

He saw Federal soldiers, prisoners under guard, and wondered why they had been brought to the city today, of all days.

At the War Department Jones was told that all workers with families were urged to remain in Richmond, and the rest to flee. There was no compulsion. Mechanics and ordnance workers were free to go if they chose.

Jones heard a rumor that General Lee had been shot. For the first time he seemed low in spirits:

> I remain here, broken in health and bankrupt in fortune, awaiting my fate, whatever it may be. I can do no more. If I could, I would.

Judge Campbell was besieged in his office by a woman friend who came seeking advice. He waved a sheaf of papers at her, grimacing and shaking his head.

"Just a minute, Judge," she said, "I'm alone at the Spotswood Hotel. What should I do?"

"Stay there, my dear lady! You'll be perfectly safe. I advise all families to remain in their own houses. Keep quiet."

The woman returned to the Spotswood and spread the advice among the families there and in houses nearby. Only at the home of the Pegram family, where they were mourning, did she turn away. The woman seemed unable to understand that the city was falling.

Naval Cadet John W. Harris, the son of a Charlottesville physician, lay abed in the Belle View Hospital, a victim of dysentery. He was not quite seventeen, but was a veteran who had fought with the raider John Mosby before entering the Navy. For all his discomfort, he was a lighthearted warrior.

At 2 P.M. a midshipman armed as an infantryman burst into the ward. Harris and his mates hooted, but their companion silenced them:

"Out of bed, the last of you, and march down to the storehouse. They'll arm you for the Naval Brigade. The Ironclad Squadron is abandoned at Drewry's." The hospital was soon emptied of all who could walk.

Admiral Raphael Semmes was waggling his spectacular waxed mustaches over late luncheon in the wardroom of his flagship, *Virginia*, at four in the afternoon, when a messenger handed him a sealed dispatch. It was from Secretary Mallory:

General Lee advises the Government to withdraw from this city, and the officers will leave this evening, accordingly. I presume that General Lee has advised you of this, and of his movements, and made suggestions as to the disposition to be made of your squadron. He withdraws upon his lines toward Danville, this night; and unless otherwise directed by General Lee, upon you is devolved the duty of destroying your ships, this night and with all the forces under your command, joining General Lee. Confer with him, if practicable, before destroying them. . . .

The Admiral was stunned, but managed for his memoirs only a mild, "This was rather short notice." He signaled his captains aboard and made plans for a busy night. His little fleet of four ironclads and five wooden ships was locked in the James just below the city, and must be sunk; he felt that he could not make a move before nightfall for fear of alarming civilians.

While his officers made stealthy preparations, Semmes sent a message from the signal tower at Drewry's Bluff to General Lee. There was no reply, though his signalman tried frantically for more than an hour.

Semmes watched from his deck a boatful of Confederate soldiers just freed from Yankee prisons, passing upstream after being exchanged. The men looked weak, but when they passed the *Virginia* they cheered the Confederate flag.

This day was a shocking welcome home for Semmes, for he had been in Richmond only a few weeks. He had come from a triumphant career of sinking Yankee shipping in the Atlantic, and had made his *Alabama* the most feared ship afloat, until she had been sunk by the *Kearsarge*, far from home.

As night came on, Semmes saw fires along the shore where departing troops burned barracks and supplies. The Admiral was astonished, for he had planned to sink the ships in quiet, rather than signal the enemy that the fleet was no more. When he saw the burning of the army's stores, he gave orders to blow up the ships.

There were hours of hard labor before the charges could be set off. Sailors swarmed through the ships, taking provisions and drawing arms. It was late when Semmes left his flagship

with fires blazing in the hold and from a distance watched her
go up. He did not seem despondent:

> The spectacle was grand beyond description. Her shell-
> rooms had been full of loaded shells. The explosion of the
> magazine threw all the shells, with their fuses lighted, into
> the air. The fuses were of different lengths, and as the shells
> exploded by twos and threes, and by the dozen, the pyro-
> technic effect was very fine. The explosion shook the houses
> in Richmond.

Fannie Walker, the copying clerk of the Bureau of War who
had read the catastrophe in a dispatch from General Lee last week,
was spending Sunday with her mother and sister, both matrons
at Howard Grove Hospital. As she walked home she met the
chief of her bureau, Captain R. G. H. Kean. The official struggled with heavy bags in each hand and bundles slung around
his neck and under his arms.

Fannie shrieked, "Where are you going, Captain? Shall I
leave town? Tell me what's happening!"

Kean did not put down his bags. "I cannot advise a lady to
follow a fugitive government," he said.

As he turned, Fannie saw tears welling in his eyes. She
hurried to her home, where she found an aunt, a Treasury Department clerk, furiously packing clothes into a bag.

The young courier Percy Hawes had been sent with a dispatch and a headquarters pass into Richmond; the boy drove his
horse to the limit of endurance.

Hawes rode to the house where General Lee's family lived,
on Franklin Street, gave a dispatch to Colonel Thomas Carter
of the 2nd Corps artillery and went across the city for a farewell
to his family. He laughed, leaving his mother and sisters, "You
look for me back here scouting, if no other way." His mother
gave him three biscuit, all the house could offer.

At the Lee house he found Colonel Carter and another
officer drinking tea with Mrs. Lee and her daughter. Mrs. Lee

was drawn with rheumatism, but chatted gaily, determined, she said, to remain in the city whatever came. The soldiers soon took their leave.

The city's streets were becoming more rowdy as crowds of flashily dressed hangers-on at the hotels and saloons emerged, looking for plunder.

The color sergeant of a Virginia regiment saw a band of women, holding hands in a chain and "singing and carousing." They passed near Capitol Square, where Major Carrington, the Provost Marshal, had his hospital stewards, clerks and convalescents on display.

Captain W. W. Blackford was an engineer who had fought with Jeb Stuart. In the late afternoon he was packing in his rented room when one of his two slaves, by name Gabe, came up from his job at the telegraph office, where Blackford had hired him out.

"What must I do, sir?" the Negro asked.

"You're free to do what you like, Gabe. You're just as rich as I am this minute. I advise you to wait here and get work with the Yankees when they come in."

Gabe left Blackford only at the crowded canalboat as the master was towed away westward, trying to catch up with Lee's army. The Negro cried pitifully at the end, and sent his love to Blackford's wife. "A more honest and faithful man never lived," Blackford wrote.

At this hour a slave dealer, one Lumpkin, appeared at the depot with a shuffling line of fifty slaves, their ankles chained. A sentinel in uniform thrust a bayonet at Lumpkin.

"There's no room here for you or your gang," he said, and turned the slaver from the station.

The furious Lumpkin was forced to unlock the Negroes in the street and watch the scattering of $50,000 worth of property—perhaps the last batch of salable slaves in the nation.

Colonel Walter Taylor's young woman friend at the Arlington lived with her mother in the increasingly painful poverty of this spring. Until today, they had clung to their faith in Lee's army; they lost it, staring from their windows as the hurrying crowds became a mob. The streets were now so full of people that carriages of officers could not pass.

Someone came through West Main Street shouting that the government commissary was open for all who wanted food. The girl did not want to fight through the crowd, though she knew that they might face starvation without these stores. One of their roomers, a Mrs. Sampson, declared that she was going for a barrel of flour, and set off despite protests that she could not carry it home. The girl and her mother felt obliged to accompany her.

The women wore their new finery—homemade hats trimmed with chicken feathers. The girl would not forget that walk in the streets: "Such a starveling mob! I got frightened and sick, and mother and Mrs. Sampson were daunted."

They went to the home of Colonel Walter Taylor's family, where they thought they might borrow the younger son, Bob, as an escort. Mrs. Taylor explained, "Why, Bob can't go, child. Walter's being married today, and all of us are working like Trojans."

"Married! How can he marry today, with all this?"

Colonel Taylor, she well knew, was one of General Lee's most active staff officers, and was engaged to her friend, Elizabeth Saunders.

Bob came to the door. "I took the dispatch to Betty while she was at church this morning," he said. "He just told her to be ready, and he'd come to town this evening for the ceremony. The army's moving west, you see, and nobody knows how long they'll be gone."

The women went off in the crowd. The girl and her mother got nothing at the commissary, but Mrs. Sampson, by some sorcery, managed to have a barrel of flour carried to their house.

In the evening the girl saw Colonel Taylor dismount at the Lewis Crenshaw home, where Betty Saunders was living. There was an affectionate reunion at the door.

Colonel Taylor found the house crowded with the two fam-

ilies and a few friends; most of the women were already in tears.
The Reverend Mr. Minnigerode greeted him effusively. Taylor
had time to do no more than brush engine cinders from his coat.
He remembered of the moment: "The occasion was not one of
great hilarity, though I was very happy. My eyes were the only
dry ones in the company."

The marriage took place after midnight, and there was the
briefest of honeymoons. Before 3 A.M. Taylor, accompanied by
his new brother-in-law, John S. Saunders, galloped off to rejoin
the army, leaving the city by Mayo's Bridge, in the glare of burning buildings.

It seemed to the watching girl at the Arlington that the
bridegroom had spent only half an hour in the house before he
emerged and left abruptly, without a public kiss or any sign of
farewell.

The girl's attention was now diverted by the increasing disorder she saw from her window:

> People were running about everywhere with plunder
> and provisions. Barrels and boxes were rolled and tumbled
> about the streets. . . . Barrels of liquor were broken open
> and the gutters ran with whisky and molasses. There were
> plenty of straggling soldiers who had had too much whisky.
> Rough women had it plentifully, and many Negroes were
> drunk. The air was filled with yells, curses, cries of dis-
> tress, and horrid songs.
>
> No one in the house slept. We moved about between
> each other's rooms, talked in whispers, and tried to nerve
> ourselves for whatever might come. A greater part of the
> night I sat at my window.

Not far from the house where this girl stared fearfully at
the city, the Naval Cadet John Harris and two companions forced
their way through the streets in a government wagon. They went
to the old tobacco factory at Franklin and Twenty-Fourth Street,
where the middies had recently been given quarters when the
foul bilge water on the river-locked ships drove them ashore.
A light led them to the top floor of the huge shed, and they

burst into the garret to find a lieutenant sitting majestically at the mahogany table from their wardroom with silver service spread before him. As if the world had not changed a trifle this week, the officer drank rum and nibbled on crackers.

"What're you doing here?" Harris said. "We heard the President had already gone, and things are about to blow up. Yanks'll be here soon."

"Nonsense," the lieutenant said grandly. "It's all going to come out all right. The middies have just gone down to North Carolina, to Chapel Hill, to set up the new academy."

Harris and his mates were half convinced and, at the order of the lieutenant, returned to the hospital and prepared for a leisurely southward journey the next day. They closed the door on the officer, who still sat with his elbows on the gleaming white tablecloth, chewing as if he would never get enough.

E. T. Watehall was fourteen years old. Tonight he prowled through the crowd of strangers, searching for food. He was on hand when the destruction of the city began.

On Ninth Street he passed great piles of paper burning, and by their light watched men in Confederate uniforms smash the door of Antoni's Confectionery, the city's famed candy shop. Women in the store begged them not to break the jars on shelves.

"Take all you want," they said, "but don't ruin us."

Young Watehall paused, but was not fatally tempted: "As this was private property, I did not try to get any of the candy, as much as I wanted it."

A nearby jewelry store window was broken and rifled by civilians.

The boy wandered to the water front, and was near General Ewell, who was furiously directing troops over Mayo's Bridge, when an explosion rocked the area. Ewell swore, "I'll shoot down the first man that puts a torch to this bridge."

Watehall looked back toward the city:

"I saw a large coal of fire fall on the steeple of the Presbyterian Church while I was half a mile away. It burned so slowly that I am sure it could have been put out if any one could have gotten to it. This church, though it stood in a thickly populated part of the city, was the only thing that burnt in that neighborhood."

There was now no light in streets except from flaming buildings; the gas had been cut off at the city works. People burned paper in the streets in order to light their way to pillage.

Captain Clement Sulivane of the Local Brigade was sent by General Ewell to muster his troops, some of the clerks and convalescent soldiers, and to supply them with food and arms. Sulivane worked all evening, herding together his men, but after hours of maddening effort he had fewer than 200 left from 1200. The battalions melted as fast as he assembled them, for heads of departments, packing for flight, called all employees and sent them westward with trunks and boxes. The carriages and wagons were gone.

The Ordnance Department clerk, Joseph Haw, was one of the fortunates ordered to the Danville depot to join the retreat by rail. When they pushed through the mob and passed the ring of midshipmen with bayonets, the Ordnance men found they were few indeed—no more than twenty, Haw estimated. Even so, they could find no place on the train then in the station. They waited for hours.

Haw heard that government stores were open and watched with a companion:

"The storehouses were wide open and filled with men, women and children, black and white. For light they were burning bits of paper and dropping them on the floor still burning. One man fell through the elevator hatch, and nobody bothered themselves about him, so bent were they on plunder."

When they returned to the depot there were more hours of waiting, but at last the Ordnance men got into a freight car, clambered over piles of pig lead and bullet molds, and were jammed in a jumble of mattresses and household furniture—the property of some fleeing officer. Joe Haw saw men atop the car, and soon realized that wounded from hospitals of the city

covered the train. At last, very late, the wheels groaned into motion and they were off.

Will Timberlake, of Company D, 2nd Virginia Reserve Battalion, was in command of a picket post on the Three Chopt
Road, outside the city. Just before dark he was told to take his
men into Richmond for emergency duty.

Their first stop was at the Provost Marshal's office on Broad
Street, where they laid aside muskets and carried armloads of
papers into the street and burned them. They then marched to
the Shockoe Warehouse on Cary Street, filled with 10,000 hogsheads of tobacco, and set it afire.

"We also took about fifteen barrels of whisky out of a cellar
on Cary Street and knocked the heads of the barrels in," Timberlake said. "We let the whisky run down the gutter."

Excited women yelled down to the soldiers from the windows of the Columbia Hotel just opposite the flaming warehouse,
and Timberlake led his men into the place to get them out. They
were busy all night.

Pretty Connie Cary, with the last of her family gone, did not
remain alone in her misery:

"I have cried until no more tears will come, and my heart
throbs to bursting. . . . All evening the air was full of farewells
as if to the dead. Hardly anybody went to bed. We walked
through the streets like lost spirits till nearly daybreak."

In the tall brick house on Franklin Street which had become
known as "The Mess," Mrs. Robert E. Lee and her daughters had
frequent visitors during the night, all urging them to flee. A
church across the street was already in flames. One man proposed
that alternate houses in the street be blown up to halt the fire, and
several people crowded around the Lee house agreed.

The house next door caught fire briefly, but still Mrs. Lee
would not budge. She sat in the parlor most of the night,
wrapped in her black shawl, and friends thought her the calmest
survivor in the city.

W. S. White of the Richmond Howitzers, who had left his cannon with a crippled soldier, spent the evening in farewells to friends, and at last went in search of his command. He noted people carrying away their loot, whisky running in the gutters, and hundreds of children in the streets after midnight. There were lights in every house.

Then, in the red light of the conflagration, came a squad of bluecoats under guard. The Federals jeered at the people as they passed, calling insults and laughing over the fall of the capital. Guards lashed at them with whips, but the catcalls broke out elsewhere in the squad, and the prisoners pushed down the street, howling, to be lost in the uproar.

White found his company on Fourteenth Street, near Mayo's Bridge, and went with it from the city.

On the crumbling front below Richmond to the southeast, under the noses of the enemy, the Ringgold Battery, under Captain Crispin Dickinson, held a few yards of the lines around Fort Gilmer. Its big guns waited during the day, without orders, though other commands had been sent to the rear.

After dark an order came: Destroy the gun carriages and spike the guns. Make ready to evacuate. Lieutenant W. F. Robinson directed the work as men cut spokes from wheels with axes and drove rattail files into the vents of the guns. They were soon hurried on the road to Richmond.

The artillerymen were given muskets as they entered the town, and marched through streets which circled the blazing districts. This was not enough for Lieutenant Robinson. He remembered his boots.

Only two days earlier he had left the boots with a shoemaker to be stretched. Robinson's father had recently paid $600 for this pair, and the boy officer was determined to keep them. He left the column at a run, found the shoeshop, kicked open the door and ran out with his boots. He caught the company as it crossed the river, going southward.

Jefferson Davis had gone home to the White House to oversee the packing. Four of the Negro servants were drunk: Robert,

Alf, V.B. and Ives. Some of the others were in a surly temper. The housekeeper, Mrs. Omelia, behaved strangely.

"Hide the groceries and bedding," Davis said. "Have it taken to the country. Mr. Grant can see to it on the farm."

Mrs. Omelia bustled in and out, but her replies were evasive. "The Missus told me to have the Sisters at the Convent to take things," she told him.

Davis was firm on one point: He had the marble bust of himself crated, and gave it to John Davis. "I'll put it where no Yankee will ever find it," the servant said.

The President turned to the paintings, looking anxiously at his favorite war canvas, "The Heroes of The Valley," wondering what was to be done with it. He was interrupted by a courier with a dispatch from the front, and sat to read it. John Davis carried the painting from the room, and while the President scratched out a message, Mrs. Omelia hurried the Negroes in their dismantling of the rooms.

Davis looked up. "I want Miss Maggie's saddle put with the rest of the tack," he said.

"I'll tend to everything, sir," Mrs. Omelia said. He saw her carry the saddle onto the porch.

Men from government departments came to him, and Davis turned briefly to each.

He gave the Confederate Treasurer, John Hendera, the check for $28,400 from the auction house, from the sale of his wife's goods.

"Have it cashed at the Bank of Richmond, if you can," the President said.

Hendera went off on his errand.

Davis walked to the porch and saw the family cow, still in the backyard, but speedily forgot her in the new rush of messages from the front. Petersburg was gone, it seemed, and the lines near the river, south and east of Richmond, were now evacuated.

James Grant, a wealthy friend, came to help carry off the mansion's treasure to his farm outside the city. "Take Mrs. Davis' carriage with you," the President urged.

Grant shook his head. "I don't believe I'd risk that, sir," he said. Davis saw that he feared to have the vehicle on his farm when the enemy arrived.

"Well, then," Davis said, "take it to the depot. I'll carry it along."

Mr. Grant left with the carriage and a wagonful of household goods. Only after he had gone did Davis notice that the cow had been left. He sent a Negro through the crowded streets with a message to Grant.

Time grew short, and though he saw in the house articles his wife had urged him to take to safety, he could not delay. "Save the inkstand," he told Mrs. Omelia. This was a gift from a war-time admirer, a work of art decorated with tiny figures of the Davis children.

"Don't you worry about anything," Mrs. Omelia said. "I'll take care of all of it." Davis seemed unwilling to leave until a messenger called him. The Cabinet was waiting.

He left the house with one of the secretaries, John Taylor Wood, and two aides, Colonel William P. Johnston of Kentucky and Governor Lubbock, the Texan. Davis wore a Prince Albert, and a weskit and trousers of Confederate gray. The streets were reasonably quiet where they rode and they soon reached the depot. The Negroes were to follow with the boxes and trunks.

The crowd opened to pass Davis and his party into the station, where they met the Cabinet. Last-minute affairs of state seized the President's attention, but he turned aside often to attend to personal details.

Hendera reported that the bank would not cash the huge check, though it was drawn by the respected firm of Elliott, Bell and Fox on the Bank of Virginia. "Take it along," Davis said. "Perhaps we can cash it in Danville, or along the route."

One of the Negroes, Robert, tugged at his sleeve. "Miz Omelia wouldn't let me pack the stuff," he said, "and they ain't much here. She even took the groceries out of the chest. I can't find Miss Maggie's saddle nowhere."

Davis had to turn from this to the carriage. Trainmen refused to put it aboard the Presidential cars, since there was not an inch of spare room. "Put it on the next train," he said, and received solemn assurance that this would be done.

A final worry was that the family treasury was empty even of the worthless Confederate money, and that he could not repay the $2,000 given him for safekeeping by the almost-white

boy Washington, son of their mulatto Ellen, who was now traveling with Varina.

As soldiers called for passengers to board the cars, Davis
found that more must be done. The Negro, Tippy, had been left
at the White House in the confusion. Another, Spencer, had come
despite Davis's orders to the contrary. A slave shouted over the
crowd to the President, "They left the spoons and forks, sir!"

Davis sent one of them, David Bradford, back to the mansion to find his wife's silver, and told him to leave the city with
General John Breckinridge, who would stay behind until the
rest of the government had moved.

The Cabinet was a striking group in the depot throng. The
loudest voice was that of Judah Benjamin, the swart, stout Secretary of State; he called orders and greetings in the silvery orator's voice that had become familiar in Richmond. Bystanders
thought they could hear in it traces of his Yale training and West
Indian birth.

The largest of them was the handsome Attorney General,
George Davis of North Carolina, also noted as a fiery orator. He
had begun as a Confederate Senator, and joined the Cabinet during the last year. At first an opponent of the President, he was now
a close adviser and warm friend. The towering lawyer had a reputation for brilliance that went back to college days, when he had
led his class at the University of North Carolina.

There was Judge Reagan, the Postmaster General, the Tennessee farmboy known as The Grand Old Roman, a frontiers-
man who had migrated to Texas when it was still a republic. His
department, perhaps the most efficient of all, had been self-sup-
porting throughout the war.

Stephen R. Mallory, of the Navy, father of the Confederate
ironclads, today had none of the distracted look of a few days
earlier, when Captain Parker of the midshipmen had found him
walking the streets with a pistol in hand.

There was George A. Trenholm, a walking legend of vast
wealth whose Liverpool office of Fraser, Trenholm and Co. had
been the most vital Southern outpost in Europe. His ships had
carried a lion's share of goods through the blockade, and his prop-
erties ran to steamer lines, railroads, hotels, cotton presses, plan-
tations, wharves, thousands of slaves. A self-trained man, the Sec-

retary of the Treasury. He was ill with neuralgia and his wife, going along to nurse him, was the only woman in the party.

Captain Parker eyed the officials carefully from his post in the line of armed sailors:

"Mr. Davis was calm, dignified as usual, and General Breckinridge, the Secretary of War, who had determined to go out on horseback, was as cool and gallant as ever—but the others, I thought, had the air, as the French say, of wishing to be off."

Breckinridge remained at the station for some time after Mr. Davis's train pulled out, and the watchful Parker admired the dignity and poise of the man who had been Vice President of the United States at the age of thirty-six, and the Democratic candidate for President in 1860. About him hung the spirit of Confederate origins.

Parker was soon called to attend the treasure, for his train was to be the next departure.

The Confederate treasure was immensely heavy. All afternoon, under guard of soldiers and sailors, its chests and boxes had been carried aboard the train under the eye of Walter Philbrook, the senior teller of the Treasury Department. It included not only Confederate funds which had, in theory, stood behind the storms of paper money showered upon the country for four years—there was also the wealth of the private Richmond banks.

In all, at least half a million dollars. Most of it was in doubleeagle gold pieces, Mexican silver dollars, silver bricks, gold ingots and nuggets, but there were also sacks and boxes of copper coins and a bewildering variety of coins of all sizes.

When the President's train had gone, Captain Parker and the sixty midshipmen drew a ring around the treasure train and the sailors stood with cocked muskets. It was duty for which the young men had been prepared when Parker told them, "You have been chosen for dangerous service, because you are brave, honest and discreet—and gentlemen." The navy men, some thought, had arrived in the nick of time to prevent the mob from looting the treasure.

Midnight came. Parker began to grow more anxious; the train gave no signs of leaving. Outside the station the captain saw "large numbers of ruffians spring into existence, suddenly, I suppose, thieves, deserters, and the like who had been in hiding. These were now breaking into stores searching for liquor. . . . We heard the explosions of vessels and magazines, screams and yells of drunken demons in the streets. Fires were now breaking out in every direction, and made it seem as though hell itself had broken loose."

Near the stroke of midnight Parker heard the rumble of artillery on a nearby bridge and sent a man to investigate. The officer came back with a report: "It's the rear guard of the army, sir. Lightfoot's Battery."

"The name's suggestive," Parker thought.

Then, to his relief, the train creaked away behind the chuffing little engine and the Confederate treasure moved on its long journey. They crossed the bridges into Manchester, and sat there, watching the burning of Richmond for a time, and then steamed away at a rate of about ten miles an hour.

IV

Monday, April 3

★

★ RICHMOND ★

HUNDREDS CROWDED the main government warehouse where whisky was being destroyed. A Richmond *Times* man watched:

> They contrived to catch most of the liquor in pitchers, bottles and basins. This liquor was not slow in manifesting itself. The crowd became a mob and began to howl. Soon other crowds had collected in front of other warehouses. . . . So frenzied had the mob become that officers in charge . . . had to flee for their lives. . . .

> Crowds of men, women and children traversed the streets, rushing from one storehouse to another, loading themselves with all kinds of supplies. . . . After midnight . . . straggling soldiers made their appearance on the streets and immediately set about robbing the principal stores on Main Street. . . . Soldiers roamed from store to store, followed by a reckless crowd, drunk as they.

Through this melee, at 1 A.M., the hearse of A. P. Hill rolled into town, jouncing uphill at last to Capitol Square. It had been almost all day on the road from the battlefield, and the general's aide and nephew, Captain Frank Hill, had gone back to the fighting. His brother, Henry Hill, Jr., had guided the body into Richmond, aided by the courier, Jenkins.

The wagon had been delayed for hours near the bridge of the James in the afternoon, and it was only in the early morning darkness that Henry found his cousin, G. Powell Hill, packing papers of the Paymaster General's office as clerks and Negroes ran in and out with bundles. Henry led Powell to the wagon.

The official stared into the ambulance in bewilderment. "I thought you'd have a coffin," he said.

The Hills left the wagon with Jenkins and ran along Twelfth Street through bands of looters into Belvin's Furniture Store, whose door, like others in the block, had been torn open. They yelled; there were only echoes in the empty building.

They found a coffin and carried it through the streets into an abandoned office, brought the general's body in from the wagon, and by candlelight washed his face and removed his gloves.

The fatal shot had blown off the thumb of the left hand and passed through the heart, emerging from his back. They stuffed the body into the coffin, which was a bit small even for the slight figure, and left the city by Fourteenth Street, over Mayo's Bridge to the south side of the river and upstream toward the farmhouse where G. Powell Hill's parents were refugees. It was slow going in the stream of vehicles and walking people. They were most of the night on the way.

G. Powell Hill rode ahead and found his mother and father at breakfast, unaware of the general's death or the collapse of the army.

They debated what was to be done with the body, since it was out of the question to carry it to distant Culpeper, and at last buried the general on the farm, in the graveyard of the Winston family. G. Powell Hill and a Negro butler made a rough case for the coffin while others dug a pit in the clay.

At about the hour A. P. Hill's body reached the city, General Josiah Gorgas departed. His overburdened ordnance train creaked from the depot across the bridge of the James, but halted in Manchester for two hours, within sight of the burning city, before it rattled off to the southwest.

The ordnance chief evidently felt no apprehension about "the brave woman," his wife Amelia, left behind; he was uneasy about the city. He had overheard General Breckinridge giving orders to burn the bridges when the troops had crossed, and Gorgas regretted that he had not interfered. More big fires would doom the city.

Amelia Gorgas and her ten-year-old son Willie spent the night stripping their apartment in the Armory. Negro servants did most of it, carting the valuables away in a carriage. Amelia Gorgas could not know that the slaves dumped the treasures in the open, atop Gamble Hill: a sewing machine, a mirror, and her prized brass fireplace set. There was not time to move the heavy furniture and the carpets.

Mrs. Gorgas feigned resignation at her general's departure: "Every wife knew that she must be separated from her husband and left to the mercy of a victorious army." Her resolution now began to fail her.

All night long, the diarist J. B. Jones noted, papers were burning in the street near the auditor's office—claims of the survivors of dead soldiers, contractors' accounts and the like.

At about 2 A.M. the city was rocked by two great explosions. The first seemed to Jones "to startle the very earth, crashing the glass throughout the western end of the city."

One report was from the arsenal, where a small mountain of gunpowder and shells went up. The magazine was near the new city almshouse, and some said that there had been no time to evacuate the last of the bedridden inmates, many of whom perished.

The shells burst for more than an hour and fragments fell within a few hundred yards of Jones's house.

The patriotic matron, Judith Brockenbrough McGuire, who was writing in her diary to soothe her feelings of alarm, was jarred by the first explosion:

> We were startled by a loud sound like thunder; the house shook, windows rattled. We did not know what it was nor care. . . . In a few hours another exploded on the outskirts, much louder, shivering innumerable plate glass windows all over Shockoe Hill. It was then daylight and we were standing out upon the pavement. The Colonel . . . had just gone. Would we ever meet again?

Judge John Campbell was shaken from sleep by the explosions. He dressed and walked to the War Office and Treasury buildings where final packing and destruction were going on and then turned down toward the riverside canal: "There were lights in the Shockoe Tobacco Warehouse resembling lamps at a distance, but in a little time there was a blaze of light and flame." The old jurist saw the fire spread to nearby flour mills and leap to stores in Cary Street. He went back to his house.

The last regular troops between the enemy and the city were in General Martin Gary's little brigade, lying on the Charles City Road under orders to wait until 2 A.M., pass through the city as rear guard, and burn the bridges leading westward. There was confusion.

Gary was a fierce old brigadier with a remnant of veteran cavalry: The 7th South Carolina, the Wade Hampton Legion's Sharpshooters, and part of the 7th Georgia, some of whom were dismounted. They came to the fringe of the city before they learned that all other troops were gone, leaving only Ewell and his hapless militia in Richmond. The horsemen were ordered to await the dismounted pickets of their rear guard. E. M. Boykin, who was in their ranks, sketched the final moments of resistance north of the James:

"We built big fires of brush wood to give light and warmth and deceive the enemy. It was cold. . . . The men . . . when they heard that the halt was to be for two or three hours, wrapped in their overcoats, with the capes drawn over their heads, and were soon sound asleep, forgetting the defeat of armies."

Two o'clock passed; there was no sign of the men from the rear. Gary reluctantly led them nearer the city. At this moment the great report from the river erupted. Boykin described it as "a tremendous explosion, lighting up everything like day, and waking every echo, and every Yankee for thirty miles around."

At daylight they came to the Turnpike Gate near the juncture of the Charles City and New Kent Roads. The sun was rising on one hand, Boykin saw, and on the other, in Richmond, "an ugly red glare" was growing. At this spot Gary settled in an abandoned earthwork to wait for his rear guard. The men soon appeared, dragging after the unaccustomed walk in their high

boots and spurs. The column wound into Rocketts, the southern section of the city. Boykin had a vivid impression:

> The peculiar population of that suburb were gathered
> on the sidewalk; bold, dirty-looking women, who had evi-
> dently not been improved by four years of military associa-
> tion; dirtier, if possible, children; and here and there were
> skulking scoundrelly-looking men . . . hard at it, pillaging
> the burning city.
> One virago stood on the edge of the pavement with her
> arms akimbo, looking at us with intense scorn as we swept
> along; I could have touched her with the toe of my boot
> as I rode by her, closing the rear of the column. She caught
> my eye.
> "Yes," she said, with all of Tipperary in her brogue,
> "after fighting them for four years y're running like dawgs."

The brigade passed into the city proper, and an even wilder
scene:

> Bareheaded women, their arms filled with every de-
> scription of goods, plundered from warehouses and shops,
> their hair hanging about their ears, rushing to deposit their
> plunder and return for more. . . .
> The roaring and crackling of the burning houses, the
> trampling and snorting of our horses . . . wild sounds of
> every description, while the rising sun came dimly through
> the cloud of smoke that hung like a pall. . . . There were
> said to be 5000 deserters in the city, and you could see the
> grey jackets here and there, sprinkled in the mob that was
> roaring down the street.

The brigade was halted by flames leaping across the street
and turned into Franklin Street, where Boykin saw at windows
"the sad and tearful faces" of women. The command circled the
burning area to Mayo's Bridge.

The cavalrymen forced their horses through a press of pil-
lagers, over the canal and in a single file across a stone conduit.
Boykin saw a struggle in the street:

"A low white man—he seemed a foreigner—was about to

strike a woman over a barrel of flour, under my horse's nose, when a stout Negro took her part and threatened to throw him into the canal."

The cavalry trotted over the planks of the main bridge, with only two sergeants and Colonel Alexander Cheves Haskell left behind to light pine faggots and burn it on command. Boykin saw about forty Federal horsemen galloping on Main Street, behind them. A few rifle shots flew over the bridge and the enemy horsemen swept from sight.

John L. G. Woods was a drummer boy of Company B, 53rd Georgia, of General Kershaw's division, a youngster who had seen most of the war's terrible days, from the Peninsula in '62, through Chancellorsville and Gettysburg. When he was not drumming, he had been put to cooking or to nursing the wounded.

Today he was one of those forgotten by the army in retreat. He started awake at dawn to find himself alone, with empty trenches stretching on either hand:

"I hastily rolled up my blanket, threw my haversack and canteen, with no provisions or water in them, across my shoulders, strapped my drum on my back, and hung an empty oyster tin to my haversack . . . and was then off on the quick step to overtake the army."

In the city he saw some men not content with rolling one barrel of plunder at a time, "but rolling several, one and then another." He met a woman loaded with as many sides of fat bacon as she could wrap in her arms, "wabbling down the street, bending under the load." He joined the crowd in the government commissary and had just filled his haversack when there was shout of "Fire!" He wriggled out the door before the crush of women and children blocked all movement and ran until he was across Mayo's Bridge.

Colonel Haskell gave the 7th South Carolina a last warning about discipline as it rode into the drunken mob: "Men, not one of you will leave the ranks. I don't want one thing touched."

On Main Street Lieutenant David Walker showed Haskell a miracle, a pair of shoes hung across the neck of his horse. "Colonel, they came out of the warehouse window and landed right there." Walker lifted a leg to show the remains of a boot tied around his foot. Haskell smiled and nodded.

The regiment came to Mayo's Bridge as the enemy advance was sighted, and only a few riders were over when the bluecoats began firing at them over the heads of the mob. Haskell ordered his men to retreat without returning fire. "If the commanding officer is a true soldier he won't massacre this mob by fighting through them," he said. The enemy fire soon died away and Haskell's men went quietly over the James, toward safety on the south bank.

Trooper Boykin looked back from the hill of Manchester at the burning of the magazine in Richmond: "It was marked by a peculiar blackness of smoke; from the middle of it would come the roar of bursting shells and boxes of fixed ammunition, with flashes that gave it the appearance of a thunder cloud of huge proportions with lightning playing through it. On our right was the Navy Yard, at which were several steamers and gunboats on fire, and burning in the river, from which the cannon were thundering as the fire reached them. The old war-scarred city seemed to prefer annihilation to conquest."

The brigade moved slowly out of Manchester, into a stream of civilians, "in some cases ladies of gentle nurture, without means of conveyance, sitting on their trunks by the roadside."

Another South Carolina soldier, Captain Charles Stevens Dwight, was sent back into the burning city about this time, ordered to find General Ewell and bring out instructions for the retreat. As he rode through the uproar he saw barrels of whisky being poured out:

"In the gutter it made a stream quite as large as would be caused by a heavy summer shower. As it rushed down the hill hundreds of men, women and boys were dipping the liquor in all kinds of vessels, even with their hands, drinking it like water—

some even lying flat and swilling it from the swift stream. . . . Our soldiers got their full share."

In front of the War Department, Dwight found Ewell and Breckinridge mounted in a crowd of civilians. "Breckinridge as he sat on his fine horse was simply magnificent, bright and cheerful, giving no sign of anguish." But Ewell was another matter. "He looked the wreck that he was, his thin narrow face wizened and worn, and twitched nervously, as did his hands and arms."

Captain Dwight could not reach Ewell, but managed to shout to an aide, and got orders to head for Amelia Court House. On the way back he ran between gushing flames that leapt from the upper stories of houses across Fourteenth Street; he got through by lying on the neck of his galloping horse. The animal was badly singed, and Dwight was "almost suffocated" when they passed.

From Manchester's hill, beyond the river, Dwight watched the burning flour mills, Haxall and Gallego, which were among the largest in the world: "They were nine and ten stories high. Out of every one of the several hundred windows and doors rushed great tongues of flame mixed with boiling black smoke; and finally, as the roofs were burned through or fell in, huge pyramids of fire and smoke shot up high above the towering walls . . . the view of the burning city was at once sublime and terrible."

In the flaming of the bridge, the shouting of the mob and the advance of the enemy, there was such confusion that no one knew which troops were the last across the bridge, but Captain Clement Sulivane saw General Joe Kershaw at the rear of his South Carolina troops at about the time General Ewell and Haskell went over.

Kershaw touched his hat to Sulivane. "All over," he yelled. "Goodbye. Blow her to hell."

Sulivane watched his men throw more lighted faggots on the planks before they fell back.

War Clerk Jones was in the streets at this hour making mental notes for his diary:

A lady sold me a bushel of potatoes in Broad Street for $75, Confederate, $5 less than the price a few days ago. I bought them at her request. And some of the shops gave clothing to our last retiring guards.

Goods at the government depots were distributed to the poor, to a limited extent. . . .

The streets are filled with pulverized glass. . . .

The doors of the government bakery were thrown open this morning, and flour and crackers were freely distributed. I got a barrel of the latter, paying a Negro man $5 to wheel it home—a short distance.

High over Richmond on the east, just across Bloody Run, was a plateau of some forty acres, all but covered with the hospital city of Chimborazo, celebrated as the world's largest. Seventy-five thousand men had passed through its cottages during the war; there were 150 one-story whitewashed buildings, 100 by 30 feet; there were five icehouses, five soup houses, a Russian bathhouse, a bakery, a brewery. The 200 cows had disappeared from the pasture, and the goats were no more; the bakery, which in other days turned out 10,000 loaves of bread daily, was now idle.

In the first daylight, Phoebe Yates Pember, matron of Chimborazo nurses, looked down from the hill on the fires of the city, on the James and its burning ships, the flame-wrapped bridges, and, beyond the line of earthworks, the dark columns of the approaching enemy.

Far below, a rickety old carriage bore Mayor Joseph Mayo and two of his men toward the Federal lines; in a small box the old man bore the seal of the city.

Phoebe had her first close look at the enemy:

"A single Federal bluejacket rose over the hill, standing transfixed with astonishment at what he saw. Another and another sprang up as if out of the earth, but still all remained quiet. About 7 o'clock there fell upon the ear the steady clatter of horses' hoofs, and winding around Rocketts, close under

Chimborazo Hill, came a small and compact body of Federal cavalry in splendid condition, riding closely and steadily along. They were well mounted . . . well fed, a rare sight. . . .

"Some advanced infantry followed, quite as well accoutered. Company after company, regiment after regiment, they poured into the doomed city, an endless stream."

One detachment wound from the line of march into the city's entrenchments, and on a battery flagpole, a U.S. flag rose in the morning air. A band played "The Star-spangled Banner"— it seemed a lifetime since she had heard that song. Phoebe heard Negroes shouting and cheering on the Federal line of march.

Colonel Taylor's woman friend at the Arlington woke up early, and in the dawn saw soldiers in the streets carrying balls of tar, which they lighted and tossed onto the roofs of houses and government buildings. She saw one thrown on the top of the house where Mrs. R. E. Lee lived, but did not see it catch fire. She, too, saw the coming of the enemy:

"As the day grew lighter I saw a Confederate soldier on horseback pause almost under my window. He wheeled and fired behind him, rode a short distance, wheeled and fired again; and so on, wheeling and firing as he went until he was out of sight. Coming up the street . . . rode a body of men in blue uniforms. It was not a very large body. They rode slowly, and passed just beneath my window. Exactly at eight o'clock the Confederate flag that fluttered above the Capitol came down and the Stars and Stripes were run up. . . . We covered our faces and cried aloud. All through the house was the sound of sobbing. It was as the house of mourning."

The streets filled with bluecoats, and Negroes ran out, dropped to their knees and clutched the soldiers, and the legs of their horses. The demonstration halted the column.

A band of soldiers entered the Arlington, searching. One of them was half drunk. "I'm Secesh," he said, "don't you worry none about me, little lady." The search was perfunctory, and the soldiers soon left the house.

Connie Cary found "the din of the enemy's wagon trains, bands, trampling horses, fifes, hurrahs and cannon" almost unbearable, but since her aunt had become seriously ill, Connie and a companion set out for Federal headquarters to ask a guard for the house. As they reached Capitol Square they saw the extent of the fire for the first time: between Eighth and Eighteenth Street, Main, Cary and Canal Streets had disappeared.

"The War Department was sending up jets of flame. Along the middle of the streets smouldered a long pile, like street sweepings, of papers torn from the archives of our beloved Government, from which soldiers in blue were picking out letters and documents that caught their fancy."

The grass on Capitol Square was already being trampled by cavalry horses. The women saw a guard posted in the yard of Mrs. Lee's house, which had by some miracle escaped the fire.

Federal officers treated the women with "perfect courtesy and consideration," and a lieutenant was sent to guide them home and identify the house; a guard was soon placed in the cellar.

When she was back home, Connie ripped out the hems of dresses, rolled into tiny tubes a dozen or more security certificates, and sewed them in the garments. The stocks belonged to her mother, and Connie had saved them by bearding her friend, a bank president, in the street yesterday, a "pale and wretched-looking" man who confessed, "I cannot vouch for the safe keeping of anybody's property. You'd best come with me and take it all." Today the bank was in ruins.

T. C. DeLeon watched Capitol Square in admiration: The Federal regiments smartly stacked muskets, were organized into fire squads and disappeared in the smoke, fighting to control the flames. For the first time since Sunday noon, order began to return. There were no reports of plunder, so far as DeLeon could learn.

"The fire was, at last, kept within bounds; then gradually forced backward, to leave a charred, steaming belt between it and the unharmed town. Within this the flames still leaped and writhed and wrangled."

Sixteen Confederate soldiers had been forgotten on the north bank of the James, a detail on "The Dead Line," set outside the trenches to catch deserters. They were four hours behind Gary's Brigade reaching the city, which was by then swarming with the enemy.

Among these men was Private S. A. Gerald. Once in the city, he was separated from his companions. He passed Federal cavalry, but they trotted by him without notice.

"I still had my gun, and I went to Capitol Square, to one of the gates, and while I was standing there with an old Texas soldier I saw our flag pulled down and the Stars and Stripes hoisted."

He went to the river, where he found the bridges had burned and fallen into the water. He walked up the canal bank, and two miles outside the city came upon the tail end of the retreat. A canalboat was so heavily loaded with women, children and piles of luggage that it was sinking; water half covered the craft. The women and children streamed from it to the bank. Young Gerald was overcome: "Everyone was crying, and being only a boy and an orphan myself, with sisters in far-off Louisiana waiting for me, I could not help crying too, the first tears I had shed since 1861, when I was 15, and left home."

The women consoled him, "Stay with us. You've got a gun. You could protect us."

"No, I'm sorry. They'd take me in an hour. There's Yankee cavalry all around us."

He went ahead of them, and soon crossed the canal and the river, going south.

Fannie Walker, the War Bureau copying clerk, was on the steps of her home when the morning explosion knocked her down; breaking glass tinkled around her. She fled from the place with her aunt, to the Valentine House, where Fannie had her first glimpse of the invaders.

"I looked down the street and to my horror beheld a Negro cavalryman yelling: 'Richmond at last!'"

The two women were terrified, but started for the Mechanics Institute, where the Bureau of War had been; flames were consuming it. They went back to their home and huddled alone.

"All day and all night we sat beside what of our belongings we could tie up in sheets, ready to leave. Parties were kept on the roof with buckets of water and wet blankets, and we were saved."

The enemy sent a guard at night, and by watching in turns, while others slept, the women of the house passed the night.

It was 8 A.M. when E. T. Watehall, the fourteen-year-old wanderer in the city streets, met the enemy. As the bluecoats marched past the boy saw a sight that stunned him:

"Some women and boys stood on the corner and waved little Union flags."

The soldiers summoned Negroes from the walks and put them to work on the fire engines. The men pumped, but they were not happy, Watehall saw, "for they had thought that now the Federals were here, the whites would have to work while they played."

At about the same hour Judith Brockenbrough McGuire met the Federals, in a street where "the rabble rushed by me in one stream." She asked a passerby what the shouting was about, and seemed to hear a hundred voices in chorus, "The Yankees have come!" Then she saw:

"I turned to come home, but what was my horror, when I reached Ninth Street, to see a regiment of Yankee cavalry come dashing up, yelling, shouting, hallooing and screaming. I stood riveted to the spot. I could not move nor speak. Then I saw the iron gates of our time-honored and beautiful Capitol Square, on the walks and greensward of which no hoof had been allowed to tread, thrown open and the cavalry dash in. I could see no more. I must go on with a mighty effort, or faint where I stood."

Amelia Gorgas made her way through the uproar to the home of her sister, a Mrs. Payne, noting sadly the contrast between the brilliant uniforms and sleek horses of the Union troops and those of the soldiers who had gone. From the Payne house they peered out at the enemy through closed blinds, "even the children shrinking from the gaze of the terrible Yankees." A shell fragment broke through shutter and window, within a few inches of her head.

The ten-year-old Willie Gorgas climbed to the roof with wet blankets to protect the house from falling sparks; the air was thick with smoke, and Mrs. Gorgas felt near suffocation. Willie soon rushed into the house.

"Yanks are robbing Mrs. Freeland next door! They've got her silver, and coming here!"

The Paynes' Negro cook plunged the household silver into a barrel of soft lye soap. Amelia Gorgas and a Negro maid opened her silver chest and tossed the pieces atop an old-fashioned shower bath, hiding them among the myriad pipes of the contraption.

The women looked from the window in relief: Bluecoat officers arrested the looters in the street and led them away. The house was safe. Mrs. Gorgas and a friend dressed in black, with heavy crepe veils, and went to Federal headquarters to ask for a guard. A sentinel faced them. "I want to see General Ord, please," Amelia Gorgas said. "He was a classmate of my husband's at West Point."

General Ord was not in; he was somewhere in the field, after Lee's army. General Weitzel commanded Richmond. But the women were treated kindly, and "a tall Prussian soldier" was sent to protect their home. The guard quickly endeared himself to Willie Gorgas and other children in the place: "Next time I come, I'll be a nice Confederate, and not a bad Yankee." A little girl threw her arms around his neck.

At the end of the day Amelia wrote, "After our little ones were asleep we three tired, heartbroken women sat bewailing the terrible misfortune that had befallen our beloved city. We tried to comfort ourselves by saying in low tones (for we feared spies even in our servants) that the capital was only moved temporarily to Danville, that General Lee would make a stand and repulse the daring enemy, and that we should yet win the battle and the day. Alas! Alas for our hopes."

The sorrowing Amelia was spared the whispered scorn of her townsmen. The good patriot J. B. Jones noted in his diary: "General Gorgas' family remain also. They are Northern born."

Southeast of the burning city the remnant of the Confederate Navy steamed up the James toward the route of escape.

Admiral Raphael Semmes, with a few sailors and naval cadets, left the exploding ironclads behind, and on a wooden gunboat ran the gantlet of the bridges; there was a wait at one bridge while the draw was held closed for crossing troops. It was dawn when Semmes neared Manchester.

He had passed the burning training ship, *Patrick Henry,* and saw blocks of the city in flame; Tredegar Foundry had caught fire when he went by. The admiral found himself in a mass of sailors, soldiers and civilians on the south shore.

"I was about the most helpless man in the whole crowd. I had just tumbled on shore, with their bags and baggage, 500 sailors, incapable of marching a dozen miles without becoming footsore."

There was no way to carry them after the army, for Semmes had not even a pack mule. A cavalryman taunted the sailors as he rode by:

"How you like navigating afoot, boys?"

Semmes saw the absurdity of the sailors' appearance: "Loaded down with pots and pans and mess kettles, bags of bread, chunks of salted pork, sugar, tea, tobacco, pipes. It was as much as they could do to stagger under the load."

Semmes sent men to fire the gunboats, which soon floated downstream in flames. The sailors then marched a few blocks, "blinded by the dust kicked up by those vagabonds," the cavalry.

They passed a railroad station, and Semmes asked some fugitives about the trains. They gaped. "Trains! Hell, they took the last train outa here 'way before day, all the Government lords."

Semmes was not dismayed. He had his men clear the packed depot with bayonets, driving herds of men, women and children from three or four old cars on a siding. The hopeful passengers squalled complaints in vain. Semmes eyed an old engine which stood nearby:

"There was no fire in its furnace, no fuel with which to make a fire, and no one to manage it."

Semmes put the sailors to work. The cars were pulled together and coupled by hand, and his own men climbed aboard.

A party of Marines attacked a picket fence from a house, chopped it into firewood, and within a few minutes had steam hissing from the boiler of the locomotive.

"Now!" the admiral shouted to the mob of civilians. "Get aboard, as many of you as we can carry."

The engine moved off at an almost imperceptible pace, and when it reached a slight grade beyond the station, halted entirely. They were still in full view of Richmond, and Semmes saw Federal cavalrymen on the hills. His engineers stoked the fire hotter, to no avail. At last one of the sailors found another engine, hidden by the railway men before flight. Semmes had it backed out of the shop building, hitched it to the first engine, and within a few minutes, with black smoke boiling over them, the triumphant party steamed away.

They went at five or six miles an hour until they reached the first railroad woodpile, and then, with better fuel, thundered along toward safety. They made dozens of stops to pick up men in uniform who hailed them. "Unattached generals and colonels in considerable numbers," fleeing from the army, Semmes said. They were miles out of Richmond, rolling at full speed, when two or three men pushed through the crowd, announced themselves as railroad conductors and engineers and asked to be put in charge. Semmes roared with laughter at the tardy volunteers. The train steamed on in the wake of the army toward Danville; it escaped enemy cavalry by an hour and took its sailors and civilian refugees to safety.

At 10 A.M. a Federal artillery battery rolled past the home of J. B. Jones near the center of Richmond, moving down Clay Street toward Camp Lee. Jones hailed an officer:

"Will you post guards to keep peace?"

"We'll do all we can to prevent disorder. The only trouble has been caused by your people." He pointed to the still-burning ruin of seventeen city blocks.

"I think it came from the warehouses," Jones said. "They were set afire hours ago."

"No doubt. We don't intend to disturb you, sir. Good day."

The officer and his staff met two Negro women loaded with

plunder. Jones watched with delight: "They wheeled them right about, and marched them off, to the manifest chagrin of the newly emancipated citizens."

Capitol Square filled with Negro cavalry and infantry, cheered by throngs of Negroes on the walks. The Square, Jones saw, was covered with parcels and bags of all sorts, dragged from houses threatened by fire. Each parcel seemed to be guarded by a Federal soldier.

A passing officer struck up a friendly conversation with Jones. "We'll picket the city with a white brigade tonight," he said. He turned to women standing on the walk. "I assure you there won't be a bit of molestation, ladies. Not a particle."

There was then an announcement in the square: "No one will be on the streets after 9 P.M. Soldiers and civilians found out after that hour will be arrested."

A young woman, Sallie Brock Putnam, came toward Capitol Square. "Long lines of Negro cavalry swept by the Exchange Hotel, brandishing their swords and uttering savage cheers, replied to by the shouts of those of their own color, who were trudging along under loads of plunder. . . . Some colored troops passed, singing 'John Brown's Body.' "

Capitol Square was also crowded with refugees from the flames, crouching among the furniture, trunks, and bags. "Fathers and mothers, and weeping, frightened children sought this open space for a breath of fresh air. But here, even, it was almost as hot as a furnace. Intermingled with these miserable beings were the Federal troops. . . . All along the north side of the Square were tethered their horses, while dotted about were seen the white tents of the sutlers, in which were temptingly displayed canned fruits and meats, crackers, cheese, and so forth."

Phoebe Pember walked the corridors of her huge hospital wards. They were almost empty.

"Every man who could crawl had tried to escape Northern prisons. Beds in which paralyzed, rheumatic and helpless patients had lain for months were empty, and the miracles of the New

Testament had been reenacted. The lame and halt compelled to remain were almost wild at being left . . . for in many instances they had been exchanged as prisoners only a short time before."

Phoebe gave these men all the comfort she could, and, "with some difficulty," their suppers. Her nurses had gone with Lee's army and her Negro cooks had deserted. She went to her room late, and was alone in her building. Federal officers had come during the day and offered help, but left no guards.

Phoebe had been asleep for an hour when a crash in the pantry roused her. She took a lamp into the room and found some men: "A set of 'hospital rats' I'd never been able to get rid of, for if I sent them to the field one week they would be sure to be back the next on some trifling pretext of sickness. The ringleader was an old enemy who had stored up many a grievance against me. . . . He was the spokesman and the trouble was the old one."

"You got thirty gallons of whisky before the army left," he said. "We know you got it. Where is it?"

"It's not yours. It's in my charge and I'm going to keep it. You're all drunk. Go out of my pantry!"

The leader was firm. "Boys, pick up that barrel and tote it down the hill. I'll tend to her."

His men were cowed by Phoebe's stern manner, and backed away. She spoke quietly, "Wilson, you've been in the hospital a long time. Do you think from what you know of me that whisky can be taken without my consent?"

"Stop that talk. Your great friends are gone, and I'll not stand for that now. Move out of the way."

The man moved toward the barrel. Phoebe stepped in front of him, and he tore at her shoulder. "Get out of the way, you bitch."

Phoebe drew a small pistol from her pocket. The click of its cocking drove the man a step backward as if he had been pushed. "You'd better leave," Phoebe said. "If I can't get you with one bullet, I have five more ready."

The men muttered together at the pantry door and trailed away. The leader shook his fist at her. "You think you're brave now, miss. But you wait an hour. Other folks got pistols, too."

When they had gone Phoebe nailed the head of a flour barrel across the door with a two-pound weight, and sat, "warm with victory," by the whisky barrel. She slept there, with matches and pistol within reach, and woke in the late morning, undisturbed.

At 3 P.M., in the first wave of men behind the leading Federal troops, a Negro correspondent of the Philadelphia *Press*, a muscular young man by the name of J. Morris Chester, pushed into the empty hall of the Confederate House of Representatives. He went to the Speaker's table, and in the quiet, began to write a story for his newspaper.

A paroled Confederate officer in uniform passed the doorway and stormed into the hall. "Come out of there, you black cuss!"

Chester looked up without replying and went on with his work.

The Confederate bellowed, "Get out of there or I'll knock your brains out!" He called obscene curses, but Chester wrote on as if he heard nothing.

The officer ran up the carpeted steps and took Chester by the collar. The writer rose quickly and knocked the Confederate sprawling in the aisle. The officer scrambled up, and to a white Union officer who had run in, said, "Lend me your sword and I'll cut this damned nigger's heart out."

"No," the Union captain said. "But if you want to fight him, I'll have a ring for you made right here, and see that there's no interference. You'll get more damnably thrashed than you ever were in your life."

The Confederate went swiftly from the room.

Charles C. Coffin, the Boston *Journal* man, was in the city by now. He went into the Spotswood Hotel while it was ringed with fire on three sides, and hailed a clerk.

"Can you give me a room?"

"I reckon we can, sir, but like enough you'll be burnt out before morning. Take any room you like. Nobody here."

Coffin signed the register beneath the names of departed Confederate officers and took a first-floor room. He looked into

Capitol Square: "It was filled with furniture, beds, clothing, crockery, chairs, tables, looking-glasses. Women were weeping, children crying. Men stood speechless, woebegone, gazing at the desolation. . . . Granite columns, iron pillars, marble façades broken into thousands of pieces, blocked the streets."

Federal soldiers on rooftops of the Capitol, the governor's house and other public buildings fought the fire; cinders still dropped through the air.

In the Square, Negro soldiers divided their rations with women and children, and Coffin made notes of it: Hot coffee, sweetened with sugar, a delicacy these people had not tasted for months. He saw ludicrous burdens; one Negro had three Dutch ovens piled on his back, and carried in one hand a stewpan and in the other a skillet. Women had bags of flour in their arms, baskets of salt, sides of bacon, pails of molasses.

C. G. Blakey, a boy about twelve years old, hung about the streets where looting continued beyond the gaze of the Union guards. A man rolling a big barrel hailed him.

"Come on, boy. Help me roll this up the hill, and I'll give you a bucket of this sugar!"

The two struggled, rolling and halting to hold the barrel against the long slope, until they reached the crest. The man broke open the end of the barrel, cursed viciously, and kicked the barrel down the hill. "Copperas!" he shouted. "Goddam copperas!" He left the boy standing in the street.

The nameless girl at the Arlington grew fearful at dusk. She huddled in a bedroom with her aunt while the house next door burned. A small boy was on the roof, working with wet blankets. Wet blankets and cloths also covered the windows, but when the wind blew, smoke and cinders blew in; the air was stifling.

After dark a girl relative of the Arlington's family of boarders was carried from a burning house on her cot; she was a typhoid fever victim, and died in the street.

The girl diarist saw a child: "a little girl who danced and clapped her hands and said she was glad the Yankees had come, because they would give her pickles and molasses and oranges and cheese and nuts and candy, 'until I have a fit and die.' She got food, and did die."

Constance Cary and some of her relatives went to services at the old Monumental Church that night. When the rector prayed for the sick and wounded soldiers, Connie wrote, "there was a sound of weeping all over the church." They sang the hymn, "When Gathering Clouds Around I View," but there was no organ, and the voice which first led the song broke down in sobs; another began and could not finish. Connie sang alone. When she came to the words, "Thou Savior see'st the tears I shed," there was a great burst of crying in the church.

"I wanted to break down dreadfully," she wrote, "but I held on and carried the hymn to the end. As we left the church, many people came up and squeezed my hand, and tried to speak, but could not."

A Federal band passed. Connie thought its fine uniforms and blaring music made a perfect mockery of the shabby congregation leaving the old gray church. She was almost overcome by grief.

★ THE ENEMY ★

CONFEDERATE DESERTERS crept into the lines every night, and the hungry, ragged men seemed as willing to surrender to Negro troops as to whites; the 25th Corps north of the James, with many Negroes in the ranks, took in hundreds of the surrendering Rebels. There were at least a dozen a night; recently, there had been a record of forty in one night.

These men came, talking freely of conditions in the Confederate army, so that George A. Bruce, who was on the staff of General Charles Devens, Jr., Commander of the 3rd Division of the 24th Corps, thought he knew as much about Rebel affairs as anyone.

They reported an air of despondency in their army. The deserters also told of buried torpedoes with which their lines were mined, and were quick with answers to all questions.

After midnight George Bruce saw a bright fire in the distance beyond the Confederate front lines, and about two hours later pickets brought him two deserters from the 10th Virginia, who said that the Rebels were pulling out of the sector. Bruce took the message to General Devens.

"Get in the Confederate works," Devens said. "If you find it can be done without too much risk, take the men you need, and go right in."

Bruce rode down the brigade fronts, taking a few men from each; they lay along the picket line until daylight. The young officer recorded the moments of waiting:

"It was a warm, still night. A soft wind, touched with the perfume of earliest flowers . . . was moving gently from the west. The sky to the zenith was free of clouds, but toward the horizon a bank of smoky mist had settled. . . . The deep baying of a watch-dog . . . was occasionally heard in the distance. Save that, all was still."

A bright fire sprang up near the city; others blazed, and the first great explosion of the morning came. Bruce saw a "huge volume of smoke like an illuminated balloon shot high into the air, followed by an explosion that shook the earth under our feet."

At that moment a Confederate deserter stumbled into the lines and Bruce turned him about. "Take us down the cleared path, man. One false step will be your last."

The bluecoats wound in single file behind the deserter, between rows of sharpened logs set in the earth and jumbles of felled trees and obstructions. Bruce saw a row of stakes, each with a strip of red cloth: Torpedoes. They found the Confederate tents empty, and filed into the earthworks.

An explosion killed a Vermont soldier who had left the path to explore on his own. When full daylight came, an orderly from Devens found Bruce.

"The General says not to advance the pickets, sir. He wants to leave that to the commander."

Bruce found Devens in front of his tent. "It's too late, Gen-

eral," he said. "My men are already in Fort Gilmer, and the whole
line is yours."

Devens put out his hand and made a quiet joke: "Hail to
thee, Count of Gilmer."

Not far away were the headquarters of General Godfrey
Weitzel, commander of the 25th Corps. Between 2 and 3 A.M.
Thomas Thatcher Graves, an aide to Weitzel, noticed the fires in
Rebel lines; the explosion erupted as he studied them. The echoes
had not died when General August Kautz, the cavalry commander
in front, sent back a prisoner, a Negro teamster. Graves questioned him:

"What's happening in the Rebel lines?"

"They began getting ready to leave after dark. They done
sent off all the teams, and the soldiers is getting out."

Graves sent a picket line forward, and found the Rebels gone.
Weitzel sent forty riders from E and H companies of the 4th
Massachusetts Cavalry down the road, under Colonel E. E. Graves
of the staff and Major Atherton H. Stevens, Jr., the Provost Marshal. Weitzel's staff followed with a line of Negro infantry behind. The road was quiet; not a Rebel was in sight.

Graves looked across open fields. "In the distance were divisions of our troops, many of them on the double quick, aiming
to be the first in the city; a white and a colored division were
having a regular race, the white troops on the turnpike and the
colored in the fields."

Explosions continued in the city.

George Bruce was in the New Market Road when the 4th
Massachusetts horsemen passed toward Richmond and he fell behind, riding at the side of his infantry pickets. He gathered a number of Confederate stragglers on the way to the city, some walking toward him, others waiting at the roadside. The first one called
gaily:

"What do you pay a man who gives up, with his gun and
blanket and all?"

Bruce shook his head; payments to deserters had been suspended today.

"I guess the Confederacy is played out at last," the deserter said.

On a hill near the inner defenses of Richmond, Bruce saw a landscape he would not forget:

"The city was wrapped in a cloud of densest smoke through which great tongues of flame leaped in madness to the skies. A few houses on the higher hills, a spire here and there half smothered in smoke, and the hospitals to the east were the only buildings that could be seen . . . ten thousand shells bursting every minute in the Confederate arsenals were making an uproar . . . but just on the verge of this maelstrom of smoke and fire cattle were grazing undisturbed . . . and I saw a farmer ploughing in a field while cinders from the burning capital were falling at his feet."

The skirmish line halted on the edge of the city, and the old barouche bearing Mayor Joseph Mayo drew up. Bruce watched the official and his brother, the latter shouting excitedly to the Federals:

"The mob is ruining the city. Nobody's trying to stop the fire, but I suppose it's as well. You'll arrest all of us and take all the property."

"No one who behaves himself will be disturbed," Bruce said.

Mayo soon became friendly, and took Bruce to his home, Powhatan, which was nearby.

"Named for King Powhatan, you know," Mayo said. "Once the capital of his tribe." He led the young Federal into the garden. "There's the rock where they laid the head of John Smith, when Pocahontas saved him from execution."

Mayo talked pleasantly for a few minutes, but Bruce observed subtle distinctions in his speech. Mayo once explained, "*My* sister married *your* General Scott."

He asked a favor of Bruce at the end: "I have no food in my house, beyond potatoes, cornmeal, and hams. Let me buy some sugar, coffee, tea and flour from your commissary. Here's a twenty-dollar gold piece, the only good money they've left me. I've kept it all through the war." Bruce took the coin and gave him $28 in greenbacks and a note to the commissary. Mayo hurried away with them.

Another of the first bluecoat officers to approach the city was Charles Francis Adams, grandson of President John Quincy Adams, a spirited young colonel of the 5th Massachusetts Cavalry, a Negro regiment which had put him into a temper this morning.

He thought his troops "the hardest body to handle" he ever saw, a grab bag of detachments from many regiments; he had no staff, and no organization beyond that he had contrived the night before, when he had gone to bed "weary and disgusted."

For all of Adams's devotion to the Union cause and his hatred of slavery, he had hard words for Negro troops on horseback. They did very good service dismounted, he thought. It was a mistake to mount them, he said, adding impulsively, "The negro is wholly unfit for cavalry service, lacking absolutely the essential qualities of alertness, individuality, reliability and self-reliance. He could not scout and he could not take care of himself in unfamiliar situations."

Adams had been up since dawn, when he had a note from his pickets that the Rebels had gone. He went down the Darbytown Road and waited. He got underway at 7 A.M. "after fretting, fuming and chafing for an hour."

He led through the enemy's deserted lines and pushed ahead without orders. He thought the Richmond fortifications were the strongest he ever saw, and the city "wonderfully defensible." The guns were still in place, unspiked, ammunition beside them.

By 9 A.M. Adams clattered into the Richmond streets with his Negro troopers. He was elated at the experience, but noted sights in the streets with the eye of a trained historian:

Of drunkenness there was necessarily a great deal, for, with an insane idea of propitiating our soldiers, the citizens actually forced liquor on them in the streets. . . . We found the slaves and poor whites pillaging freely, but that was put a stop to, and the soldiers, so far as I could see, behaved admirably.

George Bruce rode through the suburb of Rocketts with General Devens and his staff; past crowds of working people on the walks.

Handkerchiefs and strips of cotton cloth were pinned to doors and windows as flags of truce, and women and children begged for food. The soldiers could not stop, but promised to send quartermasters to feed them. As the troops neared the river a staff officer, Major William Ladd, jumped from his horse and rowed a scow into the river, where he clambered aboard a gunboat. He shinnied up the mast and ripped off a Confederate flag, stuffed it under his belt, and rowed back. As he stepped on shore the gunboat exploded behind him, spattering the river with fragments.

The column went toward Richmond and met a delegation from the Loyal League, behind which was a sea of Negroes, laughing and singing, waving to the bluecoats.

General Devens turned with tear-filled eyes to Bruce: "What a great sight—the deliverance of a race!"

The 13th New Hampshire now led the column, and as it turned into Main Street, Devens halted it to bring up the bands from every regiment; they went ahead playing "Yankee Doodle" and "Rally Round the Flag." The files wound up to Capitol Square and stacked arms.

Thatcher Graves was detained on his way to the center of the city; General Weitzel sent him with half-a-dozen troopers to free the inmates of Libby Prison. He rode recklessly through the streets, thinking of the thousands of wretched men who must be crowded in the infamous place, but found the doors open, the foul-smelling cages empty, and only a few Negroes nearby to shout:

"They's all gone, masters. Gone!"

Colonel E. H. Ripley of Devens' First Brigade was one of the commanders to report to General Weitzel, who had settled himself on the highest step of the east front of the Capitol, looking down into the roaring of the flames, coughing and wiping at his eyes, but giving a rapid fire of orders.

"I have no orders or suggestions," Weitzel told Ripley. "Just do all you can to save the city, and to help the women and children and wounded. Put down the mob the best you can, and help them with the fire."

Ripley took over Mayor Mayo, who had come back into the city, and made headquarters in City Hall; he sent his staff for the remains of Richmond fire-fighting equipment and put the men to work. "It was like a contest of innumerable artillery, like that which preceded Pickett's charge at Gettysburg," he wrote. Shells still rocketed from the burning arsenal.

Before night Ripley's patrols had filled Libby and Castle Thunder with looters and Confederate stragglers. City Hall was jammed with plunder, and officers drove themselves furiously, writing down descriptions of the confiscated articles.

One of Ripley's men was riding through the streets, gathering whites and Negroes for fire-fighting crews when a Negro called him from the front of a large brick house.

"My mistress wants to talk to you," the servant said.

The officer went into the house and met a young woman. "My mother is an invalid," she said. "She can't leave her bed. Will you help us if the fire comes this far?"

Her mother, the girl said, was Mrs. Robert E. Lee. The officer promised help, and within an hour a corporal and two men of the 9th Vermont stood guard before the house, with a waiting ambulance in the street.

The first Union flag went up on the Capitol before the city's formal surrender to Weitzel at 8:15 A.M. It seemed a long wait to Lieutenant Johnston Peyster, the eighteen-year-old son of a Federal general. For several days, in the lines outside the city, he had carried a flag on the pommel of his saddle, wrapped with care, ready to be raised over Richmond.

Peyster and a companion, Captain Loomis Langdon of Weitzel's staff, pulled down the Confederate banner and raised their own, amid cheering from the throng in Capitol Square.

George Bruce sketched the Square: "Inhabitants fleeing burning houses, men, women, children, black and white . . . bureaus, sofas, carpets, beds, bedding, baby toys, costly mirrors scattered

on the green. All the sick who could move retreated there to lie.
. . . Wind like a hurricane from the fire. . . . Rising among the
trees in the center of the square, amid this carnival of ruin, stood
the great statue of Washington, against which firebrands thumped
and rattled."

★ PETERSBURG ★

Tobacco warehouses had been burning since early yesterday
afternoon, and by midnight the streets were full of the stinging
fragrance. The blue lines had crept into sight, nearer by the hour,
but were held out by Longstreet's men until nightfall.

A meeting of the Common Council lasted much of the day,
and Mayor W. W. Townes and Councilman Charles Collier took
its resolution to General Lee. They asked Lee when he would
evacuate the city, so that they might give it up to the enemy on
good terms and protect their property.

The politicians had found Lee in no mood to parley with
them. He gave them a few moments at his new headquarters in
the Dupuy house at the edge of town.

"I will communicate with you at ten o'clock tonight," Lee
said, "at the house of Mr. Paul. That's all I can do for you."

At ten he had sent Major Giles Cooke of his staff with the
news: The troops would leave Petersburg at midnight. The mayor
and council planned rapidly. They would divide into pairs and
walk out the various entries to the city, where they would meet
the conquerors. The first to see Federal troops would surrender
the city.

The child, Anne Banister, saw her old friend General Lee as
he passed her mother's house in Petersburg—the General motioned to soldiers to leave in the Banister yard a chair he had borrowed, a "big sleepy-hollow chair" with an extended table on one
arm for writing. For months he had written orders for the Army
of Northern Virginia in this chair.

One of the marching men was young William Graham, a Georgian who was a meticulous diarist. He noted that his regiment began moving at midnight, of its destination "as ignorant as the machine which obeys the touch of the artizan upon lever or spring." He was not deceived, however. "We know this much, it is a retreat. Our gallant and hitherto invincible Army of Northern Virginia has been overcome by mere brute force of numbers."

Just outside the city Graham's regiment passed piles of commissary stores, sugar and coffee and brandy, tobacco, hardtack, bacon, corn, vinegar. Crowds of soldiers and civilians robbed them. Graham, already loaded, took only a dozen or so hardtacks and a few pounds of sugar. At a rest period soon afterward he fell asleep under a tree and woke up half-frozen in his sweaty clothes.

Captain J. C. Gorman marched with his North Carolina regiment through the midnight streets of Petersburg while enemy shells burst among the buildings. Only soldiers were in the streets now, and only a few houses seemed to be occupied. Now and then a woman thrust her head through a window.

"Boys," they called, "are you going to leave us?" Gorman thought they sounded very sad.

A few women, however, "were disposed to be merry" and these taunted the troops: "Goodbye, boys! We'll drink pure coffee with sugar tomorrow! Hard times come again no more."

Gorman's command was one of the last to cross the Pocahontas Bridge, and when it had climbed the bluff on the far bank the bridge was in flames. Rockets from the Federal line streaked redly into the sky, and cheers of the enemy rang over the firing. The regiment rested in the road for a few minutes but, as a signal gun fired, went ahead once more. The magazine of a battery of siege guns blew up behind it, and the road quivered underfoot. Magazines in other Confederate forts exploded down the long line. Gorman wrote:

> The scene was the fiercest and most imposing I ever witnessed. We left the light and pierced the midnight darkness of the rear. At each step we took some new explosion would occur. . . . The whole heavens in our rear were lit

up in lurid glare that added intensity to the blackness before us. It was as if the gases chained in the earth had at last found vent and the general conflagration of the world was at hand.

Major Henry Kyd Douglas, who had served so long on Stonewall Jackson's staff, now commanded a brigade—the old "Light Brigade" of A. P. Hill. He remained late in Petersburg, waiting for orders to move. "There was no sleeping in Petersburg that night; no night except for the darkness. It was all commotion and bustle."

During the hours of waiting, Douglas rode to several houses to say good-bye. Shells were already falling on the houses near him when he said his farewells to the pretty girl, Mary Tabb Bolling, who was to become the wife of Rooney Lee. "She uttered not a word of fear or complaint; the infinite sadness of her silence was pathetic beyond belief."

Douglas saw on his lapel by the uncertain light a forgotten flower, a faded red rose pinned there a few nights before by Robert Lee's daughter Agnes, when Douglas and other officers had serenaded her in Richmond.

The major's command fell in the line of march as temporary rear guard. They left without food.

A boy private, J. S. Kimbrough of the 14th Georgia, had known since nightfall that retreat was coming. He had seen artillery pulled out from his line, had slipped away and was soon in Petersburg. He and two friends climbed a fence into a grape arbor, spread their blankets and fell asleep. Hours passed, and the army marched within a few yards without disturbing them.

It was an hour after dawn when the cheers of Federal troops in the square woke up the Georgia stragglers. They jumped the fence with their guns and hurried by back streets to the Appomattox. They were too late. The Confederate rear guard had fired the bridge, and only smoking timbers remained. A squad of bluecoats was coming up behind them. Kimbrough broke into tears. He twisted against a stone the barrel of the Enfield rifle he had carried through the war, hurled it into the river and surrendered to the enemy.

The three Georgians were hurried through the town. "Everything was in terrible commotion. Irish women, Negro women, men and boys were running hither and thither, some with slabs of bacon on their heads and others with sacks and bundles of various sorts and sizes. We were marched in front of a regiment of Negro troops, who cursed and abused us to their hearts' content, without any protest from either our captors or the white officers who commanded them."

Private I. G. Bradwell, who marched with John Gordon's corps, also saw women at the windows in Petersburg. As he passed from the city they leaned out to call in forlorn voices, "Good-bye, Rebels, we never expect to see you again."

They passed a Confederate soldier drunk from native applejack and left him for the enemy. The column overtook an old man who tried to push a railroad handcar along the track, loaded high with provisions. A barrel of flour rolled off and burst. Bradwell joined the scramble of soldiers for this treasure, and got a haversackful of flour. Nearby, he filled his canteen from a barrel of sorghum syrup. He and his companions were among the army's fortunate few who did not go hungry on the road.

When this regiment reached the bridge they were to cross a man on the far shore waved a lantern and shouted, "Come on, boys, I'm goin' to blow her up now." The soldiers pleaded with him to wait for other troops still back in Petersburg, but the engineer was adamant. When the little column had crossed he blew up the bridge. From the hillside Bradwell looked back and saw timbers flying into the sky, which was now faintly lit by the moon.

The troops passed through Petersburg toward the open country without interruption from the enemy. Most of them got over the Appomattox and turned into Hickory Road, along the north bank of the river. General Lee supervised the end of it.

The commander rode to the mouth of the Hickory Road and stood at the roadside, Traveller's bridle in his hand, and watched the passing troops; occasional orders went out by couriers. The novelist John Esten Cooke saw him there and was struck by his manner: "His bearing still remained entirely composed, and his voice had lost none of its grave strength of intonation."

When the rear had closed up and it appeared no more stragglers would come, Lee mounted and rode off slowly with his staff. For miles they were followed by weird flashes of light and explosions.

Through Petersburg had passed some 12,000 men; in all the roads leading west, including those winding down from Richmond, were fewer than 30,000—all that was left of the Army of Northern Virginia.

★ THE ENEMY ★

MAYOR TOWNES and Councilman Collier walked the streets of Petersburg all night, pushing past regiments, then squads, then hurrying single soldiers of Lee's army, all of them moving toward the bridges leading west.

By 4 A.M., as they had agreed, the two officials walked out Dupuy Road into the country, to the corporation line near the Model Farm, where A. P. Hill's headquarters had been. They walked cautiously as daylight came, the mayor holding aloft his walking stick with a white handkerchief tied on it, though there was no one in sight.

They had reached the empty breastworks near Old Town Creek when the enemy appeared. Collier stated: "Instantaneously, as from the bowels of the earth, it seemed to me, came a mighty host of Federal soldiers, and then followed a shout of victory as seemed to shake the very ground."

These bluecoats had been massed in trenches for a final assault no longer needed, and they now swarmed past the mayor and Councilman Collier as if they did not see them. Townes and Collier shouted to the running soldiers.

"But we want to surrender the city of Petersburg, sir!" Townes shouted.

He did not halt the tide, but a trotting officer called over his shoulder, "Come along with us. We'll protect your people."

The *Herald* reporter Cadwallader came riding through the troops; to him the mayor and councilman seemed only "old men in homespun, butternut clothing . . . bearing an improvised flag of truce that looked suspiciously like a dirty linen table cloth. They came along at a sober gait, as if attending a funeral."

When the officials saw Cadwallader, with the insignia of a staff officer on the harness of his horse, they gave him an absurd salute and one of them began to shout in a pompous voice:

"On behalf of the municipal government, and the people of the city of Petersburg, I have the honor of tendering its formal surrender."

The reporter tried to escape, but the old men would not be shaken off. Cadwallader lost his temper:

"I'd have been glad to take your damned city any time the last nine months. It's too late now we're in. General Grant will accept no surrender, nor will anybody else. I advise you to go home and wait."

"But, sir, will private property be respected?"

"Will you observe the rights of unarmed citizens?"

Cadwallader rode away, and still the old men called after him.

The dignified officials trailed in the ranks of the conquering army, and when they reached the courthouse, saw the whole building, steeple and all, covered with small American flags.

H. G. Young of the *New York Times*, who ran the last miles "like greased lightning," was among the first reporters into Petersburg with the invading army. Two New York *Herald* men had put up at the Jarratt House at almost the same hour, and were followed by Charles A. Page and T. C. Grey of the New York *Tribune*, who summoned the grinning black chief steward and asked for breakfast. There was some hesitation, but at last the meal was brought forth, "scraps of dry bread and some indigestible scraps of bacon."

Page and Grey offered a bale of Confederate bills in payment.

"God bless ye," the Negro said. "I got more of that than a mule could tote. Hasn't you any Yankee money?"

"Now look here, John," Page said. "This is over $500 just for breakfast, that surely should pay you."

"I know it's a heap of money, sir. But, I don't want it, and youall are welcome to your breakfast, if that's all you got."

The *Tribune* men gave him a $5 bill "of the Union persuasion."

Meade's staff was amused by two small Petersburg boys who hung about bug-eyed. One of them was loudly protesting his friendship for the invaders.

"I'm not a Rebel atall," he said.

His companion swung at him. "Oh, you've changed your tune since yesterday—and I can still lick you, whatever you are!"

They fell to the ground, tussling.

General Grant had gone to bed late, still resisting urging of his staff to launch a night attack on Petersburg's inner lines. "They will evacuate tonight," he had said, "and there's no need for sacrifice."

This morning the first word came about five o'clock and found Grant awake: Troops were already pouring through the town. He dressed quickly and went out for a talk with Meade. Before six they finished their conference, and both men rode toward the fallen city.

Colonel Theodore Lyman, who rode at Meade's side, seemed to miss nothing on the way into the city whose steeples he had so long seen from afar. He saw the place with the eye of a Massachusetts patriot:

"The outskirts are very poor, consisting chiefly of the houses of Negroes, who collected, with broad grins, to gaze on the triumphant Yanks; while here and there a squalid family of poor whites would lower at us from broken windows, with an air of lazy dislike. The main part of the town resembles Salem, very much, plus the shiftlessness and minus the Yankee thrift . . . here and there an entire building had been burnt, and everywhere you saw corners knocked off, and shops with all the glass shattered."

Grant and Meade found enemy sharpshooters still working at the rear of the town, and crouched behind a house, peering out occasionally, though the bullets, Grant noted, were "flying thick and fast." Confederate divisions were still massed in the distant streets, and along the shore of the Appomattox, waiting to cross a bridge.

Grant thought of bringing up artillery to blow apart the tempting targets, but dismissed the idea. "I was sure Lee was trying to make his escape, and I wanted to push immediately in pursuit. At all events I had not the heart to turn the artillery upon such a mass of defeated and fleeing men, and I hoped to capture them soon."

The enemy had filed from sight when a lone Confederate came to Grant:

"I'm an engineer for the Army of Northern Virginia," he said. "I can help you end this. Lee's taken the army to new fortifications just out there—he's been working on them for weeks. He'll be waiting."

Meade became excited at the prospect and wanted to cancel the orders of the morning. Grant refused. He had already sent the infantry in the tracks of Sheridan's troopers, going west along the south bank of the Appomattox, and it was already making progress. He did not believe the story of the "engineer." "I knew that Lee was no fool, as he would have been to have put himself and his army between two formidable streams like the James and the Appomattox rivers."

Grant decided that Lee had sent the man as a ruse, to lead him off the trail. "He will have to give up Richmond," Grant told Meade, "and the Danville Road is the only way he can go."

"If he's going that way, we can follow," Meade said.

"We don't want to follow. We want to get ahead of him and cut him off, and if he'll just stay where you think he is, I want nothing better. If I get to the Danville Railroad where it crosses the Appomattox, and he's still between the rivers, we'll close him up."

Grant turned to find temporary headquarters. He rode through a few cheering Negroes to a comfortable-looking brick house. A man emerged and introduced himself as Thomas Wallace. Grant went to his porch with several officers.

Wallace invited him into the parlor, but Grant declined. "I'm smoking," he said, and sat facing the street, where his troops passed. The yard and walk were soon crowded with staring Southerners. An officer rode in with a dispatch from Sheridan, which Grant read immediately. The cavalryman was already on the open roads to the west, and had passed Namozine Creek, where he was near the Confederate supply trains.

Grant was anxious to go to the front, but he had a telegraph message from the President, arranging to meet him in Petersburg; he waited.

Lincoln had been in the hut which served as the telegraph office at City Point when word of Petersburg's fall came in. He had collected all the dispatches and piled them before him, tracing the army's rapid movements on a little chart. He was especially interested in the cavalry.

"Here," he said to Admiral Porter. "Here they are at this point, and Sheridan is just starting off up this road. That will bring about a crisis."

Finally the President said, "Now let us go to dinner. I'd like to peck a little." He was soon back at the telegraph post, however.

The Petersburg news came while Lincoln was playing with three kittens in the hut. He lifted the animals to his table, where they tumbled over his chart.

"You poor, little miserable creatures," he said, "what brought you into this camp of warriors? Where is your mother?"

"The mother is dead," an officer said.

"Then she can't grieve for them as many a poor mother grieves for sons who have fallen in battle—and who will still grieve if this surrender does not take place without bloodshed. Ah, kitties, thank God you are cats, and can't understand this terrible strife."

The President took out his handkerchief and wiped the eyes of the kittens. He turned to an officer, "Colonel, get them some

milk, and don't let them starve. There's too much starvation going on in this land anyhow."

He was interrupted by a midshipman knocking at the door
with a message for Porter: "Vice President Johnson and Mr. Pres-
ton King are on the *Malvern,* sir, and wish to pay their respects
to the President."

Lincoln jumped from his chair and shouted at the young
sailor. Porter thought he had never seen such a change in a man.
"The President was greatly excited, and the habitual benevolent
expression had left his face. He was almost frantic."

"Don't let those men come into my presence," Lincoln said.
"I won't see any of them. They have no business here, anyway,
no right to come down here without my permission. I never want
to lay eyes on them. I don't care what you do with them, but don't
let them near me." He sat down, and Porter thought he "looked
like a man it would be dangerous for anyone to anger."

Porter sent the midshipman back with orders to provide
champagne and liquors for the gentlemen aboard the *Phlox,* a dispatch boat, and to take them anywhere they wished to go, except
to Mr. Lincoln. The President listened calmly, and went on
playing with the kittens as if nothing had happened.

They went up to Petersburg by boat, and took with them
the President's twelve-year-old son, Tad, who was in his Army
uniform, as usual. The boy had remained at the front with his father and the White House guard, W. H. Crook, when Mrs. Lincoln
left them on her recent return to Washington.

At the Petersburg landing was Lincoln's older son, Robert,
who was a captain on Grant's staff. Robert had brought horses.

They rode through streets filled with shouting Negroes, and
came to the house where Grant sat.

General Horace Porter watched from his place beside Grant.
"Mr. Lincoln . . . dismounted in the street and came in through
the front gate with long and rapid strides, his face beaming
with delight. He seized Grant's hand as the general stepped forward to greet him, and stood shaking it for some time and pouring
out his thanks and congratulations."

"Do you know, General," Lincoln said, "I've had a sort of sneaking idea for some days that you intended to do something like this, though I thought you would maneuver so as to have Sherman come up and co-operate with you."

"Yes," Grant said. "At one time I thought that Sherman might advance far enough to be in supporting distance." He told Lincoln that he had thought it better for the country to let the Army of the Potomac, Lee's old adversary, finish the task, rather than create sectional jealousies by calling in the Western army at the kill.

"I see," Lincoln said. "I never thought of it in that light. In fact, my anxiety has been so great that I didn't care where the help came from, so long as the work was done."

They talked of the troubles that would come in the wake of victory. Lincoln spoke for more than half an hour, in a rambling way. Horace Porter said, "Thoughts of mercy and magnanimity were uppermost in his heart."

One of the officers noticed that Tad was fidgety, and intuitively came to his rescue with a bag of sandwiches. "Here, young man, I guess you must be hungry."

Tad seized them "as a drowning man would seize a life preserver" and yelped, "Yes I am. That's what's the matter with me."

Lincoln laughed and paused in his talk. Grant turned aside to write a telegram to General Weitzel, in command at Richmond, asking for news. He showed the dispatch to Lincoln. "I had hoped to be able to hear before leaving you that Richmond was ours, but I must get to the front."

Grant and Lincoln shook hands, and the little officer was soon out of the city, riding in search of General Ord's column. Officers with him noticed flowers in bloom as they left the city: violets, trillium, hepatica and cowslips.

The reporter Morris Schaff admired the landscape:

> The road, having cleared the mild ascent . . . which overlooks Petersburg, leads on, bordered here and there by lonely, tapering cedars, its roadside fences, old and gray, masked by rushy thickets and tangled vines. On by old fields with peanuts and corn, through woods, by old plantations . . . the dreaming silence broken every once in a while by cow bells.

Lincoln turned back through the city and spent the day there, besieged in the streets by Negroes who came out in such numbers as to force the President into doorways to escape the press.

The tobacco warehouses and stores were open and mobs and soldiers helped themselves. In the warehouses the leaf was bundled in three-pound bales. Admiral Porter tied four of these to his saddle, and the President and Tad took several for themselves.

As they rode back to the river, regiments recognized the President and cheered. One voice rang out, "We'll get 'em, Abe, where the boy had the hen. You go home, and sleep sound tonight. We boys will put you through."

Lincoln went to the waterside in a wave of cheering, and during the rest of the day rode up and down the James with Porter in the admiral's barge, towed at the end of a long line by a swift little boat.

When he got back to headquarters the President found a telegram from the anxious Secretary Stanton in Washington:

> I congratulate you and the nation on the glorious news. . . . Allow me respectfully to ask you to consider whether you ought to expose the nation to the consequence of any disaster to yourself in the pursuit of a treacherous and dangerous enemy like the rebel army. If it was a question concerning yourself only I should not presume to say a word. Commanding generals are in the line of duty running such risks; but is the political head of a nation in the same condition?

Lincoln replied:

> Thanks for your caution, but I have already been to Petersburg. Staid with General Grant an hour and a half and returned here. It is certain now that Richmond is in our hands, and I think I will go there tomorrow. I will take care of myself.

One of the first regiments in Petersburg had been the 116th U.S. Regiment of colored troops, which went in at dawn behind

a band playing "John Brown's Body." Major Alexandria S. Johnson, riding at their head, saw a small girl, about ten years old,
waving a United States flag at the roadside.

The regiment was hurried out after an hour in the city,
westward after the Rebel army. The road was strewn with plug
tobacco for a mile or more.

The 116th camped sixteen miles out, and Johnson and other
officers had supper in a nearby farmhouse. They ate corn pone
and bacon, sorghum molasses, and "a solution of something called
coffee." They paid their host $1 each.

When their host came onto the porch and saw Negro soldiers camped on his land he swore angrily, and was so overcome
that tears ran down his cheeks. "Poor old Virginia!" he said. "Poor
old Virginia that I should have lived to see this day."

★ FLIGHT ★

JOHN WISE was the eighteen-year-old son of General Henry Wise,
the aging ex-Governor of Virginia. For some weeks he had been
on duty at Clover Station, a cluster of houses on the Richmond
and Danville Railroad, some eighty miles southwest of Richmond
in Halifax County.

Wise had hung about the telegrapher in the tiny depot almost without respite, and heard the news of disaster from the
chattering key. Last night, the first of the trains came through,
and by midnight they had become a procession. Most of them
stopped for wood or water, and Wise listened eagerly to the Confederate officials who came out to reassure the little crowd.

"The army's not beaten or demoralized," one said. "It's retreating in good order. Lee is now out from under the burden of
defending those long lines. Why, he'll draw Grant from his lines,
like the master he is, and whip the Yanks yet. Wait and see!"

Wise heard much of this, and he was cheered. At 3 A.M., however, the train bearing Jefferson Davis and the Cabinet drew into

the torchlit station, and, with a glimpse of the President, Wise felt despair.

Davis sat at a window of the train, waving a hand and smiling to acknowledge the cheers of the crowd, but, Wise said, "His expression showed physical and mental exhaustion."

Beside Davis sat his military advisor of the last months, General Braxton Bragg, whose striking appearance drew Wise's attention. "His shaggy eyebrows and piercing eyes made him look like a much greater man than he ever proved himself to be."

Wise saw his brother-in-law in the car, a Dr. Garnett, who was physician to the President. The young cavalryman went in for a moment, and learned that his mother had been left at the family home in Richmond. The train soon pulled away, and Wise watched its lanterns dwindle away in the direction of Danville.

There was a secret source of merriment and comfort in the Presidential car which Wise failed to discover—Secretary George Trenholm had managed to bring aboard two well-filled hampers of old peach brandy, and the invalid became the most popular member of the Cabinet.

Mallory of the Navy, at least, was won, and proclaimed, "Our fugitives recovered their spirits."

Several other trains followed. One was filled with papers of the archives and employees of the Treasury Department; another bore the Post Office and another the Bureau of War. Wise hailed many old friends. The procession convinced him that all was lost:

"I saw a government on wheels. It was the marvelous and incongruous debris of the wreck of the Confederate capital. There were very few women on these trains, but among the last in the long procession were trains bearing indiscriminate cargoes of men and things.

"In one car was a cage with an African parrot, and a box of tame squirrels, and a hunchback. Everybody, not excepting the parrot, was wrought up to a pitch of intense excitement."

The last train brought the final bit of news. A man called from the platform, "Richmond's burning. Gone. All Gone."

It was after dark of the long day that this last train went by, and Clover Station, Wise thought, was "now the Northern outpost of the Confederacy."

Robert Lee had come up from Petersburg on Traveller along the River Road, on the north side of the Appomattox. This track was followed by the corps of Longstreet and A. P. Hill, after their crossings at the pontoon bridge near Battersea Factory.

John Gordon's corps, which had left the city just east of this point, over a railroad bridge and big Pocahontas Bridge, had come west on the Hickory Road a bit farther north; the two roads joined less than ten miles from Petersburg.

Lee did not seem depressed, and in the morning, when John Esten Cooke, the novelist, rode near the commander, he found his bearing remarkable: "His expression was animated and buoyant, his seat in the saddle erect and commanding, and he seemed to look forward to assured success."

Lee told his staff, "I have got the army safe out of the breastworks. In order to follow me, Grant must leave his lines, and he'll get no more benefit from railroads or the James River."

Cooke noted that the troops themselves were "in excellent spirits" during the spring morning.

Colonel Walter Taylor rejoined the staff about midmorning, and there was a laughing reception for the bridegroom. Taylor was struck by the lack of energy in the enemy's pursuit, for there was not a sign of a bluecoat. The army's wagons were slow in this road, but the staff seemed unconcerned.

General Armistead Long of Lee's staff observed the same phenomenon, especially among the troops:

"A sense of relief seemed to pervade the ranks at their release from the lines where they had watched and worked for more than nine weary months. Once more in the open field, they were invigorated with hope, and felt better able to cope with their powerful adversary."

Little more than twelve miles out of Petersburg, on Winterpock Creek in Chesterfield County, was Clover Hill, the country home of Judge James H. Cox, once Speaker of the Virginia House, and first chairman of the Secession Convention. His house was a rambling English cottage studded with gables and dormers, its porches overgrown with roses. Even in the months of famine,

Clover Hill had imported wines in the cellar, bags of Java coffee, pipes of sherry and French brandies.

The family had only yesterday learned of the collapse of the army. The judge's daughter Kate was startled to see graycoats wandering in the woods—and when she had returned from church, she found the house crowded with friends, all refugees from Petersburg.

It was midnight before the Coxes knew the retreat had begun in earnest; one of the judge's sons, a captain, drove up in a wagon with General William Mahone's wife and children. At almost the same hour the vanguard of Lee's infantry column reached the neighborhood, at a settlement called Summit. Lee and Longstreet, so officers said, would halt there during the day.

Osmun Latrobe, a Lieutenant Colonel on Longstreet's staff, rode through the woods to see Kate Cox, who was an old friend of days in Richmond and Petersburg. Judge Cox welcomed him with an invitation.

"I want you to bring General Lee and General Longstreet and all their officers here," he said. He sent servants for the commanders, and Clover Hill bustled with "large preparations."

Lee and Longstreet and a large party arrived in an already overcrowded house. Kate wrote: "The confusion was terrifying, but as General Lee entered the house, everything and everybody was under the spell of his presence and dignity."

There was a wait before the meal could be served, and Judge Cox led the officers into his drawing room. Kate talked briefly with Lee.

"General, we will still win. You will join General Johnston in North Carolina, and together you will win."

The General gave her a weary smile. "Whatever happens, no men ever fought better than mine."

A butler brought mint juleps. Lee took his glass and gave Kate a taste from it. He hardly touched the drink, she noticed, but took a glass of ice water while his officers had their juleps.

"Do you know," he said, "this glass of water is far more refreshing than those drinks they're enjoying so much?"

Lee led Kate into the dining room on his arm.

She protested. "No, we've decided that every morsel cooked today should be for you and your men."

Lee insisted, and she went, "only too glad to comply."

Longstreet sat opposite her, with one arm still helpless from the wound he had suffered in The Wilderness last spring. The butler took Old Pete's plate to Kate, who cut up his food for him.

Judge Cox asked his daughter to sit by Longstreet and help him, but Lee put a hand on her arm. "No, don't leave me," he said.

The meal was "good and abundant," and followed by coffee. Kate turned to Lee in surprise:

"My, General, do you take cream in your after-dinner coffee?"

"I haven't had coffee in so long that I wouldn't dare take it in original strength."

When she spoke of this to a staff officer, she was told, "The General sends all his coffee to the hospital."

Kate wrote of the farewell:

> Well, our great hour came to an end, and our beloved chief had to shake hands, mount Traveller, and turn his back on us. The procession, as it rode up the quarter of a mile of lane clear of trees and with clover fields on each side, made a most imposing picture. General Lee on horseback was a wonderful sight. . . . I have the most vivid picture in my mind of him going down the lane, his gray cape lined with red thrown back from his shoulders.

Kate cried as they went from sight.

When he had gone a mile from Clover Hill, back to the road junction at Summit, Lee found that the nearest bridge of the Appomattox, Bevil's, was impassable because of high water. He led the staff north, and within four miles came to Hebron Church, near the village of Skinquarter. Here he had further bad news from the river: Far ahead, where the Appomattox looped northward, there was trouble at the Genito Bridge. Lee was concerned about Ewell and the men coming down from Richmond by that route.

He camped at Hebron Church for the night. At 6:30 P.M. he sent Ewell a message:

> When you were directed to cross the Appomattox at Genito Bridge, it was supposed that a pontoon bridge had

been laid at that point, as ordered. But I learn today . . .
that such is not the case. Should you not be able to cross at
that point or at some bridge higher up, you must take the
best road to Rudd's Store on the Goode's Bridge road, and
cross the Appomattox. . . .

This portion of the army is now on its way to Goode's
Bridge, the flats at Bevil's Bridge being flooded by high
water. Notify me of your approach to the bridge and passage
of the Appomattox by courier to Amelia Courthouse or
wherever I may be.

To the South of the Appomattox, far behind Robert Lee,
Lieutenant J. F. J. Caldwell herded westward the remnants of
his South Carolinians from McGowan's Brigade. He reported:

"There was an attempt to organize the various commands, to
no avail. The Confederacy was considered as 'gone up,' and every
man felt it his duty, as well as his privilege, to save himself. There
was no insubordination . . . but the whole left of the army . . .
struggled along without strength, and almost without thought.

"So we moved on in disorder, keeping no regular column,
no regular pace. When a soldier became weary, he fell out, ate
his scanty rations—if, indeed, he had any—rested, rose and resumed the march. . . . There were not many words spoken. An
indescribable sadness weighed upon us. The men were very gentle toward each other."

One soldier divided a last scrap of bacon with Caldwell, a
piece about two inches square. The man offered his bread, but
Caldwell refused it. The lieutenant had lost his pipe, however,
and accepted one from his benefactor.

There were no wagons or artillery with this band of stragglers, and they could move as swiftly as they wished. Caldwell
led them toward Appomattox near Deep Run, but they were
turned back. A horseman met them:

"No sense going down there. The bridge is half under water, and you'd have to swim horseback to get up on the south
end of it."

They stumbled into General McGowan in the afternoon, as
the brigadier directed weary men in rebuilding a bridge over

Deep Run. A few timbers were in place when a body of Confederate cavalry charged up, shouting, "Yanks after us! Run!"

The infantry crowded on the unfinished bridge and sank into the swift water, General McGowan among them. The troops floundered out, swimming desperately, and landed on both banks of the creek. McGowan recalled that he had "a sharp little swim of it."

About midnight Caldwell's troops moved beyond Deep Run, near exhaustion. "They fell about, and slept heavily, or else wandered like persons in a dream. . . . It all seemed to me like a troubled vision. I was consumed by a fever, and when I attempted to walk I staggered like a drunken man."

Captain William Brunson, of McGowan's Sharpshooters, was at the Deep Run crossing and, though he was one of the stronger survivors, barely made it over the stream. He was so exhausted when he crawled out on the opposite shore that he could do no more than hug the ground under a fury of Federal fire.

Some distance to the east of them, on the banks of the Appomattox, Major Dunlop and his handful were marching toward Petersburg as Federal prisoners. They had met disaster at dawn.

Dunlop had kept the Sharpshooters probing the circling Federal line all night, but they found no gap. He wrote of the end:

> The search was continued until daylight, when we again hid ourselves in a dense cedar brake. All our efforts to avoid capture were fruitless, so about nine A.M. a heavy skirmish line combed out the fatal cul de sac and took us in. I surrendered my sword to an officer of the 26th Michigan Infantry. We were treated with marked courtesy by our captors, and were marched off with the Federal column under guard.

The ordnance reserve train, under Captain Fred Colston and Lieutenant Joseph Packard, made good progress during the day; they had taken the River Road used by Robert Lee, just north of the Appomattox, and the commander passed them in the morning. By daylight Packard and Colston had caught up with their wagons, after raiding the abandoned quartermaster stores in Petersburg, and the day passed without incident.

They discovered more passengers among the shells and ordnance equipment: Judge G. D. Camden, of West Virginia, with his wife, two young children and a Negro nurse, rode in one wagon. The judge's son-in-law was a captain with the Ordnance Reserve.

There were other strangers, "a black-coated Baptist preacher and quite a pretty black-eyed Miss R., who was trying to get to her home, somewhere in Southern Virginia."

The party pushed on until almost dark, when they neared Judge Cox's home at Clover Hill. There was an argument here, for other officers wanted to halt and allow the women and children to rest; Packard and Colston warned that they should ride all night, since the enemy might come at any hour. They were overruled, and camp was made far in rear of the army's column. They were almost unarmed, but were not molested, though stragglers wandered past in the road all night.

Dr. Claiborne's hospital train had moved north from Petersburg toward Chesterfield Courthouse, about halfway to Richmond, where it could turn to the west. A dog delayed it at the start.

The surgeon owned a bobtailed yellow "Scotch Terrier," one Jack, a twelve-year-old veteran of Petersburg scandals. He was, Claiborne confessed, "Irritable, selfish, self-asserting, frail as to virtue . . . but full of faith in his master."

The doctor had warned the ambulance driver to bring Jack, whoever else might be left behind. "He thinks too much of himself to walk, and he's ridden thousands of miles, fallen out of more carriages and been run over oftener than any other dog on earth."

When Claiborne overtook the wagons, Jack was missing, and he sent his driver back into Petersburg to bring out the animal or be captured by the enemy. The man went reluctantly. "I never expected to see him again," the doctor wrote.

The hospital train was delayed by broken-down cannon on the road to Chesterfield Courthouse, and there were many halts. The teams were bad, the roads worse and the drivers profane.

Only four miles from the city the artillery traveling with them was forced to leave two caissons mired in the road. It was after 9 P.M. when the party camped. Claiborne's driver appeared on a stolen horse, leading old Jack by a rope made of white handkerchiefs he had taken from stores broken open by Petersburg mobs. He reported that crowds were looting the town.

They were roused from sleep by cannon fire which seemed so near that Claiborne had the men put in the road again. One explosion terrified Jack, who leapt from the blanket at the doctor's side and disappeared into the night, out of the final campaign of the war.

The smallest fragment of the retreating army moved west by way of Chesterfield Courthouse—the men of General William Mahone from the trenches at Bermuda Hundred, on the James between Richmond and Petersburg. Their road lay between the other streams of Confederates, but would join Robert Lee's some twelve miles to the west.

Private W. L. Timberlake of the 2nd Virginia found himself in this road after falling back from Richmond. The first stop of his company was at Chesterfield Courthouse, where he saw some of his friends from the Surrey Light Artillery.

As he left Richmond, Timberlake had been issued a pound of coarse corn meal and a third of a pound of old bacon. He and a friend, one Private Marshall, built a fire, made bread of the corn meal and water from a nearby creek, and poured batter into a frying pan.

A bugle blew.

"Oh, God," Timberlake said, "we've got to get. Marshall, I'm going to throw this away."

"No, don't. We'll have to eat the damned thing anyway."

"A peculiar blessing," Timberlake thought, "on the last rations we had." He was to have nothing to eat for three days except sassafras buds and an ear of parched corn.

They hurried into column, and were off on "such a march as we had never experienced."

Not far away in Chesterfield County was Major Robert Stiles, the pious artilleryman, with his footsore gunners. They had marched surprisingly well, Stiles thought. In the first moments, while they were still in sight of the James, the ships and magazines on the riverfront had blown up:

"It seemed as if the very dome of heaven would be shattered down upon us. Earth and air and the black sky glared in the lurid light. Columns and towers and pinnacles of flame shot upward to an amazing height. . . . After this I could never more be startled."

Stiles walked in the rear of his column to catch those who were straggling; he saw demoralization in the pale faces of his men. "I felt that a hare might shatter the column."

They halted at daylight to let other troops pass, and his men fell as if dead, sleeping by the road. Stiles walked to a nearby farmhouse porch and talked with an old man and woman and their daughter, a soldier's widow, who wore black. The widow saw that the major's coat was torn and had him take it off. While she mended it another woman appeared, a pretty girl whose face was red with weeping.

"Tell him if he passes here he's no husband of mine," she said to the old woman.

Stiles stood in front of her. "You're sending your husband word to desert. You can't do that in front of my men."

The troops in the yard began to crowd about.

"Is he your husband or mine?"

"He's yours, but these are my soldiers. We belong to the same army as your husband."

"Army! You call this mob of retreating cowards an army? Why don't you stand and fight the savage wolves that are coming down on us defenseless women and children?"

"We have to obey orders, Madam, but if the enemy came on that hill this minute, you'd see these men are soldiers."

"Talk's cheap, the Yankees aren't here, and won't be until you've got your precious carcasses out of the way. There's no government or country for anybody. My husband owes allegiance to me and his starving children, and if he doesn't come when I need him, he needn't try when he wants me."

Stiles and the young woman shouted for several minutes,

surrounded by soldiers, most of whom, the Major thought, sided with the girl.

At last he asked, "What command is he in?"

"The Stonewall Brigade!" There was pride in her voice. "He joined in 'sixty-one."

The woman had surrendered. She drew a paper from her dress. "If you doubt it, look at that."

Stiles read a worn furlough pass signed by General Lee for "Extraordinary gallantry in battle." He yelled to his men, "Take off your hats, boys, and listen to this." He read it aloud while the woman wept.

The Major remembered the final melodramatic moments of the exchange on the farmhouse porch:

" 'This little paper is your most precious treasure, isn't it?'

" 'It is.'

" 'And yet, for the brief ecstasy of one kiss, you would disgrace this hero-husband of yours . . . and turn this priceless paper to bitterness; for the rear guard would hunt him from his own cottage, in half an hour, a deserter and a coward.'

"Not a sound could be heard save her hurried breathing. . . . Suddenly she snatched the paper from my hand, put it back hurriedly in her bosom and turning once more to her mother said: 'Mother, tell him not to come.' "

As the woman turned away the men about Stiles yelped cheers.

The command went on, with men dropping out to sleep at such a rate that Stiles could not rouse them all. He had two horses, which he used to carry officers along the column, to help exhausted men, and to send their doctor about. The Major had to walk, in any event, since he could rouse the sleepers only on foot. He organized a rear company to halt the melting away of the little command.

On the northernmost road of retreat the troops of Generals Ewell, Custis Lee and Joe Kershaw fought their way through streams of Richmond's refugees. The nondescript division of the commanding general's eldest son was soon broken into segments. The moon had set at 2 A.M., and Custis moved his men from the trenches then, taking off even the giant guns without arousing the enemy. Most of the artillery had been abandoned at Chaffin's Bluff, but the crews were off safely.

Captain McHenry Howard of the staff was hopeful; he was well shod at least, in a pair of new boots for which he had paid $800 last week—about six months' pay. He marched with the head of the column behind Kershaw's troops, and by daylight they were several miles out on the road toward Amelia Court House. They saw the water-front explosions behind them about this time.

The division had lost its wagon train, which went through Richmond toward an upper ford and disappeared. The 1400 clerks and gunners pushed ahead. For miles, just outside the city, they left the roads and went through "almost interminable woods . . . ankle deep in mud and water." When the rear guard caught up, Custis gave them a two-hour halt, in which the men lay, half asleep, watching smoke rise over the capital. The newcomers were full of tales of ruin in the city.

They had made fifteen miles by dusk, and Custis got supper for himself and the staff from a nearby farmhouse. Captain Howard found it a welcome change from the uncooked corn he had chewed for breakfast and lunch. There was also fodder for the horses. The staff galloped at sunset and overtook the main body of troops, but was lost among strange commands for an hour before riding across country to find their men in camp at Tomahawk Church.

Howard wandered, lost in a grove, even then, and did not find his companions until a dog, the pet of the company, barked from beneath a pile of blankets. Howard fell asleep at 2 A.M.

The rear guard on this road was the band of South Carolina cavalry which had kicked dust into the faces of Admiral Semmes and his seamen in the morning.

Young E. M. Boykin, who was still with them, wrote:

"Already we began to come upon pieces of artillery mired down, the horses dead beat, the gun left, and horses double teamed to the remaining pieces."

The rear guard camped after a long day's march of only

eleven miles, sleeping by squadrons in a woodland, with horses picketed near each fire for immediate use. The horses had corn, and the men ate from a small supply of bread and bacon.

The regimental surgeon, a Dr. McLaurin, got into his ambulance and passed out coffee and "some not very salt James River herring." There were not many such feasts in the army that night.

Late in the night, near the advance of the scattered Confederate columns, General Rufus Barringer and his 1st North Carolina Cavalry turned out of the road at last. They found half-a-dozen strange soldiers to guide them into a comfortable campground, and settled down gratefully.

Within half an hour the accommodating guides had disappeared; they were the scouts of General Sheridan's enterprising Major Young, complete as to gray uniform and Virginia drawl.

The main body of Lee's army had made almost twenty miles in the first day of flight to the west.

★ PURSUIT ★

GRANT and Meade left Petersburg in the early afternoon, riding along the heavy column, and the combined staffs were as big as a cavalry troop as they splashed at the roadside.

They were at Sutherland's Station on the Southside Railroad, nine miles out, by midafternoon. The westward road forked here, and the fields were full of wagons, waiting for the army to choose its route.

An orderly handed Grant a dispatch from Weitzel:

> We took Richmond at 8:15 this morning. I captured many guns. The enemy left in great haste. The city is on fire in two places. Am making every effort to put it out.

Grant read it to the staffs and said calmly, "I'm sorry I didn't get this before I left the President. But I suppose he has the news by now. Circulate the word among the men."

News of the fall of the Rebel capital brought bands out to play, and there was shouting and laughter. There were catcalls from veterans who had been so often deceived, but most men joined the celebration. One yelled, "Stack your muskets and go home!" and another said, "I feel better than I did after that fight at Gettysburg."

Grant was impatient to push ahead, since there was still light to travel, but the bad roads and big wagon trains up ahead forced a halt. Two of the corps were out of rations, and none could come up on the crowded road during the night. Grant did not seem perturbed. "The Army of the Potomac, officers and men, were so elated . . . that they preferred marching without rations to running a possible risk of letting the enemy elude them."

At 4 P.M. Grant had a dispatch from Sheridan, who was out ahead, by now at Namozine Church; it was a cheering description of the litter of a rout:

> The enemy threw their ammunition on the sides of the road and into the woods, and then set afire the fences and woods through which the shells are thrown. The woods are strewn with burning and broken down caissons, ambulances, wagons and debris of all descriptions. Up to this hour I have taken about 1200 prisoners from A. P. Hill's corps and all accounts report the woods filled with deserters and stragglers.

Grant studied his maps in the evening, but without Meade, who had become ill—acute nervous indigestion, it appeared to be.

The commander saw an opportunity of trapping Robert Lee within the next two days: The Confederates were moving west along roughly parallel roads north of the Appomattox, the columns from Petersburg and Richmond joining along the route; Lee had several bridges on the river—but the main road, as well as the Danville Railroad, crossed the Southside Railroad at Burkeville Junction. This spot was about halfway between Petersburg and Lynchburg, and Sheridan would surely be there before the

Confederates could come up. Sheridan had cut up or scattered the Rebel forces isolated south of the Appomattox in the retreat.

Grant was already about as far west as Lee. Tomorrow, he decided, he would turn Meade into the north fork of this westward road, leading nearer the Appomattox in Sheridan's trail. Ord would move by the southward fork, almost parallel. The forces would meet at Burkeville. The commander left orders to put the troops in motion at 3 A.M.

Sheridan spent the night at the home of a Mrs. Cousins, on a road leading to Amelia Court House; he was halfway to Jetersville, with his troopers camping in front of him at Deep Creek.

There had been light skirmishing all day, with the regiments scattering all opposition. General Wesley Merritt had driven some Rebel cavalry out of the path and an incipient fight sputtered near sunset, but the enemy crossed Namozine Creek and escaped. Sheridan watched troopers pick up a few stragglers.

The vital orders for the night went to General George Crook, who would move his cavalry at 3 A.M., and to General Charles Griffin, who would push toward Jetersville at 5 A.M. with his infantry.

Far in the rear, at City Point on the James, more than 4500 imprisoned Confederates roosted glumly in a pen. The 114th Pennsylvania, musicians and all, had been called out to help do guard duty.

Officers shouted offers of freedom to the Confederates: "Step aside, all who want to take an oath of allegiance! We'll give you full protection!"

After a long time, only 100 of the graycoats had come out, and they left their companions in a storm of hooting and howling, "Traitors! Cowards!"

The repentant Rebels were marched to a steamer and sent on the journey north, to rejoin the Union.

V

Tuesday, April 4

★

MEDIEVAL RAPINE was in the minds of Richmond's women, Colonel Ripley concluded. He had been besieged through the night by frantic women seeking guards for their houses. Few of them asked for food.

The colonel had barred Richmond's men from his City Hall quarters. If the houses must have protection, the women must apply. He found their "imaginations inflamed" from years of reading in Richmond newspapers lurid descriptions of the barbaric hordes of the Union army. Ripley sent a guard with every woman who applied.

At 2 A.M., when quiet fell, Ripley trotted through the streets to inspect his new wards. He saw no sign of life, except his sentries, standing against buildings, or pacing on the dim walks. The fires were still flaring in hulks of buildings, but were now under control. He wrote:

"The silence of death which brooded over the city so lately in the hands of that wild mob was only broken by the occasional explosion of shells in the ruins."

The young woman at the Arlington, who had slept little this night, awoke in a world of bluecoats. She and her friend went into the street and saw soldiers asleep on the sidewalks "and everywhere there was a place for weary men to drop down and rest."

The boarding house was out of food, and she came now to her decision:

"In all this time of horror I don't think anything was much harder than making up our minds to draw rations from the Yankees. We said we would not do it. We could not do it."

Hunger overcame pride.

The venerable Mrs. Sampson, who lived in the house, declared war. "I'll take anything I can get out of the Yankees," she said. "They haven't had any delicacy of feeling in taking everything we've got. I'm going for rations."

The girl did not go, but sent Mrs. Sampson and her mother, who spent hours standing in line. They came home with two dried fish.

The girl wrote, "As each stately matron came marching in, holding her codfish at arm's length before her, Delia McArthur and I fell into each other's arms laughing."

Phoebe Yates Pember had fought off Confederate stragglers to save her hospital whisky, only to be beset by the invaders. Early this Tuesday morning her steward reappeared.

"Our stock is gone, Miss Phoebe. The Yanks say we can't draw no more rations from our commissary."

Phoebe dressed for the streets: Untanned leather boots; a homespun dress sent her from Georgia, in a pattern of black and white blocks—the white of cotton yarn, the black of old silk which had been scraped into pulp with broken glass, then carded and spun; a hat of plaited rye straw gathered from the field behind the hospital.

She described her quaint gloves: "Knitted worsted of three shades of green, the darkest bottle shade being around the wrist while the color tapered to the loveliest blossom of the pea at the finger tips. The style of the make was Confederate."

She walked into the Federal office at City Hall and shouted to an officer:

"Do you intend to starve the captured sick?"

The officer was polite. "We can't get transports up the river, Miss. As soon as we do, the hospital will be cared for."

"In that case, sir, you'll give me back my ambulance, which you've put under lock and key."

"Well, I didn't know."

"If you'll turn it over to me, sir, I can take some coffee I've hidden away and exchange it for animal food."

"Where does the coffee come from?"

"I saved it from rations and private donations."

"Why hasn't it been turned over?"

Phoebe only glared at him.

The officer wrote out an order so that she could reclaim the vehicle.

"Are you a native of Virginia?"

"No. I was a South Carolinian when war broke out. I tried to help suffering where I could, in the hospital."

"I lost a brother in South Carolina."

"It's the fate of war. Self-preservation is a law of nature. As a soldier you must recognize our right to defend our soil."

"Well, I'm sorry about the food supply. I hope we can soon end this war. I can see in the pale, pinched faces of the women here how much you've suffered in the war."

"If my features are pinched and pale, it's not because we couldn't feed ourselves—it's anguish because we failed."

The officer responded with generous treatment of the angry Phoebe, and she soon drove her wagon from Chimborazo, slapping the mules with the reins; in the rear were the bag of coffee and keg of whisky. She traded them in the market for a live calf.

Phoebe then intimidated the Federal guards stationed before her commissary building. She walked between them, firmly pulled aside their bayonets and, as they stared, unlocked the door. She emerged with a basket of sugar.

"If you want to arrest me," she said, "I'll be in my quarters."

The Federals thereafter ignored her coming and going, and she took all the supplies she needed.

Connie Cary went through the crowds of soldiers to the home of Judge Campbell. She passed by the White House; its porch was crowded with Federal soldiers and politicians, and the street in front was packed with curious Negroes whom Connie said, "appeared in swarms like seventeen-year locusts."

Miss Cary read the Richmond *Whig* after her visit with the Campbells, the first issue under the direction of General Weitzel and his officers. She read with scorn Weitzel's telegram to Secretary of War Stanton: "The people received us with the wildest joy." She thought to herself: "That scene in Monumental Church looks like it, doesn't it?"

There were signs of returning life in the newspaper: R. D'Orsay Ogden would open a play in the city theater tonight— *Don Caesar de Bazan.*

Along Broad Street, Connie saw shops already reopened, doing "a flourishing trade in greenback currency." She went into the State Library and noted that many books, coins, and medals had been stolen. A collection of captured Yankee battle flags had disappeared.

As Connie went back to her home she was halted by a commotion in the street—a rumor of a Yankee defeat, somewhere out to the west where the armies were. "Oh, if I dared believe it!" she wrote.

As she peered out the window a strange sight rewarded her —"A young woman wearing a costume composed of United States flags."

Connie noticed that other houses were shuttered like her own, while crowds of soldiers and Negroes went by, the latter "decked in the spoils of jewelry shops." But when an occasional Confederate passed, still in uniform, the blinds opened and women called greetings.

The family gathered for prayers in the afternoon, and Connie's uncle read the usual service. He read rapidly, and did not hesitate when he came to the blessing of "the President of the United States." When they rose from their knees, Edith, his younger daughter, said, "Oh, Papa. You prayed for the President of the United States!"

"Did I?" the old man said. "Devil fetch him!"

They laughed together.

But Connie's sadness returned and she was often in tears during the day. The mood had begun last night, late, when she had been awakened by a Federal band playing "Annie Laurie" so beautifully that she thought she was still dreaming—until the soldiers played "The Star-Spangled Banner," which she had not heard for four years. "In one minute I was broad awake and weeping. Oh, that such a noble air should send such a pang to rend me!"

With gentle understanding she tried to cheer another tearful girl in the house next door, who told Connie, "The only comfort I have is singing 'Dixie' with my head buried in a feather pillow."

Judge Campbell went out in the morning to report to an old acquaintance, General George F. Shepley, whom Weitzel had given the title of Military Governor.

In the old days when Campbell sat in the U. S. Supreme Court, Shepley had argued cases before him, and the Federal welcomed Campbell as if nothing had changed. He gave the judge an order to protect his family and talked for a long time about the future of the South.

The Federal Government, Shepley was certain, would treat the people kindly.

"President Lincoln is down the river at City Point, you know," he said.

Campbell responded quickly. "I want to go and see him."

"I'll ask Weitzel," Shepley said. "And I'll send Lincoln a telegram if he agrees."

John Beauchamp Jones, the idle war office clerk, walked around the burned section of the city in the morning. Seven hundred burned buildings, he recorded for his diary, made a black ruin from Main Street to the riverside canal, including banks and the best stores. The Federal soldiers met with his tentative approval:

> The troops do not interfere with the citizens here any more than they do in New York—yet.

Jones saw thousands of Negroes, most of them women, idle in the streets and in Capitol Square.

There were also hundreds of employees of the Confederate departments who had been left behind by their superiors, "a shameful abandonment," he thought.

T. C. DeLeon, the equally enterprising diarist, was at Federal headquarters during the day when a little old woman appeared. "Dickensesque," DeLeon said. She was short, wrinkled and bent, in an old-fashioned black bombazine dress which was rusty with age. She was "Aunt Sallie," a character from Henrico County noted for her sharp tongue.

The old woman's eyes glittered under her poke bonnet as a flippant young officer approached her.

"What do you wish, Madam?"

"What do I wish?"

"That's what I asked, Madam!"

"I wish all you Yankees were in hell!"

Judith Brockenbrough McGuire had not slept, and after breakfast she went to her room and lay, exhausted, until the afternoon. When she woke, a frightened neighbor warned her that Yankee soldiers were prowling about the place.

Judith went toward City Hall with a woman companion. The sight of the building gave her new courage, for her father had sat there as judge for many years, and she had known all the attorneys and officials. Judith saw many of these men in the waiting crowds, forbidden even to enter and beg for food.

She went to a large table where officers were talking with women.

"I want to see the Provost Marshal," Judith said.

"I'm the commandant, Madam."

"To whom can I apply for a guard at my house?"

"You don't need one, Madam. Our troops are under perfect discipline. They wouldn't dare enter your premises."

"I'm sorry to be obliged to undeceive you, sir," Judith said. "When I left home seven of your men were in the yard of the house next door, and one had already been rummaging in my kitchen."

The officer's surprise seemed genuine. "Then you're entitled to a guard, Madam." He sent a captain with her to see that the house at the corner of First and Franklin Streets was not molested.

Judith was once more trying to rest when someone knocked on her door: The guard was drunk in the yard, and threatening to shoot the servants.

Judith went to headquarters once more, and a new guard, a corporal, took away the reeling soldier. Almost every house in the neighborhood was now guarded, Judith saw. She wrote in her diary at night:

The streets are now perfectly quiet. The moon is shining brightly on our captivity. God guide and watch over us.

She heard that President Lincoln had come to the city in the afternoon and gone into the Davis house. She wrote:

Ah, it is a bitter pill. I would that dear old house, with all its associations, so sacred to Southerners, so sweet to us as a family, had shared in the general conflagration. Then its history would have been unsullied.

The channel of the James had been cleared by 8 A.M., and Admiral David Porter set small boats to sweeping the river from City Point toward Richmond, fishing for torpedoes.

Mr. Lincoln was soon aboard the *Malvern* with young Tad; he was elated by reports from occupying troops in the city.

"Thank God I have lived to see this," he said. "It seems to me that I have been dreaming a horrid dream for four years, and now the nightmare is gone. I want to see Richmond."

"If there's any of it left," Porter said. "That black smoke is still there—but before we can go up, the torpedoes must be cleared."

When they got underway the *Malvern* was not alone. A dozen or more boats steamed ahead, eager to be the first into the city. These ran aground, and the *Malvern* passed into the lead, until at last she grounded. Porter took Lincoln into his barge, and with a tug ahead and a party of Marines on board, they went upstream.

Porter sent the tug to help free a boat stuck under a bridge, and went on with Lincoln in the barge, rowed by the Marines after having set out in an armada of vessels.

"Admiral," Lincoln said, "this puts me in mind of a fellow who once came to ask me to appoint him as a minister abroad. Finding he couldn't get that, he came down to a more modest position. Finally he asked to be made a tide-waiter. When he saw he couldn't get that he asked me for a pair of old trousers. But it is well to be humble."

Lincoln saw the Boston reporter, Coffin, at the waterside and shouted, "Do you know where General Weitzel is?"

"Yes," Coffin said. "I'll show you."

Porter landed the boat at a tiny landing near which several Negroes were at work.

Coffin turned to one of the men. "I suppose you were a slave."

"Yes, boss."

"Would you like to see the man who gave you your freedom —Abraham Lincoln? There he is."

"Is that Master Lincoln sure enough, boss?"

"That is he."

The man rushed toward the President, shouting, "Bless the Lord! The great Messiah! I knowed him soon as I seen him. He's been in my heart four long years. Come to free his children from bondage. Glory, hallelujah!"

The old man fell on his knees and kissed the President's feet, and others crowded about him. The President seemed embarrassed.

"Don't kneel to me," Lincoln said. "That's not right. You must kneel to God only, and thank him for liberty. . . . But you may rest assured that as long as I live no one shall put a shackle on your limbs."

Porter tried in vain to move the Negroes from the President's path.

The old man continued to shout, "We means no disrespect to Master Lincoln. We means all love and gratitude."

The Negroes joined hands in a ring and sang:

"Oh, all ye people clap your hands,
And with triumphant voices sing;
No force the mighty power withstands
Of God, the universal king."

Lincoln stood quietly, listening, looking up the hill, which was now covered with Negroes. Porter had the Marines surround the President with bayonets, but still they could not move in the crush of people.

"My poor friends," Lincoln said, "you are free—free as air. You can cast off the name of slave and trample upon it; it will come to you no more. Liberty is your birthright. God gave it to you as he gave it to others, and it is a sin that you have been deprived of it for so many years. But you must try to deserve this priceless boon. Let the world see that you merit it. . . . Learn the laws and obey them; obey God's commandments and thank him for giving you liberty, for to him you owe all things."

The quiet was complete.

"There, now," Lincoln said. "Let me pass on. I have but little time to spare. I want to see the capital."

The Negroes moved, and Lincoln went between them up the hill, mopping sweat from his forehead. They were half an hour reaching Libby Prison. Lincoln halted to look at this, and the Negroes yelled anew, "We'll pull it down!"

"No," Lincoln said. "Leave it as a monument." He passed on.

Porter got an impression of a not-unfriendly city:

"The people could not have had a gala day since the Confederates occupied Richmond as headquarters, judging from present appearances. They certainly were not grieving over the loss of the government which had just fled.

"There was nothing like taunt or defiance in the faces of those who were gazing from the windows or craning their necks from the sidewalks to catch a view of the President. The look of everyone was that of eager curiosity—nothing more."

W. H. Crook, Lincoln's bodyguard, who was caring for Tad, found the crowd hostile. The only sign of welcome he saw was from a young woman on a bridge connecting the Spotswood Hotel with another hotel. She had an American flag over her shoulders. Crook saw, or imagined, danger:

"The blinds of a second story window of a house were partly opened, and a man dressed in gray pointed something that looked like a gun directly at the President. I dropped Tad's hand and stepped in front of Mr. Lincoln. I was sure he meant to shoot."

Coffin walked with the party, behind the Marines, who appeared to him as "six sailors, wearing round blue caps and short jackets and baggy pants." The reporter also saw glowering looks on the faces of white men in the crowd.

The only incidents, however, were harmless. A white man in shirt sleeves ran toward Lincoln so swiftly that Porter started to draw his sword. The man halted, pulled off his hat and yelled: "Abraham Lincoln, God bless you! You are the poor man's friend."

The man tried to force his way to Lincoln's side, and Porter was forced to "treat him rather roughly" before he gave up his effort to shake the President's hand. When the admiral saw him last, he was tossing his hat into the air.

A pretty girl pushed through the crowd and gave Lincoln a bunch of roses. The admiral noted that there were no cheers or growls from the crowd, but that curious people questioned the girl when she returned to the sidewalk.

Lincoln once put his hand lightly on the head of a baby held in his path by a mother. A Negro woman screamed from a doorway, "Thank you, dear Jesus, for this! Thank you, Jesus!"

Coffin noted a few white women waving handkerchiefs, but they were few. "One lady in a large and elegant building looked a while, and then turned away her head as if it was a disgusting sight."

Thomas Thatcher Graves, General Weitzel's aide, now came upon the procession:

"I saw a crowd coming, headed by President Lincoln, who was walking with his usual long, careless stride and looking about him with an interested air and taking in everything."

Graves saluted.

"Is it far to President Davis' house?" Lincoln asked.

Graves took him to the White House.

Lincoln peered at everything in the Confederate White House. Captain Graves had been there earlier in the day, and had been shown over it by Mrs. Omelia, who had been left behind by the Davis family.

Graves led Lincoln into the reception room. "Their housekeeper said this was Mr. Davis' office," he said.

Lincoln sat at a desk. "This must have been President Davis' chair," he said. He gazed out a window with what Graves thought "a serious, dreamy expression," but soon turned back.

"Is the housekeeper here now?"

"No, sir."

Lincoln jumped up. "Let's go," he said in a boyish voice. "Let's look at the house."

Graves led him upstairs, repeating what Mrs. Omelia had told him about the rooms and their furnishings. Lincoln seemed interested in all of it.

General Weitzel ran in the front door as they descended. The commander was out of breath. Graves noticed that Lincoln's face "lost its boyish expression" when he saw that work must be done.

Some Confederate officials came in, among them Judge Campbell and General Joseph Anderson, the Tredegar Foundry director. Lincoln spoke with them, General Shepley made a speech to crowds from the front porch, and the party was served lunch. Lincoln talked with his visitors in the parlor, behind closed doors.

Campbell had seen Lincoln in Washington before the war, and during the past winter had met him at Hampton Roads with other Confederate peace commissioners in a vain effort to end the fighting. They had a pleasant meeting this morning. Campbell saw that Lincoln expected some official message from him, perhaps a formal surrender.

"I have no commission to see you," Campbell said. "When General Breckinridge left here—the Secretary of War—I told him I would stay in Richmond, and that I would see you at the first opportunity.

"I asked him for some kind of commission to speak to you on the subject of peace. I got nothing from him."

Campbell, however, thought they might make peace between them without waiting for word from the racing armies in the field. The judge recorded the conversation:

"I then told the President that the war was over, and all that remained to be done was to compose the country. . . . I told him that he should talk to the public men, and get Virginia back into the Union."

"Who do you have in mind?" Lincoln asked.

Campbell called the names of several prominent Richmond men: Ex-Governor Letcher, Rives, Hunter, Baldwin, Caperton, Holcombe—and General Lee himself.

"Your principles are right," Lincoln said. "The trouble is,

how to apply them. I want to have another talk with you. I'll remain in Richmond tonight."

The officers, especially Admiral Porter, would not hear to Lincoln's spending the night in the city, and the President left. He invited Campbell to visit the *Malvern* the next day.

Lincoln went back to the river in a carriage, and on the way left a memory with Captain Graves of Weitzel's staff, when they stopped for closer looks at Libby Prison and Castle Thunder.

Weitzel asked Lincoln what he should do about the captive people of Richmond.

"I don't want to give any orders on that, General," Lincoln said, "but if I were in your place, I'd let 'em up easy. Let 'em up easy."

The party went into the halls of the Confederate Congress, but stayed only a moment. Porter saw only "dreadful disorder, with Confederate scrip and . . . documents lying on the floor."

On the way back down the river, Lincoln and Tad and the Marines saw dozens of huge torpedoes which had been taken from the river. They lay on the banks "like so many queer fish basking in the sun," Admiral Porter said.

After dark, when it was quiet on the *Malvern*, there was a hail from shore: "Ho, *Malvern!* Dispatches for the President. Send a boat!"

Porter was cautious. He sent a boat with orders to bring in the message, but to leave the man on shore. The Marine returned.

"He won't send the dispatch. He says he must deliver it in person."

"All right," Porter said. "Go get him. Watch him."

The Marine found that the mysterious caller had disappeared.

The silence was soon broken by another call from the bank: "I'm a sailor off the *Saugus*. Let me come on." There was no such vessel in the fleet. Porter sent a party in a boat; this man also disappeared.

Lincoln seemed to feel uneasy after these hails, and did not protest when Porter placed a Marine outside his stateroom door for the night.

★ FLIGHT ★

By seven o'clock in the morning Robert Lee had ridden the half-dozen miles from his camp at Hebron Church to the crossing of the Appomattox at Goode's Bridge and was waiting by the stream when the courier he had sent to Ewell the night before reported: Ewell was not to be found.

The commander wrote on the note and sent the rider to continue the search:

P.S. 7:30 A.M., April 4th. The courier has returned with this note, having been able to learn nothing of you. I am about to cross the river. Get to Amelia Courthouse as soon as possible, and let me hear from you.

Longstreet's men were crossing Goode's Bridge, and Lee ordered that Mahone's troops, when they came up, remain here to hold the crossing for Ewell.

The army was now concentrating. Pickett and Richard Anderson had led survivors of the march along the south of the Appomattox, and had already crossed at Goode's.

Lee went over the stream soon after sending his dispatch to Ewell; he had not lost his keen eye for the condition of his men.

A young Virginia staff officer, Thomas G. Jones, rode up to report to the commander. His troops were in good condition, he said, and he wanted orders. Lee gave him a stern look.

"Did those people surprise your command this morning?"

"No, sir. Did you get such a report?"

"No," Lee said, "but judging from your appearance something urgent must have prevented you young men about headquarters from making your toilets this morning. I thought you must have been surprised by the enemy."

Jones looked in dismay as Lee pointed to his boots—one leg of his pants hung outside his boot, and the other was stuffed inside, with the look of a huge bologna sausage.

Jones saluted with a wry expression and turned away.

Lee called him back.

"I meant only to caution you as to the duty of officers, especially those who are near high commanders. You must avoid anything that might look like demoralization while we are retreating. I know you're a good soldier. You must not take my caution so much to heart."

Lee heard scattered musket fire ahead, where Longstreet's advance was pushing back Federal cavalry. Grant's infantry would be up within a few hours. He rode into Amelia Court House, a sleepy village of unpaved streets, most of the houses behind board fences over which tumbled roses or honeysuckle. Around a grassy square in the center were the courthouse and a rambling stage tavern. A row of huge oaks shaded the common. A railroad station was nearby.

Lee reached the station at about eight thirty and made a stunning discovery. He had ordered the Richmond reserve supply of 350,000 rations sent here to feed the army on its retreat. Instead there were carloads of supplies and ammunition—hundreds of boxes of artillery shells, caissons, and harness for artillery teams, but no food.

John Esten Cooke was near Lee at this moment, noting expressions of dismay among the officers and men in the village; the look of defeat. Lee for once lost his self-control, and the disaster could be read on his features. Cooke wrote:

> No face wore a heavier shadow than that of General Lee. The failure of the supply of rations completely paralyzed him. An anxious and haggard expression came to his face.

There was by now a steady drizzle of rain. Lee sent troops on the far side of the village to form a line and turned several regiments into the already destitute country, foraging for food. He issued a plea to the country people:

> To The Citizens of Amelia County, Virginia.
>
> The Army of Northern Virginia arrived here today, expecting to find plenty of provisions, which had been ordered to be placed here by the railroad several days since, but to

my surprise and regret I find not a pound of subsistence for man or horse. I must therefore appeal to your generosity and charity to supply as far as each one is able the wants of the brave soldiers who battled for your liberty for four years. We require meat, beef, cattle, sheep, hogs, flour, meal, corn and provender in any quantity that can be spared. The quartermaster of the army will visit you and make arrangements to pay for what he receives or give the proper vouchers or certificates. I feel assured that all will give to the extent of their means.

Lee also sent a telegraph message along the railroad to Danville, asking that 200,000 rations be rushed to Amelia. The dispatch went by horseback to Jetersville, seven miles below the village, before officers found wires intact.

The wagons creaked away into the country, seeking food.

Despite the spreading depression, the army responded to Lee. The Second Corps cheered him with the old vigor in the streets of Amelia. And William Owen, a gunner with the New Orleans Washington Artillery, noted this morning: "I saw General Lee and Longstreet. As usual they both looked confident."

Another of his soldiers, Captain J. D. Cummings, wrote:

> Here I saw General Lee for the last time. . . . I had never seen him look so grand and martial and handsome on horseback. He was the finest specimen of a man I ever looked at, then apparently about 60 years of age, deep brown eyes, clear skin, a well-shaped Roman nose, abundant gray hair, silky beard and mustache, well and neatly trimmed, wearing a gray coat and soft hat, his uniform buttoned up and fitting to perfection. He was a picture worth seeing. . . . General Lee and staff rode up and rested a few minutes under the slight shade of the new leaves . . . presently the party moved on . . . and when he disappeared it seemed as if a great light had gone out.

Lee settled in Amelia; more troops arrived during the day. The commands had shrunk, but they came on, including Hill's corps and a division under Wilcox; General Heth had rounded up the survivors of Sutherland's Station, among others. John Gordon's men were now in camp, just five miles out.

Lee had his tent pitched in the yard of a Mrs. Francis Smith, and made headquarters. Fred Colston had passed here in February and talked with Mrs. Smith, whose husband was a relative of General Lee.

"We haven't seen him all through the war," she told Colston.

"You might see him before it's over," the ordnance captain said. "He might tent in your yard."

Reports from the wagons were distressing from the start, and many rattled back empty long before dark.

Private W. L. Timberlake of the 2nd Virginia Battalion, who had thrown away his morning corn bread yesterday, was Lee's companion under fire in Amelia.

The general and the private were in the road together when an explosion went off. Both moved swiftly in the direction of the sound, and Lee went ahead to investigate. It was the first of dozens of caissons blown up in Amelia during the day; there was no longer use for them, and too few teams to pull them.

Lee was soon drawn to the western edge of the village, where Federal cavalry was skirmishing with troopers of the 14th Virginia, of Rooney Lee's division. The commander rode into the midst of the action as the graycoats countercharged a Union squadron; Traveller took him directly toward the enemy. The bluecoats reined aside as the Confederates galloped, except for a lone rider who came on without faltering.

The troopers aimed pistols at the Federal, but Lee shouted, "Don't shoot." A moment later a cavalryman caught the enemy rider's bridle and saw that what Lee had suspected was true; the bluecoat was wounded and unable to control his horse.

Most of the army was safe at hand by dusk—if it could be fed tomorrow there was still hope. Enemy troopers had come within a mile of Amelia on more than one road, littering them with burning wagons and debris, but by now the remnants of the commands of Anderson, Wise and Pickett had come in, shielded for the last few miles by cavalry.

Lee had reassuring word from Ewell at 9 p.m. Crews were laying planks over the railroad span at Mattoax Bridge and the troops of Ewell and Custis Lee would soon cross the Appomattox. Gordon was at Scott's Shop, about halfway in from Goode's Bridge, and Mahone was behind Gordon.

Candles burned late in the headquarters tent in Mrs. Smith's yard. Gusts of wind lashed the canvas with showers.

On the route of retreat, three miles from Amelia Court House, was the plantation house Winterham, home of the Jefferson family. Young George Jefferson was there today, aiding women and servants as they buried silver, hitched horses in the swamps and hid the remaining food. The boy had heard terrifying tales of Yankee looting, but it was not the enemy who came today. George wrote:

> We were soon overrun by our half-starved soldiers who had eaten little or nothing for several days. Aunt Prudence, our good old cook, worked faithfully day and night until entirely exhausted, when the boys were furnished with salt and corn meal and told to help themselves.

George heard tales of the soldiers, who gave him an endless variety of opinions:

"General Lee's making a strategic retreat. We'll whip 'em yet."

Others shook their heads. "It's all done. We may as well go back home, and try to save the home place."

George's older brother Eugene, one of Lee's gunners, soon came to the house and joined the soldiers around the kitchen shed. Eugene had been separated from his companions of the Otey Battery. When the feasting men heard explosions in the direction of Amelia Court House and hurried away, Eugene mounted one of the best of Winterham's remaining horses and followed them. He attached himself to a cavalry company.

Custis Lee's men had begun the day miserably. Captain McHenry Howard stirred before dawn in the cold drizzle and helped to herd the men into column. There was no breakfast. For the first time the road was clear, and in midmorning the men were cheered by a report that they might find provisions at Mattoax Bridge.

Custis ordered an hour's halt at noon, and the few who had food in knapsacks cooked it, sharing rations more liberally than usual. A long artillery train overtook them, and when they were within a mile of Mattoax the Richmond troops were halted once more.

At 4 P.M. a couple of supply wagons appeared; fires sprang up, and there were a few meals of johnny cake made from gray flour.

They crossed the bridge after dark to the chant of soldiers posted with torches, "Watch your step. Walk right in the middle, or them planks will throw you."

The loose boards lay across the rails on the high trestle, rattling endlessly under the feet of the troops, who went over with locked arms to steady themselves. It was late when the rear guard reached the south bank of the river, and after midnight when the division camped. The last miles were over a winding track through woods and fields, in search of a dry campsite. The exhausted men fell asleep under trees before fires could be built.

The Georgia private William Graham, who had so nearly frozen in his sleep outside Petersburg, was also up and marching at 3 A.M., without rations. "Great demand for hard-tack," he wrote, adding that no one provided it. They were halted for several hours while officers organized a rear guard for their wagon train.

As usual, Graham noted, men of the signal corps claimed exemption from work. One of them pulled out a spyglass and another a copper signal torch, showing officers that they should not be sent to such menial duty. The provost marshal's men had no mercy, however, and Graham recorded: "The redoubtable flag-floppers were much to their chagrin and disgust turned into infantry."

Not even this diversion could cheer Graham for long. His diary entry for late this night:

Sore and weary and O, so hungry, we reached the Appomattox where we camped. Had pretty good luck today. Got a couple of biscuit and a piece of raw bacon which made a small though I thought at the time a princely meal.

When we got to the bridge found a soldier, one of the bridge guard, with meal and potatoes to sell. Bought two quarts of meal and one of the potatoes which we—Feild, Finley and I—proceeded to cook. Made ash cakes which were superb. Ate heartily and turned in.

About 12 o'clock was roused by some one who informed me that we were about to draw rations. They were the first we got since leaving Petersburg—and consequently a great desideratum but I was actually too tired and sore to get up—so told Feild to draw mine and he might have them.

Lieutenant Caldwell of McGowan's Brigade was so hungry that the thought of food nauseated him, but he could not put it from his mind even in the turmoil of the morning. The scattered command still struggled along both banks of the Appomattox, and officers were busy rounding up the strays. At last, when Orr's South Carolina Rifles got to the south bank of the river, there were 500 survivors of the brigade to march together toward Amelia.

They came upon a few supplies; Caldwell forced himself to eat and was soon "greatly improved." He helped the little force beat off occasional forays by Federal cavalry, which hung in the rear, apparently content to hurry them on.

They reached Amelia about noon and drew a meager ration of meat from the brigade wagons—less than a day's supply for each man. At first, Caldwell said, the very sight of the main body of the army relieved their "forlorn and desolate feeling," but in the evening, when they watched the rear guard arrive, their darkest suspicions of the army's plight were confirmed. Gordon's corps came, "a mere skeleton," and the worn, hungry men of Pickett, Johnson, Heth and Wilcox looked as if they might not be able to leave this camp.

Captain William Brunson, of the Sharpshooters of Mc-
Gowan's Brigade, took command of a few of his old men when the
fragments of the regiment reorganized. Most of the higher officers
were gone, and Major Dunlop was presumed lost. Brunson
wrote:

> From this time forth the army was little more than a
> mob. We fought day and night without much system, sur-
> rounded by Yankee cavalry. The Sharpshooters were ordered
> from one flank to another, and from front to rear.

The little party of Georgians and Carolinians entered Amelia.

Some troops were taken by the enemy within sight of Amelia.
R. M. Doswell, a Virginia private, was on the muddy road with a
dispatch when he saw a wagon train under the guard of Confederate Negro troops. "A singular sight to me," Doswell wrote.

The wagons were halted, and in the rear, no more than a
hundred yards away, a Federal cavalry regiment was forming for
a charge. The bluecoats fell into line on a hillside and galloped
down on the wagons. The Negroes fired rapidly and drove them
off.

While Doswell stared in admiration at the colored troops,
the Union cavalry wheeled back into sight, this time in a determined charge that broke up the train and turned the vehicles
from the road. The Negro soldiers were quickly captured.

Doswell thought of his own plight only when the last of the
captives were being rounded up; he galloped away without drawing the attention of the enemy.

Dr. Claiborne, the Petersburg surgeon, was far behind with
his hospital train. He passed through Chesterfield Courthouse between the lines of General William Mahone's veterans, who
cheered him on.

Claiborne was ordered to hurry toward Amelia, but had
camped on the north side of the Appomattox, thinking that Mahone's men were still behind him, as a shield against the enemy.
He passed a plantation house and saw, sitting under trees on its

lawn, General Mahone and his staff, evidently awaiting a meal. Mahone hailed the doctor. "Come in, Claiborne, and have a bite with us."

They ate hungrily when servants brought them fried chicken, ash cake and buttermilk, but had hardly finished when Mahone hurried them into the saddles.

"It's time we were off," he said.

Claiborne looked to the rear and was astonished to see blue lines of troops. "What does that mean?" he asked.

"Yankees, I suppose," Mahone said. "We'll have to stop about here somewhere."

Claiborne left the tiny general and hurried to his train, which had passed ahead in the road. He took his leave almost timorously.

"General Mahone," he said, "you have a very good surgeon on your staff?"

"Yes. There's Wood. A good man."

"Well, then, as you have no need for my services, I'll go along to my people."

"You'll be sorry you didn't stay with Mahone," the general said.

Claiborne camped with his wagons about a mile out of Amelia, and spent the rainy night undisturbed.

Young E. M. Boykin of the 7th South Carolina Cavalry found this the slowest day of the march. His men did not move until nine o'clock, since their horses could quickly overtake the column. It was after dark when they went over Mattoax Bridge, with their mounts shying and going gingerly on the uncertain footing.

They camped about a mile from the river, on the south bank, amid some of Longstreet's infantry.

The most striking sight was a boy with food:

"One of the young men attached to our mess . . . had his pockets filled with ham and biscuits near the crossing by some good Samaritan he had met, and so our herring grilled by one of the couriers on the half of a canteen was helped out by this addition."

The troopers went to sleep early, but one of the fires spread into a field of drying grass in which they slept, and a blaze flashed through their camp. Boykin said:

"There was a general jumping up and stamping it out. One of the men created quite a sensation by shaking his India rubber, which was on fire; it flew into pieces in a shower of flame." Blankets were burned and equipment was charred.

In the village of Amelia, as the enemy cavalry pushed near, a North Carolina private, Thomas P. Devereux, Grimes' Division of Gordon's Corps, had a glimpse of one of the latest of Confederate military marvels—a sharpshooter with a globe sight.

Devereux found General Fitzhugh Lee, General Grimes and other officers staring through field glasses to the southwest, studying a distant Federal officer who sat a white horse in the open. The generals were debating as to how far away the man was. Fitz Lee interrupted, "I have a man who is a capital judge of distance."

Someone called up a trooper, who dismounted, carrying a rifle with a globe sight.

"Can you hit that man?" Lee asked.

"I think I can, sir." The trooper lay in the field and took long aim. He fired and officers shouted, "You got him! They're carrying him away."

Devereux gaped in wonder at the riderless white horse. The marksman estimated the range at 1000 yards.

The Washington Artillery of New Orleans rolled into Amelia in the afternoon, and its biographer, William Owen, noted that the men had not eaten a meal since Sunday. They had marched for forty-four hours with hardly a halt.

Like other soldiers, Owen found a pleasant surprise at the Appomattox bridge, where one of his men gave him a handful of parched corn and a bit of raw bacon. Owen wrote: "I thought it an excellent breakfast, and tasted as nice as a tenderloin steak garnished with mushrooms in Victor's best style."

In Amelia, Owen saw the first signs of the army's end; dozens of men were straggling off to find food. As the stream grew, those who were left became demoralized.

Owen learned of the missing rations and heard a rumor that the train General Lee had expected was sent into Richmond and used to carry off Confederate documents. He wrote in his diary: "Who cares for archives now? It is food we need. The result of this mismanagement is that the army is without subsistence for man or beast."

During the day President Davis, who had paused in Danville, issued a final call to arms to the people of the Confederacy.

Since it could not be sent to Richmond or to Lee's army, the proclamation could travel only southward. The few Confederates who saw it read in wonder:

> . . . It would be unwise, even if it were possible, to conceal the great moral, as well as material injury to our cause . . . from the occupation of Richmond by the enemy. It is equally unwise and unworthy of us, as patriots engaged in a most sacred cause, to allow our energies to falter, our spirits to grow faint, or our efforts to become relaxed. . . .

> We have now entered upon a new phase of the struggle, the memory of which is to endure for all ages, and to shed ever increasing lustre upon our country. Relieved from the necessity of guarding cities . . . with our army free to move from point to point . . . and where the foe will be far removed from his own base . . . nothing is now needed to render our triumph certain, but . . . our own unquenchable resolve. . . .

> I will never consent to abandon to the enemy one foot of the soil of any one of the States of the Confederacy. . . . Virginia, with the help of the people, and by the blessing of Providence, shall be held and defended, and no peace ever made with the infamous invaders. . . .

> Let us not then despond, my countrymen, but relying on the never-failing mercies and protecting care of our God, let us meet the foe with fresh defiance, with unconquered and unconquerable hearts.

★ PURSUIT ★

THE COUNTRY had begun to change. The reporter Morris Schaff, who rode near the head of the blue column, wrote of the roads winding westward along the Appomattox:

> The main roads wind through much deep and pondering forest, cross many creeks and runs . . . clayey ridges, fields of wheat, tobacco and blading corn. The river itself curves often . . . with old trees, leaning, tangled with grape vines, almost meeting over the stream. . . . There are deep, winding, tree-roofed creeks and runs . . . where wood ducks nest.

Of this landscape, little changed for generations afterward, a native wrote:

> A gray loneliness, the loneliness of tired silent cedars brooding up rural lanes to the doorways of gray plank houses and quiet broken but occasionally by the cry of crows, the sound of an axe chopping wood or a distant cowbell. Slow brown creeks come to sight and die from the sight in screens of bushes. Broomstraw fields lie about, useless and silent . . . a perfect setting for a Greek tragedy.

George Meade rattled off in his ambulance after Sheridan's cavalry at dawn, his face pale beneath the scraggly gray beard. The wagon plunged to the northwest in the direction of Jennings Ordinary and Jetersville, where the vanguard hoped to bar Lee's army from the railroad to Danville. Grant rode with him at first, but soon turned south in the route of the bulk of the infantry, which struck for the Southside Railroad junction at Burkeville.

The day was cold and overcast, with a drizzle for hours on

end, and the commander of the Army of the Potomac rode with
eyes closed, his grim lips tight against the jarring of the ambulance.

Schaff wrote of the scene:

> Streams rose, and had to be bridged, and the water in
> pools, low places and tussocky swales was up to the hubs of
> the wheels. It was almost impossible to move the trains,
> which doubled up teams. . . . Poor, exhausted, floundering
> animals blocked the way, and miles of the road had to be
> corduroyed for them. But on, regardless of the weather,
> water spurting from their shoes at every step, rain dripping
> from the soaked brims of their hats, went the gallant in-
> fantry.

Colonel Lyman recorded a moment of humor. There was
cheering, and a band blaring "Hail to The Chief," and a cavalry
squadron trotting by.

Lyman and Meade's other officers assumed that Grant was
approaching: "But lo, as they drew nearer, we recognized the
features of Colonel Mike Walsh (erstwhile a sergeant of cavalry) who, with an admirable Irish impudence, was acknowledging the shouts of the crowd that mistook him for Grant!"

Meade's caravan rolled on. Near noon it got official word of
the fall of Richmond, and marching men cheered for an hour
or more as they hurried through gusty showers.

Meade halted at 5 P.M., at the farmhouse of a Mrs. Jones,
near Deep Creek. The staff grumbled over prospects of a cold,
hungry night, for the wagons were far in the rear and there
seemed nothing to do but bed down in the wet grass of the yard.

Meade went over the creek to visit General Andrew Humphreys of the 2nd Corps, and at dusk came back with him in tow.
Humphreys provided food for the staff, and supper fires were
soon blazing.

Meade was seized by chills and fever, followed by nausea.
Lyman said that the fever "excited him greatly, though it did
not impair the clearness of his head."

At 7 P.M. the rain ceased and skies cleared. Meade had a
dispatch from Sheridan, brought by Colonel Newhall:

The Rebel army is in my front, three miles distant, with all its trains. If the 6th Corps can hurry up we will have sufficient strength.

I will hold my ground unless I am driven from it. I understand that Humphreys is just after the 5th Corps. My men are out of rations, and some rations should follow quickly. Please notify General Grant.

P.S. The enemy are moving from Amelia Courthouse via Jetersville and Burke's Station to Danville. Jeff Davis passed over this railroad yesterday to Danville.

Meade had the message read to him, and went to bed, but soon called for Newhall. He questioned the aide sharply about the situation in Sheridan's front.

"If you will drop everything but ammunition wagons," Newhall said, "we can stop Lee where he is, and he must surrender."

Meade was deeply impressed. He dictated a ringing order to the troops:

The Major General commanding feels that he has but to recall to the Army of the Potomac the glorious successes of the oft-repeated contests with the Army of Northern Virginia, and, when he assures the army that, in the opinion of so distinguished an officer as General Sheridan, it only requires these sacrifices to try and bring the long and desperate conflict to a triumphant issue, the men of this army will show that they are willing to die of fatigue and starvation as they have ever shown themselves ready to fall by the bullets of the enemy.

The infantry was ordered to take the road again at 3 A.M. At 10:45 P.M. Meade sent a copy of this order to Grant, who was below him on the Southside Railroad, at Wilson's Station, twenty-seven miles west of Petersburg.

Scores of scouts prowled the country in front of Sheridan, dressed as Confederates, civilians and Federal troopers. They looted farms, joined marching files of Lee's army and swarmed along roads and rails between the converging armies. One of them galloped into a party of Sheridan's officers at a remote settlement called Scott's Mills, on West Creek, shouting excitedly, "The Rebels are in Amelia Courthouse, and coming down the railroad. Thousands of 'em."

The officers agreed to carry the message to Sheridan.

They soon sighted a road filled with Confederate stragglers, men moving wearily westward. An occasional mounted officer in gray emerged from the woods and joined the passing infantry, evidently coming from hiding to the protection of the column.

The party of Federals trotted near the railroad and saw puzzling signs of distress from the mounted Confederates; the graycoats made covert signals for them to keep away. At last two of these riders turned from the road and met the Federals.

"Keep back," the men in gray said. "We're Major Young's scouts. The Major's down the road a way with a whole corral of Johnnies. We're taking him more."

The officers discovered the ambush when they came upon the legendary Major Young in the undergrowth by the railroad tracks, his horses tied to trees behind him, and below the embankment a regiment of Confederate prisoners. A dozen or more scouts kept them quiet with cocked rifles. A stream of new prisoners came, led by the gray-coated decoys.

Phil Sheridan had been in the saddle since dawn, hurrying his men into position. His cavalry was split into two forces, one under General Crook heading for the railroad between Amelia and Burkeville, another under General Wesley Merritt toward Amelia Court House. The infantry of the 5th Corps, which was nearby, was being pushed toward Jetersville, some six miles southwest of Amelia on the Danville railroad.

Sheridan drove himself. He rode for ten hours across country with an escort of the 1st U.S. Cavalry—about 200 troopers— and near 4 P.M. rode into Jetersville and put his handful of men into line at the crossroad until the heavy column of infantry could come up. He intercepted a Confederate message he would long remember:

"Just as the troopers were deploying, a man on a mule, heading for Burkeville, rode into my pickets. He was arrested, of course, and being searched there was found in his boots this telegram in duplicate, signed by Lee's Commissary General:

" 'The Army is at Amelia Courthouse, short of Provisions. Send 300,000 rations quickly to Burkeville Junction.' "

Sheridan saw that one copy was meant for Rebel officers in Danville, and the other for Lynchburg. He reasoned that telegraph lines north of Burkeville must have been cut by General Crook after Lee wrote the dispatches. It was clear that Lee was concentrating his troops at Amelia.

Sheridan sent fresh dispatches to his commanders: Crook was to come up the railroad to Sheridan at Jetersville, Merritt was to leave a small force in the enemy rear and close in on Jetersville, and the 5th Corps, under General Griffin, was to speed its march.

Sheridan attempted a ruse to entice the Confederates to send rations for his own hungry men. He sent four of Major Young's scouts to Burkeville, where they were to separate, taking roads leading to Danville and Lynchburg. When they found telegraph lines open, they would send the messages and perhaps lead the unwary Rebels to send supplies into Sheridan's trap.

By 5 P.M. the head of the 5th Corps infantry came into Jetersville, and Sheridan soon had the weary men digging trenches and throwing up a line of rail breastworks. He waited for attack at dusk.

VI

Wednesday, April 5

★

★ RICHMOND ★

JUDITH BROCKENBROUGH MCGUIRE walked through city streets where bluecoat sentries kept order, into Franklin Street, and entered the home of the Robert E. Lee family. Mary Lee was in her invalid's chair, still knitting clothing as she had throughout the war. She refused to carry on a gloomy conversation.

"The end is not yet," she said. "Richmond is not the Confederacy."

Judith left her with the feeling that life would go on, somehow.

A woman who had a "sky parlor" at the Spotswood Hotel took a morning walk with a young man from the hotel:

"I passed General Lee's house. A Yankee guard was pacing to and fro before it—at which I felt an impulse of indignation—but presently the door opened, the guard took his seat on the steps and proceeded to investigate the contents of a very neatly furnished tray, which Mrs. Lee in the kindness of her heart had sent out to him."

Phoebe Yates Pember, the Chimborazo matron, was shocked by the change on Richmond's streets. The steamboats coming upriver brought throngs of new people:

"Squads of mounted male pleasure seekers scoured the streets. Gaily dressed women began to pour in also, with looped-up skirts, very large feet, and a great preponderance of spectacles."

Nor was that all. Women of Richmond's leading families opened their doors to friends who had come on pleasure trips to the mourning city. Phoebe thought it bad taste for them to enter the threadbare parlors dressed in the latest New York fashions, chattering away of the "manifold sins" of the South in the four years of war.

At the hospital Phoebe seemed to have vanquished the invaders:

"I had quite won the heart of the Vermonter who had been sentry at my door, and though patriotic souls might not believe it, he paid me many compliments at the expense of the granite ladies of his state. The compliments were sincere, as he refused the drink of whisky my gratitude offered him."

One of the hospital errand boys who had been fraternizing with Yankee sutlers told Phoebe of a tribute to her:

"The Federal surgeon in charge thinks that woman in black had better go home. He's awful afraid of her."

John Beauchamp Jones, the war clerk, had spent the night with his next-door neighbors, all women, who had been afraid to stay alone despite the Federal guards.

Jones rose early and found the day bright and pleasant, with the streets quiet. "So far," he wrote, "the United States pickets and guards have preserved perfect order."

The chief topic of conversation in the streets was yesterday's visit by President Lincoln. Jones surmised that the cheers for Lincoln came from Negroes and Federals "comprising the great mass of humanity."

Richmond's people, Jones said, were annoyed that Negro troops should be stationed there, and concluded that it was purposely done to keep alive animosity.

Jones made an inspection of the burned district, which, he said: "includes all the banks, money-changers, and principal speculators and extortioners. This seems like a decree from above."

In the morning he saw thousands of Negroes and white women about the Federal headquarters begging for food. He saw none of them being fed, and noted only disappointment on their faces.

He wrote: "It is said all the Negro men, not entering the army, will be put to work, rebuilding bridges, repairing railroads, etc."

By 4 P.M. Capitol Square was almost empty of Negroes. A

Federal officer told Jones, "We expect to put them in the army in a few days. The Northern people do not really like Negro equality any better than you do."

Two rumors raced through the streets late in the day: Lee had won a great victory on Monday—and Lee had surrendered, with 35,000 men.

The *Evening Whig* was markedly changed, though William Ira Smith was still its proprietor. It was, abruptly, a Yankee newspaper, and its columns bore only a few advertisements, long dispatches from Northern papers and official orders from the headquarters of the city's conquerors.

An announcement on the front page read:

> We hope, in the course of the next few days, to secure the services of one of the most brilliant and vigorous writers in Virginia, who will take charge of the editorial conduct of the paper and address its readers daily in that eloquent and inspiring style which characterizes him as a writer. Until his arrival, we will be unable to present much editorial matter, the duties of the other departments of the journal requiring almost the undivided attention of the force now employed.

There was also in the *Whig* the brief mention of a milestone, the revival of the city's trade:

> The Sutler's Stores—Sutler B. F. Smith, of the 139th New York Volunteers, was the first to offer for sale, in this city, a stock of desirable goods. He opened Tuesday at 118 Franklin Street, first door above Metropolitan Hall.

Someone was curious about details of the city's life in the coming of Secession and the years of war, for there was a plea which perhaps came from the historian Francis Parkman, buying for the Boston Atheneum:

> Wanted—Files of the *Whig, Enquirer, Dispatch* or *Examiner,* since 1860, for which liberal price will be paid in greenbacks. Enquire at this office.

★ MR. LINCOLN ★

JUDGE CAMPBELL appeared at the side of the *Malvern* in a small boat at 10 A.M.; he had brought with him General Weitzel and an eminent Richmond lawyer, Gustavus Myers.

They were in the President's cabin an hour or more, and Admiral Porter, who came up as they parted, thought they "seemed to enjoy themselves very much, to judge from their laughter."

Lincoln hailed Porter, "Admiral, I'm sorry you weren't here when Mr. Campbell came on board. He's gone ashore happy. I gave him a written permission to allow the State Legislature to convene in the Capitol since there's no other government."

Porter stared, and in Lincoln's hurried explanation the officer divined that Campbell had shrewdly played on the President's good nature. Campbell had promised, Lincoln said, that he would vote Virginia back into the Union, and have all Virginia troops lay down their arms. "It would be a delicate compliment to Virginia," Lincoln said.

"But Richmond's under martial law, Mr. President," Porter said. "No civil authority could be set up without the sanction of the commanding general of the army. It should go through General Grant. He would surely protest this arrangement with Campbell."

"Weitzel made no objection," Lincoln said, "and he commands here."

"That's because he's Campbell's particular friend, and wanted to gratify him."

Lincoln saw the mistake, Porter recorded. "Run and stop them," the President said, "and get my order back."

Porter asked him, instead, to write an order to Weitzel canceling the meeting of the Virginia legislature. The Admiral took the dispatch ashore himself and hurried a waiting driver into the city:

"Kill the horse if you have to, but catch the carriage with

General Weitzel and Mr. Campbell and deliver this to the General."

The carriage whirled away, and Lincoln's proclamation welcoming Virginia into the Union, scot free, was soon back on board.

Within an hour another visitor appeared, a fantastic figure in gray homespun who came to the landing with a huge stick in his hand and bellowed:

"I'm Duff Green, and I want to see Abraham Lincoln. My business concerns me alone. You tell Abraham Lincoln that Duff Green wants to see him."

The officer of the deck took the message to Lincoln in his cabin. "Let him come," the President said. "Duff is an old friend of mine, and I'd like to talk with him."

Green came on deck, scowling at the United States flag and at Admiral Porter. "I want to see Abraham Lincoln," Green said.

"When you come in a respectful manner, the President will see you. Throw away that cord of wood before you go in."

"How long is it since Abraham Lincoln took to aping royalty? Man clothed in a little brief authority cuts such fantastic capers before high heaven as to make the angels weep. I expect airs from a Naval officer, but not from a man with Abraham Lincoln's horse sense."

Green at last threw his staff overboard, growling, "Has it come to this, that he is afraid of assassination? Tyrants generally get into this condition."

Porter went in and told Lincoln of Green's ranting. "Let him come down," Lincoln said. "He always was a little queer. I shan't mind him."

Lincoln rose with an outstretched hand as Green entered. Green did not take it.

"No," he said. "It is red with blood. I can't touch it. When I knew it, it was an honest hand. It has cut the throats of thousands of my people, and their blood, which now lies soaking in the ground, cries aloud to heaven for vengeance.

"I didn't come to see you for remembrance sake, but to give you a piece of my opinion. You won't like it, but I don't care, for people generally don't like to have the truth told to them.

You have come here, protected by your army and navy, to gloat over the ruins and desolation you have caused. You are a second Nero, and if you'd lived in his day you'd have fiddled while Rome was burning."

Lincoln continued to smile at Green with his hand reaching out to him, but Porter saw the smile fade as Green's tirade went on, and when the old voice rose to a shout, "Shame on you! Shame on you!", Lincoln's finger stabbed under Green's nose. The President spoke fiercely.

"Stop, you political tramp! You, the aider and abettor of those who have brought all this ruin on the country, without the courage to risk your hide in defense of the principles you say you espouse—a fellow who stood by to gather up the loaves and fishes, if any should fall to you. A man who had no principles in the north, and took none south with him.

"A political hyena, who robbed the graves of the dead and took their language as his own. You have all cut your own throats, and unfortunately have cut those of many more. You miserable impostor, go before I forget myself and the high position I hold.

"Go, I tell you, and don't desecrate this national vessel another minute."

Porter wrote:

"Green's . . . courage failed him. He fled out of the cabin, never stopping until he reached the deck, and looked to shore to see if he could swim to the landing."

Porter had him sent ashore.

A quarter of an hour later when the Admiral went to Lincoln's cabin he found the President as calm as if nothing had happened.

"This place seems to give you annoyance," Porter said. "Would you like to go ashore to City Point where we might see some friends?"

"Let's go," Lincoln said. "I seem to be putting my foot into it here all the time. Bless my soul, how Seward would have preached to me if he had been here when I gave Campbell permission for the legislature. I'd never have heard the end of it. Seward is a small compendium of international law himself, and laughs at my horse sense, which I pride myself on.

"And yet I put my foot into that thing about Campbell

Ruins of Mayo's Bridge, by which Confederate troops left Richmond April 2-3. Photo of May, 1865.

he Fall of Richmond according to the popular Currier & Ives rendition. Though e picture is fanciful, details of buildings were drawn from photographs.

Dead Confederate gunner at Fort Mahone, April 2. Much of his equipment is captured, bearing the insignia "U.S."

Ruins of Richmond, seen across the James, April, 1865. By Mathew Brady James Gardner.

General George E. Pickett, CSA.

General Bryan Grimes, CSA.

General William Mahone, CSA.

Henry A. Wise, when he was Governor of Virginia.

Colonel William Pegram, the 23-year-old gunner who was fatally wounded at Five Forks, April 1.

General John B. Gordon, the unquenchable Confederate who survived Sayler's Creek and was stoutly defiant three days later at Appomattox.

Mary Custis Lee, the arthritic invalid who remained in burning and fallen Richmond, refusing to give up, and was carefully protected by Federal troops.

Phoebe Yates Pember, the courageous matron of Chimborazo Hospital.

General Ambrose Powell Hill, killed by a Federal infantryman April 2, then carried in a macabre funeral procession.

General James Longstreet, though nearly insubordinate in earlier stages of the war, was almost the last to accept surrender at Appomattox.

Admiral David D. Porter, commander of the Federal fleet at City Point, articulate companion of Lincoln during the final scenes.

Admiral Raphael Semmes, master of the famed *Alabama,* and at the last commander of foot sailors and a train thief.

The younger Lees: W. H. F. (Rooney) and G. W. Custis, *top left and right*, the general-sons of R. E. Lee, both taken in the Confederate collapse. Custis was captured at Sayler's Creek. Their cousin, Fitz Lee, *below*, escaped Appomattox with some of his cavalry to retain a few days of freedom.

General Thomas T. Munford, a gifted cavalry commander during the final scenes, and able postwar controversialist.

General Thomas Rosser, the dashing cavalryman whose shad bake at Five Forks became famous. A fierce fighter to the last.

General George Gordon Meade, the testy commander, Army of the Potomac, who chased Lee to Appomattox in an ambulance.

General Seth Williams, who carried the truce messages from Grant to Lee.

Colonel Ely S. Parker, Grant's Indian aide.

General George A. Custer, leader of the final dash on Confederate artillery and infantry at Appomattox Station which doomed the Army of Northern Virginia. A spectacular and controversial figure during the last moments of surrender negotiations.

General Philip Henry Sheridan, chief of pursuing Federal cavalry, whose relentless pressure halted Lee for the kill.

General U. S. Grant at his City Point headquarters, with his son, Jesse, and his wife Julia Dent Grant.

Head Quarters Armies of the United States,

City-Point, April 7. 11. Am. 1865

Lieut Gen. Grant.

Gen. Sheridan says "If the thing is pressed I think that Lee will surrender." Let the thing be pressed.

A. Lincoln

The original dishatch sent by Mr. Lincoln to me, Aph. 7th 1865.

U. S. Grant

Chicago Historical Society

[Li]ncoln's famed telegram of April 7 to Grant: "Gen. Sheridan says 'If the thing is [pr]essed I think that Lee will surrender.' Let the *thing* be pressed." Grant's certifica-[ti]on of authenticity at bottom. Original in the Chicago Historical Society.

The Bettmann Archive

Grant's baggage wagons, of which he was deprived during the gallop to Appomattox. Miles of such wagons made up the supply trains of both armies.

Varina H. and Jefferson Davis, whose flight from Richmond took them out of the path of the armies, to temporary safety.

Libby Prison in Richmond, 1865.

e McLean House, Appomattox, with the McLean family on the porch.

pomattox Court House, a posed scene with Federal soldiers who are already
ßy aware of the presence of history in the village.

Tad Lincoln and his father, in a photo of April 10, the day after they returned to Washington from Virginia.

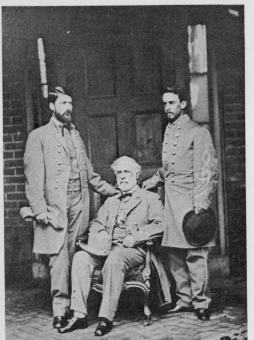

Robert E. Lee on the rea porch of his Richmond home, soon after Appomat tox, in the familiar pose flanked by his son Custis left, and his aide, Colone Walter Taylor. Brad photograph.

with my eyes wide open. If I were you, Admiral, I don't think I would repeat that joke yet awhile. People might laugh at you for knowing so much more than the President."

On the way to the docks Lincoln's barge passed a transport on which more than a thousand captured Confederate soldiers were under guard.

The Rebels rushed to the railing, craning for a glimpse of Lincoln.

Porter said: "They seemed perfectly content; every man had a hunk of meat and a piece of bread in his hand, and was doing his best to dispose of it."

The prisoners yelled to Lincoln.

"That's Old Abe," one said. "Give the old fellow three cheers."

"Hallo, Abe," another shouted. "Your bread and meat's better than popcorn."

Porter thought the Rebels good-natured and kindly, and found them no different from Federal soldiers, except for their leanness and ragged clothing. "They were as happy a set of men as I ever saw," he wrote.

Lincoln gazed at the Confederates. "They will never shoulder a musket in anger again," he said. "And if Grant is wise he will leave them their guns to shoot crows with, and their horses to plow with. It would do no harm."

★ FLIGHT ★

ROBERT LEE spent the rain-swept morning in Amelia, withholding marching orders until almost noon, while the army's predicament became clearer and more grim by the hour. There was a report that the wagon train going west toward Paineville had been attacked by Federal horsemen; if that was true, the enemy was swinging around them, dangerously close.

More wagons creaked back from the country, almost empty of food. Lee issued orders:

Burn the surplus ammunition and the caissons at the depot,

and push the army toward Jetersville, on the way to Danville.

Rooney Lee's cavalry led the way, and the infantrymen of Field and Mahone were close behind, but several brigades waited at the Court House. Soldiers left the village about 1 P.M., with exploding ammunition popping near the depot and black smoke hanging over the trees as if the place were burning.

The vanguard followed the road southwest, parallel to the Danville Railroad, until, about seven miles from Amelia, there was musketry ahead. Lee rode to the front with Longstreet, and with his glasses looked carefully at the terrain.

The wooded country rose above a small stream on his right, and to the left, the railroad cut through a forest. A few bluecoats were in sight. Robert Lee turned to his son Rooney.

Reconnaissance had revealed only the skirmishers in the front line, Rooney reported. These were dismounted enemy cavalry, but infantry might be among them. Beyond, at any rate, Federal infantry was coming up, and was digging trenches around Burkeville. If Rooney had scouted as accurately as usual, the army's path to Danville was blocked. His father spent a long time with his decision.

Rooney was a heavily built young man of about six feet four, his florid face half concealed by a black beard. He had huge hands and feet, and was awkward except on horseback; John Wise had wondered how Rooney found horses strong enough to carry him. Rooney spoke in a soft, cultivated voice; he had been schooled at Harvard, where he came under the critical eye of Henry Adams:

> Tall, largely built, handsome, genial, with liberal Virginia openness toward all he liked, he had also the Virginian habit of command. . . . For a year, at least . . . was the most popular and prominent man in his class, but then seemed slowly to drop into the background. The habit of command was not enough, and the Virginian had little else. He was simple beyond analysis; so simple that even the simple New England student could not realize him. No one knew enough to know how ignorant he was; how childlike, how helpless before the relative complexity of a school.

Today, however, Rooney rode with the commander, giving quick answers to questions about the enemy position; they paused frequently as Robert Lee gazed through glasses. They were so long at the task that Longstreet became impatient; troops had filed off the road and were waiting in position. Old Pete seemed to favor attack.

The commander was forced at last to give up his line of march. The way to Danville was closed. He gave orders to Longstreet, and the first of the gray files moved off. They must circle now, by way of Amelia Springs to the north, until they struck the Southside Railroad, which crossed the Danville tracks at Burkeville, then led westward, through Farmville, to Lynchburg.

Lee soon discovered that reports of the morning about the burned wagon train were true, for the infantry was forced out of roads by the halted wagons, and it was long after dark before the vehicles were moving again. There was worse: A bridge over Flat Creek, near Amelia Springs, had broken down.

Lee stopped at the home of Richard Anderson for supper, a farmhouse known as Selma. Before he was served he advised his hosts to take refuge in the cellar, since an enemy attack might come at any moment. The family, instead, defended him from all comers, so that he could eat in peace. A young woman guarded the door, turning aside dispatch bearers. Colonel Charles Marshall of the staff, who came with a message for Lee, was refused by the young woman until he wrapped himself in a Confederate flag and asked for admission. There was an important dispatch from General Gordon.

Daylight brought signs of the army's disintegration. Creed Davis, a young gunner with the Richmond Howitzers, counted fifteen men missing from his company, all of whom had slipped away during the night. Almost a whole company of the 9th Virginia Cavalry had disappeared.

An officer of Fitz Lee's division entered Amelia in the first moments of dawn: "I beheld the first signs of dissolution of that grand army . . . when looking over the hills I saw swarms of stragglers moving in every direction."

The signs lay behind, too, on every road leading into the village. Muskets stood in the fields, their bayonets thrust into the mud, or leaned against fences and trees. Haversacks and canteens were strewn about. An occasional haversack hung from a tree limb.

The Georgia soldier, William Graham, who had spent the night a few miles short of Amelia, began the day's march at dawn, "utterly worn out." It was soon hot on the route, with a blazing sun overhead. Graham wrote:

> Great demand for water. Few with canteens. Those without sponging upon those who have. Too tired to carry water for others so refuse several thirsty flag-floppers a drink who have more than once drained my canteen on the march.
>
> A few miles from Amelia C.H. pass an ice house near the road. While we are refreshing ourselves there is a sudden whipping up of teams and general hurrying among the stragglers. The Yankee cavalry are close upon us. Off we start at a double quick forgetting our sore feet. Broadus in the lead—a great bull calf of a fellow who had thrown away his gun, blankets and everything that he could get rid of— and pretended to be half dead. When the cry of Yankees was raised, he trotted off as nimbly as it was possible for such a clumsy chap to move.

Graham's regiment got into Amelia at noon, rested for an hour or more and pushed on. There was a rumor that his outfit had been attached to Longstreet's corps; Graham noticed that this caused "quite a depression" among the signalmen, who dreaded the very thought of being dragooned into the infantry. Graham wrote: "Your true signalman is essentially a stationary animal, not gregarious like your infantryman, but he likes a quiet retreat—ladies, etc.—far from the turmoil and dangers of battle fields—near good pastures where buttermilk is plenty— and neighbors kind—and being turned over to the infantry had ever been his great bug bear."

This command had been turned into provost marshal guards, and the men were told off to guard prisoners, several hundred of whom tagged along. Graham escaped this duty, since he had a sprained ankle. He went into camp at 11 P.M. and

drew rations of a half pound of flour and a third of a pound of
bacon.

Dr. Claiborne and his hospital train had slept undisturbed
almost within sight of the courthouse in Amelia, and he knew
nothing of the disastrous loss of the rations until he rode into
the town. The doctor stopped at the campfire of some officers,
among them a couple of generals. He recognized a friend, a
Major Branch, of Atlanta, Georgia, who told him of the missent
rations. "Somebody's blundered," he said, "and the supplies went
on to Richmond. I expect they'll feed the Yankees."

The railroad beyond the courthouse village was also torn up,
Branch explained, and the enemy was probably down the line,
blocking the advance in that direction.

"We're expecting a fight if we take the road that way,"
Branch said.

Firing broke out at that moment. Major Branch and Claiborne rode out the road on which the hospital train had entered, now full of quartermaster wagons, ambulances and stragglers. Claiborne wrote:

"I got my wagon, ambulance, buggy into line, after some
scrouging and swearing, and we took up our march, we scarcely
knew whither."

He knew only that they would be less exposed to the enemy
than on the left-hand road, where firing increased. Claiborne had
a stroke of good fortune; he met an impressment officer with a
fine black mare and exchanged his worn mount for her. The mare
was too spirited for artillery use and the impressment man
seemed happy to be rid of her.

The hectic march had given Claiborne little opportunity to
know all of those in the remarkable band he led.

In his buggy was his slave boy, Romulus, with a young
civilian named Venable and Joseph V. H. Tucker, an attaché of
the Petersburg hospital. There were three doctors, Hume Field,
Richard E. Lewis and J. P. Smith. In the wagon were Captain
Riddick, the wounded soldier, and his sister, his faithful nurse.
Claiborne did not learn their full names.

There was a fat chaplain whose identity Claiborne con-

cealed in his memoirs, and an orderly named Burkhardt, a
Moravian boy who had been conscripted when he refused to
fight because of religious scruples. He was, the doctor said, faithful, honest and fearless, and "the greatest forager I ever saw."

Burkhardt left the train this morning in search of food.

Claiborne had an uneasy feeling that they were to be
attacked by cavalry. He rode half a mile back down the line and
found Romulus.

"Boy, no Yankee shall ever claim that he gave you freedom.
I'll set you free right here."

The doctor sat at the roadside and wrote out a document
certifying the freedom of the slave. He gave Romulus a bit of
money and a knife as "a memento of his master."

"You stay with me as long as you want to, and as long as
it's safe," Claiborne said. "But when things get too hot, skedad-
dle."

Romulus put the treasures in a pocket, but took the affair
as a joke and went laughing to his place in the buggy. Claiborne
halted at a spot where he saw fodder, and unbridled and fed his
mare. He was there when shouts came from ahead:

"Yankees!"

Teamsters and stragglers ran for the rear and wagons
jammed together, with horses squealing and rearing. The road
was no more than twenty feet wide, running between thickets of
blackjack oak and second growth pine so thick that no cavalry
could push through.

Claiborne caught his mare, remembering the warning of the
impressment officer that she was hard to bridle. "If this mare is
a fool, I'm a goner," the doctor thought. She took the bit quickly,
and he was in the saddle by the time bluecoat riders appeared;
there were about fifty of them, riding hard down the line of
wagons, shooting horses and mules. Claiborne galloped until he
found an opening in the oak scrub, left the road, and went
parallel to it until he saw that the enemy had not been reinforced, and that they were only trying to halt the caravan by
dropping the animals.

Hundreds of Confederates streamed through the woods,
and Claiborne tried to rally them.

"There's only a handful, men! Make a stand and save the wagons!"

They tore on as if they heard nothing, until one old soldier halted and yelled, "If you're fool enough to believe it, you stop. I'm agoing on."

A quartermaster captain tried to help Claiborne: "Shoot just one time," he yelled. "Them Yankees'll run away."

"I got no gun," a fleeing man called.

The captain mounted a stump to shout. "Stand, men! Right here! Five real men can stop this. For General Lee's sake. For my sake. For the country's sake!"

The quartermaster captain fell with a shattered arm.

The rush slowed only when the road climbed a steep hill, from which Claiborne saw an infantry column approaching. For a moment it appeared to be Federal, but a graycoat rider, Captain Stephen W. Jones, came up with news that it was a North Carolina regiment. The panic was over, Jones reported. He had mustered a few teamsters and driven off the Yankee troopers with musket fire.

The wagon train was a shambles; more than a hundred vehicles were in flames, and the road was blocked for hours. The bait which had drawn the Federal horsemen, Claiborne learned, was six new Brooke guns, which they had carried off.

The hospital train had suffered. Romulus, Venable and Tucker had been captured, though the buggy survived. Doctors Field, Lewis and Smith had taken to the woods, and soon reappeared. The wounded Captain Riddick had been taken prisoner, but the wagon from which he had been carried was saved; his sister had stubbornly refused to leave the vehicle, and the Federals had not burned it. The fat chaplain had disappeared.

"He got away through the woods," Miss Riddick said. "He made the best time I ever saw."

The chief ambulance driver was gone. The orderly, Burkhardt, returned from his foraging expedition with a superb four-year-old thoroughbred.

Aside from this horse and the mare Claiborne rode, only one animal was left to them, a Confederate Government mule which had been hitched behind the buggy, but had escaped in the firing. There was also one servant, a young Negro. Claiborne sent the slave and the mule to a nearby house, with "a silly note" addressed to "The Gentleman Who Lives on the Hill. When I return may he be there still."

Claiborne's clothes had burned in the ambulance, among them a fine new imported coat of Confederate gray which had cost $1500. "A greater loss," he said, "was my diary, which dated back to the last days of the Charleston Convention of 1860."

There were recruits, however. A wagon joined them, driven by a North Carolina quartermaster and bearing two handsome young women—a Miss Dimitry, the daughter of Professor Alexander Dimitry of New Orleans, a former U.S. Minister to Nicaragua and finance officer of the Confederate Post Office; and the former Miss Florida Cotton, identified by Claiborne only as "Mrs. S." The doctor put Miss Riddick into his wagon and the procession moved on in the direction of Amelia Springs.

Captain Fred Colston and Lieutenant Joseph Packard were near this scene with the remnants of the reserve ordnance train. The wagons had started north from Amelia Court House at 8 A.M., taking a road to the left some five miles out. About two hours later, when Packard was at the rear issuing ammunition to some cavalry officers, they met the enemy.

Packard ordered the wagons into fields on either side of the road and trotted toward the front. He had his last sight of his passengers, Judge Camden and the black-clad Baptist preacher, who "perched on the fence like a crow."

Packard found the wagons emerging into a narrow creek bottom. A bridge was ahead, and as the lieutenant reached the wagons Federal cavalry pounded over the thundering boards; they were no more than a hundred yards away. Packard ran into the woods, where he wandered for some time. When he returned the enemy had been driven off by Confederate troopers, but some of the wagons had been blown up and many horses were dead.

Packard wrote:

> Toward evening, having hitched up all the animals we could find, we started again with some twenty wagons along

with the troops. We moved along during the night in the slow way that is enforced upon a train moving with troops over bad roads. Sometimes I slept on horseback; and once, as I recollect, I lay down for about half an hour on the porch of a house in a village through which we were passing. I don't know the name of the village.

The young Second Corps courier, Percy Hawes, was worn almost beyond endurance. He could not later recall on what day he passed through Amelia Court House. One memory remained clear: "I know this, that in my riding to and fro I was constantly in the saddle, with the exception of a few hours on the first night."

Nor did he forget the desperate hours on the road when the enemy pecked at the trains of wagons:

"The poor famished horses and mules would stop to drink when getting to a stream, which we had orders not to allow, but with poles and sticks to drive them through the water without giving them a chance to halt the column. The indifferent country bridges broke down with our artillery and wagons; the half-starved mules and horses stalled in the mudholes and creeks."

It seemed an age ago to Lieutenant W. F. Robinson that he had helped to drive files into the touchholes of the guns of the Ringgold Battery, and to chop down their wheels. He could not accept the fact that it was only two days before that he had kicked in the shoemaker's door in Richmond and seized his new pair of $600 boots.

He was on horseback, but his company of artillerymen, un-accustomed to marching, had suffered greatly. Since leaving the burning capital he had eaten only hardtack, huge "Yankee Crackers" as large as dinner plates.

He had a bag of peas to keep his horse alive, and carried it in front of his saddle, doling out a handful morning and night. The route of retreat led by the farm of his uncle, Dr. Thomas Robinson, and the lieutenant paused briefly. His uncle filled the lieutenant's canteen with sorghum molasses, and had time for a word of news: Two of the doctor's sons had been taken in a cavalry fight, and were Federal prisoners.

The boy, George Jefferson, spent a memorable day at Winterham, the family home outside Amelia. Ambulances came with wounded Confederate soldiers, casualties of a caisson explosion in the courthouse village the evening before. Chaplains prayed over them as they were carried into the farmhouse.

George's Uncle Garland raised a yellow hospital flag over the roof as protection against Yankee foragers. Straggling and crippled soldiers swarmed in. At noon a detachment of thirty Federal horsemen trotted up, carbines ready. George remembered one of them: "The gallant lieutenant in command had captured a long-necked gander from the Widow Quinn, at the Courthouse, and carried it swinging to his saddle."

The yard of Winterham cleared quickly. A couple of dozen able-bodied Confederates went into the woods, hid in the garden, or crawled into bed with the wounded. Many were captured, but Garland Jefferson stood belligerently at his doorway, pointing to the yellow flag, and the Federals did not enter. The bluecoat lieutenant snatched a new felt hat from Jefferson's head and forced him to remove his fine calfskin boots, and left his Union army brogans in exchange.

When they had rounded up the prisoners from the woods, taken all the eggs from the barn and outbuildings, and drunk up a little keg of whisky, the Federals rode away. Young George Jefferson said, "I don't think I was ever as scared in my life."

Lieutenant Fletcher T. Massie marched with Lieutenant Colonel John Cheves Haskell's artillery battalion on the northernmost road, coming down from Richmond and across the Appomattox at Clementown Bridge. Massie was with Lamkin's Battery, from Nelson County, Virginia; they had mustered about a hundred men at the start of the march, experts who had been firing the big tubs from Fort Harrison on the entrenched line.

Now they had eight or ten of the huge iron mortars in wagons, dragged by straining horses which were constantly under the whips. The gunners walked alongside, unarmed, since there were neither swords nor muskets for them. They entered Amelia County and were approaching Flat Creek when

a horseman in a Confederate uniform directed them into the
road leading to the village of Painesville. The strange officer
then rode away.

The wagons were near Flat Creek, still without infantry
support, when several hundred bluecoat troopers dashed among
them. "I did not have time to count them," Massie said.

Ramsey's North Carolina battery got one fieldpiece into
firing position, but the charging Federals were too fast, and
overran it; men scattered. The enemy took four fine British guns
from Ramsey's battery, as well as all the mortars. Many officers
were captured.

Massie escaped into the woods; when he returned the wagon
wheels had been chopped down, the teams were gone, and only
ten men of the battery were left. The lieutenant had them take
from the wagons all the provisions they could carry, and they
went on foot to the west.

The man who gave the train its order to head for Painesville,
Massie thought, must have been a Yankee scout in disguise.

Captain James N. Lamkin, the commander, was captured
during this skirmish. At first glimpse of the charging bluecoats he gave his horse to a courier and sent him off to General
E. P. Alexander with some vital maps.

Two privates of the battery were nearby, and one of them,
H. R. Irvine, recorded the moment:

"Being crippled with rheumatism, the captain could not
move around. He ordered me to skip—and I did. Chastain
Cocke tore the battery flag from the staff and put it in his bosom.
We came to a turkey blind made of cedar brush. Cocke pulled
me into this and adjusted the brush over us, and the cavalry
charged around us."

When the enemy horsemen had gone past, Irvine and Cocke
emerged. They met their sergeant major, George Cary Eggleston,
and two brothers of the battery, Billie and Tommie Booker, and
"gathered in as quail after a flush." The five survivors found
Ramsey's remaining guns moving in the road and joined with
them. They slept a little during the night on the front porch of
the Booker home, which was on the route, and were soon moving

westward again. Tommie and Billie Booker took their mother's carriage horses to make the march easier.

The South Carolina trooper, E. M. Boykin, recovered quickly from loss of sleep in his scorched camp of the night. He rode with General Gary's cavalry toward the west until, near Amelia, the brigade was ordered into a clover field to graze the horses, keeping the regiments as closely together as possible, in the event of a raid. Boykin sat on the steps of an old house to eat breakfast with two colonels, Alexander C. Haskell of the 7th South Carolina and William T. Robins of the 24th Virginia. A friend had filled Haskell's knapsack, and he provided food.

They were watching the men and horses when a courier brought an order:

> Mount the brigade and move up at once.

An enemy force had blocked the infantry's path toward Burkeville, and cavalry had struck the wagon train some three miles away.

Boykin wrote:

> So there was mounting in hot haste, and off we went at a gallop. We soon reached the point they had first attacked and set fire to the wagons—the canvas covers taking fire very easily. Their plan of operation seemed to be to strike at the train, which was several miles long, at a given point, fire as many wagons as they could, then making a circuit and striking it again, leaving an intermediate point untouched. . . .
>
> The burning caissons, as we rode by, were anything but pleasant neighbors, and were exploding right and left, but I do not recollect any of our men being hit.
>
> We could hear the enemy ahead of us, as we pressed our tired horses through the burning wagons and the scattered plunder which filled the road, giving our own wagon rats and skulkers a fine harvest of plunder. Many of the wagons were untouched, but standing in the road without horses, the teamsters at the first alarm taking them out and making for the woods, coming back and taking their wagons again after the stampede was over, sometimes to find them

plundered by our own cowardly skulkers, that I suppose belong to all armies.

The cavalry column came upon the enemy beyond a creek on the way to Amelia Springs; the bluecoats had formed a line in an open field. Boykin had a diversion as they trotted toward action.

A pretty woman stood by the road, a Mississippi girl who had ridden from Richmond in an artillery wagon, only to be put out into the road when the enemy took the vehicle and its horses. "She was much more mad than scared," Boykin said, "and she stood there in the mud and gesticulated as she told her story, making up a picture both striking and peculiar."

There was no time to hear her story, but Boykin and his friends sent her to a nearby farmhouse, called assurances that they would punish the culprits and galloped after the column. The enemy lay in ambush at a turn of the road, and swept the Confederate advance with fire. Four or five men of the leading party of the 7th South Carolina fell, among them a famed scout, one Mills, who was struck in the spine and pitched backwards from his horse, screaming in agony. The troopers picked up several Federals as prisoners during a brief saber fight in the roadway.

General Gary dismounted his men and pushed the Federals across a field and ravine to the top of a hill, where the enemy lay behind a rail fence and held him off, yelling familiar taunts to the Confederates, "Come get your greenbacks, boys!"

Fitz Lee came up with his division and drove the enemy about two miles to their main body. At sunset the brigade went into camp at Amelia Springs, where they found a few rations of flour and bacon at a mill on a creek. Boykin joined some officers at a white house on a hillside. Fitz Lee was on the porch issuing orders for the troops, and men thronged the yard, filling canteens at the well.

Boykin cadged a drink from a lieutenant of the Hampton Legion, and got a delightful surprise:

"I took a large swallow and discovered it was excellent old apple brandy. I had eaten nothing since a very light breakfast, had been working hard in the saddle all day, had the breath

knocked out of me by a spent ball on the chest at the end of the
charge in the woods; the excitement of the fight was over, and I
was lying over the pommel rather than sitting on my saddle,
but as that electric fluid went down my throat I straightened
up like a soldier at the word of command, ready for what was
to come next."

The music of Federal bands floated up the hill to the cavalrymen, and Boykin thought they were mocking the desperate
condition of the Confederates; the troopers, however, seemed
to enjoy the music as much as if it were their own. The camp
settled for the night.

Boykin's luck had not run out. A sergeant shook him awake:
"Sir, would you like a canteen of old apple brandy? One of
the couriers found a barrel over in the woods and let a few of the
boys in on it."

"Would I? Man, if we ever get out of this scrape, I'll recom-
mend you for promotion."

Boykin wrote: "The canteen came full, and proved to be
of the same tap as the 'long swallow' of which I had partaken.
That canteen of apple brandy was meat and drink for the rest
of the time I was a soldier of the Southern Confederacy."

Somewhere near this spot survivors of McGowan's infantry brigade were halted at dusk. They had marched a wandering trail all day, driven from the roads by cavalry attack,
halted by smoke clouds ahead, forming battle lines, and then
marching on once more.

Their historian, Lieutenant J. F. J. Caldwell, was in the
advance when they stopped:

"When dark had fairly set in, we were instructed to keep
profound silence, and then put again in motion. We moved
briskly and noiselessly, not a canteen being allowed to rattle. We
soon came in sight of the bivouac fires of the enemy, crowded
together in a large basin, as it were, below the high circle of
hills on which we marched. We went, by a wide detour, around
them, and I expected that we should attack the force there en-
camped; but we did not. We hurried past them and bore westward. We were not halted until just before dawn."

Farther in the rear, with a little wagon train that had come from Richmond, Corporal M. W. Venable of the 1st Engineers had his first brush with the enemy—a party of bluecoats which galloped down on the wagons, scattering drivers and guards. "They tore up things pretty generally," Venable reported, but they were driven off by mounted men gathered from broken units by a general officer. The big man with the metallic voice of command, Venable learned, was Secretary of War Breckinridge, the only combatant from the Confederate Cabinet, the one-time Vice President of the United States. The Kentuckian had long, gleaming jet hair, and called commands as fiercely as the hotheaded boy field officers. He led his victorious little band westward when the Union cavalry had disappeared. The train camped near the settlement of Deatonsville, to the west of Amelia Springs.

Robert Stiles, the praying major, left his marching gunners this morning. His mother was in a house a little more than a mile from the road where his command marched, a refugee in the country home of an elderly Richmond businessman.

The host greeted Stiles at the door:

"Ah, Bob, my dear boy. It's all over!"

Stiles responded in the spirit of his training—he was a Yale graduate of '59, a winner of the DeForest gold medal:

"Over, sir? It's just begun. We are now where many of us have longed to be. Richmond gone, nothing to take care of, footloose, and, thank God, out of those miserable lines. Now we may get what we have wanted for months—a fair fight in an open field. Let them come on, if they're ready, and the sooner the better."

The Richmond clerks and militia of Custis Lee's division, perhaps the most weary men in the Confederate swarm, did not meet the enemy during the day.

McHenry Howard, the Maryland captain who marched with them, found food in the morning, and also time to stop and broil his treasure—two fine slices of ham. The road seemed shorter, but as darkness came on his adventures began:

"Night came and found us toiling on at a snail's pace. Nothing is so fatiguing and demoralizing to soldiers as an irregular step and uncertain halts. About 9 P.M., just as the head of the division was crossing the railroad through a deep cut, with a wood in front, the column was suddenly fired into.

"Most of the men became panic-stricken, broke and sought cover behind trees or fences, while not a few skulked disgracefully to the rear. They began to discharge their pieces at random, in many instances shooting their own comrades."

It was a long time before officers could calm the men, halt the firing and reform the ranks. Howard was told that a small party of the enemy had fired from ambush to cause a panic. Just as the line was getting underway once more Howard's horse shied at sight of the body of a horse in the road and plunged wildly. The head of the column again disintegrated in flight. The officers, now alert, shouted, "Don't shoot! Hold it, men!" They could not control the armed civilians.

Howard wrote:

"With a sickening feeling I saw in the moonlight a number of bright barrels pointed directly at me, and many bullets passed close by."

He could not dismount from the plunging horse, and remained exposed until the firing stopped. There were a dozen casualties, among them Major Frank Smith of Norfolk, who was killed. The wounded were taken to a farmhouse and left behind.

Howard said: "The whole division was disheartened by this unhappy occurrence and for some time marched on, discussing it in subdued but eager tones, presently relapsing into a gloomy silence."

J. C. Gorman, a North Carolina captain, noted that his command averaged no more than half a mile an hour in the night march, but he saw with "intense satisfaction" that the wagons were becoming lighter.

"The heavily laden quartermaster, doctor's and commissary wagons began to cast up their plunder. The jaded horses and mules refused to pull, and for miles the roads were strewn with every convenience, comfort and luxury that 'Sunday soldiering' could devise."

Gorman felt that but for the slow wagons, the army would easily escape the oncoming Federals.

The army's chief artillery train, under General R. L. Walker, had been sent west from Amelia Court House in the morning, in advance of most wagons, in the hope of saving it from the enemy cavalry. There was a brief halt as Walker destroyed surplus equipment; almost a hundred caissons were blown up with ammunition which could not be carried.

The wagons and guns were heavy enough, however, and the road in the rear was littered with broken-down vehicles. A staff officer who rode with General W. N. Pendleton, chief of artillery, wrote of the march:

"No note was taken of day or night; one long, confused, dreadful day. There seemed to be no front, no rear, for firing might be heard ahead and behind, and on both sides at once. There were no headquarters except where the ambulance happened to be."

William Owen of the New Orleans artillery fought through the cavalry raids of the day and at night entered in his diary:

Marched all day and nearly all night. When the batteries halt to rest, the men throw themselves upon the ground and immediately go to sleep. When the order is given to move forward, the horses often move on without their drivers, so hard is it to arouse the men. Tired and hungry we push on. It is now a race for life or death. We seldom receive orders now. The enemy has the shortest line to Danville and Burkeville, and is heading us off.

From Clover Station in Halifax County, more than fifty miles southwest of the army, young John Wise helped in a futile effort to get news of the chase. The telegraph wires were clear to Jetersville in the morning, but Amelia did not reply to the tappings of the telegrapher from the outpost at Clover.

The Jetersville station soon fell quiet, and General H. H. Walker, in command of the outpost, got a report that the wires had been cut. Burkeville, ten miles south of Jetersville, remained open.

Walker was studying a map in the tiny depot when he heard this report, and quickly divined Robert Lee's problem. "They're pressing him off the railroad," Walker said. "They'll force him to fall back by the Southside to Lynchburg."

Messages came from Danville to the west, calls from President Davis for news of Lee's army. Walker replied that wires were down, and Davis sent a more urgent call:

> Can you send trustworthy man on engine to Burkeville
> to try communicate General Lee, get position and plans and
> report to me?

John Wise was in the depot when the message arrived; the older officers were out on duty, and the boy begged Walker to send him on the errand. The general hesitated, but told him to get ready for the trip. He sketched the terrain on his map for Wise, who had often passed through the country where the armies were now marching.

"You move slowly and take heed," Walker said. "In all probability, they will have forced Lee to the west here, and I expect you'll find Yankees already in Burkeville. If they're not there, you'll have to use your own judgment. You could switch the engine to the Southside tracks and run it west, or leave the rails and take a horse.

"If they've already taken Burkeville, and I'm afraid they have, reverse the engine and come back down to Mcherrin Station. You can get a horse from there and find General Lee."

Before Wise mounted the waiting engine Walker had a final warning: "I think the Yanks are in Burkeville, John. I got several telegrams from there, signed by General Lee, asking for rations to be sent there. It sounds like a trick to me, but I might be wrong. Make sure of things before you go too close, and don't get yourself captured."

Walker handed him an order from President Davis which authorized him to impress men, horses or food he might need.

The engineer was a strong young man who seemed to know

his work. Walker ordered him to obey Wise, shook hands, and waved them off. The train chuffed away in the dark. It was 8 P.M. There was only the engine, its tender, and a single rickety car. Wise remembered of it:

"I carried no arms except a navy revolver at my hip, with some loose cartridges in my haversack. The night was chilly, still and overcast. The moon struggled out now and then from watery clouds. We had no headlight nor any light in the car. Our train was the noisiest I had ever heard. The track was badly worn and very rough. In many places it had been bolstered up with strap iron, and we were compelled to move slowly. The stations were deserted. We had to put on our own wood and water. I lay down to rest, but nervousness banished sleep. When we stopped at a water tank I swung down from the car and clambered up to the engine. Knowing that we might have to reverse it suddenly, I ordered the engineer to cut loose the baggage car and leave it behind. This proved to be a wise precaution."

At midnight they were still puffing slowly through the dark toward the enemy.

★ PURSUIT ★

PHIL SHERIDAN began puzzling over Robert Lee's intentions at dawn; he rode up and down the lines at Jetersville within sight of gray cavalry, wondering why the Confederates did not advance in strength. As the hours passed and the enemy only felt his line, Sheridan's anxiety grew. He ordered General Crook to send cavalry to the left, thrusting toward Amelia. Crook sent General Henry Davies with the 1st Brigade, troopers from New York, New Jersey and Pennsylvania.

Davies had gone but three or four miles when he neared a crossroad and found Confederate wagons moving west. The leading regiment raised a fox-hunting cry and went in, breaking the line, burning wagons and halting traffic. By the time gray infantry arrived, the work was done.

Davies trailed back into Jetersville with his loot: 1000 prisoners, five cannon and several hundred thin mules. He reported some 180 wagons destroyed, among them the headquarters wagons of Robert and Fitzhugh Lee. At the end of Davies's foray he was struck sharply by Confederate cavalry, and was forced to call for help. It was now clear that Lee was turning west, and that he would hold the one remaining lifeline of the Danville Railroad at all costs.

Sheridan saw that more Confederate infantry had come out to face him at Jetersville. He saw through Lee's plan, but there were conflicts in the Federal command. Sheridan wrote:

"It being plain that Lee would attempt to escape as soon as his trains were out of the way, I was most anxious to attack him when the 2nd Corps began to arrive, for I felt certain that unless we did so he would succeed in passing by our left flank, and would thus again make our pursuit a stern-chase; but General Meade, whose plan of attack was to advance his right flank on Amelia Court House, objected to assailing before all his troops were up."

Meade had left his camp near Deep Creek at 9 A.M., still sick in his ambulance; he rode along the main road for some miles, then had the driver strike out across fields toward Jetersville, clenching his teeth against the furious plunging of the wagon. At ten o'clock he got word that the enemy were still in Amelia, and Meade leaned from the back of his wagon, shouting to infantry regiments as he passed, trying to hurry them along.

By 1:30 P.M. Meade was at the home of the Childers family a mile south of Jetersville, where Sheridan had headquarters. His aide, Colonel Lyman, wrote:

"Though he was not fit for the saddle, General Meade insisted on riding out beyond the lines to talk with Sheridan. He treated him very handsomely and did not avail of his rank to take command over his cavalry, but merely resumed the 5th Corps—a generosity that General Sheridan has hardly reciprocated!"

Sheridan's own version revealed the hostility between the commanders of the pursuit:

"Meade expressed a desire to have in the proposed attack all the troops of the Army of the Potomac under his command,

and asked for the return of the Fifth Corps. I made no objections, and it was ordered to report to him."

In the afternoon, with the 2nd Corps infantry already in position beside Sheridan's cavalry, and Meade's larger force at hand, the Federal army faced Lee's little shielding force while the Confederate wagons and other troops marched away.

Sheridan's impatience was increased when his men brought him a captured Confederate letter:

> Dear Mamma:
>   Our army is ruined, I fear. We are all safe as yet. Shyron left us sick. John Taylor is well—saw him yesterday. We are in line of battle this morning. General Robert Lee is in the field near us. My trust is still in the justice of our cause, and that of God. General Hill is killed. I saw Murray a few minutes since. Bernard, Terry said, was taken prisoner, but may yet get out. I send this by a negro passing up the railroad to Mecklenburg. Love to all.
>
> Your devoted son,
Wm. B. Taylor, Colonel

Sheridan called a scout, one Campbell, and gave him a note to Grant, who was to the south near Nottoway Courthouse. Sheridan explained more fully than he had in earlier dispatches the raid of Davies and the movement of Lee's wagons, and added:

> I wish you were here yourself. I feel confident of capturing the Army of Northern Virginia if we exert ourselves.

Campbell folded the message inside tin foil and popped it into his mouth in a wad of chewing tobacco. On second thought, Sheridan sent Grant the captured letter from the Confederate colonel. Campbell rode off in a Confederate uniform.

Soon after the scout left him, Sheridan went along his line with the half-sick Meade; it was near 3 P.M., and the 2nd Corps infantry was still settling into position. Colonel Lyman reported a near-panic among the horsemen which he seemed to find amusing:

"Mr. Sheridan (and still more his officers) had a stampede

that Lee was coming on top of us. For once in my life I will say I knew better than that, and laughed the cavalry staff to scorn; for I was dead certain it was only a demonstration, to protect their trains and find our strength. In truth they never came even in sight of our infantry pickets."

Grant marched through the day with General Ord's infantry; he was near Nottoway Courthouse when the first of Sheridan's messages made it clear that Lee had been blocked at Jetersville. He sent officers to read the news at the head of every brigade, and though the men had marched fifteen miles, they broke into cheers and moved on more quickly after this.

Grant and his staff studied maps for half an hour or more, then rode along the column, now moving parallel to the Southside Railroad. At dusk, when they were about halfway between Nottoway and Burkeville, a rider in gray came from the woods. Some infantrymen fired at the horseman, but Horace Porter of Grant's staff recognized him as Sheridan's scout.

"How are you, Campbell?" he called.

Campbell produced his dispatch from the foil and tobacco wrappers and Grant read it in the dying light. The commander dismounted from his pony, Jeff Davis, and stood as he wrote a message to General Ord, using the back of his mount as a desk. He then changed mounts, and climbed on his larger Cincinnati, a long-legged thoroughbred bay sired by Lexington, "The King of the Turf."

"We'll follow you, Campbell," Grant said. A small party rode off with him in the dark toward Jetersville: Grant's surgeon, General Rawlins, Porter, and the New York reporter, Cadwallader, and an escort of fourteen troopers. They rode under a dim moon through woods and over fields. Dogs bayed at them from farmhouses. Cadwallader wrote of it:

"The ride was lonely, somewhat hazardous, and made at a slow pace part of the way. The scouts, or couriers acting as guides, riding from one to two hundred yards in advance, in perfect silence. At all forks or crossings of roads one remained till we caught up, when he spurred forward and joined his companion."

They found Sheridan in his headquarters—a log cabin in a tobacco patch. His staff was at work by candlelight, but Sheridan was in the loft, trying to sleep on the floor, until he heard them and clambered down a ladder in his shirt sleeves. He pointed out the situation at Jetersville on his map and showed Grant the roads in Lee's rear by which the Confederates were probably now escaping to the west.

Cadwallader remembered: "Sheridan . . . ended by declaring this to be the final battle ground. Meade's troops must be forced to certain positions during the night, and then not a man of Lee's army could escape. He was enthusiastic, positive, and not a little profane in expressing his opinions."

The reporter saw that Grant was "brimming over with quiet enjoyment" of Sheridan's tirade.

Grant spoke quietly, "Lee's surely in a bad fix. He'll have to give up his line of retreat through here. But if I were in his place I think I could get away with part of the army. I suppose Lee will."

"He'll not take off a single regiment if we move," Sheridan said.

"We're doing very well," Grant said. "Everything's in our favor now. Don't expect too much at once. We'll do all in our power."

Grant sent a note to Meade, who was nearby:

> I would go over to see you this evening, but I have ridden a long distance today. Your orders directing an attack tomorrow will hold in the absence of others, but it is my impression that Lee will retreat during the night, and, if so, we will pursue with vigor.

Sheridan retained a different impression of the commander's state of mind this evening:

"Grant stated that the orders Meade had already issued would permit Lee's escape, and therefore must be changed, for it was not the aim only to follow the enemy, but to get ahead of him, remarking . . . that he had no doubt Lee was moving right then."

VII

Thursday, April 6

★

FEDERAL ARMY bands had played in Capitol Square every day, but though there were newspaper notices of the concerts and the bluecoats made every effort to attract crowds, the conquered people of Richmond did not appear.

Phoebe Pember noted it:

"When the appointed hour arrived, except for Federal officers, musicians and soldiers, not a white face was to be seen. The Negroes crowded every bench and path."

Later newspapers announced that Negroes would not be admitted to the concerts. The next day there were only the bands and Federal troops. Phoebe said, "The absence of everything and anything feminine was appalling."

The ingenious Federals then advertised that Negro nurses would be admitted, if they brought white children as their charges. The Square was packed with them the next day, each white child surrounded by a dozen or more well-dressed Negro women.

In two or three days, however, the music was abandoned, Phoebe wrote, "the entertainers feeling at last the ingratitude of the subjugated people."

Phoebe found the Federal troops courteous, and was pleased to see that they made "no advance toward paternalism." Many bluecoats spoke warmly of their Southern sympathies, but the hospital matron saw that they did not understand the feelings of defeated Virginians. She wrote:

> Bravely-dressed Federal officers met their old classmates and enquired after relatives to whose homes they had been welcomed in days of yore, expressing the desire to call and see them, while the vacant chairs, rendered vacant by Federal bullets, stood by the hearth of the widow and the bereaved mother. They could not be made to understand that their presence was painful.

There were few men in the city at this time, but the

women of the South still fought their battle for them, fought
it resentfully, calmly, but silently. Clad in their mourning
garments, overcome but hardly subdued, they sat within
their desolate homes, and when compelled to leave, went
with veiled faces and swift steps. By no sign or act did the
possessors of the fair city know they were even conscious of
their presence. If they looked in their faces they saw them
not; they might have supposed themselves a phantom army.

It was not easy for the new shopkeepers in the atmosphere
of gloom. Small shops were set up in rows along the main
streets, with circus booths and other entertainments among them.
Miss Pember complained:

"The small speculators must have supposed that there were
no means of cooking left in the city from the quantity of canned
edibles they offered for sale. They inundated Richmond with
pictorial canisters at exorbitant prices, which no one had money
to buy."

The new shopkeepers would trade only in greenbacks, and
since these were scarce, many of the stores soon closed.

Phoebe made a last defiance of Federal authority on Chimborazo Hill during the day. She was ordered to transfer her
Confederate patients to Camp Jackson, some distance away,
leaving the vast wards of Chimborazo for Federal soldiers.

Miss Pember insisted that the men were in no condition to
be moved and the officers retreated, leaving her to care for the
last of her wounded; she was alone now, without a surgeon or
a servant to help. She worked with the remaining Confederates
in a ward crowded by sick Federal soldiers.

The diarist T. C. DeLeon was fascinated by the sutlers,
peddlers, and hucksters who arrived on every river steamer—
like locusts, he thought. He walked among their crowded stores
on Broad Street, where he saw "every known thing that could
be put up in tin."

These tradesmen were strangely Southern in sympathy, he
found.

"The war was a damned shame," one of them said. All of
them curried favor with Richmond's people, but their customers

were only Negroes who could somehow obtain greenbacks, or the "stamps" issued by Federal authorities. DeLeon wrote of these merchants:

"They had calculated on a rich harvest, but they reckoned without their hosts. There was no money in Richmond to spend with them, and after a profitless sojourn, they took up their tin cans, and one by one returned north—certainly wiser, and, possibly, better men."

Showers fell during the morning, but John Beauchamp Jones, the enterprising war clerk, was in the streets. He talked with Federal officers about the future, but found them unable or unwilling to predict Richmond's fate. "Reticent," Jones thought.

Most of the town had assumed a philosophical attitude, prepared to accept the new order.

But Jones knew some women who would not surrender, and some of these seemed hysterical to him. All he could hear from these friends was an insistent chatter that they would leave Richmond this very day, and set out on foot for "The Confederacy," a fast dwindling land.

Charles Francis Adams, the Massachusetts soldier-historian, had been just outside the city for three days on picket duty with his Negro cavalry regiment. He found the place as "quiet and orderly" as any Northern cities, with none of the incidents usually reported from fallen cities in foreign wars.

In the afternoon he was surprised by an order to take his troops to Petersburg. He called in his pickets and "made a moonlight flitting." It was midnight when he left camp on the march through Richmond's streets, and Adams found "that conquered city quiet and silent as a graveyard. I believe I saw but one living being in the streets—a single sentry on his beat—and I did not hear a sound."

⋆ FLIGHT ⋆

GENERAL JOHN B. GORDON, the lean Georgian, herded the Confederate rear guard west from Amelia, looking often behind him. The view was not reassuring, he said:

"On and on, hour after hour, from hilltop to hilltop, retreating, making one almost continuous shifting battle."

A scout brought Gordon two prisoners, both in gray uniform. The scout, a veteran named George, insisted that these were spies.

"General, they say they belong to Fitz Lee, but I say they're Yankees. I want you to examine them."

Gordon questioned the men at length, but found no reason to suspect them; they were obviously at ease, as if amused by this comic error. They called off names of Fitz Lee's commanders, down to the companies, and gave the names of those in their own mess.

"They seem all right to me, George," Gordon said.

"They're not, General. I saw them in the dark counting your files."

"Yes," one of the boys said. "We were trying to get an idea of our force. We've been on sick leave, and wondered if we had an army left."

Gordon's suspicions were aroused by this and he had them taken to a fire so that he could read their furlough papers. As they entered the bright light of a roadside blaze, George shouted, "They're Yankees, General! They're the two who caught me two months ago, at Grant's headquarters."

The prisoners laughed and pointed to the papers, whose signatures seemed genuine.

"They're forged," George said. "That's an easy trick—or maybe they captured them. Make them get down, General, and I'll search them."

The scout found nothing in the clothing of the prisoners until he pulled off their boots, cut open the lining and saw a folded dispatch—an order from General Grant to General Ord which bore an ominous dateline:

Jetersville, April 5, 1865—10:10 P.M.

The order directed Ord to move at 8 A.M. to guard roads between Burkeville and Farmville to the west. It was clear that the Union strength was at hand, for Ord's Army of the James had come by the longest march, from east of Richmond, its arrival unsuspected by the Confederates. The dispatch ended:

> I am strongly of the opinion that Lee will leave Amelia tonight to go South. He will be pursued at 6 A.M. from here if he leaves. Otherwise an advance will be made upon him where he is.

Gordon turned to the prisoners: "Well, you know your fate. I'll shoot you at sunrise."

The oldest of the two boys was about nineteen. "We knew what we were doing, General. You have the right to shoot us, but it would do you no good. The war can't last much longer."

Gordon sent them away and hurried the captured dispatch to Lee, who was to the northwest at a crossing of Flat Creek. The engineer, Colonel T. M. R. Talcott, was there, just after 3 A.M., when Gordon's message arrived.

"The county road bridge over the stream had given away, so that neither artillery nor wagons could cross it. General Lee . . . considered the situation critical enough to require his personal attention . . . and did not leave until he was assured that material for a new bridge was close at hand."

Lee sat to write instructions to Gordon, three long pages in pencil, outlining the infantry and wagon routes, telling Gordon to burn bridges behind him. He added, "You must, of course, keep everything ahead of you, wagons, stragglers, etc. I will try to get the head of the column on and to get provisions at Rice's Station or Farmville."

Gordon's aide passed a verbal request to Lee as he took the dispatch from the commander:

"What should General Gordon do with the spies? They admit everything. They're in Confederate uniform, and subject to execution. Should they be shot?"

Lee hesitated. "Tell the General that the lives of so many of our men are at stake that all my thoughts now must be given to disposing of them. Let him keep the prisoners until he hears further from me."

Lee rode ahead to the resort hotel at Amelia Springs where Fitz Lee's cavalry had camped, and was now stirring. The bridge over Flat Creek was built under Talcott's direction, and guns and wagons were soon crossing. At sunrise a Federal artillery battery came into sight and opened fire, but by then only engineers and a Negro work gang were within range.

Lee met his Commissary General, I. M. St. John, at Amelia Springs and got a report on the confusion which had cost the army its rations yesterday—blocked railroad lines, the swift Federal advance on Richmond, and, finally, the capture of supply wagons at the Clementown Bridge of the Appomattox. There was one hope:

"I have eighty thousand rations for you at Farmville, General. Do you want them left there, or brought up the tracks nearer the army?"

"I can't say," Lee said. "The enemy cavalry is along all these roads, no longer in the rear. They might strike the railroad at any point."

At daylight Longstreet's infantry was well on the way toward Farmville, by way of Rice's Station. Behind him were the commands of Anderson and Ewell, with Gordon in the rear. Fitz Lee's troopers went toward Rice's Station, outdistancing the column and its wagon trains. Ewell reached Amelia Springs at 8 A.M.

The nineteen miles of road from Amelia Springs to Farmville lay reasonably straight until it joined the old Genito Road at the village of Deatonsville, some three miles away. It then ran on westward, making a series of loops to avoid streams which fed the Appomattox, over and around hills at the marshy heads of creeks, past tilting fields, through ravines, between thickets of wild plum and azalea, now in bloom. The ruts were deep from weeks of rain, and a heavy shower at sunrise sent red torrents foaming under the wheels and feet of the army.

West of Deatonsville two roads spraddled over the valley of Sayler's Creek, a narrow lowland with shouldering bluffs, its walls cut by twin branches of the stream. The valley was 600 to 800 yards wide, with the main bed of the creek to the west, a shallow, inconspicuous stream lined with willow and alder, its miry banks overgrown with sedges.

The main road crossed the southern end of this valley by a flimsy pole bridge, passing the plantation house of the Hillsman family; the second road looped northward some two miles away. Thick growths of pine and sassafras screened the hillsides, above the mouths of gulches known as The Devil's Tavern. Rice's Station was just to the south and west of this landscape, perhaps four miles along a road lined with drifts of dogwood.

At 9 A.M. John Gordon climbed the hill west of Amelia Springs with the rear guard, able to look into the distant valley of Sayler's Creek—and to see on the flanks of the marching army lines of blue cavalry. The enemy struck him in the first of the day's crackling skirmishes.

Colonel Walter Taylor, the bridegroom of Lee's staff, had ridden ahead with the commander, leaving headquarters wagons behind. He gave precise orders to the drivers about papers they carried, especially those in a chest with rope handles—the archives of the Army of Northern Virginia, orderbooks, letterbooks and other valuable documents: "If the Yankees crowd you, take this chest with you and leave the wagon. They must not have these papers."

But when the blue cavalry pounded from a side road into the path of the wagons, excited clerks took the chest from the wagon and burned the papers. A few minutes later the enemy was driven off and the wagon was saved.

The Georgia private, Willie Graham, was roused at 3 A.M. by the voice of his commander, Major James Milligan, "Come, Bullies, get up! Rise, Bullies!" They marched by the ruins of two miles of wagons, burned by enemy cavalry the night before, some 400 wagons and ambulances. Graham said:

"After marching ten or fifteen miles we struck the lines of battle. The Yankees had massed their troops and disputed our passage. The prisoners were marched by the right flank at a double quick almost; through fields, swamps, over gullies, fences, briers—nothing seemed to be in the way. We carried them in this style several miles until the danger was passed. But the poor signalmen who were nearly dead before, were now fagged out. . . . I walked wearily on alone amongst thousands and soon came to the Appomattox River which here is a small stream. The bridge was worn out and they were trying to ford. The passage of the stream was so slow that the wagons had accumulated by the hundred waiting their turn. About this time there was a cry of 'Yankees!' Such a stampede I never witnessed. The teamsters cut loose their teams and here they came by the hundred. The whole bottom is soon covered by them seeking a crossing! Presently I hear a cry, 'Come back! False alarm! Being sick and lame I thought it best to hasten away as best I could. So I plunged into the stream and forded it—the water being about three feet deep."

Captain McHenry Howard of Custis Lee's division breakfasted just before dawn: "I first parched a handful of corn in a frying pan, borrowed with some difficulty, and was then preparing for a nap, when the drum beat the assembly and we took the road once more."

They were separated from a part of the command, and began squeezing past the wagon train:

"By this time the command was fearfully reduced in numbers, and men were falling out continually. They were allowed to shoot from their places in the ranks pigs, chickens, or whatever of the sort came in their way, commanding officers looking on without rebuke."

W. L. Timberlake, of Company D, was one of the few survivors of the 2nd Virginia Reserve Battalion with the strength to perform special duty. The men had slept for an hour just before dawn, but their commander, Lieutenant Colonel R. T. W. Duke, roused them at a drum roll and they shambled ahead, worn, hungry, all but exhausted.

They had marched about two miles within sound of enemy cavalry attacks when Duke sent Timberlake ahead with a companion to search for food. They caught three sheep, slaughtered and skinned them, and were dividing them when enemy cavalry came, shouting and firing.

Timberlake lost part of his sheep to Colonel Duke, who wrote of this attack:

"We at once fell into ranks, moved on, and in the excitement of the moment forgot our mutton, except that I pulled off a kidney and put it in my haversack."

Soon afterward, during a pause, Colonel Duke broiled the delicacy over a bed of coals.

About 2 P.M. these troops neared Sayler's Creek as part of the army's swarm. Unknown to them a gap had opened in the gray column between the tail of Longstreet's corps, which was Mahone's division, and the head of Anderson's corps, made up of Pickett's survivors. Enemy cavalry was slashing at this spot.

The 2nd Virginia Reserve Battalion passed over Sayler's Creek on a few fence rails. Duke saw an important party:

"I came to a group of mounted officers, consisting of Generals Ewell, Custis Lee, Barton and others. In a few moments the artillery of the enemy opened on us. I felt somewhat excited, but General Ewell remarked in his ordinary tones, 'Tomatoes are very good. I wish I had some.'"

Duke was calmed by the absurdly irrelevant remark, and had to restrain his laughter. Duke dismounted and gave his horse to an orderly, and after a walk of half a mile his men were halted just below the crest of a hill, with a higher ridge opposite them, across Sayler's Creek. Duke lay on the left of the corps line, with a battalion of Naval cadets under Commodore John R. Tucker and some infantry under Colonel Stapleton Crutchfield on either side. Duke's own men now numbered only ninety.

Firing broke out and bluecoats came into the valley. The action at this spot was not severe, and within half an hour

Duke saw the enemy retiring. He watched anxiously, however, as another blue column, at least a brigade strong, marched around to his left.

Captain Fred Colston, who rode with the reserve ordnance toward this valley, lost his personal belongings today. Federal cavalry came down on the wagons, and his Negro driver, Tom Peters, drove a wagon into a tree in his excitement, refusing to pull from it clothing or the records of the command. Colston and his friend Bob Burwell drove a wagon beside the smashed vehicle, threw Colston's belongings into it, and lurched away after the scattered wagon train. Colston came to the ridge overlooking Sayler's Creek and halted behind a snarl of wagons at the bridge.

General Ewell was there, shouting curses:

"Double up them teams! If they don't get on, we'll get caught right here."

Colston dived into his wagon to rescue his good uniform coat and emerged into a hail of fire from the enemy:

"One man next to me was struck, the bullet making a loud whack. We crowded on the bridge and had to take it at a slow pace under the heavy fire. . . . When I got across I looked back and saw the enemy setting fire to our wagons. Thus I lost all of my treasures of the war, for which I had risked my life only a few hours before."

Colston rode up the hill beyond the fighting in the creek valley, and came upon Robert Lee:

"He was reclining on the ground and holding Traveller's bridle. He was entirely alone and looked worn. I was then 'dead beat' in mind and body. I had been more than forty consecutive hours from Amelia Courthouse in the saddle, practically without food or sleep."

Colston rode on; the firing behind him grew louder.

Dick Ewell, still strapped to the lean gray Rifle, led his troops into the valley blindly, following General Anderson. Men in his ranks were chewing raw fresh meat as they marched. Ewell wrote of this hour:

"On crossing a little stream known as Sayler's Creek, I met General Fitz Lee, who informed me that a large force of cavalry held the road just in front of General Anderson, and were so strongly posted that he had halted a short distance ahead. The trains were turned into a road nearer the river, while I hurried to General Anderson's aid. General Gordon's corps turned off after the trains."

At that moment, however, no one seemed to know that Gordon's rear guard had left the main route of the infantry; the enemy pressed from almost every direction, and confusion grew.

Ewell consulted Anderson.

"At least two divisions of cavalry up in front," Anderson said. "We can get out two ways. Unite our forces and break through, or turn to the right through the woods and strike a road running to Farmville."

"I say go to the woods," Ewell said, "but you know the ground and I don't."

Before Anderson put troops into motion a Federal infantry column appeared behind Ewell.

"I'll charge in front," Anderson said. "You hold them off here."

Ewell drew his men into line across a ravine, with General Kershaw on the right, Commodore Tucker's Naval battalion in the center, and Custis Lee on the left. The Federal artillery pounded away at the waiting men from a field across the creek. Ewell had no guns to challenge them, and the enemy came closer with their batteries. The cannon fired for half an hour before the blue infantry moved in.

Ewell rode to the front just as the enemy wave came forward:

"General Anderson made his assault, which was repulsed in five minutes. . . . General Anderson rode rapidly toward his command. I returned to mine to see if it were yet too late to try the other plan of escape.

"On riding toward my left I came suddenly upon a strong line of the enemy's skirmishers. This closed the only avenue of escape, as shells and even bullets were crossing each other from front and rear over my troops. My right was completely enveloped.

"I surrendered myself and staff to a cavalry officer. At my request, he sent a messenger to General G. W. C. [Custis] Lee, with a note from me telling him he was surrounded, General Andersons's attack had failed, I had surrendered, and he had better do so, too, to prevent useless loss of life."

Custis Lee had been captured before the note reached him.

General Joseph B. Kershaw's men were literally driven to the battlefield. They had pushed back two Federal cavalry attacks when Gordon's rear guard appeared, also under fire. He did not see Gordon's column take the right-hand fork of the road. Kershaw said:

"I was not informed that Gordon would follow the wagon train as he did, and was therefore surprised on arriving at Sayler's Creek to find that my rear was menaced."

He dismounted General Gary's cavalry, added a little infantry brigade, and sent them to hold off the enemy while his column crossed the creek. His entire command was fewer than 2000 men.

Charles Stevens Dwight, the South Carolina captain on Kershaw's staff, had been sent to the rear to save the headquarters wagons. Dwight found the train halted, with teamsters refusing to cross an open space where enemy shells were bursting. He stationed guards from the train along the road with orders to shoot any driver who hesitated. Dwight wrote:

"They moved! A shell burst harmlessly over the first team. The next shell burst under the wheel horses of the second wagon, blowing them to pieces, badly wounding the teamster and upsetting the wagon. A panic resulted, of course, but the choice between Yankee shells at long range or Confederate miniés at short range kept the wagons moving, at least as long as I could stay there. That was my last sight of Confederate Army wagons."

This train was burned by the enemy after Dwight had returned to General Kershaw.

The captain found the general watering his horse in Sayler's Creek, talking with Ewell and Custis Lee; troops were already under fire in their line on the ridge. Colonel Stapleton Crutchfield, the gunner who had served with Stonewall Jackson, reported to the generals.

"I haven't even one battery left," he said. "We barely got through the attacks with the men, and the guns that got past the cavalry stuck in the roads, or had to be left when the horses gave out."

The officers came under fire.

"Gentlemen," Kershaw said, "they've noticed this group. We'll have to scatter now."

A shell struck Crutchfield in the right thigh, passed through his horse and his left leg, and exploded shortly beyond. Horse and rider fell into a heap. Captain Dwight and another staff officer knelt by Crutchfield, who could barely speak.

"Take my watch and letters for my wife," the gunner said. "Tell her how I died, at the front." He was dead.

Dwight and his friend removed Crutchfield's body from the horse and left him lying in the open by the creek. The enemy infantry was coming.

Dwight ran to Kershaw's forming line, which was only one man deep, with the soldiers many feet apart. Downhill, nearing the creek, the Federal infantry was massed elbow-to-elbow, two men deep, and firing rapidly. Over the heads of these men enemy cannon dropped shells from the ridge. Dwight sketched the action on this front:

"General Kershaw gave strict orders to hold fire until the enemy was within 50 yards, and to aim low. The lines neared, and there was a flash and a roar. The big column hesitated and then with a Rebel Yell the thin line charged them. The Yankees broke and fled, closely pressed. A supporting column came up in good order and drove us slowly back. The first enemy line, broken but now repaired, came in a second attack. It was like the first."

Captain Dwight saw Custis Lee walking calmly along the line, a sheathed saber lying flat on his left arm, "in perfect dignity and composure" which seemed natural in the son of the Commander-in-Chief.

Dwight saw the big Federal flanking column and knew that the end had come. Kershaw ordered the line straightened at all costs, but it was too late. Dwight grabbed a flag from the color-bearer of a Georgia regiment. "Tell the men to follow me," he yelled.

The color-bearer snatched back the staff. "No, Captain," he said. "You can't have this flag. Show me where you want it put and I will put it there, but I must do it."

Dwight lost sight of the man. The right flank had been driven in, and blue cavalry galloped behind the Confederate line. General Kershaw and Custis Lee and several brigadiers were quickly rounded up.

Dwight was riding along the hill when a bluecoat cavalry-man locked knees with him, holding him fast.

"Halt!"

"Who're you?"

"Oh, I'm a Yankee soldier and you're my prisoner."

"I'm not sure about that," Dwight said. He looked around for a chance of escape.

"You needn't look. We've got you tight."

A Confederate private ran past them and did not halt when the enemy horseman called to him. The Federal dropped him with his carbine, not twenty yards away.

"That's how I'd have done you," he said to Dwight, "if you had run. I guess you'll surrender."

"You're a private, aren't you?

"Yes."

"I'm damned if I'll surrender to you."

"The hell you won't. I'll have to shoot you."

"Shoot and be damned. I'll not give up to a private. Bring an officer and I'll surrender to him."

"Well, you're a hell of a fellow."

The trooper hailed a passing Federal officer. "Major, here's a Rebel officer says he'll be damned if he'll surrender to a private."

The major halted. "He's perfectly right," he said. "Captain, I see you're a staff officer. Whose staff are you on?"

"If you want to know, find out. I don't give information to the enemy."

"You're right again, Captain. I should not have asked. You see the situation here. It's hopeless. Will you give me your parole not to escape?"

"I will. There's no other way."

"Well, just ride aside. Dismount if you like, and await events."

Dwight dismounted and leaned against a tree. His horse shied and tore away from him, disappearing on the hillside. Dwight broke down:

"I wept as never before or since. I had one pervading, overwhelming regret that I had survived the division, the Army of Northern Virginia, and the Confederate States. Why could I not have fallen like so many war-long veterans?"

After a time Dwight fell asleep under the tree above Sayler's Creek.

Not far from Kershaw's sector of the front, Major Robert Stiles, the gunner, settled his battalion on the hill. Next to him, to his amusement, Commodore Tucker shouted orders to his Naval battalion. The old seaman called to the sailors, "To the starboard, march! Grand moral combination!" There were choruses of "Aye, aye, sir!" as the men went into position.

A staff officer rode to Tucker.

"May I help put your command in position, sir?"

"Thank you, young man," the commodore said. "I understand how to talk to my people."

The enemy was already shelling the ridge, and one of the bursts struck among the artillerymen. Major Stiles wrote:

"My men were lying down and ordered not to expose themselves. I was walking backward and forward just back of the line, talking to them whenever that was practicable. . . . A twenty-pounder Parrott shell struck immediately in my front, on the line, nearly severing a man in twain, and hurling him bodily over my head, his arms hanging down and his hands almost slapping me in the face as they passed."

Stiles recognized the victim as young Blount, who had been

so tearful at the reading of the Soldier's Psalm on Sunday night that now seemed so long ago.

Federal fire was so accurate that Stiles thought his men might bolt: "They did not appear to be hopelessly demoralized, but they did look blanched and haggard and awe-struck."

Federal infantry came up the hill at a walk and Stiles called to his men, "When I say ready, rise on the right knee. Aim at their knees. Fire together when I call. Obey every order instantly."

In the last yards of the Federal approach the field was "still as the grave," Stiles thought. Some of the enemy officers had white handkerchiefs in their hands, and waved to Stiles, telling him to surrender. The major gave the order to fire, with results which surprised him:

"The earth appeared to have swallowed up the first line of the Federal force in our front. . . . The second line wavered and broke.

"The revulsion was too sudden. On the instant every man in my battalion sprang to his feet and, without orders, they rushed, bare-headed and with unloaded muskets, down the slope after the retreating Federals. I tried to stop them, but in vain, although I actually got ahead of a good many of them. They simply bore me on with the flood."

Stiles caught up with his color-bearer, whom he yanked backward with a tug at his rolled blanket.

"What do you mean, advancing the colors without orders?"

An artillery shell knocked down the flag-bearer, and when Stiles reached for the colors, the dead man's brother grabbed for them. "They belong to me now, Major!" he yelled. The second man was shot through the head almost as he took the staff.

Another of the color guard jumped up. "Give 'em to me, Major!" This man also fell. Stiles said:

"There were at least five men dead and wounded lying close about me, and I did not see why I should continue to make a target of myself. I therefore jammed the color staff down through a thick bush, which supported it in an upright position, and turned my attention to my battalion."

Stiles saw that his men could not remain in the open, and

led them through a ravine to their old position; many were missing when they were once more in place. He saw the bloody end of it:

"Quicker than I can tell it the battle degenerated into a butchery and a confused melee of brutal personal conflicts. I saw numbers of men kill each other with bayonets and the butts of muskets, and even bite each other's throats and ears and noses, rolling on the ground like wild beasts. I saw one of my officers and a Federal officer fighting with swords over the battalion colors, which we had brought back with us, each man having his left hand upon the staff. I could not get to them, but my man was a very athletic, powerful seaman, and soon I saw the Federal officer fall."

Stiles had warned his men against wearing the captured blue enemy overcoats in battle, but today many had them on. Stiles saw one of his men blow open the head of his most intimate friend, failing to recognize him in the blue coat he wore. This moment impressed Stiles:

"I was wedged in between fighting men, only my right arm free. I tried to strike the musket barrel up, but alas, my sword had broken in the clash and I could not reach it. I well remember the yell of demoniac triumph with which that simple country lad clubbed his musket and whirled savagely upon another victim."

The fury around Stiles ceased suddenly and he ran. Within a few yards he met a Federal force and was captured. He said, "I was not sorry to end it thus, in red-hot battle."

Private Timberlake, watching from a few yards away, saw:

"Near the end the 37th Massachusetts had the fiercest literally savage encounter of the war with the remnant of Stiles' battalion and the Marines. I was next to those Marines and saw them fight. They clubbed muskets, fired pistols into each other's faces and used bayonets savagely."

Commodore Tucker, who fought stoutly in his first land battle, did not give up until the blue lines had overrun his band from every side. He was astonished: "I never before got into a fight like this. I thought everything was going on well."

Timberlake was soon captured. He fired at a Federal who came up with a flag of truce before he understood his purpose, but missed him.

"You're surrounded," the bluecoat said. "We have lines all around you. Give it up."

As the 2nd Virginia Reserve Battalion's survivors surrendered, Timberlake threw down a musket so hot that it burned his hands. He wrote:

"I went to the rear, thirsty, but the water was bloody in a ditch I tried. Custer's cavalry was gathering prisoners. I jumped from the ditch and scared a Yank's cavalry horse. He cursed me. The next one came along at a gallop."

"You hungry, Johnny?" the trooper said.

"That's a pretty question to ask a Rebel."

"Never mind. You got a knife?"

"Yes."

The bluecoat turned the horse and Timberlake saw a ham strapped to the saddle.

"Cut you a piece, Johnny."

Timberlake took a thick slice and the Federal gave him a piece of hardtack.

"God bless that Yankee," Timberlake said. "He saved my life."

Captain Thomas Blake, of Company E of the artillery battalion on the hillside, also found the enemy abruptly friendly when he had surrendered:

"The infantry which we had so recently repulsed came up with smiling faces. They showed no resentment, but opened their haversacks and offered to share their hard tack with us, saying, 'You Johnnies sure put up a good fight.' . . . It was only when we fell into the hands of the provost guard that any harshness was shown."

General Henry Wise, the one-time Governor of Virginia, led a small brigade from Anderson's corps into the outer edge of the melee at Sayler's Creek. The enemy fired from behind a plantation house and outbuildings and the stone wall of a graveyard, but Wise drove the bluecoats from this cover, chased them about two miles, and, he said, "broke them thoroughly." He got no support from Pickett's men, who were nearby. There was an order to retreat. Wise said:

"We had hardly formed and begun to move in his rear before Pickett's whole command stampeded, leaving their artillery in the enemy's hands, and they were exploding caissons in a lane in our front."

Wise led his men over the west fork of Sayler's Creek and found himself surrounded. A neighboring brigade broke, but the former governor gave not a thought to surrender: "We pressed up a hill in our front, halted behind a worm fence on the crest, fired three volleys to the rear . . . poured three volleys obliquely to the left and front, broke the enemy and got out."

The well-drilled veterans of Colonel William K. Perrin's 26th Virginia saved Wise. They rallied and formed ranks in sight of the Federal column, and Wise formed his entire brigade about it. A strange scene followed. When Wise's men fired into adjoining woods, a white flag emerged, and the South Carolina brigade of General William Wallace came out of hiding. Wise put these men in front of him and hurried them rearward, toward Farmville.

Colonel R. T. W. Duke was sent into the creek valley by General Barton during a lull in the firing, to meet a Federal flag of truce. The enemy officer was Colonel Oliver Edwards.

"Generals Ewell and Custis Lee and several others have surrendered," he said. "Lots of men and officers are dead. We want you to give up and stop this useless bloodshed."

"We can't do that," Duke said. "We've had no orders. We'll fight on." He went back up the hill to report to Barton, but had hardly arrived when a bluecoat cavalry squadron surrounded them. Duke gave up his dress sword with reluctance; his great-grandfather had carried it in the Revolution. Duke carefully took down the name and address of the officer who relieved him of the weapon.

The Federals carried General Ewell to the headquarters of General Horatio Wright, commander of the 6th Corps. Ewell freely answered questions about the strength of the two divisions he had lost: some 6,000 men had left Richmond with him, but the figures of 2800 prisoners and 150 killed or wounded at Sayler's Creek were as accurate as he could make them. Thousands, he said, had straggled away during the march.

At his request the Federals found Major Robert Stiles among the prisoners and brought him to Ewell. Stiles wrote:

"In the presence of half a dozen generals [Ewell] said that he had summoned me to say, in the hearing of these officers, that the conduct of my battalion had been reported to him, and that he desired to congratulate me and them upon the record they had made."

Survivors of the afternoon's fighting began to scatter, and many did not follow the trail of the main army west toward Farmville.

Private W. S. White and a few companions of the 3rd Company, Richmond Howitzers, waited until dark and buried the few cannon left to them. Then, around a campfire, they discussed the future:

"It was now apparent to all that we could hold out but a few hours—men and horses were utterly worn down by fatigue, loss of sleep and hunger. Thousands were leaving their commands and wandering about the devastated country in quest of food, and they had no muskets."

Private John L. G. Woods, the drummerboy of the 53rd Georgia, had beat the long roll for his regiment in the morning and then, as a noncombatant, gone to a hospital wagon as his companions went into line of battle.

In the lull before the wounded came back, Woods wandered, visiting farmhouses in search of food. He was trading for provisions when a civilian shouted to him:

"The Yanks have surrounded Longstreet's corps, and their cavalry is on the road just behind you and will soon cut off the bridge."

Woods was incredulous, but the man insisted that he had seen the enemy troops, and the drummer hurried for the bridge. He was none too soon, for he reached the far bank as bluecoats appeared. He walked among disorganized stragglers in the road. After dark these men were thrown into a panic by a mounted officer or courier who galloped among them yelling, "Halt! Yanks in front!" The column halted and many left the road, but the report was soon found to be false, and the soldiers concluded they had been misled by a Yankee scout.

Woods went on into Farmville, and spent the night under a tree.

Corporal M. W. Venable and the 1st Engineers were a bit to the west of Sayler's Creek when the battle came on; they had driven off cavalry and were retreating when they met General Eppa Hunton's brigade of Pickett's division, lying along the road awaiting orders. As the engineers passed, shells dropped near this infantry, and Hunton soon ordered them up and into battle.

An hour or more later Venable met a man hobbling back in a stream of wounded. "I'm the last of Hunton's men," the cripple said. "They got all the rest, dead, wounded or captured. They got General Hunton, and Ewell and Custis Lee and lots of others."

The engineers marched toward Farmville by way of the chief crossing of the Appomattox east of the town—High Bridge. They had orders to destroy both the lofty railroad bridge and the lower wagon bridge beneath it, but only after the infantry had passed. By 8 P.M. the engineers had reached the bridge and Company G was detailed to stand by until ordered to burn it. The bridge was built of a dozen wooden trusses atop towering brick pillars, and the dry pine frames would burn like giant torches. Troops poured over the bridge.

Major Henry Kyd Douglas, the young survivor of Stonewall Jackson's staff, brought the remnants of The Light Brigade to High Bridge, only 500 of them in the ranks. Douglas had narrowly escaped during the day.

His brigade was caught in the rear of Gordon's fight near Sayler's Creek, and held a hill until artillery and wagons had crossed the stream. Lieutenant Colonel Wilfred Cutshaw, who had left Petersburg with six batteries in his artillery battalion, reported to Douglas with a handful of men, armed with muskets. Their cannon were gone.

In the fighting Cutshaw's leg was torn off by a shell, and Douglas was knocked from the saddle by a spent musket ball which struck a button on his chest.

Near High Bridge there was an even closer call for the major. He was asleep when the enemy came near, and staggered groggily after his men had shaken him. He was fully awake only when a shell burst overhead, tearing his shoulder with a painful wound from a fragment. A doctor halted the bleeding, gave Douglas a stout drink of brandy, and put him back into his saddle. He retreated with his arm in a sling.

Robert Lee rode up from Rice's Station in the afternoon, apprehensive at the sound of firing, aware that the broken valley of Sayler's Creek held dangers for the column. He learned that Gordon had been attacked, but that he evidently was not marching with the main body. A Virginia captain approached Lee as he studied the valley with binoculars, holding Traveller's reins with one hand.

"Are those sheep or not?" Lee asked.

"No, General," the soldier said, "they are Yankee wagons."

"You're right," Lee said slowly. "But what are they doing there?"

There was only one answer: The enemy wagons were following Grant's infantry, which must have overtaken the rear segment of the Confederate column. Lee soon met General William Mahone, and was riding with the tiny Virginian when Colonel Charles Venable, Lee's aide, came up swiftly.

"Did you get my message, sir?"

"No," Lee said. "What message?"

"The enemy's taken the wagon train. At Sayler's Creek."

"Where is Anderson?" Lee said. "Where is Ewell? It is strange that I can't hear from them."

The commander turned to Mahone. "I have no other troops. Will you take your division to Sayler's Creek?"

Mahone soon had the men on the way, and went with Lee to a knoll overlooking the site of defeat. Mahone wrote:

"The scene beggars description—hurrying teamsters with their teams and dangling traces, retreating infantry without guns, many without hats, a harmless mob, with the massive column of the enemy moving orderly on.

"At this spectacle General Lee straightened himself in the saddle and, looking more the soldier than ever, exclaimed, as if talking to himself:

"'My God! Has the army been dissolved?'"

Mahone was ready. "No, General. Here are troops ready to do their duty."

"Yes," Lee said. "There are some true men left. Will you please keep those people back?"

Men of the retreating brigades swarmed around Lee, who held a battle flag in one hand. Mahone took the flag from him.

The commander agreed, at Mahone's suggestion, to send Longstreet by the river road into Farmville during the night, and allow Mahone, Gordon and other survivors to march north to the river and cross at High Bridge. Once over the bridge, Mahone was to use his own judgment as to a course.

"What shall I do with the bridge when I've crossed?"

"Set fire to it," Lee said.

Mahone asked him to send Colonel T. M. R. Talcott of the engineers to direct the burning.

Lee put a few of Mahone's men into line within sight of the approaching enemy and rode Traveller about in the dusk as if impatient for action. The writer, John Esten Cooke, watched admiringly:

"An artist ought to have seen the old cavalier at this moment, sweeping on upon his large iron-gray, whose mane and tail floated in the wind; carrying his field glass half-raised in his right hand; with head erect, gestures animated, and in the whole face and form the expression of the hunter close upon his game. He rode in the twilight among the disordered groups, and the sight of him aroused a tumult.

"Fierce cries resounded on all sides, and, with hands

clenched violently and raised aloft, the men called on him to lead them against the enemy. 'It's General Lee! Uncle Robert! Where's the man who won't follow Uncle Robert?' I heard this on all sides—the swarthy faces full of dirt and courage, lit up every instant by the glare of burning wagons."

Lee told an officer, after he had looked at the scene of the rout of Ewell, Pickett and Custis Lee, that "half of the army has been destroyed."

At dark there was a dispatch from John B. Gordon:

> I have been fighting heavily all day. My loss is consider-able and I am still closely pressed. I fear that a portion of the train will be lost as my force is quite reduced & insuffi-cient for its protection. So far I have been able to protect them, but without assistance can scarcely hope to do so much longer. The enemy's loss has been very heavy.

Gordon, at least, was safe. Lee could not know that the fierce Georgian lost about 1500 men as prisoners when the enemy broke his line at dusk—or that Confederate losses for the day were near 8000, excluding the stragglers who would be seen no more.

Lee rode at nightfall to Rice's Station, and in a field beside the railroad tracks, with only an orderly or two and a staff officer, made headquarters as the army moved toward Farmville in re-treat. He handled many dispatches during the night; in the early hours Longstreet's men were forced to fend off enemy attacks, but the situation was not serious, and fighting died away.

Young John Wise, who had been stalking the enemy in his locomotive, forced his engineer into Burkeville in the early morning hours and came upon hundreds of Federal soldiers working on the rails by firelight, widening the tracks to accom-modate Grant's big trains.

There was hardly time to surmise the obvious fact that the enemy held Burkeville, for blue cavalrymen charged the light-less locomotive which had so startled them.

"Reverse the engine!" Wise yelled. His engineer seemed to be paralyzed.

"It's no use, Lieutenant," the man said. "They'd kill us before we got underway."

Wise put his pistol behind the engineer's head. "Reverse or you're a dead man," he said. The engineer pulled a lever and the engine slowly backed away. Federal riders opened fire. Wise and the engineer lay down and let the locomotive go. She gathered speed and rocked away so swiftly that Wise feared she would jump the rotten track.

When they were safe, the engineer turned to Wise:

"Lieutenant, would you have blowed my brains out, sure enough?"

"I would that."

"Well," the engineer said. "I don't want to travel with you no more."

Wise left him at Meherrin Station, not far down the tracks, and with the aid of his pass from Jefferson Davis, took a fine mare from a cavalryman on furlough and rode on in search of General Lee and the army. He heard the fighting at Sayler's Creek, outran a couple of enemy cavalry parties and was almost ambushed by Confederate scouts. He rode through Farmville, having gone far out of his way, then southeast toward Rice's Station.

Wise found Lee in the field, standing by a fire. Colonel Charles Marshall was in a headquarters wagon, writing dispatches on a lap desk as Lee dictated.

The boy gave Lee his message, telling him of President Davis's request for information.

"I hardly think it is necessary to prepare written dispatches," Lee said. "They may be captured. You may say to Mr. Davis that, as he knows, my original purpose was to adhere to the line of the Danville road. I have been unable to do so, and am now trying to hold the Southside road as I retire toward Lynchburg."

"Have you chosen a place to make a stand?"

Young Wise long retained his memory of Lee's reply: "No, I'll have to wait for developments. A few more Sayler's Creeks and it will be all over—ended—just as I have expected it would end from the first."

Lee sent the boy toward Farmville, where he might join his father for a night's rest.

Between Sayler's Creek and Farmville, not far from High
Bridge, Fitz Lee's cavalry ran into the enemy. It was near noon,
before the opening of battle at the creek.

Trooper E. M. Boykin missed the action, but saw the prisoners, about 900 fresh Yankee infantrymen just come to the front,
gobbled up by Fitz Lee's regiments. Boykin saw them going to
the rear:

"Their coats were so new and blue and buttons so bright,
and shirts so clean, that it was a wonder to look upon them by
our rusty lot."

These prisoners were the harvest of a sharp skirmish in the
Confederate rear. General Longstreet had discovered enemy
infantry marching toward High Bridge and guessed that its mis-
sion was to destroy the bridge before Lee's army could cross.
He sent Tom Rosser after it with a division of horsemen; he soon
reinforced him with Tom Munford, leading Fitz Lee's men.

Rosser found the bluecoats about 1 P.M. and charged as
they lay behind a fence at the fringe of a woodland. Munford's
men joined, and it seemed that the Federals would be quickly
overrun, until bluecoat cavalry slashed in upon the flank of the
attack. The columns met at great speed, and there was close work
with sabers and pistols.

One of Rosser's commanders was young General James
Dearing, of the Laurel Brigade, who led troopers upon the enemy
at the fence and ran into a saber duel with the Federal commander, General Theodore Read, of Ord's staff. Dearing dropped
Read from the saddle with a fatal body wound, but, as he
turned, the Federal's orderly shot Dearing, who fell to the
ground.

The charge was pressed home by Colonel Elijah White of
the 35th Virginia Battalion, and the enemy was driven. White's
Comanches herded prisoners back toward the army, but the
colonel did not leave the scene—Watson's Farm—until he had
visited the mortally wounded Dearing.

The boy general had been carried into a farmhouse. When
White entered, Tom Rosser sat by the bed, nursing a fresh
wound of his own. Dearing was failing rapidly. He pointed to

the new stars of a brigadier on his collar and whispered weakly to Rosser, "These belong on his collar." He nodded toward White in one of the final gestures of his life.

There were other casualties among Confederate officers. Major James Thomson, the fearless chief of horse artillery, had been shot through the neck in the charge and had died instantly. The 5th Virginia had lost its colonel, Reuben Boston. The Federals had lost both General Read and Colonel Francis Washburn, a cavalryman who had been at West Point with Dearing.

William Owen of the New Orleans artillery was sitting near High Bridge when the cavalry came in with the prisoners. A familiar voice called, "Where would I find General Longstreet, friend?"

Owen was surprised to see Tom Rosser, whom he had not seen in months. The horseman was full of news. "Oh, we captured these people who were going to burn the bridge, and took them all in. But we lost Jim Dearing. He cut General Read from his horse, but was shot down. It was a gallant fight."

Rosser had some trophies.

"This is Read's horse, and this is his saber. Both beauties, aren't they? But I must see Longstreet."

Owen joined Rosser after he had reported to Old Pete, and they rode toward Farmville. Owen wrote: "It was 10 P.M. when we took the road again. It was axle-deep in mud. It was a fearfully trying night."

Trooper E. M. Boykin rode with his command toward Farmville, living on the country. Broken-down commissary wagons were the best supply, but some riders stopped at farmhouses and were given food. They rode through Farmville and camped in a grove outside the town.

They built a big campfire, for the night was cold. When the flames died down "there was a general awakening and a building up" of the fire. In one of these late stirrings Boykin and Colonel Haskell were surprised to find two strangers bedded down between them, a colonel and a lieutenant from Pickett's command who did not know what had become of their regiment, or even the division. For the first time Boykin realized that the famous fighting unit had been destroyed.

★ PURSUIT ★

General Meade was off on a false scent at 6 A.M., following his three massed corps of infantry on Amelia Court House. Meade still rode in his ambulance, but Colonel Lyman wrote:

"We are pelting after Old Lee as hard as the poor doughboys' legs can go."

Grant was not misled: "It turned out that the retreat began the evening of the 5th and continued all night. Satisfied that this would be the case, I did not permit the cavalry to participate in Meade's useless advance."

Grant put the troopers on a road leading west, from Deatonsville to Rice's Station, with Crook and Merritt leading. They soon struck Rebel wagons and the squadrons raced in; smoke rose over the roadway, but the bluecoats were driven off by infantry. Grant moved as calmly as if he were playing checkers:

"So, leaving Stagg's brigade and Miller's battery about three miles southwest of Deatonsville—where the road forks, with a branch leading north to the Appomattox—to harass the retreating column and find a vulnerable point, I again shifted the rest of the cavalry toward the left, across-country, but still keeping parallel to the enemy's line of march."

The leading Federal cavalry had crossed Sayler's Creek when Merritt and Crook saw their chance. They went into the road to Rice's Station, cut the Confederate train, burned several wagons, took hundreds of prisoners and sixteen guns. Longstreet's corps had marched on ahead of this break, but Ewell and Custis Lee were behind. The little force Grant had posted near Deatonsville had pushed John Gordon out of the main road, and was striking Ewell's rear. The Confederate line of march was snarled.

Colonel Lyman watched the start of it from Jetersville

when Meade had returned from his early-morning march. Lyman could see the fighting four miles away:

"At that point was a bare ridge, a little above Deatonsville, and there, with my good glass, I could see a single man very well. It was just like a play of marionettes. . . . At first I saw only the Rebel train, moving along the ridge toward Deatonsville, in all haste; there now goes a pygmy ambulance drawn by mouselike horses, at a trot. Here come more ambulances and many wagons from the woods, and disappear in a continuous procession, over the ridge. Suddenly—boom! boom! and the distant smoke of Humphreys' batteries curls above the pine trees. At this stimulus the Lilliputian procession redoubles its speed. . . . Ah, here come the infantry. Now for a fight! Yes, a line of battle in retreat, and covering the rear. There are mounted officers; they gallop about, waving their tiny swords."

At 8:30 A.M., when he discovered at last that the Rebels were streaming westward, Meade turned the infantry in their path, and Humphreys, Wright and Griffin pushed the men hard.

It was the 26th Michigan which first sighted the Rebels—a glimpse over the valley of Flat Creek, near Amelia Springs. It was ten thirty, and the troops they saw made up the rear of John Gordon's column. Griffin's men were swung wide, north of the enemy's route. Humphreys hurried the 2nd Corps after Gordon. Humphreys wrote:

"A sharp, running fight . . . continued over a distance of fourteen miles, during which several partially entrenched positions were carried. The country was broken, wooded with dense undergrowth and swamps, alternating with open fields . . . for miles the road being strewn with tents, camp equipage, baggage, battery forges, limbers and wagons."

By noon, with the massed infantry closing in and Sheridan hurrying along the flank into the Confederate path, the cavalryman sent to Grant a dispatch on the plight of the enemy:

The trains and the army were moving all last night and are very short of provisions and are very tired indeed. I think now is the time to attack them with all your infantry. They are reported to have begged provisions from people of the country all up and down the road as they passed. I am working around farther to the left.

Until 2 P.M. Sheridan's rear force under Stagg and Miller worried the Confederates. By then General Wright's 6th Corps marched into sight, and at three thirty these men looked down from a ridge to see Ewell's troops turning in confusion. Morris Schaff, the Federal reporter, sketched the scene from the hill above Sayler's Creek:

"The Confederates could see the regiments pouring into the fields at double quick, the battle lines blooming with colors, growing longer and deeper at every moment, and batteries at a gallop coming into action in the front. They all knew what it meant. . . . Batteries right and left of the Hillsman house opened on Ewell's line, a rapid and destructive fire."

Sheridan watched the opening of the fight from beside a barn on a hillside, shading himself from the hot sun.

Colonel Oliver Edwards, of the 3rd Brigade, 1st Division, reported to him. Sheridan pointed across the creek, to the steep hillside.

"The enemy are there," he said. "I want you to form your brigade in one line, cross the creek and carry the heights." He indicated the left of the enemy line held by Custis Lee.

"Can my flanks be covered?"

Sheridan roared, "Never mind your flanks! Go through them. They're as demoralized as hell!"

The attack moved slowly, the men wading the creek without drawing Rebel fire—some of them went to their armpits in the water. A volley broke the line and hand-to-hand fighting covered the slope.

The 37th Massachusetts, of the same 3rd Brigade, was late in arriving. Like most units today, it had marched twenty miles at a fast pace, but when word came that the Rebels were at bay, the sweating men checked the magazines of their Spencer repeating rifles, began flinging aside knapsacks, blankets, canteens and heavy clothing, and for the last three miles went at a run. They came to the hillside where the Confederates were fighting for their lives, and the men of the 37th, most of them from the Berkshire hills, crashed through the undergrowth to meet the remnant of Stiles' battalion and the Confederate Marines.

Schaff said: "They clubbed their muskets, fired pistols in each other's faces and used the bayonet savagely. One Berkshire man was stabbed in the chest by a bayonet and pinned to the ground as it came out near his spine. He reloaded his gun and killed the Confederate, who fell across him. The Massachusetts man threw him off, pulled out the bayonet, and despite the awful wound, walked to the rear."

Federal cavalry hacked away at the gray line in the rear, and the end soon came. Bluecoats began working on a mass grave in the ravine by the creek.

Just to the west, Custer had snapped up an artillery battery of Colonel Frank Huger, his West Point classmate. With the divisions of Crook and Merritt, the Federals cleared away infantry guards, and in the midst of a panic began rounding up prisoners. Generals Corse and Hunton of Pickett's division were taken. Pickett, Fitz Lee and Dick Anderson escaped on fast horses. General Bushrod Johnson did not wait to see the stout defense of his lieutenant, General Henry Wise, but "fled up the road in the midst of a panicky swarm of soldiers and teamsters toward Rice's Station."

As night fell Humphreys' men were pecking at Gordon's force, which managed to cross the double bridges of Sayler's Creek and escape. To the south and west, General Ord's Army of the James approached Rice's Station, but it was too late for a full-scale attack on Longstreet's corps.

Sheridan sent a staff man, Colonel Redwood Price, to Grant with news of the victory. On his way Price stopped at the headquarters of Meade. Meade was astonished when he read the dispatch, for he had known nothing of the scale of victory at Sayler's Creek. He seemed even more surprised that no infantry general had observed the formality of reporting to him, and that Sheridan had claimed full credit. Colonel Lyman noted in his diary:

"There comes a staff officer with a dispatch. *'I* attacked with two divisions of the 6th Corps. *I* captured many thousand prisoners, etc. P. H. Sheridan.'

" 'Oh,' said Meade, 'so General Wright wasn't there?' 'Oh, yes,' said the staff officer, as if speaking of some worthy man who had commanded a battalion, 'Oh, yes, General Wright *was* there.' Meade turned on his heel without a word, and Cavalry Sheridan's dispatch proceeded—to the newspapers!"

Thus the squabbles among the high command raged before Grant learned of his victory. Sheridan wrote of his aide's halt at Meade's camp:

"On his way Price stopped at the headquarters of General Meade, where he learned that not the slightest intelligence of the occurrence on my line had been received, for I not being under Meade's command, he had paid no attention to my movements. Price gave the story of the battle, and General Meade, realizing its importance, sent directions immediately to General Wright to make his report of the engagement to the headquarters of the Army of the Potomac, assuming that Wright was operating independently of me in the face of Grant's dispatch of 2 o'clock, which said that Wright was following the cavalry and would 'go in with a vim' wherever I dictated. Wright could not do else than comply with Meade's orders in the case, and I, being then in ignorance of Meade's reasons for the assumption, could say nothing."

Meade was soon consoled by getting a report from General Humphreys. Colonel Price rode into the night and found Grant at Burkeville. It was midnight when the commander-in-chief read the stunning lines of Sheridan's dispatch:

Up to the present time we have captured Generals Ewell, Kershaw, Barton, Corse, Hunton, Dubose and Custis Lee, several thousand prisoners, 14 pieces of artillery and a large number of wagons. If the thing is pressed, I think Lee will surrender.

Grant sent a telegraph message to President Lincoln at City Point and hurried a note to Meade: "Every moment is now important to us."

He sent the infantry westward by several roads, to cut off Lee around Farmville. The troops were to move early.

Sheridan's camp was not far from Sayler's Creek. Colonel Newhall of his staff sketched the cavalry commander:

"He is lying on the broad of his back on a blanket, with his feet to the fire, in a condition of sleepy wakefulness. Clustered about are blue uniforms and gray in equal numbers, and immediately around his campfire are most of the Confederate generals. Ewell is sitting on the ground hugging his knees, his face bent down between his arms."

Ewell was not talkative, but he made a brief comment to General Horatio Wright, who invited him to share his quarters, "Our cause is gone. Lee should surrender now, before more lives are wasted."

George Custer was at hand, a boy general of twenty-six, resplendent in a suit of olive corduroy, his long yellow hair on his shoulders, a scarlet neckerchief over his coat. The South Carolina Confederates, General Kershaw and Colonel Huger, were Custer's guests for the night.

Colonel George Forsythe of Sheridan's staff came to report that headquarters had been set up in a fine orchard, with tents pitched and a hot supper ready. The officers followed him, and the cavalry command settled for the night. Federal generals shared their blankets with their captives. They slept for no more than an hour before Sheridan was up, busy with plans for the chase.

★ THE LINCOLNS ★

Mrs. Lincoln returned to her husband about noon, when her river steamer nudged into the busy harbor at City Point; she had been almost exactly twenty-four hours steaming from Washington down the Potomac, through the Chesapeake and up the James. She had brought a rather exotic party:

One of them, to his lingering surprise, was the young French count, Adolphe de Chambrun, who had known the Lincolns little more than a month, and was in his third month of learning English. The Count had impeccable manners, was an impassioned partisan of the principles of Union, and paid homage to Mary Lincoln with subtle flattery. He had scratched in his diary: "Mrs. Lincoln must have been very pretty when young."

Others in the party were Lincoln's old enemy, Senator Charles Sumner; James H. Harlan, new Secretary of the Interior, with his wife, daughter, and an undersecretary. There were also Mrs. Lincoln and her maid, Elizabeth Keckley, a former slave who had been seamstress to Mrs. Jefferson Davis in prewar days in Washington.

The party went immediately to the President's boat, and Lincoln took them, with boyish enthusiasm, into the saloon where he had met with Judge Campbell and the other Confederate commissioners in the futile peace conference of the winter.

Secretary Harlan, an old friend of Lincoln's, had until lately been a Senator from Iowa, a sturdy schoolmaster of pioneer days who had become in turn a college president. He was amazed at his first glimpse of Lincoln today:

"His whole appearance, pose and bearing had marvellously changed. He was, in fact, transfigured. That indescribable sadness which had previously seemed to be an adamantine element of his very being, had been suddenly changed for an equally indescribable expression of serene joy, as if conscious that the great purpose of his life had been achieved."

Mary Lincoln was "much disappointed" when she heard that her husband had already visited fallen Richmond, Elizabeth Keckley noticed. Mrs. Lincoln had wanted to go to the Rebel capital herself and announced plans to do so the next day.

Lincoln turned to business. He was drawn by the dilemma of trying to make peace with Campbell and other Virginia leaders while Grant was in chase of Lee; he could not put it from his mind, and now dealt with it more subtly than Admiral Porter suspected. Lincoln telegraphed General Weitzel in Richmond:

> It has been intimated to me that the gentlemen who have acted as the legislature of Virginia, in support of the rebellion, may now desire to assemble at Richmond, and take measures to withdraw the Virginia troops, and other support from resistance to the General Government. If they attempt it, give them permission and protection until, if at all, they attempt some hostile action to the United States, in which case you will notify them and give them reasonable time to leave; & at the end of which time, arrest any who may remain. Allow Judge Campbell to see this, but do not make it public.

The President also telegraphed Grant, explaining his effort to entice Virginia from the war; there was little chance that his maneuver would bear fruit, he said, but added, "I have thought best to notify you, so that if you should see signs, you may understand them."

There was a bit of further news for him to send Grant: Secretary of State Seward had been dangerously injured in a carriage accident, and Lincoln must soon return to Washington.

VIII

Friday, April 7

★

★ FLIGHT ★

PERCY HAWES, the 2nd Corps courier, was ordered out of the plodding column sometime after midnight, as he neared High Bridge, and detailed to remain at a small bridge over a creek, where he would halt an artillery brigade moving toward Farmville.

He was so exhausted that he turned his mare sidewise across the bridge and fell asleep. A shout roused him:

"Wake up, boy! What do you want us to do, anyhow?"

Hawes passed marching instructions to the gunners and rode off. He found corn for himself and the mare in an overturned wagon and traded some of the corn to a passing soldier for a bit of fat meat. The two made "a very hearty meal."

Hawes wrote: "After eating all I could, I went in the creek and filled myself with water, congratulating myself that for once I was full."

He lay down by his mare and slept soundly, but was driven from this place when the campfire escaped into leaves, burned his hat and singed his hair. He went back into the path of the column.

Lieutenant Joseph Packard and "a miscellaneous crowd" pushed through the retreat in the night; Packard got a glimpse of Robert Lee on Traveller, looking "as grand and serene as ever." A battery was passing, and an Irish sergeant yelled to his men:

"Do ye hear, boys? 'Tis the General himself that wants us."

As Packard passed on, this battery was getting into position to guard the column. When the moon was high in the sky Packard saw High Bridge arching over the valley of the Appomattox, but traffic at the bridge was so slow that he and his friend Bob Burwell rode across country toward Farmville in search of food.

They robbed a barn of a few bundles of fodder and some corn, and reached the town just before midnight.

Packard knocked at a house on the edge of town. A woman emerged. General Breckinridge and his staff were there, she said, and they filled her house. She could offer nothing to eat. Burwell soon so ingratiated himself that she gave them some cold corn bread and molasses, "a treat indeed."

The ordnance men had no place to keep their horses while they slept, and feared they would be stolen. The woman expressed regrets: "There's no place but the henhouse."

Packard and Burwell squeezed their mounts in the low door of the hen coop, fed them and locked them up. They slept on the back porch, heads on saddles. Before daylight the daughter of the house nudged Packard with her foot. "General Breckinridge has been gone an hour. They heard Yankees were on the edge of town. Mother thinks you'd better go."

They saddled and rode through town, and at the railroad station found wagons they had lost the day before; Packard filled them with corn meal and grain from the quartermaster stores at the depot and they went rapidly over the bridge of the Appomattox and turned westward.

Captain Fred Colston caught up with them, and on the march had a talk with one of Pickett's wandering staff officers who was "very gloomy over the situation."

Packard wrote:

"While I was thinking of this General Breckinridge and his staff rode by, and his calm, buoyant manner was very impressive. The last time I had seen him he was presiding in the Senate chamber as Vice President of the United States."

Dr. Claiborne, of the sadly reduced hospital train, neared Farmville:

"Our road carried us back to the main road, on the right, along which the wagons, as many as were left, were dragging their slow length. We marched all night, or rather crept along with them, until at some creek a panic occurred, and there was crowding and confusion and worse confounded. How many ever came out, I do not know. Being light of baggage ourselves we got ahead of them. . . .

"General Lee was riding slowly along the line of inextricably tangled wagons, as if going to the rear, no one with him, as far as I can remember, and I was near enough to look into his face. He rode erect, as if incapable of fatigue, and with the same dignified mien that I had so often noted on the streets of Petersburg. From his manner no man would have discovered that which he so well knew, that his army was melting away, that his resources were exhausted."

Claiborne found the night extremely cold, and when his friend Dr. Richard Lewis met a North Carolina quartermaster, one Captain Oates, who had some whisky, the surgeon gratefully took the proffered canteen. "It was the first drink I had taken in many months, and I suspect the whisky was as good as any, but it had the most peculiar effect upon me. I had congratulated myself that up to that night I had not suffered from fatigue, from hunger, from want of sleep, from fear. Yet in ten minutes after I took that drink of whisky I was hungry, tired, and scared, and so sleepy that I had to get off my horse and walk to keep awake."

Before daylight he stumbled into Farmville, wrapped his horse's reins about his body and fell to sleep on the sidewalk.

Robert Lee was in Farmville before the sun rose, and got a few hours of sleep in the home of Patrick Jackson. Mrs. Jackson gave him tea for breakfast as he left. The commander also made a call on the widow of Colonel John Thornton, who had been killed in the Sharpsburg campaign, and then rode to inspect the work of quartermaster clerks at the depot, who were giving out the scanty rations to troops.

Dr. Claiborne was there and saw that there was little ceremony in the issuing. The officer in charge, Major Frederick R. Scott, handed him a side of middling meat at his request and the doctor rode away, followed by his orderly, Burkhardt, the Moravian driver.

Another of Lee's soldiers who arrived at the depot at this

time was Private A. C. Jones, who had joined a race down the riverside, within sight of a Federal column in pursuit on the opposite bank. The rations, Jones saw, would not wait:

"There were a few barrels of meal and a few middlings of meat scattered along the sidewalks. Without orders, the men charged that meal, with which they filled their pockets and any other available receptacles. The meat was seized upon and slashed into pieces as they ran. Several of the men stuck their bayonets into middlings and bore them proudly aloft."

Just outside the town, pushed by a heavy Federal force, was the 35th Virginia Cavalry Battalion, with Captain Frank Myers commanding the lead squadron. A bluecoat came up with a white flag.

"Letter from General Grant to General Lee," he said.

"Nothing doing," Myers said. "I won't take it unless that line of infantry stops where it is."

The Federal rider went back, and the troops were halted half a mile away. Myers sent a rider into Farmville with the dispatch.

It was good news for Robert Lee—Custis was a Federal prisoner, alive, unwounded and well.

Robert Lee's young nephew, George Taylor Lee, had marched in the retreat from Richmond since the disbanding of the cadets of the Virginia Military Institute on Sunday. He had made one detour to visit his family in Powhatan County, and today had returned to the army. He found his uncle in Farmville soon after sunrise.

Lee was talking with some officers when he caught sight of the boy. The commander turned, holding in one hand a slice of bread and a leg of fried chicken.

George wrote: "He looked very grave and tired and there was a tone of distress in his voice."

"My son," Lee said, "why did you come here?"

"I thought it my duty," George said.

"You ought not to have come. You can't do any good here."

"If I'd stayed home, they'd have taken me prisoner."

Lee gave him a fatherly look. "No, I don't think they would do that."

"Where is Custis?"

"I'm afraid he's been captured. Have you had any breakfast?"

"No, sir."

Lee gave him the bread and chicken. "Go somewhere and eat it. I have to meet these officers now."

George lost sight of him.

Robert Lee rode north out of Farmville a short distance, by one of the town's two bridges across the Appomattox, seeking troops which survived Sayler's Creek. Among the first men he met was General Bushrod Johnson, who had fled yesterday's battle.

Johnson reported to Lee that his division had been destroyed. Lee could see that this was untrue as the troops of General Henry Wise approached them in the road. Wise was a remarkable sight. He wrote of it himself:

"We were overcome by exhaustion, and without food. There was no water but the pools, as red as brick dust, in the soil of that region. Colonel J. Thomas Goode and myself washed our faces and hands in the same pool, and neither of us had a handkerchief or towel to wipe with, and consequently the paint of the red water remained on our faces at the edges of our hair."

During the night, too, a soldier of Wise's command had found the old man sleeping without cover and had draped a tattered gray blanket about him, fastening it around his neck with a wire pin. Wise said of his entry into Farmville:

"With a face painted like an Indian, with the gray blanket around me, and with the Confederate Tyrolese hat on, and muddy all over, I put myself on foot at the head of the two brigades and marched . . . across an open field to where General Lee was sitting in his saddle, with General B. R. Johnson on his horse a little in the rear.

"The latter had fled from Sayler's Creek and reported me as killed and the whole division cut to pieces and dispersed. As

I moved up with the two brigades I saw General Lee suppressing a laugh. I knew he had a sub-vein of humor, which he was hardly concealing when he saw my appearance—like that of a Comanche savage."

Wise approached Lee angrily. "General Lee, these men shan't move another inch unless they have something more to eat than parched corn taken from starving mules."

Lee smiled. "They deserve something to eat, sir. Let them, without taking down the fence, move to the trees on that hill, and they shall be filled for once at least."

When the men were marching, Lee said to Wise, indicating some disorganized men in the way, "You, sir, will take command of all these forces."

Wise protested. "I can't take such a command. I have no horse."

"Get a horse and make all the stragglers fall into your ranks."

"It will ruin my brigade to take in those men."

"You must obey orders, General."

"I will, sir," Wise said, "or die trying, but first I must understand them." He looked directly at Bushrod Johnson. "It's not the men who're deserting the ranks, but the officers who are deserting the men who're disorganizing your army. Do you mean to say that I must take command of men of all ranks?"

Lee turned his head to hide a smile. "Do your duty, sir," he said.

Wise went off to feed his men and give them another hour or so of sleep.

Wise's son John, who had come so far across country from Clover, at last found his father in Farmville:

"The troops were lying there more like dead men than live ones. They did not move, and they had no sentries out. The sun was shining upon them as they slept. I did not recognize them. Dismounting, and shaking an officer, I awoke him with difficulty."

This was an old friend, who pointed out General Wise. "He's over there. Oh, we've had a week of it. Yes, this is all that is left of us." The officer led John to his father. John was moved by pity:

"Nearly sixty years old, he lay, like a common soldier, sleeping on the ground among his men."

Old Wise started awake: "Great Jehosaphat, what are you doing here? I thought you, at least, were safe." John hugged his father and told him about his message from Jefferson Davis to Lee.

"Where is General Lee?" the Governor shouted. "I want to see him again. I saw him this morning about daybreak, when I'd washed in a puddle, and he said, 'General, go wash your face!'" Wise laughed and went with his son to find Robert Lee.

John wrote of the streets of Farmville:

"The roads and fields were filled with stragglers. They moved looking behind them, as if they expected to be attacked. . . . Demoralization, panic, abandonment of all hope, appeared on every hand. Wagons were rolling along without any clear order or system. Caissons and limber-chests, without commanding officers, seemed to be floating aimlessly upon a tide of disorganization. Rising to his full height, casting a glance around him like that of an eagle, and sweeping the horizon with his long arm and bony forefinger, my father exclaimed, 'This is the end!' It is impossible to convey an idea of the agony and the bitterness of his words and gestures."

They found General Lee on the rear porch of a Farmville house, drying his beard with a towel over a tin basin of water. The Governor and Lee talked for a few minutes, Wise still profanely denouncing Bushrod Johnson. Lee assumed a stern air.

"General, are you aware that you're liable to court martial and execution for insubordination and disrespect toward your commanding officer?"

"Shot?" Wise said. "You can't afford to shoot the men who fight for cursing those who run away. I wish you would shoot me. If you don't, some Yankee probably will within the next twenty-four hours."

"What do you think of the situation?" Lee asked.

"There is no situation. Nothing remains, General Lee, but to put your poor men on your poor mules and send them home in time for spring ploughing. This army is hopelessly whipped. They have already endured more than I thought flesh and blood could stand. The blood of every man who is killed from this time is on your head, General Lee."

Lee gestured impatiently. "Oh, General, don't talk so wildly. My burdens are heavy enough. What would the country think of me, if I did what you suggest?"

"Country be damned! There is no country. There has been no country, General, for a year or more. You're the country to these men. They have fought for you, without pay or clothes or care of any sort. There are still thousands of us who will die for you."

Lee looked out into the fields for a moment and made no reply. He turned at last to John Wise, and wrote a dispatch for him to take to Jefferson Davis—a few words to the effect that he had talked with the boy, and sent the message itself verbally.

"Deliver this to the President," he said. "I'm afraid to write anything in case you're captured. Those people are already several miles above Farmville. You must keep on the north side of the river to a ford eight miles above here, and be careful about crossing even there."

John Wise left them for his long ride to Danville.

Longstreet's infantry was streaming into Farmville over the bridges, with some of Rosser's cavalry in the rear. Most of these men drew two days' rations at the depot, and turned quickly to cook, for it was their first issue since leaving Richmond.

Longstreet wrote: "They were just ready to prepare a good breakfast, when General Lee rode up and said that the bridges had been fired before his cavalry crossed, and that part of the command was cut off and lost, and that the troops should hurry on to a position at Cumberland Church."

Longstreet's men dumped everything into their wagons, eating as they fell into ranks. The teamsters, as usual at the very mention of cavalry, lashed their teams and went off among the trees in a panic, blindly seeking a road of retreat. Lee urged Old Pete to put his troops at the double-quick, and went to the head of the column himself on Traveller, urging the men forward. There was already the sound of cavalry fighting on the outskirts of town, and one of Longstreet's divisions, under General Harry Heth, was turned back to meet this threat.

Colonel Armistead Long of Lee's staff noted that the commander lost his temper this morning—the only such lapse on the retreat. Lee's face became red with anger when he found the reason for the sudden appearance of the bluecoat cavalry, and the absence of some of his own: High Bridge and its companion wagon crossing had not been burned in time, and the enemy had poured over the Appomattox in hot pursuit.

The burning of the bridges, assigned to Mahone's command, had been left in the hands of experts. Colonel T. M. R. Talcott, Lee's staff engineer, had arrived, as had Captain W. W. Blackford, the engineer who had won fame with Jeb Stuart. The work itself was left to Company G, 1st Engineers, under Captain William R. Johnson.

The engineers had lain by the bridge for hours, waiting for the retreating men to pass. Near dawn, when the last of the artillery and wagons seemed to have gone by, Talcott became impatient to light his fires. There was, however, no order from General Mahone, and Talcott had been told to await final, specific word. Talcott sent Captain Blackford toward Farmville in search of Mahone.

Blackford found the general about four miles away and galloped back with permission to burn the bridge; he reached the span as Federal infantry came into sight.

Captain Johnson's men put torches to the pine timbers, and they soon roared with flame. It was clear that two or three of the frames would drop into the river before the enemy could come in. The wagon bridge was another matter; its hardwood planks did not burn so readily. Moreover, Confederate troops ran belatedly to the crossing. One of them, a sixteen-year-old private, had a memory of it:

"We crossed a high bridge when nearing Farmville, one end of which was on fire, and a little beyond as we walked along the road I went into such a sound sleep, marching with my musket on my shoulder, that I fell and was only awakened when my tired body struck the earth."

The enemy rushed the bridge and some of the bluecoats stamped out the burning boards while the artillery and riflemen drove back the Confederate engineers. Talcott and Blackford led a swift retreat toward Farmville.

One of the rear guard here was Thomas Devereux, the North Carolinian in Bryan Grimes' division. He left a glimpse of the bridge burning:

"We kept the enemy off until it was in a light blaze and then struck out for Farmville. One or two spans had fallen in before we lost sight of it. About a mile down the road we came to a cluster of farmhouses and tobacco barns."

Devereux passed a row of hogsheads with their heads knocked out and good tobacco spilling into the road. Their owner, an old man, shouted to the troops:

"Help yourselves, for the damned Yankees will get it if you don't."

Robert Lee crossed the Appomattox at Farmville as the enemy pressed near the town, riding in a swarm of men, wagons and guns on the twin bridges. As his artillery opened from the north bank of the river to check the Federals, he called to him General E. P. Alexander, the young Georgia gunnery chief.

They leaned over a map as Lee explained:

"The enemy has crossed downstream at High Bridge, and will come into our route of retreat about three miles ahead of us. I want you to send some batteries to the crossroads up here, and cover it until we're past. You must also hold these bridges until the troops are over. Destroy them when we have crossed. I leave them in your personal charge."

Alexander held Lee a bit longer, pointing out on the map a shorter route to Lynchburg than the commander had chosen. After some discussion Alexander called up a native to confirm his argument that the new road was better.

By this time a cavalry skirmish crackled in the Farmville street, where Fitz Lee fought off bluecoat troopers.

Young E. M. Boykin was roused with the rest of Gary's brigade when the call came for help. He rode with the South Carolina squadrons down the long main street of Farmville, past a boarding school for young ladies. The girls waved and cheered from the porch of their building. Boykin was touched:

"We greeted the waving handkerchiefs with moist eyes, while cheer after cheer rose from our men. They did not know, as we did, that their friends and defenders were soon to pass by, leaving them so soon in the hands most dreaded by them. They saw us going to the front; our men were excited by the circumstances and the prospect of a fight, and the light of that wild glory that belongs to war shone over it all. The rough, grey soldier, the tramping column, and the groups of tender girls, mixed with it like flowers on a battlefield. . . .

"The shells were bursting over the town, and in the street occasionally, while the good people of Farmville, in a state of great though natural alarm, were leaving with their goods forthwith. We told them we were going at once, and were not to make a fight in the town, to keep quiet in their houses, and it was not probable that they would be interfered with."

Captain Haskell of Boykin's command took thirty troopers to destroy a railroad bridge on a nearby creek; they finished the work under enemy fire and joined the command at the Appomattox. Their guide had misled them, and they almost lost the first men and horses in deep water.

There was a squabble with ambulance drivers, who had pushed to the waterside.

"What the deuce are you doing here? Your place is in the rear!"

"We go in the rear when you advance," one of the drivers yelled, "but in front when you retreat."

Boykin lost patience. "So be it," he said, "in with you."

The wagons plunged into the difficult ford of the swift stream and only after a struggle did their horses scramble up the northern bank.

Dr. Claiborne was among the last to cross on the Farmville wagon bridge.

"As we reached the river there were . . . the Yankee prisoners who had been captured on the route. I judged that there were more than a thousand of them, and a sorry-looking set they were. A good many of them carried large pieces of meat, sides of middling, such as that I had just drawn as the last issue of rations to the Army of Northern Virginia."

Claiborne saw signs of the end:

"A short distance farther on they seemed to be lightening the load of headquarters wagons by destroying papers and letters. . . . Here, for the last time, I saw Dr. Lafayette Guild, General Lee's medical director, and Mrs. Guild, who was trying to make her escape with the army into friendly lines, and General Lee's carriage and horses, which I never saw him use, though I was told he did ride in the carriage once or twice during the retreat."

They now passed on a new road cut through pines by engineers, and the way was difficult.

"You'd better stay with us," Dr. Guild told Claiborne.

"I think I will, Doctor," Claiborne said—but in the next hours of confusion he became separated from the headquarters party, and went his own way. He did not see Guild again.

The army wound along the north bank of the Appomattox toward the west, followed by Federal troops in its rear and raced by a heavy blue infantry column on the opposite bank. Robert Lee watched the men pass near some coalpits north of Farmville; he was still an inspiration to the troops.

Thomas G. Jones, an Alabama officer, overheard an argument in his ranks:

"The Yanks gobbled up Ewell's corps somewhere back there yesterday," one man said.

There was an indignant reply, "Didn't you see Marse Robert when he rode by just now? Did he look like Ewell's folks had been captured?"

As Robert Lee neared the coalpits, Federal cavalry broke through, and infantry from Bryan Grimes' division helped to beat off the attack.

William Owen of the New Orleans artillery sketched the climax:

"Our column was moving through an old field parallel to the road, bullets began to whistle around our ears, and presently the Laurel Brigade of our cavalry appeared on our flank, crying, 'They're coming! They're coming!' "

Owen gave immediate orders to the gunners: " 'Tention! Fire to the left, in battery!" The guns were wheeled, horses led off, and the battery was ready to fire when bluecoat cavalry came over a hill.

"With shell cut for close range, and canister, our twelve guns were let loose, and such a scattering I never saw before."

A file of infantry ran toward the Federals, and Owen went out with his saber to lead it, but General Walker, who was with his troops, yelled, "Gentlemen! I'll lead my men myself!"

Walker's troops returned with a captive Federal cavalry general, John Gregg. William Owen noted that the officer looked "quite chagrined."

"He said he thought he would have had an easy time of it destroying our moving trains, and had not expected to run into the jaws of a whole park of artillery."

The repulse kept the enemy from the road where Robert Lee and his staff were riding. Captain J. C. Gorman of a North Carolina regiment saw:

"As Grimes' division entered the road, they met General Lee and his staff. He stopped, took off his hat and saluted them for the lesson they had just given the pursuers, and he received in return a rousing yell that demonstrated plainly that it mattered not how the balance of the army felt, there was the same old mettle in that division still."

William Owen left the scene on a pleasant errand. Two companions beckoned him into the bushes, produced a canteen of "medical supplies," and gave him a long, heartening swallow to provide strength for the road.

Robert Lee saw his son Rooney as cavalry passed after the skirmish, and stopped to congratulate him. He had a cheery voice, but John Esten Cooke took note of the fact that the commander mentioned the possibility of surrender for the first time:

"Keep your command together and in good spirits," the commander told his son. "Don't let them think of surrender. I will get you out of this."

At Cumberland Church, north of the coalpits, Lee ordered Mahone's infantry into line. John Gordon now approached with his survivors and turned through a woodland to join Mahone's flank. The roads near the site of this stand were enough to convince veterans that the army must soon succumb. Francis Lawley, a British correspondent, sketched it:

> Every mud-hole and every rise in the road choked with blazing wagons—the air filled with the deafening reports of ammunition exploding and shells bursting when touched by the flames, dense columns of smoke ascending to heaven from the burning and exploding vehicles, exhausted men, worn-out mules and horses, lying down side by side—gaunt Famine glaring hopelessly from sunken, lacklustre eyes— dead mules, dead horses, dead men everywhere.

Yet the army rallied once more, near dusk, when the enemy came on. E. M. Boykin rode with his troopers to the sound of firing, past a line of infantry—all that remained of the famous Texas Brigade, now only 130 men. These infantrymen yelped to the Carolina horsemen:

"Forward, boys! Tell 'em by God Texas is coming!"

The cavalrymen fought briefly with muzzle-loading muskets, in an effort to screen passing infantry, but at sundown rode into an open field; firing still went on near them. Boykin wrote:

"It had been a tiresome day, and though not an admirer of strong drink, I fell back upon and fully appreciated the contents of my canteen—the famous apple brandy of Amelia Springs."

Lee had watched the action from a knoll, using field glasses. A staff officer who rode across the open to take him a message got a stern reprimand:

"You came up the wrong side of the hill. You must not expose yourself unnecessarily."

"I would be ashamed to take shelter when you are so exposed," the young man said.

There was tartness in Lee's reply: "It is my duty to be here. I must see. Go back the way I told you, sir."

The 54th North Carolina Infantry, who found the commander on their front during the skirmish, had to restrain him as he tried to lead a charge. The soldiers took Traveller's rein and one of them shouted, "No, no, but if you'll go back, we'll do the work."

At the end of the dusk fighting, the bluecoats fell back from Cumberland Church, but Lee's retreat had been slowed. Longstreet's men had been called back to help in the defense. There were more than 300 new prisoners in the hungry horde traveling with the column, and these would also encumber the flight.

Lee went, after dark, to a cottage near Cumberland Church, in Longstreet's lines. They were close to the rear now, with the wagon trains and other corps marching westward ahead of them. Gordon had been relieved of his rear-guard duty.

At 9 P.M. a Federal with a flag of truce appeared in Longstreet's front. Captain James W. English, who was in charge of the picket line in this sector, reported the flag to division headquarters. Colonel Herman H. Perry was sent to investigate. He walked out cautiously, buckling on a revolver and saber.

The moon was rising as Perry emerged into an open field, stepping around enemy dead and wounded. He halted about fifty yards beyond his picket line and called:

"Flag of truce! Here!"

Someone shouted from the dark woodland. A Federal officer approached.

"My worn Confederate uniform and slouched hat, even in the dim light, would not compare favorably with his magnificence," Perry said. "But as I am six feet high I drew myself up as proudly as I could and put on the appearance of being perfectly satisfied with my personal exterior."

The Federal spoke first.

"I'm General Seth Williams, of Grant's staff."

Perry introduced himself, and Williams pulled a silver flask from his pocket.

"I hope you won't think it an unsoldierly courtesy for me to offer you some very fine brandy."

Perry wrote: "I wanted that drink awfully. Worn down, hungry and dispirited, it would have been a gracious Godsend if some old Confederate and I could have emptied that flask between us. But I raised myself about an inch higher, if possible, bowed and refused politely, trying to produce the ridiculous appearance of having feasted on champagne and pound cake not ten minutes before, and that I had not the slightest use for as plebeian a drink as fine brandy."

Williams pocketed the flask with a courteous murmur, for which Perry was thankful: "If he had taken a drink, and my Confederate olfactories had obtained a whiff, it is possible that I should have caved. The truth is, I had not eaten two ounces in two days, and I had my coattail then full of corn, waiting to parch it as soon as an opportunity might present itself."

"I have been sent up to receive any communication offered," Perry said. "I can't properly accept or offer courtesies."

Williams handed him a letter.

"This is from General Grant to General Lee," he said. "General Lee should have it immediately, if possible."

"Is that the only business between us?"

"It is, sir."

The two officers bowed and went back toward their lines, but Williams called after Perry, and asked him to come back and meet another officer. A colonel appeared and handed Perry a number of captured papers, letters and pictures from General Mahone's family, to be given to the general.

The officers also agreed to exchange a few wounded men now lying on this front, and as he went back into the Confederate lines Perry sent Captain English and a squad of men to carry some of the casualties to the enemy.

Within twenty minutes after Perry reached division headquarters a courier was riding toward General Lee's cottage near Cumberland Church with the letter from Grant.

Longstreet's infantry was moving westward again, when, at about nine thirty, Robert Lee opened the dispatch:

Headquarters Armies of the United States
April 7, 1865—5 P.M.

General R. E. Lee,
    Commanding C.S. Army:

General: The results of the last week must convince you of
the hopelessness of further resistance on the part of the Army
of Northern Virginia in this struggle. I feel that it is so, and
regard it as my duty to shift from myself the responsibility of
any further effusion of blood, by asking of you the surrender
of that portion of the C.S. Army known as the Army of
Northern Virginia.

Very respectfully, your obedient servant,
U. S. Grant,
Lieutenant-General
Commanding Armies of the United States

Lee read the sheet and passed it to Longstreet without a
word. Old Pete looked for a long moment and handed it back.
"Not yet," he said.

Lee scratched out a reply by candlelight in the cottage:

7th Apl '65

Genl
    I have recd your note of this date. Though not enter-
taining the opinion you express of the hopelessness of further resistance on the part of the Army of N. Va.—I recipro-
cate your desire to avoid useless effusion of blood, & therefore before considering your proposition, ask the terms you
will offer on condition of surrender.

Very respy your obt. Servt
R. E. Lee
Genl

Lt. Genl U. S. Grant
Commd Armies of the U States

By 10 P.M. General Seth Williams, waiting in the moonlight,
had the reply, and was on his way back to Grant's headquarters.

Longstreet had no need to ask what Lee's decision had been,
since orders for the night meant continued retreat, and battle if
necessary.

During the late afternoon half-a-dozen of Lee's generals had held a private council. Three courses had been debated:

1. To disband and permit the troops to escape to some distant rendezvous as best they could.

2. To abandon all wagons, concentrate the army, and cut a way through Grant's lines.

3. To surrender immediately.

Surrender, the generals decided, was the only way out. To disband the army would complete the ruin of the countryside and scatter the fighting force beyond reclamation; there could be no resistance, either, without the wagons. The officers thought they should help General Lee shoulder the moral burden of surrender, and chose a representative to advise him of their decision.

They picked General W. N. Pendleton, the chief of artillery, a West Point trained officer who had been a prewar Episcopal rector.

General Pendleton sought Lee in vain during the night march.

Longstreet left a record of the movement in these hours:

"Broken down caissons and wagons abandoned and sometimes not even pulled out of the road before they were fired. . . . One of my battery commanders reported his horses too weak to haul his guns. He was ordered to bury the guns and cover their burial-place with old leaves and brushwood."

★ PURSUIT ★

WHEN GRANT learned of Sheridan's victory, about midnight, he gave new orders for the chase of Lee:

General Griffin's infantry would hurry to Prince Edward Courthouse, a village seven miles south of Farmville, to close the way to Danville. A cavalry column, led by General MacKenzie, would strike for the same spot. The bulk of the infantry would follow Lee's two routes into Farmville.

Grant had just finished an interesting conversation in his Burkeville headquarters with a Dr. Smith, an old Army surgeon who had resigned at the outbreak of war. Smith was related to Dick Ewell, the captured Confederate.

"Ewell told me during the winter that the Confederacy was lost," Smith said. "He has thought all this while that Lee should ask for peace."

Grant listened intently.

The night was very dark in the early hours. Federal troops found their march the most difficult of the week, but as they began, toward dawn, to find squads of unarmed Confederates waiting to surrender, the blue infantry took heart. One veteran wrote:

"Men were singing, laughing, joking, and apparently happy. Along the road were evidences of the rapid retreat of the enemy, all sorts of ammunition strewn around loose, dead horses, and here and there a dead soldier."

A marcher in Humphreys' 2nd Corps remembered: "We began to come upon whole parks of wagons, burned as they stood, artillery ammunition scattered at the roadside, and caissons partially destroyed."

Grant and his staff left Burkeville at 7 A.M., riding swiftly on the main road toward Farmville. Horace Porter watched as the army caught sight of its chief:

"The columns were crowding the roads and the men, aroused to still greater efforts by the inspiring news of the day before, were sweeping along despite the rain that fell, like trained pedestrians on a walking track. As the general rode among them he was greeted with shouts and hurrahs on all sides, and a string of sly remarks, which showed how familiar swords and bayonets become when victory furnishes the topic of their talk."

Grant overtook Wright's corps, whose troops also cheered. Warren Keifer, one of Grant's generals, at first thought the commander was wearing a tarpaulin suit:

"He was even to his whiskers so bespattered with mud, fresh and dried, as to almost prevent recognition. He then, as always, was quiet, modest, and undemonstrative. A close look showed an expression of deep anxiety."

It was not long after noon when Grant entered Farmville, just as the Confederate cavalry trotted from the town; the bridges at the far edge of the village still burned. The commander made headquarters at the Farmville Hotel, a rambling building with a broad porch, where a swarm of couriers and aides clustered about.

General Crook reported his cavalry fighting against heavy odds north of the river, and Horace Porter was sent to see what was needed there. Porter found General Humphreys' corps also on the far bank, cut off from the rest of the army. On Porter's return, Grant hurried Wright's men as reinforcements.

General Wright was delayed while his engineers rebuilt the burned railroad bridge, and came to headquarters. He reported a conversation with Ewell of the night before:

"Ewell said they were lost as soon as they crossed the James, and that it was Lee's duty to negotiate then, while they could still demand concessions."

"Yes," Grant said. "I talked about that with Dr. Smith last night."

The commander held a private conference with Wright, Ord and Gibbon, and afterward dictated his first dispatch to Robert Lee. By then, or soon thereafter, he had opened an insistent message from President Lincoln, urging that things be brought to a head.

Grant handed his note to General Seth Williams, his adjutant general. "Take it to Humphreys' front. He's closest to the Rebel rear. Have it sent into their lines. I'll stay here tonight."

Williams was off on a long ride. He was forced to go the four or five miles downstream to High Bridge, cross the river, and then turn westward again. It was dark before he was well started on his way.

Phil Sheridan had started early for the open country. He led the divisions of Custer and Merritt through morning showers toward Prince Edward Courthouse, but had sent Crook with his division toward High Bridge. Morris Schaff sketched Crook: "An open-faced blue-eyed man with a splaying tawny beard and an aquiline nose." He was also an aggressive field officer; this morning, when he reached High Bridge and found it burning, with the 2nd Corps fighting the flames, Crook hurried his men forward, seeking action with the main body of the enemy.

Sheridan veered across country toward his objective. As Custer's division passed a band of Confederate prisoners, there was a reunion.

Custer recognized Kershaw and Huger, his Rebel guests of the night before and lifted his hat to them. Kershaw lifted his in return and yelled: "There goes a chivalrous fellow. Let's give him three cheers." Custer responded to this by turning to a regimental band with a signal, and the blue column of troopers wound away to close the trap on Robert Lee with the musicians blaring "The Bonnie Blue Flag." A chorus of Rebel Yells followed it.

By 3 P.M. Sheridan was at Prince Edward Courthouse, a settlement of three or four stores and thirty houses. The winding road had led them twenty miles during the day.

Sheridan went to the porch of a village house to study his maps and had an adventure with a Confederate patriot, an old man who was ensconced in a rocker on the porch. The host wore long gray hair behind his ears, tumbling to his collar, an old-fashioned swallow-tailed coat, a brown linen vest, nankeen trousers and red morocco slippers. A starched cambric frill circled his neck. He bowed to Sheridan, who gave him a nod.

"Any of Lee's troops passed here?"

"Sir," the old man said, "as I can truly say none has been seen by me, I will say so. But if I had seen any I should feel it my duty to refuse to reply to your question. I cannot give information which might harm General Lee."

"How far is it to Buffalo River?" Sheridan asked.

"I don't know."

"The devil you don't. How long have you lived here?"

"All my life."

"Very well, sir. It's time you did know."

Sheridan called an officer, "Captain, turn this gentleman over to the guard, and when we move, walk him down to Buffalo River and show it to him."

Sheridan turned to a Negro boy and completed his questioning. He then led a force of the troopers to Prospect Station, west of Farmville, and by sundown got word from a scout that excited him: A string of railroad cars was at Appomattox Station, full of Confederate supplies. Sheridan advised Grant.

Grant replied at 7 P.M., and sent Colonel Newhall across country with the dispatch: Sheridan would drive for Appomattox Station. He had already sent Lee a note, urging surrender. The 5th Corps, now going into camp at Prince Edward, would be put on the road to Appomattox immediately; the 24th Corps would leave from Farmville.

Sheridan scoffed to Newhall at mention of the note from Grant to Lee. The cavalryman thought the Confederates would march on until they were cornered.

The main body of Federal infantry had a full day. Humphreys had the 2nd Corps on the road at 5:30 A.M. going along the Appomattox River, taking roads which seemed to have been used by the largest bodies of Rebels. Even General Meade, kept to his ambulance by illness, was moving by eight o'clock. The observant Colonel Lyman took careful note of the enemy's trail near Sayler's Creek:

"The way was completely strewed with tents, ammunition, officers' baggage, and, above all, little Dutch ovens—such a riches of little Dutch ovens never was seen! I suppose they bake hoecakes in them. You saw them lying about, with their little legs kicked up in the air, in a piteous manner. . . . Wagons, ambulances, cannon filled the hollow near the bridge. This hillside was white with Adjutant-General's papers; here and there lay a wounded Rebel, while everywhere lay broken boxes, trunks, ammunition cases and barrels. It was strange to see the marks on the wagons, denoting the various brigades, once so redoubtable."

The head of Humphreys' column reached High Bridge long before Meade rolled into sight. The lead regiment was the 19th Maine, woodsmen who had won a fearsome reputation for fighting in The Wilderness. The Maine men rushed the bridge, put out the flames started by the Rebels, and set a line of riflemen to hold off the enemy rear guard.

Colonel Lyman could hardly believe his eyes when he came in sight of this bridge:

"Nothing can more surprise one than a sudden view of this viaduct, in a country like Virginia, where public works are almost unknown. It is a railway bridge, nearly 2500 feet long, over the valley of the Appomattox, and is supported by great brick piers, of which the central ones are about 140 feet high. The river itself is very narrow, perhaps 75 feet wide, but it runs in a fertile valley, a mile in width, part of which is subject to overflow."

Bluecoats streamed over the wagon bridge below High Bridge at 9 A.M. and moved on both banks of the river in pursuit of the Rebels. Humphreys stumbled onto the Confederates in battle order on a long, open slope north of Farmville, about 2 P.M. and, after a flank attack was beaten back, called on Grant for help. There was a long delay.

Crook's cavalry forded the stream and attacked what seemed to be a helpless wagon train, but was driven back with losses, among them a promising young commander, John Gregg.

Infantry fighting broke out at dusk around Cumberland Church, where Humphreys had sent in a crack division under General Miles. The fight was brief, but heavy. Veterans who heard the roar of it knew that the bulk of Lee's infantry was close at hand.

Officers at Grant's headquarters in Farmville found the commander's calm maddening. When General Wright came to explain excitedly that he could not yet cross the river over the ruined railroad bridge, and that Gregg's cavalry was being whipped, Grant replied, "The cavalry are doing very well. I'm hoping General Lee will continue to fight them. Every hour's delay lessens his chance of escape."

When he had reports of Gregg's losses, however, he ordered the troopers to recross to the south bank, and the action was ended. Now, when it was almost dark, General Wright took his infantry over the Appomattox, the men walking to the north bank in single file over the rebuilt bridge.

Horace Porter watched men of this corps in Farmville as they moved:

"Notwithstanding the long march that day men sprang to

their feet with a spirit that made everyone marvel at their pluck, and came swinging down the main street of the village with a step that seemed as elastic as on the first day of their toilsome tramp."

These men caught sight of Grant on the porch of the hotel and there followed what Porter thought the most dramatic scene of the campaign:

"Bonfires were lighted at the sides of the street. Men seized straw and pine knots and improvized torches. Cheers arose from throats already hoarse with shouts of victory. Bands played, banners waved, arms were tossed high in the air and caught again. The night march had become a grand review with General Grant as the reviewing officer."

Someone began singing "John Brown's Body" and the whole corps took it up, making the streets ring.

Grant went in to the hotel and asked for a place to sleep. He was shown a room. "General Lee slept here last night," a man told him. The commander disappeared without comment.

It was after midnight when Seth Williams returned to him, tapping at the door, offering the reply of Robert Lee to his call for surrender.

★ THE LINCOLNS ★

The Navy took Mary Lincoln and her party into Richmond in the morning. Count de Chambrun went along, but seemed little impressed by the city. He noticed only the Confederate White House, now occupied by General Weitzel, and the Hall of the Rebel Congress.

Senator Sumner picked up a souvenir—a gavel from one of the houses of the Congress, which he took off as a gift for Secretary of War Edwin Stanton.

Elizabeth Keckley accompanied Mrs. Lincoln, and was the most appreciative sightseer of the party. She took note of papers strewn about the Confederate Senate chamber, and looked at them closely enough to find a copy of a law forbidding freed slaves to enter Virginia. She also saw "ladies scowling darkly" when the party entered the Confederate White House. Everything pleased Elizabeth, who thought it a "delightful visit."

Below them, at City Point, Lincoln spent the morning at the telegraph office. By eight thirty he had passed on to Stanton in Washington the good news from Sheridan, ticking off the names of Confederate generals captured at Sayler's Creek.

At 11 A.M. his impatience for victory appeared in an official dispatch to Grant:

> Gen. Sheridan says "If the thing is pressed I think that Lee will surrender." Let the *thing* be pressed.

The Presidential party dined on the *River Queen* after dark, amid the lights of the fleet. A young officer of the Sanitary Commission, who sat near Mary Lincoln, attempted conversation.

"Mrs. Lincoln, you should have seen the President on his triumphal entry into Richmond. He was the cynosure of all eyes. The ladies kissed their hands to him, and waved handkerchiefs. He's quite a hero when surrounded by pretty ladies."

Mary Lincoln glared. "Your familiarity is offensive to me, young man."

She erupted into one of the tantrums which had become familiar to headquarters officers during the war. The young Sanitary Commission officer flushed with embarrassment at the display of jealous temper he had so innocently set off.

Elizabeth Keckley wrote: "Quite a scene followed."

★ RICHMOND ★

THE WAR CLERK, John B. Jones, went exploring into the burned section of the city despite the light showers. He peered down into the "awful crater" of the magazine, where powder and shells had blown up.

He found that a veritable stream of fire and flying bricks

had knocked down the wall of the adjoining cemetery, and stones, bricks and other debris lay everywhere. Gravestones had been knocked down and broken, and trees and shrubs demolished.

Jones picked up threads of the day's gossip:

The few men in Richmond talked covertly of Judge Campbell and his visit of Wednesday to Lincoln on the Federal warship. Some said that they had negotiated terms for peace, and that affairs would soon be settled, with Virginia rejoining the Union.

There was scornful talk of Ira Smith, the owner of the *Whig*, who was now known to Jones and his friends as a tailor first and a newspaper publisher second, since he had continued the journal as "a Union paper."

There was a more serious matter:

> Negotiations are in progress by the clergymen, who are directed to open the churches on Sunday, and it was intimated to the Episcopalians that they should pray for the President of the United States. To this they demur, being ordered by the Convention to pray for the President of the Confederacy. They are willing to omit the prayer altogether, and await the decision of the military authority on that proposition.

★ PETERSBURG ★

CHARLES FRANCIS ADAMS and his Negro troopers of the 5th Massachusetts were among the first to occupy the scarred old battleground of the nine-month siege of Petersburg. The young historian had his picket line through both the Union and Confederate lines, with earthworks stretching out of sight on either hand. He wrote:

> It is a curious region of desolation. I have ridden all through it and it seems to have been swept with the besom of destruction. All landmarks are defaced, not only trees

and fences, but even the houses and roads. It is one broad
tract, far as the eye can reach, dotted here and there with
clumps of trees which mark the spot where some headquarters stood, and for the rest covered with a thick stubble
of stumps of the pine.

You ride through mile after mile of deserted huts, marking the encampments of armies, and over roads now leading
from nowhere, nowhither. Large houses are gone so that
even their foundations can no longer be discovered. Forts,
rifle pits and abattis spring up in every direction, and in
front of Petersburg the whole soil is actually burrowed and
furrowed beyond the power of words to describe. There it
all is, freshly deserted and as silent as death; but it will be
years and years before nature must bring forth new trees
and a new race of men must erect other habitations.

IX

Saturday, April 8

★

★ FLIGHT ★

GENERAL E. P. ALEXANDER, the Georgia gunner, found the pace too much for him in the hours after midnight:

"It was the third consecutive night of marching, and I was at last scarcely able to keep from falling off my horse for sleep. So, with my staff, I left the column and went a quarter of a mile, or more, off to our right through old broom grass and second growth pines, by cloudy moonlight, until we found a secluded nook by an old worm fence and there we all laid down and slept for three or four hours."

Alexander hid his staff well, to prevent the stealing of the horses, for he had seen thieves cut the bridles of mounts from the hands of dozing officers at the roadside.

When morning came, with bright sunshine and no sign of the enemy, many soldiers took heart. Alexander was not cheerful. He knew that the army was moving toward Appomattox Station, twenty-six miles west of Farmville, and that the enemy might cut across their trail. He described the watershed over which the column toiled: "A jug-shaped peninsula between the James River and the Appomattox—and there was but one outlet, the neck of the jug at Appomattox Court House, and to that General Grant had the shortest road."

The 7th South Carolina Cavalry was roused from two comfortable camps in succession, and at 10 P.M. Trooper Boykin and his companions were on the way once more.

Noncommissioned officers rode down the line, passing a handkerchief full of cartridges to each man. That began "the most weary night march that will always be remembered," Boykin thought. They plodded around wagons in the cruel road until dawn, when they caught up with their own wagon train, the first time they had seen it since Richmond. They were not expected. Boykin wrote:

"They were camped in a fine grove, with good fires and a glorious smell of cooking permeating the air. Our servants (never expecting to see us again, I suppose) were cooking on a large scale from our private stores for half a dozen notorious wagon rats of the genteeler sort. Of course as we rode up our boys declared they expected us and were getting breakfast ready."

Boykin saw the longing glances of the discomfited stragglers at a pot of cooking rice as they left the place. The troopers had a big meal. Boykin said:

"Our breakfast and rest had so refreshed us, short as that rest was, that we resumed our march and the work before us cheerful and ready."

The road became wider, and the wagons now rolled two abreast. So far there was neither sight nor sound of the enemy. Near noon the 7th South Carolina stopped to water horses in a stream, and Boykin made an amusing error.

A Captain Allen of the 24th regiment of this brigade, a gray-bearded man of about sixty, bore a striking resemblance to Robert E. Lee. Boykin watered his horse in the stream, watching a rider approach on a gray horse.

It was Captain Allen, he thought, the perfect type of a veteran soldier. Boykin wrote:

"He got within a few feet of me when I changed my intended rather familiar, but still most respectful, salute, meant for the Captain, for the reverence with which the soldier salutes the standard of his legion—as I discovered that it was General R. E. Lee himself, riding alone, not even an orderly in attendance. He returned our salute, his eye taking it all in, with a calm smile, that assured us our confidence was not misplaced."

Boykin thought the commander bore his burdens lightly this day.

A few minutes later the trooper moved on with his regiment. At the foot of a hill they crossed the Appomattox River, here little more than a creek. Boykin noted with surprise that it was not knee-deep on his horse.

Even in the absence of the enemy there were signs of disintegration in the infantry ranks. Private H. M. Wharton, the sixteen-year-old soldier who had fallen asleep in the road near High Bridge, dropped from the column and shot an ox in a pasture. He hacked meat from the carcass with his pocket knife, and carried a raw chunk on his bayonet as he rejoined the march.

Corporal M. W. Venable of the 1st Engineers had a pass from his captain to visit his family, whose home was only four miles from High Bridge.

Venable got home at 2 A.M. and spent three hours there, leaving with a warning to his parents that the enemy were in the neighborhood. He took with him a full knapsack with a side of bacon and "about a peck of biscuits," and planned to treat the men of his mess to one last meal, but could not find his company again in the procession of stragglers. He met an engineer officer of his acquaintance and marched with him as a guard in headquarters train.

Only in the afternoon, when he arrived in the village of Appomattox Court House, did Venable remember that today was his eighteenth birthday.

In the late morning, enemy cavalry surprised a few men of the column at a crossroad, and in a brief fight took a handful of prisoners and left some casualties. The skirmish was heard only by marchers near the spot.

One of the prisoners was Private J. M. Finley, of Company C, 14th Alabama, who had dropped behind his regiment to get a few winks of sleep. He was roused by sounds of fighting, and as he got to his feet was surrounded by Federal troopers. A bluecoat chased him along a fence, snatched his gun and shouted, "If you don't keep up with my horse I'll kill you."

Finley managed to keep up, though the cavalryman kept his horse at a gallop, and after a little while the Federal halted. "Give me your money, or I'll blow you through."

Finley gave him all he had, $7 in Confederate. The bluecoat also robbed two nearby Confederates and marched the trio before him. When they came to a Federal skirmish line one of the enemy called to the prisoners:

"You're lucky to get out of it. He's the meanest bastard in the army, the worst man we've got. He robs all his prisoners and kills most."

Finley did not learn the identity of his captors but remembered that they treated him kindly, once he was rescued from the robber.

Somewhere nearby, a line of Federals ran down a lean North Carolina private who had strayed, seeking food. "Surrender!" they yelled to him. "We've got you."

"Yes," the Tar Heel said, "and a hell of a git you got."

Young Percy Hawes, the courier, saw that the enemy attack only stiffened the resistance of those who remained in the column.

A friend spoke quietly to Hawes, "You can go back to the staff if you like, but you go without me. I'm going home. I think the game's up, and I don't intend to be captured or killed if I can help it."

Federal cavalry charged into the road at that moment, and the boy who had planned to desert began firing with his captured carbine, helping to drive off the enemy.

Hawes wrote: "His spirits seemed to be revived, and I never heard anything more about his deserting."

General Pendleton rode up and down the column, discussing with commanders the delicate matter of proposing surrender to General Lee. He found E. P. Alexander and John Gordon in agreement with the verdict of last night's council; surrender seemed to be inevitable.

When Pendleton took the problem to Longstreet, he got the fierce reaction of a disciplined old soldier.

"I've been asked to tell General Lee about the council we had last night—we decided there's nothing left but to surrender. We think it's wrong to have men killed on either side now, and we don't feel that General Lee should be left to bear the burden of initiating the idea."

Old Pete said, "Don't you know that the Articles of War provide that officers or soldiers asking commanders to surrender should be shot?"

"I think it's my duty to take their thoughts to General Lee," Pendleton said.

"If General Lee doesn't know when to surrender until I tell him," Longstreet replied, "he'll never know."

In the end, as Pendleton recalled it, Longstreet became more agreeable, and said he thought he should be represented in the council when the idea was presented to Lee.

Pendleton had a vivid impression of his interview with Robert Lee:

"General Lee was lying alone, resting, at the base of a large pine tree. I approached and sat by him. To a statement of the case he quietly listened, courteously expressing thanks for the consideration of his subordinates in desiring to relieve him in part of existing burdens."

But of surrender Lee told Pendleton firmly, "I trust it has not come to that. We certainly have too many brave men to think of laying down our arms. They still fight with great spirit, whereas the enemy do not. And besides, if I were to intimate to General Grant that I would listen to terms, he would regard it such an evidence of weakness that he would demand unconditional surrender, and sooner than that I am resolved to die. We must all determine to die at our posts."

"We're perfectly willing for you to decide," Pendleton said. "Every man will cheerfully die with you."

After noon Lee sent out orders confirming his action of the night before: The army was reduced to two corps, with Longstreet and John Gordon in command. Since there were no longer troops for them, George Pickett, Bushrod Johnson and Richard Anderson were relieved of their commands. There was no mention of their roles at Sayler's Creek.

The commander got a report from his nephew, Fitz Lee, about 1 P.M. that deepened his anxiety: Only Federal infantry was in the rear of the column, coming on steadily. The cavalry, Fitz suspected, was racing far in advance, and the horseman wanted to go after them, leaving a small mounted rear guard with the main army. Squadrons began hurrying forward.

General Pendleton moved in the same direction, going up

to find General Lindsay Walker and his reserve artillery, which had been ranging ahead of the army for two days.

The afternoon dragged on in quiet.

Soldiers noted that the march became easier and swifter after noon, when they struck the improved road. Near darkness, when the head of the column reached Appomattox Court House, J. C. Gorman, the North Carolina captain, congratulated himself that the race was over, and that the army would reach Lynchburg in safety tomorrow, since the town was only twenty-four miles beyond.

He went into camp early, worn from nights of endless marching; he noted that many regiments had dwindled to mere skeletons: "One fact, a strange one, too, it appears to me, was that our higher officers did not try to prevent this straggling. They seemed to shut their eyes on the hourly reduction of their commands, and rode in advance of their brigades in dogged indifference."

Near the very front of the army rolled the buggy of Dr. Claiborne, now without a hospital train. There was nothing to halt him, and for hours there was no enemy in sight.

"There were increased signs of demoralization and disintegration all along the roads. Soldiers whom I knew had been soldiers of steadiness and courage were straggling and sleeping, unarmed and apparently unconcerned. I attributed it to fatigue and hunger and exhaustion. Officers of the line seemed to be doing the same thing—colonels, generals, even lieutenant generals. And I saw a member of the staff of one of Lee's most distinguished lieutenants throw himself on the ground and swear an oath that he would never draw his sword from his scabbard."

Claiborne also saw more small arms thrown aside, muskets stuck into the earth by bayonets. But, the doctor said, like thousands of others, he had not given a thought to surrender.

He rode for a long time with broken artillery sections, most of which were out of ammunition and under orders to march to Lynchburg. Claiborne met Colonel Henry Peyton, Lee's Inspector

General, who was placing some infantrymen in position on an open knoll. A few bluecoat riders sat a couple of hundred yards away, watching the road. Peyton had no more than 200 men to place.

"What command is this?" Claiborne asked.

Peyton's voice was slow: "That's what's left of the 1st Virginia, and that's the only guard for the left flank of the Army of Northern Virginia."

"Does General Lee know how few soldiers are left, and to what extremities they're reduced?"

"I don't believe he does," Peyton said.

"Then whose business is it to tell him, if not his first inspector's?"

"I cannot," Peyton said. "I cannot."

Claiborne's confidence began to fail for the first time. He was choking with tears as he returned to his small party. "I can't see what further use we can be here. Let's push on. Maybe we can get to Johnston's army, or maybe beyond the Mississippi someone will fight on."

Thomas P. Devereux, of Grimes' Brigade, found a couple of ears of corn in the road in the morning, his first food in two days, except for a bit of bread he picked up in Farmville. His horse, Trumps, carried him faithfully, and though Devereux often fell asleep, he managed to keep up with the column.

Two men with the 45th North Carolina stirred his admiration: The Rev. E. H. Harding, its chaplain, marched today with a musket. He had picked up the gun at Sayler's Creek, had somehow escaped, and clung to the weapon, saying, "This is no time for noncombatants." The other was Colonel John R. Winston, who had got a head wound at Sayler's Creek to match one he carried from Fort Damnation, and now rode bareheaded in front of his regiment, his bandaged head making it impossible for him to wear a hat.

These North Carolina troops were halted for a few minutes at hourly intervals. Devereux wrote: "It seemed that every one was asleep before the bugle sound for the halt had ceased to reverberate, but at the command most of the men rose and staggered forward. Some (and who could blame them?) failed to respond to the call of duty, and we saw them no more."

The remnants of the artillery and the wagon train were just ahead, but Devereux could not see or hear them.

Young John L. G. Woods, the Georgia drummerboy, managed to escape the army's pickets and found a hospitable farmhouse. The family fed him well.

"Lee's army is surrounded," the farmer told him. "He's going to have to give up. You stay with us and I'll hide you from the Yanks. When it quiets down, you can go home. You could help me protect the house, too."

"I can't stay, thank you," Woods said. "I want to get to Joe Johnston's army if I can. If I can't, I'm going home."

Woods walked westward beyond Appomattox toward Lynchburg in a road with disorganized cavalry and other stragglers. At nightfall the drummer found a little herd of abandoned horses, took one of them, and rode to the camp of some cavalrymen, who invited him to their fire. He fell asleep.

The diary entry of the young Georgia infantryman, William Graham, left a clear picture of this sunny Saturday:

> Spent a writched night. The ground was as cold as a stone—and I awoke after a disturbed sleep stiff and sore in every joint. It will be a mercy if I escape a severe sickness. Breakfast time and nothing but raw meat to eat. Trade a piece of meat for a piece of bread of equal size. Also gave another piece for a cup of flour. 12 oclk . . . stop at a house to rest. Get my flour cooked—a very small thin cake. . . . Woman begged me for my pocket handkerchief. Inexorable no. Proceeded 3 or 4 miles further and night approaching we concluded to stop for the night and have a pot of soup made—which would at least satisfy hunger—but the woman's pot was in use and she (a negro woman) said she didn't know when it would be at our service—so we determined to go off the road and try to get something to eat.

Graham and three companions were directed to the home of a wealthy planter, John Davidson, three miles off the line of march. They hurried, hoping to arrive before other troops found the place, but found Confederate cavalry in the yard. "These men are ubiquitous," Graham wrote. "Go where you may in front or rear of the army and the cavalry either are or have been there."

The Georgians approached Davidson:

"Sir, can you give four hungry soldiers a piece of bread?"

"No."

"Well, can you give or sell us a little meal?"

"No."

"We understand you have brandy. Will you sell us a quart?"

"No."

"Can you give us a drink?"

"No."

Graham said, "It was on the end of my tongue to give the old dog a genteel blowing up," but he thought of the woman of the house and went to her. When she heard Graham's story, Mrs. Davidson brought food, and another soldier in the meantime persuaded her husband to part with a quart of brandy for $75. Graham wrote:

> So we all took a dram and before long we sit down to a plate of ash cake and sorghum syrup—a bountiful repast. I have some coffee which I have been saving for sickness. Thinking this a good opportunity I get it parched and ground.

The men went back on the road, and a mile or so beyond were invited to spend the night in a house. They declined and crawled into a hayloft, thinking it would be safer in case of a Yankee raid.

William Owen and the New Orleans artillery passed through the village of New Store, in Buckingham County, early in the day. They ate enough to keep them marching by pooling supplies. Some surgeons furnished coffee and sugar, and Owen and his friends cooked their meat. They marched all night without orders, with men falling asleep at each halt.

At a rest near New Store the battery commander's cook

reported the food all gone, and they took up the march without breakfast. A few minutes later, however, Owen saw an instance of official greed: "Riding to the front I was not a little surprised to see the Colonel and his Adjutant eating breakfast in a fence corner."

Owen finally got food for the morning from Colonel Edmund Pendleton of the 15th Louisiana, who shared his breakfast, and in addition gave Owen "three large slabs of desiccated vegetables for making soup." They went into camp on Rocky Run, only a mile from Appomattox.

In the enemy cavalry's brief attack during the day, Captain J. D. Cumming's battery lost a few men and two or three cannon. When the skirmish was over and the files were moving on, Cumming rode back to his men.

A braying laugh came from the quiet column, and the captain went to investigate.

"What do you mean by acting like this, and making so much noise?"

The private laughed again. "Oh, Captain," he said, "I'm so damned glad to be alive I've got to laugh."

Cumming could not quiet him, and rode back to the front. He wrote: "It seemed a very ludicrous thing."

Colonel Magnus Thompson, of the 35th Virginia Cavalry Battalion, found the scene in the army's wake distressing as he rode with the rear guard:

"The few men who still carried their muskets had hardly the appearance of soldiers—their clothes all tattered and covered with mud, their eyes sunken and lusterless, and their faces peaked and pinched from their ceaseless march through storm and sunshine without food or sleep. . . . Many of the men, from exhaustion, were lying prone upon the ground, only waiting for the enemy to come and pick them up, while at intervals horses and mules lying in the mud had struggled to extricate themselves until exhaustion had forced them to be still and wait for death to glaze their wildly staring eyes. And yet through all these scenes the remnant of that once invincible army still trudged on, with their faith still strong, only waiting for General Lee to say where they were to face about and fight."

At the extreme rear of the army was the 2nd Squadron, 35th Virginia Cavalry Battalion, under Captain Marcellus French. Colonel Elijah White had shaken him from his blanket before dawn to give him orders:

"Stay here until daylight, then take your boys along for rear guard. Captain Myers will be just ahead of you with the First Squadron. Watch the enemy."

French saw that the men changed once the march began: "We rode along silently, gloomily; not merrily, as was the custom of the cavalry. The jokers were hushed, the songsters and even the whistlers were silent."

They had been riding for three hours when they entered an open creek valley, where French fell behind with two men, Lieutenant C. A. James and Corporal Jimmy Terrell. The three watched a distant drama:

From a woodland a party of Federals rode with flags of truce and were fired upon. One man fell, and three others turned back, hesitantly. French saw that Captain Myers's men were shooting, evidently in ignorance of the fact that they had killed a man with a flag of truce. French wrote:

"The flag was found by the body of the dead man. The flags were too small to attract attention, not being larger than good-sized handkerchiefs, and they were not as white as new-fallen snow."

The surviving Federals saw French with his two men, and a bluecoat rode toward them, shouting, "Flag of truce!"

"Bring it over!" French yelled.

The Federal rider was pale.

"General Williams, of Grant's staff, has a dispatch for General Lee," the horseman said. "Your men have shot three of our orderlies this morning."

"Go tell Williams to stop the advance of his troops and bring the dispatch," French said.

The enemy infantry halted in plain sight, with men perching on fences like flocks of blue birds. Three horsemen approached, one of them carrying a white flag. The Federal officer was at first hostile.

"Captain, you've fired on my flag of truce and three men have been shot trying to deliver it."

"That's the first and only flag of truce I've seen today," French said. "And I haven't fired on that."

The Federal's manner changed and he spoke "in a most gentlemanly way":

"I'm General Seth Williams from Grant's staff, and I have a second letter from Grant to Lee. Can you deliver it?"

"I can get it to my division commander, General Rosser."

"That will do." Williams took a letter from his coat and handed it to French. He then produced a flask, and smiled: "Here's some very fine brandy cocktail from Grant's headquarters. Have a drink, Captain."

French and Lieutenant James each drank a small cup of the liquor, "without etiquette or ceremony."

The Federal orderly paid no attention to the third thirsty Confederate, Corporal Terrell. French wrote:

"Without noticing Terrell, who was near him, the man returned the flask to his haversack. To Terrell the snubbing was of small consequence in comparison to the deprivation of such a select drink, over the loss of which he was inconsolable. . . . He commented on Yankee manners. He did not understand that the intercourse between officers and enlisted men in the Union army was very different from that to which he had been accustomed."

The Federal orderly passed the flag of truce to Terrell, and the party galloped in the path of the Confederate infantry, taking the dispatch on its way to General Lee.

The sun set before six thirty, and Robert Lee halted with his staff in a woodland just east of Appomattox Court House. In the new darkness men saw ominous reflections in the clouds, a ring of the campfires of the enemy, closed about them on every side but the north.

A second message from Grant had come through Mahone's lines, and Lee opened it in the early night, with Colonel Venable peering over his shoulder by the light of a candle:

April 8, 1865

General R. E. Lee
Commanding C.S.A.

Your note of last evening in reply to mine of same date, asking the condition on which I will accept the surrender of the Army of Northern Virginia is received. In reply I would say that, peace being my great desire, there is but one condition I would insist upon, namely: that the men and officers surrendered shall be disqualified for taking up arms again against the Government of the United States until properly exchanged. I will meet you, or will designate officers to meet any officers you may name for the same purpose, at any point agreeable to you, for the purpose of arranging definitely the terms upon which the surrender of the Army of Northern Virginia will be received.

U. S. Grant
Lieutenant General

"How would you answer that?" Lee asked.
"I would answer no such letter," Venable said.
"Ah, but it must be answered."
The commander dictated a reply:

8th Apl '65

Genl

I recd at a late hour your note of today. In mine of yesterday I did not intend to propose the surrender of the Army of N. Va.—but to ask the terms of your proposition. To be frank, I do not think the emergency has arisen to call for the surrender of this army, but as the restoration of peace should be the sole object of all, I desired to know whether your proposals would lead to that and I cannot therefore meet you with a view to surrender the Army of N. Va.—but as far as your proposal may affect the C. S. forces under my command & tend to the restoration of peace, I shall be pleased to meet you at 10 A.M. tomorrow on the old stage road to Richmond between the picket lines of the two armies.

Very respy your Obt. Servt.

R. E. Lee

Genl

Lt. Genl U. S. Grant
Commd Armies of the U.S.

Lee held a council of war soon afterward. John Gordon described it:

"It met in the woods at his headquarters, and by a low-burning bivouac fire. There was no tent there, no table, no chairs, and no camp-stools. On blankets spread upon the ground or on saddles at the roots of the trees, we sat around the great commander."

Gordon thought that a painter might do justice to the scene, but that no writer could catch the anguished expressions of the generals as they sought signs of reassurance in Lee's haggard face.

Pendleton, Fitz Lee and Longstreet were there, and a number of staff officers whom Gordon took no trouble to remember. Lee told them of the exchange of notes with Grant, and the officers fell into a discussion of the fate of the Southern people in the event of surrender.

Some officers urged forcing a way through the Federal lines, so that part of the army could carry on guerrilla warfare until Washington wearied of the struggle.

Gordon kept a close watch on Lee: "We knew by our own aching hearts that his was breaking. Yet he commanded himself, and stood calmly facing and discussing the long-dreaded inevitable."

The council ended with a desperate decision: The army would disregard the surrender notes and make an effort to break through beyond Appomattox Court House. Fitz Lee's cavalrymen would lead the way, and Gordon's infantry, only 4000 strong, would hold the route open. Longstreet's rear guard would follow.

Gordon left them, but sent a staff officer back with a question for General Lee: "General Gordon wants to know if you have any orders as to where he should halt tomorrow night."

Lee was still able to summon a smile. "Yes," he said. "Tell him that I'd be glad for him to halt just beyond the Tennessee line."

That was more than 200 miles beyond. Gordon interpreted Lee's joke to mean that there was little chance of breaking through the Federal army, and that if he did escape, his campsite was of little moment.

At headquarters, Fitz Lee made a final request of his uncle:

"Before there's a surrender, will you notify me? I want to take my men to unite with Johnston in North Carolina, and fight on."

"All right," Lee said.

The conference ended about midnight.

The Tar Heel soldier, Captain Gorman, got a glimpse of the session:

"The general officers were consulting together, and their looks plainly indicated a depressed state of feeling; besides, before we had completed our meal the rumbling of distant cannonading sounded warningly in front, and I closed my eyes and went to sleep to its music."

Gorman and his men had gone into camp to a remarkable accompaniment—the regimental bands on every side played favorite tunes, and cheering troops hailed them as usual. Gorman wrote:

"The old spirit seemed to be returning. As for myself, I had emptied my haversack . . . and wrapped my blanket around me, and was in sound slumber before darkness set in, intending to have one more good nap sure, as I did not exactly like the look of things."

One of the day's strange moments was noted by Lee's staff officers sometime before the commander retired, when Robert Lee glimpsed George Pickett passing in the army's swarm and stared after him and said, as if to himself:

"I thought that man was no longer with this army."

From the tone of his voice, he might have been speaking of a stranger.

Most of the troops went to sleep in ignorance of affairs at the front. Near dusk the enemy fell upon an unsuspecting band of artillerymen, quartermasters and surgeons at Appomattox Station, some four miles southwest of the courthouse village. In its state of exhaustion the army's vanguard gave little heed to the cannon fire ahead.

Lieutenant J. F. J. Caldwell had camped with McGowan's Brigade four or five miles east of the courthouse, but in the late afternoon rode into the village:

"The confusion exceeded anything I had ever witnessed in the army. Wagons and artillery were crowded on either side of the road, and struggling cavalry and infantry either thronged about or wandered loosely over the fields. We lay in a basin surrounded by a wide circle of hills and the country was generally cleared on each side. . . .

"Despite the disorganization of troops there was little movement or noise of any description. A horrible calm brooded over us, only intensified by the living figures around us. . . . Troops were moving up constantly, their faces haggard."

A little band of about 250 men came to the rear of McGowan's Brigade.

"What regiment's that?" a Carolinian yelled.

An officer gave him a wry smile. "It's Kershaw's division," he said.

Caldwell noted that one brigade in his corps numbered only eight men.

As the sun went down the silence was broken by a roar of guns on the railroad. Caldwell misinterpreted it: "It was rambling fire, vague, purposeless."

Dr. Claiborne and his party halted near the courthouse in the late afternoon, but when he heard that a wagon train full of wounded men was at the depot, Claiborne went there. The doctor helped several more wounded men into the wagons and watched the caravan of casualties pull away to the west.

Claiborne's party, including Drs. Field and Smith and the faithful Moravian wagoner, Burkhardt, rode back toward the courthouse, passing on the way some artillerymen making camp.

The doctor dismounted with his party, fed his mare some captured fodder and lay with his head on his saddle, quickly asleep. He had no more than dozed off when firing woke him, and Burkhardt was shaking his shoulder:

"Doctor, the Yankees be upon thee!"

Claiborne saw the other two doctors disappearing through a forest of scrub blackjack oaks, and Burkhardt running in the road toward Lynchburg, his horse still hitched to a tree behind him. From the direction of the depot a band of Federal cavalry charged in, yelling. Claiborne had no time to mount; he snatched a shawl, climbed a fence and retreated into the oaks, where he hid, listening to "a pretty smart firing" of carbines and artillery, a Rebel Yell, a scurrying retreat of horsemen, then more irregular firing, as if the skirmishers had scattered.

Claiborne and a few others made beds in piles of leaves in a fence corner: "We concluded that, ignorant as we were of the topography of the country and the relative positions of the contending forces, we had better remain still until daylight."

General Lindsay Walker's artillery had reached the depot about 4 P.M. and gone carelessly into camp. There was no need to post pickets, since the enemy was known to be following in the rear of the army, many miles behind. No one anticipated a blow from the front after the quiet march of the day.

As soon as they halted, men began to wash themselves and prepare for cooking. There were sixty cannon from three batteries at the depot: The Washington Artillery of New Orleans; the Donaldsonville Cannoneers, made up of Louisiana Creoles; and a Virginia battery detached from the 7th South Carolina cavalry.

General Pendleton, the artillery chief, rode up on his tour of inspection and climbed down from his horse. He was talking with General Walker, who was in the process of shaving, when a bugle call sounded charge and Federal troopers galloped into the roadside camp, firing carbines. Walker coolly put into line the men of two batteries whose guns had been abandoned; they fell in across the road with muskets. The general went through the woods shouting comically from his still-lathered face, giving orders until the big guns began firing. Fighting became confused. General Pendleton, who fled back toward the courthouse, narrowly escaped capture by a Federal squadron.

Major W. M. Owen of the New Orleans battery was in camp a few hundred yards to the rear of General Walker, and saw the fighting erupt:

"Long trains of wagons came tearing down the road from the front, their drivers whipping up their mules and shouting lustily. I mounted my horse and rode forward to see what was the matter."

Owen passed the artillerymen fighting with muskets, and in the woods came upon men of his own battery digging holes in which to bury their guns, while others chopped down wheels, destroyed carriages, and prepared to ride away westward, fleeing both armies to avoid what seemed certain capture.

Trooper E. M. Boykin and Gary's Brigade were in the midst of this fighting almost from the start. He had been in a woodland just west of the courthouse near sunset, watching the regiment's foragers come in with hay and fodder on their saddles, when a shell burst near the railroad station, followed by general firing. An officer galloped out of the road, shouting to the 7th South Carolina:

"The enemy are down yonder! Are you going to stand here and let them cut us up?"

The regiment fell into column and hurried down the road; the officer still shouted behind them. In the first gray of twilight, their vision dimmed by the early-rising moon, the Carolina horsemen rode into carbine fire. They dismounted and pushed through woods to the batteries, and into hand-to-hand fighting.

Some guns were lost, and bluecoats dragged them away; at other points knots of the enemy were blown apart by blasts of the big guns. Boykin was on the spot:

"Then began one of the closest artillery fights, for the numbers engaged, during the war. The guns were fought literally up to the muzzles. It was dark by this time, and at every discharge the cannon were ablaze from touchhole to mouth, and there must have been six or eight pieces at work, and the small arms of some 300 or 400 men packed in among the guns. It seemed like the very jaws of the lower regions.

"They made three distinct charges, preluding always with the bugle, on the right, left and center, confusing the point of attack. Then, with a cheer, up they came. It was too dark to see anything under the shadow of the trees but a long dark line. They would get within 30 or 40 yards of the guns and then roll back. Amid the flashing and the roaring and the shouting rose the wild yell of a railroad whistle, as a train rushed almost among us, as we were fighting around the depot, sounding on the night air as if the devil himself had just come up and was about to join in what was going on."

There was a lull in the fighting, and General Gary sent an officer to gather the horses, left behind in the road; at the same time men were put to work at the guns, trying to pull them back to safety. He put the 7th South Carolina in the rear of the procession, and all went back toward the courthouse in the moonlight. The enemy pressed behind, made bolder by the silent Confederate guns, and the cavalrymen in the rear ranks were constantly halting to wheel and fire behind them. The darkness concealed the small numbers of the Carolinians, and they escaped.

Boykin overheard a conversation when cannon fire ceased, and one soft, drawling voice called, "Tout perdu." He recognized the unseen battery as that of the Donaldsonville Creoles.

Half an hour of confused skirmishing, charge and countercharge went on in the road. At last, when it seemed that their way to the courthouse must be clear, Federals rushed ahead at a gallop. Boykin saw them ambushed by a party of the 5th Squadron from his regiment, with several saddles quickly emptied. These, Boykin thought, were the last shots of the night.

The bluecoats rode slowly, feeling their way just to the west of the courthouse village. The 7th South Carolina left the road and circled the village, trying to get back to the main body of the army.

A number of Confederate casualties in the blackjack scrub fell before their own guns. Two batteries, Ringgold and Otey, were unpacking near the depot when the Federal cavalry came. They lost their baggage wagons, but the men began firing on the enemy.

Lieutenant W. F. Robinson, with the Ringgold men, was caught in it:

"Both batteries moved forward to drive back the advance of Custer's cavalry when, to our surprise, our reserve artillery opened fire on the enemy with grape and canister, forgetting we were between them and the enemy, shooting down Dave Herndon, killing Bob Ruffner and wounding R. E. Butler. Captain Dickinson and Peter Ragsdale ran back to our reserve artillery to stop them from shooting us. I never saw Captain Dickinson any more."

Lieutenant William Lipscomb, second in command of the Ringgold Battery, had been captured the day before, and Robinson found himself in command. He gathered infantry stragglers in the oak scrub and charged a band of the enemy, driving it some distance. Robinson hid his company behind a barn, and when a single cannon came to his aid, he held the enemy in check on his front until it was fully dark.

Robinson resorted to subterfuge to hang onto his post:

"During the battle I could plainly see General Custer sitting on a white horse in the center of a long line of cavalry, and he was heard urging his men to charge, telling them that there was only a handful of Confederates opposing them. I urged my men to take good aim and shoot at General Custer, and I shot at him a number of times myself.

"All of us hallooed at the top of our voices: 'Bring up the Second Brigade! Hurry up the Division,' and so on, and the enemy evidently believed we were the head of Lee's infantry. We loaded and fired so fast with our muskets, and Captain Martin with his cannon, protected by a large house, that Custer couldn't get his cavalry to charge us."

These men kept up their resistance, after dark firing at the enemy by the flash of their guns, until, at nine o'clock, they trailed off on the road to Lynchburg—where Robinson thought the army would follow and make a stand.

James W. Albright, of the 12th Virginia Battalion, was jarred awake at the opening of the skirmish at the depot:

"Notwithstanding the gravity of the situation, I could scarcely help smiling as I heard a kettle drum beating the long roll, and a man riding on horseback beating it furiously and calling for men with muskets to go into the dense forest of black-jack oaks, and drive back the cavalry. Who beat the drum? It has always been a source of curiosity to me."

His battalion lost two wagons and saw hundreds more lost in the road. Albright destroyed all the letters from his mother which he had carried for months, and tore his name from his pocket diary: "So that no Yank could say he had a Rebel's diary by the name of Albright."

This unit marched all night after the skirmish, moving toward Lynchburg. There was nothing to eat except "corn taken from the poor, half-starved horses."

The wandering survivors of Lamkin's artillery, now adopted by Ramsey's Battery, were among the refugees of the attack from the depot.

Private H. R. Irvine had crawled under one of the guns to sleep just before dark with Tommie and Billie Booker. The brothers had just come back from a stunning success as foragers, bearing a great hunk of corn bread and some country molasses. The three burst open a canteen and used its sides for plates, then fell asleep, contented. They were soon aroused by an order: "All keep quiet. Yanks down at the depot. Don't stir."

The quiet was broken by a rush of horsemen and a bugle call, and as Irvine crawled from beneath his gun, it fired. He scrambled up, to seek George Eggleston:

"Everything was pell-mell and hurry-scurry. Several horses with harnesses dragging passed me, but I could not catch them. I came upon a mare and colt, dazed by the noise. I got upon the mare's back and started, guiding her with my hands until I reached Booker, who gave me a strap from his saddle and helped me get it attached to the mouth of the beast."

He and the Bookers outran the mare's colt and came to a hillside at twilight, where a crowd of Confederates watched the skirmishing below. It was becoming dark, and Irvine thought he must have a bridle for escape:

"I shoved the mare up into the midst of some riders and unbridled an officer's horse while he was busily explaining what would probably be done next. I backed out and joined Eggleston and party and advised them that I knew the way to Lynchburg."

The little band escaped, going west from Appomattox Court House; as they approached Lynchburg, Private Irvine stopped at his family home and left the war. "A sad goodbye," he said.

John E. Bouldin, a Virginia cavalryman, passed through the courthouse village at dusk and saw the bodies of several dead Yankees in the road. The regiment continued marching until late, with frequent halts. It left the road and went across country, keeping to woods most of the time.

Word was passed down the line almost constantly: "Keep quiet. Do not speak above a whisper." They rode for a long time over the rough country, covering few miles, and were stopped for the night. Bouldin remembered:

"Finally we halted in a dense wood with orders not to unsaddle, speak out nor make a light, and to sleep on arms. Weary and worn, and hungry as wolves, each man threw himself on the ground, and, with halter strap around his wrist, was soon dreaming of loved ones and good things to eat."

General Breckinridge, the Secretary of War, who had left the army the day before, was now far to the west, on his way to Roanoke. During the day he had telegraphed President Davis in Danville, from a station called Red House:

I left General Lee at Farmville yesterday morning, where he was passing the main body across the river for temporary relief. . . . The straggling has been great, and the situation is not favorable.

★ PURSUIT ★

GRANT'S STAFF thought he had been up most of the night, for he appeared about dawn at the Farmville hotel, ready with his reply to Lee's note. The message was given to Seth Williams, who was off again on a long cross-country ride to Rebel lines.

After the staff had breakfasted a lean "hungry-looking gentleman in gray" appeared, a Confederate colonel.

"I'm the proprietor of this hotel," he said. "My regiment crumbled, and I was the only man left. I thought I might as well stop off at home."

Horace Porter thought his "story was significant as indicating the disintegrating process that was going on in the ranks of the enemy."

Grant prepared to leave Farmville. He had, until today, marched with the column pushing westward on the south flank of Lee's retreat, but since he expected a reply to his second call for surrender, he turned north across the Appomattox. In the Rebel rear, he decided, he could be more easily found by dispatch bearers from Lee.

As he left Farmville, Grant sent orders to Sheridan and Ord to push on toward Appomattox. The Federal forces were now widely separated, but moved so as to completely cover the valley of the Appomattox River:

Sheridan's cavalry was at Chickentown, not far from Prospect Station, fifteen miles southwest of Farmville, on the southern bank of the river. The 5th and 24th Corps of infantry were close behind him. To the north of the river and in rear of the Rebel column was the 2nd Corps, with the 6th Corps just behind and a bit to the south, closing the gap to the riverside. Far behind all was the 9th Corps, still at Burkeville.

As they rode, General Rawlins lectured Grant on Lee's plight:

"He was mighty careful in that last note. He's stalling for

time, and his officers consulted with him on every word. He's going to hold off, trying to get good terms for his general officers, so they won't get the punishment they've got coming to them."

Grant seemed to agree and in the morning's leisurely ride sent frequent dispatches to keep the columns moving up the watershed with all possible speed. The day's reports were encouraging.

Colonel Lyman wrote in his diary for the morning:

"Last night was a white frost, as my toes, under the blankets, suggested to me. We left betimes, before six, for we had to get all the way back to High Bridge and then begin our march."

The ambulance had to ford the river beside the partially burned bridge, and when Meade had clambered back in on the north shore, they plunged through pine groves and an old woods road, into the main road near the Piedmont coalpits, scene of the fight of the evening before. Here they came upon the striking sight of a commander eager for battle. Lyman wrote:

"We found General Humphreys, wearing much the expression of an irascible pointer, he having been out on several roads, ahead of his column, and getting down on his knees and peering at foot-tracks, through his spectacles, to determine by which way the main body had retreated."

Humphreys was not in a joking mood, and he proclaimed that the Rebel end was near:

"When we held Lee here last night, he was finished. He lost time he can never recover, night marching or no. It will cost him supplies, if Sheridan gets ahead of him—and the cavalry will surely catch him now. Question of a little time."

Meade's staff first learned of the exchange of notes between Lee and Grant at this place, and there was a good deal of whooping about the wagon; there were many predictions that surrender would come immediately. The latest gossip was even more promising: Seth Williams was out under a flag of truce with the second note from Grant.

Meade's staff now trotted along what had once been a fine stage road, rutted by the passage of the Rebels and worn by rains until stones three feet high protruded. They passed many burned wagons.

Meade's young men were soon set to whooping again, for they sighted Grant and his entourage ahead. Grant was in high spirits, and astonished the officers by riding up, calling to Meade, "Hello, old fellow!" It was a new high in amity among the commanders.

The day passed pleasantly in the enemy's rear, and except for a few faint, brief snatches, there were no sounds of firing.

Phil Sheridan moved at daybreak as the squadrons of Merritt and MacKenzie joined Crook at Prospect Station and merged into a heavy blue column going west. They passed from woodlands into open, rolling country, with glimpses of the winding river and long vistas of the railroad tracks ahead. George Custer's men led the way over sandy roads drying under the sun, and the column went at a fast trot toward Appomattox Station. For the first time in the campaign the cavalry could show its speed. Sheridan got good news from the front.

One of his gray-clad scouts, a Sergeant White, rode in with a report on a tempting target—the trains of Confederate supplies lured from Lynchburg by Sheridan's ruse. Sheridan wrote:

"Sergeant White, who had been on the lookout for the trains ever since sending the dispatch, found them several miles west of Appomattox depot, feeling their way along, in ignorance of Lee's exact position. As he had the original dispatch with him, and took pains to dwell upon the pitiable condition of Lee's army, he had little difficulty in persuading the men in charge of the trains to bring them east of Appomattox Station."

Sergeant White urged haste, however. "They'll find out how things stand before long," he told Sheridan. "And they'll run the trains back to Lynchburg before we can get at them. We've got to cut the track west of the station. You'll have to hurry."

It was late in the afternoon when Custer's lead squadron saw smoke over the trees at Appomattox Station. The first regiments were turned off to circle the woods to the left, while Custer led the column down the main road. The circling regiments had orders to tear up tracks to the west, in rear of the Rebel trains, and prevent their retreat.

Custer's men drove down upon the station. There was a sharp fight with the guard, but Custer was driving off these Rebels and taking guns when a battery opened on him from a woodland. Some of Custer's men jumped aboard the engines and moved the trains east of the station as fighting broke out in the thickets.

Sheridan arrived as the trains pulled out and the fury in the woodland reached its height. General Devin was sent into line with Custer, and slowly the Rebels were pushed back and the station made safe. Devin's line went along a woods path to the right and emerged in a wide field. The line pushed toward Appomattox Court House as the sun set; firing continued after dark.

Sheridan wrote: "I then forced the enemy back on the Appomattox road to the vicinity of the courthouse, and that the Confederates might have no rest, gave orders to continue the skirmishing throughout the night."

After a time, however, the front line halted near the village and fighting ceased. Sheridan settled for the night in a frame house just south of the railroad station.

Reports of the action were cheering: The Rebels were cleared out for a mile or so, with twenty-five pieces of artillery taken, in addition to a hospital train and a large park of wagons which had been pushed ahead of the Confederate army in hope of their reaching Lynchburg.

Sheridan sat on a bench in the parlor of the cottage, before a wood fire, writing a dispatch to Grant. He was interrupted:

"The captured trains had been taken charge of by locomotive engineers, soldiers of the command, who were delighted evidently to get back at their old calling. They amused themselves by running the trains to and fro, creating much confusion, and keeping up such an unearthly screeching with the whistles that I was on the point of ordering the cars burned. They finally wearied of their fun, however, and ran the trains off to the east toward General Ord's column."

Sheridan completed his report to the commander:

Cavalry Headquarters
April 8, 9:20 P.M.

General.

I marched early this morning from Buffalo Creek and Prospect Station on Appomattox Depot, where my scouts had reported trains of cars for Lee's army. A short time before dusk General Custer, who had the advance, made a dash at the station, capturing four trains of supplies with locomotives. . . .

Custer then pushed on toward Appomattox Court House, driving the enemy, who kept up a heavy fire of artillery, charging them repeatedly. . . .

If General Gibbon and the 5th Corps can get up tonight we will perhaps finish the job in the morning. I do not think Lee intends to surrender until compelled to do so.

P. H. Sheridan,
Major General

Sheridan did not go to bed, and kept the staff officers up, sending dispatches by the dozen in an effort to hurry the infantry. There was an endless relay of riders from General Sheridan's cottage, going out to Ord's column and to General Grant.

The cavalryman wrote of it: "If the infantry could get to the front, all knew that the rebellion would be ended on the morrow. Merritt, Crook, Custer and Devin were present at frequent intervals during the night, and everybody was overjoyed at the prospect that our weary work was about to end so happily."

Grant had come, at the end of the day, to the settlement of Curdsville, some ten miles northwest of Farmville, and at least twenty miles east of Appomattox Station in a direct cross-country line. Making camp was a simple affair, for the headquarters wagons were somewhere south of the river, rolling in Sheridan's wake.

General Meade made headquarters in the farmhouse of a Stute family, near a big, rambling white frame house known as Clifton House. Grant and his staff ate supper with Meade and borrowed blankets from him.

Grant had suffered one of his numbing headaches all after-noon, but remained patient during the hour or so he spent in Meade's headquarters. Colonel Lyman wrote:

"To show how really amiable he is, he let the officers drum on the family piano a long while before he would even hint he didn't like it."

About sundown the officers heard faint cannon fire from the west; they knew Sheridan had struck, but nothing more.

After supper Grant and his staff went to the Clifton House, which was deserted except for two or three Negro servants left behind to guard the property. The rooms had been stripped, and there was but one remaining bed, in an upper room, which was shared by Grant and Rawlins.

The rest, including the New York correspondent, Sylvanus Cadwallader, slept on the floors. The reporter used his field glasses as a pillow, and did not stir until about midnight, when a guard called out a challenge and boots thumped through the hall:

"Dispatches for General Grant!" someone yelled.

The awakened men were quickly alert, listening as the boots went upstairs. The parlor door opened and Cadwallader and his companions eavesdropped. It was not difficult.

Rawlins read aloud the note from Lee to Grant, and as he read his voice rose and became angrier. At the end Rawlins cursed:

"He did not propose to surrender!" Rawlins shouted. "Diplomatic, but not true. He did propose, in his heart, to surrender. Now he's trying to take advantage of a single word by you, to extend such easy terms. He wants to entrap you into making a peace treaty. You said nothing about that. You asked him to surrender.

"He asked your terms. You answered with the terms. Now he wants to arrange a peace—to take in the whole Confederacy. No, sir! You can't do it. It's a positive insult. It's an underhanded way to change the whole correspondence."

Grant's quiet voice came down to the listeners:

"It amounts to the same thing, Rawlins. He's only trying to get let down easy. I can meet him in the morning as he says, and settle the whole business in an hour."

"No!" Rawlins said. "You can't presume to teach Lee the use of the English language. He's arranged this meeting to gain time, and get better terms. He deserves no reply whatever. 'He don't think the emergency has arisen!' Now that's cool—but a lie. It's been staring him in the face for forty-eight hours. If he hasn't seen it yet we'll soon show it to him. He'll surrender. He has to surrender. By God, it'll be surrender and nothing else!"

Grant tried to calm him. "We've got to make some allowance for the trying place Lee is in. He's got to obey orders of his government. It all means exactly the same thing, Rawlins. If I meet Lee, he'll surrender before I leave."

"You've no right to meet General Lee or anybody else to arrange peace terms," Rawlins said. "That's for the President, or the Senate. Your business is to capture or destroy his army."

There was more of it, but Rawlins at last subsided and went back to bed. Grant stayed up.

Horace Porter persuaded the commander to take a hot foot bath, plunging his feet into steaming water laced with mustard. He also put mustard plasters on his wrists and the back of his neck, but nothing seemed to relieve the headache, which had grown worse.

★ RICHMOND ★

PRIVATION HAD brought Richmond's families closer together. John B. Jones wrote: "The people are kinder to each other, sharing provisions, etc."

There was little enough to share, beyond the stores from the Federal commissary, and there was still quiet in the bright, pleasant weather.

Jones noted that there was uncertainty as to the fate of the city's people; he did not know whether they would be forced to take oaths of allegiance.

He heard more talk of the peace settlement. Judge Campbell

had been joined by other prominent Richmonders, Gustavus Myers, General Joseph Anderson and N. P. Tyler; they would call a convention to withdraw Virginia from the Confederacy—a second Secession.

Jones recorded one of the first reports of turncoat Confederates: General Roger A. Pryor was said to have remained in Petersburg when the army fled, and had announced "his abandonment of the Confederate cause."

In truth, Pryor had been left behind as under parole—but had been re-arrested by almost every passing Federal division in the swarm past his home.

★ MR. LINCOLN ★

PRESIDENT LINCOLN led his party into a coach on the military train in the early morning, and they were off to Petersburg: Mary and Tad, Senator Sumner, Secretary Harlan and his family, the Count de Chambrun, the bodyguard William H. Crook, Elizabeth Keckley and a few officers. Three or four Negro waiters from the *River Queen* went along; they sat quietly at the rear of the car as the train rattled over the flat landscape.

A crowd gathered in Petersburg and people stared and pointed at Lincoln. They pushed through the people and went into the town in a carriage, stopping once to allow Lincoln to admire a great oak tree; he reminisced about the vast forests of his youth. Sometime during the day he and Mary left the party and rode into the country. They passed a cemetery. Mrs. Lincoln remembered:

"It was a retired place, shaded by trees, and early spring flowers were opening on nearly every grave. It was so quiet and attractive that we stopped the carriage and walked through it. Mr. Lincoln seemed thoughtful and impressed. He said, 'Mary, you are younger than I; you will survive me. When I am gone, lay my remains in some quiet place like this.'"

On the way back to Petersburg, Lincoln saw a terrapin from

the train window, sunning itself on a bank beside the track. He had the train stopped and a man brought the terrapin to him. Elizabeth Keckley wrote:

"The movements of the ungainly little animal seemed to delight him, and he amused himself with it till we reached the James River, where our steamer lay. Tad stood near, and joined in happy laughter with his father."

Lincoln went into the army's camps and hospitals in the afternoon, and was late returning to the *River Queen*. Elizabeth Keckley thought he had a "tired, weary look." He sought Mary Lincoln.

"Mother," he said, "I have shaken so many hands today that my arms ache. I almost wish I could go to bed now."

Dusk came, and Elizabeth Keckley was enchanted:

"As the twilight shadows deepened the lamps were lighted and the boat was brilliantly illuminated; as it lay in the river, decked with many-colored lights, it looked like an enchanted floating palace."

A military band had come aboard, and as it played, Lincoln sat with de Chambrun. The President asked the band to play the "Marseillaise" in honor of the Count, and had it repeated.

"You have to come over here to hear it," Lincoln said. The Frenchman nodded wryly, acknowledging the decline of democracy and patriotic airs in the Second Empire.

A few minutes later Lincoln was called on for a speech and stood, stretching wearily:

"You must excuse me, ladies and gentlemen. I'm too tired to speak tonight. We have a long trip to Washington. And now, by way of parting from the brave soldiers of our army, I call upon the band to play 'Dixie.' It has always been a favorite of mine, and since we have captured it, we have a perfect right to enjoy it."

De Chambrun thought the musicians looked startled, but they blared away, and were applauded loudly.

Between ten and eleven o'clock the *River Queen* got underway, sliding around the Federal craft in the harbor and heading cautiously down the James, her captain still fearful of torpedoes and debris. There was for a long time an odor from bodies of hundreds of horses on the banks.

De Chambrun wrote:

"Mr. Lincoln stood for a long while gazing at the hills, so animated a few days before, now dark and silent. Around us more than a hundred ships at anchor gave visible proof of the country's maritime strength. . . . Mr. Lincoln remained absorbed in thought and pursued his meditation long after the quickened speed had removed the lugubrious scene forever from our sight."

X

Sunday, April 9

★

★ FLIGHT ★

THE STAFFS of Robert Lee, Longstreet and Gordon slept in a dense woodland without blankets or tents. The wagons were lost, most of them burned. The officers lay under their coats, heads on saddles, their feet to the campfires.

Colonel Charles Marshall, the Baltimore lawyer of Lee's staff, fell asleep soon after midnight. Marshall was Lee's literary aide; he had composed many of the famous orders and addresses of the war, revealing the talent of his legendary family, one of whom was Chief Justice John Marshall. The colonel suffered from extreme myopia, and since he was helpless without his thick spectacles, wore them in sleep. He soon pulled the cape of his overcoat around his head to shut out the chill, but not even that deadened the sounds of the hungry horses, gnawing bark from trees.

Within an hour Marshall sat up, listening intently. Troops marched in a nearby road, perhaps Federal infantry, since the position was almost surrounded. Marshall's doubts were soon dispelled. The men began chanting a Texas version of a scriptural parody—they were from the remnant of John Hood's brigade:

> "The race is not to them that's got
> The longest legs to run,
> Nor the battle to that people
> That shoots the biggest gun."

Headquarters broke camp. There was nothing to do but to put on hats and to saddle horses, though a few of the younger officers made an emergency meal. Someone found a tin shaving can, and water was soon boiling. An officer produced a bit of corn meal and, as Marshall wrote:

"Each man in his turn, according to rank and seniority, made a can of corn meal gruel, and was allowed to keep the can until the gruel became cool enough to drink. General Lee, who reposed as we had done . . . did not, as I remember, have even such refreshment. This was our last meal in the Confederacy."

By the time this meal was over, infantry was moving up in earnest, pressing through the courthouse village in the effort to break through enemy lines.

General Pendleton reported to Lee to tell him of his narrow escape of the night before, when he had jumped his horse over a fence and skirted the village to avoid the enemy. He was shocked by Lee's appearance at the campfire this morning, "dressed in his neatest style, new uniform, snowy linen." It was the only uniform left to the commander.

"I'll probably have to be General Grant's prisoner," Lee said, "and I thought I must make my best appearance."

At Lee's urging that he get some rest, Pendleton left headquarters; the thought crossed his mind that Lee might be dressing himself for death. Pendleton recalled Lee's headlong charge toward the enemy long ago, in The Wilderness, when soldiers had seized Traveller's bridle and taken him rearward.

Robert Lee mounted Traveller and went toward the village. It was near 3 A.M. In his front, strung about the village, were 5,000 of Gordon's infantry; in the rear, Longstreet commanded perhaps 3,000. Thousands more wandered nearby, an unarmed mob seeking food.

Dr. Claiborne left his bed in the thickets in the first light and sought the army. With the survivors of his hospital train, Drs. Hume Field and Richard Lewis, he approached a horseman who sat with a big Navy revolver across his saddle. Claiborne walked within ten yards of the trooper:

"We're friends," he said. "Only three lost Confederate surgeons. Which way are Lee's lines?"

The horseman waved them ahead with his pistol, but when they moved Claiborne heard the cocking of the pistol, and saw that the rider's uniform was blue.

"About face, march," the Federal said. They turned and shambled back, the horseman riding near Claiborne, and the pistol bobbing near the doctor's head.

"Sergeant, you'll shoot me presently."

"I don't care a damn if I do," the rider said cheerfully.

"I care very particularly," Claiborne said, but the weapon did not move until the doctor presented a bribe:

"Sergeant, those are poor spurs you're wearing, for so fine a trooper. I have a beautiful pair in my pocket, taken from the old Merrimac you people sunk in the Gosport Navy Yard. If you'll let me stop I'll make you a present of them."

The rider took the spurs and put his pistol away, leading the party toward Federal lines. Claiborne looked ruefully at the spurs, which he had owned since he was "playing soldier" in trenches below Norfolk at the opening of the war; he had removed them from his boots last night to hide them in case of capture.

They passed a big frame building resembling a country church, where a Federal officer was surrounded by staff and couriers. Claiborne recognized General Sheridan:

"He was splendidly mounted, and a number of his officers, all well-dressed and with caparisoned steeds, presented quite a different appearance from our poor, broken cavalry."

Sheridan called to the Confederate physicians: "Now, boys, you're going to see something grand."

Bluecoat cavalry went toward the Confederate lines, where firing had broken out. The enemy's infantry called obscenities and jeered at the troopers, Claiborne noted, just as in the Confederate army.

"Oh, you'll be back pretty soon," an infantryman yelled to the cavalry. It was an accurate prediction, for the horsemen came swarming back a few minutes later, riding "pellmell" to the rear.

Claiborne was hurried to the rear with other prisoners.

"We met the Yankee infantry advancing—and such numbers! They seemed to come out of the ground. We had to give them the road to let them pass."

Since three o'clock Gordon's corps had been stumbling toward Appomattox Court House, and at the first graying of dawn had spread through the village. Captain J. C. Gorman, the North Carolinian, passed with his men, threading the trains of wagons and artillery. He saw a strange tableau in Appomattox:

"The whole cavalry force drawn up in mass, and the troopers apparently asleep mounted. The fields, gardens and streets of the village were strewn with troops, bivouacking in line of battle."

The column marched west of the village and sharpshooters went out. The fog lay heavily below them, and visibility was poor. Gorman was startled.

"The careless positions of things did not seem alarming, and I was not prepared to believe an enemy was so close, when the picket informed us that the Yankees were in that woods, some 200 yards in front."

Bryan Grimes was a thirty-six-year-old North Carolinian who had been a Brigadier General for six weeks, a square-faced man with eyes set far apart, and penciled brows, a fiery commander determined to die before surrender. This morning he led the front division of Gordon's corps. He wrote of his movements:

"I had my command aroused and passed through the town of Appomattox Courthouse before daylight, where, upon the opposite side of the town, I found the enemy in my front. . . . I reconnoitered and waited the arrival of General Gordon for instruction, who, a while before day, accompanied by General Fitz Lee, came to my position, when we held a council of war."

"Nothing out there but cavalry," Gordon said. "Fitz, you should give them a go."

Fitz Lee studied the distant figures through his glasses and shook his head. "Infantry," he said. "I can't budge them. Your boys will have to attack."

Grimes fretted as the two argued.

"They discussed the matter so long that I became impatient, and said it was somebody's duty to attack, and that immediately."

Grimes volunteered, "We can drive them from that crossroads, where you want the wagon train to go, and I'll try it."

"Well, drive them off," Gordon said.

"I can't do it with my division alone. I need help."

"You can take the whole corps," Gordon said.

Fitz Lee led his cavalry toward the enemy flank. Grimes rode to his left a short distance and gave orders to General James A. Walker, who had the remnants of Jubal Early's old division. Skirmishers were already firing, and artillery began to echo through the village, adding black clouds to the mists. Far ahead, behind rails where the enemy lay, winking lights signaled the opening of a fight.

Grimes rode into the open. The enemy's artillery saluted him:

"I remember well the appearance of the shell," Grimes wrote, "and how directly they came towards me, exploding and completely enveloping me in smoke. I then gave the signal to advance."

His infantry went out briskly, over the enemy breastworks, driving blue figures to the rear. Men came back with prisoners, and a party dragged in two Federal guns. Some of the prisoners had a chilling message: On the flank lay the whole Army of The James, some 10,000 of General Ord's veterans, ready to strike. Grimes reacted as if the war had only begun:

"Halting my troops, I placed the skirmishers, commanded by Colonel J. R. Winston, 45th North Carolina, in front, about 100 yards distant . . . I placed Cox's brigade, which occupied the right of the division, at right angles to the other troops, to watch that flank. . . . I then sent an officer to General Gordon, announcing our success, and that the Lynchburg road was open for the escape of the wagons, and that I awaited orders."

Gordon watched from a position in rear, and took little comfort from the quavering of Rebel Yells as his men drove the Federals:

"I discovered a heavy column of Union infantry coming from the right and upon my rear. I gathered around me my sharpshooters, who were now held for such emergencies, and directed Colonel Thomas H. Carter to turn all his guns upon the advancing column. It was held at bay by his shrapnel."

Almost immediately a Federal cavalry column appeared on a hillside, ready to strike between Gordon and Longstreet.

In the moment Gordon saw the new threat he was approached by Colonel Charles Venable of Lee's staff:

"General Lee wants to know if you can cut a way through."

"Tell General Lee I've fought my corps to a frazzle, and I can do nothing unless Longstreet can support me."

Venable disappeared, and Gordon sent Grimes an order to withdraw. Grimes refused to obey. He wrote:

"He continued to send me order after order to the same effect, which I still disregarded, being under the impression that he did not comprehend our favorable location."

He at last got a command to pull back from Lee himself, and gave orders to General Cox:

"Hold your line right here, and keep the men down. Don't show one man until we have pulled the rear line back a hundred yards or more. Then fall back to protect us."

The enemy came forward as Grimes retreated, but broke back into the woods as Cox's men rose from hiding and fired. The gray division withdrew unmolested and the field became quieter.

Grimes found Gordon:

"Where shall I form my line?"

"Anywhere you choose."

"What does that mean?"

"We're going to be surrendered."

Grimes shouted angrily, "Why didn't you tell me? I could have got away. I'm going to tell my men. I'll take them with me."

Gordon took Grimes by the shoulder: "Are you going to desert the army and tarnish your honor as a soldier? It will be a reflection on General Lee and an indelible disgrace."

"All right," Grimes said. "All right. I'll tell them nothing."

When he reached the infantry, however, men swarmed around Grimes. "General, are we surrendered?"

"I'm afraid it's so."

One man tossed away his musket and yelled, "Blow Gabriel, blow! My God, let him blow! I'm ready to die."

Trooper E. M. Boykin was awake early, and one of his first thoughts was that spring had come: "The oak trees were cov-

ered with their long yellow tassels." The South Carolina horsemen saw enemy troops swarming over the valley beyond them,
but calmly built fires. Boykin wrote:

"They all seemed to have something to eat, and to be amusing themselves eating it. . . . We waited for the performance
to commence. You would not have thought that there was anything special in the situation. They all turned all the responsibility over to the officers, who in turn did the same to those above
them—the captain to the colonel, the colonel to the brigadier,
and so on."

It was late before Boykin and his men went into action:

"The blue jackets showed in heavy masses on the edge of the
woods. General Gary, riding up, put everything that had a horse
in the saddle, and moved us down the hill, just on the edge of
the little creek that is here the Appomattox, to wait under cover
until wanted.

"I then lay down, with my head, like the luxurious High-
lander, upon a smooth stone, and, holding my horse's bridle in
my hand, was soon in the deep sleep of a tired man. But not for
long, for down came the General in his most emphatic manner."

Gary yelled, "Mount, men, mount!" Boykin jumped up, still
half asleep, and got into his saddle.

"I found myself maneuvering my horse with his rear in
front. We soon had everything in its right place, and rode out
from the bottom into the open field, about 250 strong, to see the
last of it."

There was sharp infantry fighting beyond them, and Boykin saw that they were already almost surrounded by Federal
cavalry.

The Virginia cavalryman, John Bouldin, started awake at
the first cannon shot, and with his companions waited in their
woodland hiding place until Rooney Lee came up with his staff.
The order came down the line: "Mount! Form fours! Forward,
march!"

They trotted to a field, across which were two enemy cannon at the edge of a pine grove. Infantry supported the guns.

Bouldin wrote: "Across the field we dashed right up to the

guns, shooting the gunners and support down with our Colt's
Navies. Just as our colors were planted on the guns, out of the
woods on our left flank came a regiment of Yankee cavalry in
fine style. With empty pistols and disorganized as we were, every
man wheeled his horse to the left, and we drew sabers and
went at them with steel. . . . We soon sent them back in great
confusion. . . .

"Our attention was now called again to the infantry, who
had abandoned their works and fallen back and from behind
trees were picking our boys off their horses. One dash was sufficient. We rode through their camp just in rear of their guns.
They were preparing breakfast."

Bouldin passed cooking ham and eggs and beefsteak and
caught the odor of real coffee boiling in cans. He overcame a
powerful temptation to fall out of the charge. The riders rounded
up several hundred prisoners and dragged back two captured
Napoleon guns. Bouldin captured four men at one time.

These men of the 9th and 14th Virginia Cavalry had hardly
returned to the village, however, before the end came for them:
"The Yankees soon rounded us up, took our guns and prisoners,
and sent over to us wagonloads of bacon, hard-tack, and some
sure-enough coffee, which I hadn't tasted for four long years."

Other cavalrymen at the front thought that they made the
final charge on the enemy. Colonel Magnus Thompson, of
Elijah White's 35th Virginia Battalion, stood in battle line with
his command near a swamp until after sunrise. Colonel White
rode up with stunning news: The army was about to be surrendered, and General Rosser would take his army through the
lines to escape. Rosser had them moved forward half a mile,
where these riders were waiting when Gordon's fight erupted.
Thompson wrote:

"Rosser now put White's brigade in front and moved
promptly upon the enemy, who seemed not to understand exactly what was expected of them, and as Colonel White took
position on a hill in an open field about four hundred yards from
a division of Federal cavalry the latter only looked, but made no
hostile movement. After a while a column of about 400 Yankees

moved from the division and formed on the hill near the remnant of the Laurel Brigade. This was too much for Colonel White, and he ordered a charge."

"Mix with 'em, boys!" White shouted. "Unjoint 'em!"

The attack drove the Federals to their reserves, who fled in turn, and the blue wave broke. Thompson saw it: "Again, but for the last time, the avenging sabers of the Laurel Brigade flashed fiercely over the Yankee cavalry, many of them being killed or wounded, but no prisoners were taken."

The chase went on for two miles before White dismounted his men and fought them as infantry.

Lieutenant Fletcher Massie, of Lamkin's Battery, had ten men left, most of them unarmed. They marched in rear of General Field's infantry and settled near the courthouse. Massie looked out at the front line of the army, talking to a lieutenant from a nearby battery:

"It looks mighty slender. Look, how many holes are in the ranks."

Their attention was diverted by a captured Federal gun being wheeled through the town, a brass Napoleon from Company M, U.S. Regular Artillery; a caisson followed, each of the vehicles drawn by six horses. Federal gunners rode the lead horses, under guard of gray cavalrymen.

Massie saw General E. P. Alexander in the road.

"I'm sorry you don't have your guns with you, Massie," the Georgian said. "I'm putting the batteries in line now to meet the enemy."

"I've got ten men here ready to serve a gun, and I saw a Yankee piece just come through, and I'd like to have that. My men can handle it."

"Very well. Come along and I'll turn it over to you."

Massie sent the Federal crew to the provost marshal and prepared to wheel the gun into position.

Percy Hawes, the young courier, found himself near the guns of Colonel Alexander Stark's battalion when the enemy attack came. Bluecoats overran them, but Stark remained on horse-back, and his gunners fought until cut down by bayonets. Stark then called off survivors and left the guns to the Federals.

Just to the rear were eight guns of the old Poague Battalion, commanded by Major Thomas H. Brander. Hawes was sent back to ask Brander to drive off the enemy. A blast of fire cleared the spot. The courier wrote:

"The enemy had not gotten more than thirty feet away from the mouth of Stark's guns when Stark ran up at the head of his cannoneers, took charge of the guns, and, turning them on the enemy, killed many of them almost at the mouths of the pieces."

Robert Lee had watched since daylight from a position be-hind Gordon, peering through the fog with glasses. Venable returned with Gordon's grim message.

Lee spoke after a moment, "Then there is nothing left for me to do but go and see General Grant, and I would rather die a thousand deaths."

One of the officers said, "Oh, General, what will history say of the surrender of the army in the field?"

"Yes," Lee said. "I know they will say hard things of us: They will not understand how we were overwhelmed by num-bers. But that is not the question, Colonel: The question is, is it right to surrender this army? If it is right, then I will take all the responsibility."

The staff noted that Lee was on the verge of losing his self-control. The commander all but moaned, "How easily I could be rid of this, and be at rest! I have only to ride along the line and all will be over. But it is our duty to live. What will become of the women and children of the South if we are not here to protect them?"

Longstreet and Mahone came up. Old Pete wrote of the commander at this moment: "He was dressed in a new uni-form . . . and a pair of gold spurs. At first approach his com-pact figure appeared as a man in the flush vigor of forty sum-mers, but as I drew near, the handsome apparel and brave bearing failed to conceal his profound depression."

Lee asked Longstreet's advice on surrender.

"Can the sacrifice of the army help the cause in other quarters?"

"I think not," Lee said.

"Then," Longstreet said, "your situation speaks for itself."

The tiny Mahone shivered by a fire, his worn brown linen duster covering him completely, concealing even the point of his sword. Mahone was about forty, thin, frail-looking, with a sallow sharp face.

"I don't want you to think I'm scared," Mahone said. "I'm only chilled."

Lee asked his advice, and Mahone chattered away for several minutes. Longstreet did not listen carefully, but he heard that Mahone, too, thought the commander should ask Grant for terms.

Lee asked Longstreet once more, point-blank, if he should surrender. Old Pete merely nodded his head.

Lee delayed, standing by the fire, and when E. P. Alexander approached, led him to a seat on a fallen log. The gifted artilleryman had irregular features, a scraggly beard and "a decidedly ugly mouth," but there was an unmistakable air about him, a hint of the talents the army had so often used. Lee bent over a map with him.

"Well, here we are at Appomattox, and there seems to be a considerable force in front of us. Now what shall we have to do today?"

"If you see a chance to cut our way out, I'll answer for the artillery. We'll fight as well as ever. The boys were yelling to me on the road just now not to surrender any ammunition, whatever else we gave up."

"The trouble is lack of infantry," Lee said. "There are just two divisions left that haven't been worn to pieces, and they're so small."

"Well, sir, we have two alternatives. We must surrender or scatter in the woods and bushes and rally to General Johnston in North Carolina, or each man report to the governor of his own state. Scattering would be best."

"Well, what would you hope to gain by that?"

"If there's any hope for us, it's in delay. If you surrender, every other army will give up as soon as the news reaches it. The only thing left for us to fight for is to get some kind of terms, so we won't be at their mercy. A little blood more or less now makes no difference. Your men have the right to ask you not to make an unconditional surrender."

"If I took your suggestion, how many men do you suppose would get away?"

"Two thirds of us. We'd scatter like rabbits and partridges in the woods, and they couldn't scatter to catch us."

"The men would have no rations, be under no discipline. They're already demoralized. They'd have to rob and plunder. You young men might afford to go bushwhacking, but the only proper course for me would be to surrender and take the consequences."

Alexander talked with him for several minutes, but though Lee said he expected honorable terms, without unconditional surrender, he ordered the artilleryman to the front to aid Gordon. Alexander rode off to place the remaining batteries.

Colonel Walter Taylor came to Lee, reporting that he had done his best to bring up the wagon trains during the night, as he had been ordered.

"Well, Colonel, what are we to do?" Lee asked.

"I'm afraid we'll have to abandon the wagons, sir, and then the army might escape."

"Yes," Lee said. "Perhaps we could. But I have had a conference with these gentlemen, and they agree the time has come to surrender."

"Well, I can only speak for myself. To me any other fate is preferable."

"That's my own thinking," Lee said.

"Of course, General, it's different with you. You have to think of these brave men, and decide not only for yourself, but for them."

"Yes," Lee said. "It would be useless and cruel to provoke more bloodshed, and I've arranged to meet General Grant with the view to surrender, and want you to accompany me."

Lee rode into the old stage road with a small party, in search of Grant: Taylor and Charles Marshall, riding behind Sergeant G. W. Tucker, General Hill's old courier. Tucker car-

ried on a stick a flag of truce—a dirty handkerchief. Marshall
noted that the troops "cheered General Lee to the echo, as they
had cheered him many a time before." Lee waved his hand to
halt the cheering, fearing that the men would attract fire from
the enemy.

When they had passed the picket line, Tucker and Marshall
rode ahead of them until he reached a bluecoat picket. A
Federal rider emerged:

"Lieutenant Colonel Charles Whittier, General Humphreys'
staff," the enemy officer said.

Whittier shook his head, obviously puzzled, when Marshall
asked about a meeting between Grant and Lee, and then surprised the colonel by holding out a letter. "A dispatch from
General Grant to General Lee. I'll wait, in case General Lee has a
reply."

Marshall took the letter back to Lee, opened it and read:

> General R. E. Lee,
> Commanding C.S. Armies:
> General: Your note of yesterday is received. As I have
> no authority to treat on the subject of peace the meeting
> proposed for 10 a.m. today could lead to no good. I will
> state, however, General, that I am equally desirous for peace
> with yourself, and the whole North entertain the same feel-
> ing. The terms upon which peace can be had are well un-
> derstood. By the South laying down their arms they will
> hasten that most desirable event, save thousands of human
> lives, and hundreds of millions of property not yet de-
> stroyed. Sincerely hoping that all our difficulties may be
> settled without the loss of another life, I subscribe myself,
> very respectfully your obedient servant,
> U. S. Grant,
> Lieutenant General U.S. Army

Lee at last spoke to Marshall. "Write a letter to General
Grant and ask him to meet me to deal with the question of surrender of my army, in reply to the letter he wrote me at Farmville.

Marshall sat and wrote as Lee dictated:

General:

I received your note this morning on the picket line, whither I had come to meet you and ascertain definitely what terms were embraced in your proposition of yesterday with reference to the surrender of this army.

They were interrupted by a flying horseman, Colonel Jack Haskell, a reckless one-armed rider who had come from Longstreet. Haskell reined sharply.

"What is it?" Lee said. "What is it? Oh, why did you do it? You have killed your beautiful horse."

"Fitz Lee has found a way out," Haskell said. "The army can get away if we hurry."

Lee questioned Haskell briefly and turned back to his letter as if he gave no further thought to the situation at the front. He continued dictating:

I now request an interview in accordance with the offer contained in your letter of yesterday for that purpose.

Very respectfully,
Your obt. servt.
R. E. Lee

Marshall passed the dispatch to Lee for signing and took it to the waiting Whittier at the Federal lines. Whittier returned to the spot within five minutes:

"I've been directed to say that an attack has been ordered here, and that the commander on the front has no discretion. General Grant left General Meade some time ago, and the letter cannot reach him in time to stop the attack."

"Ask Meade to read General Lee's letter," Marshall said. "Perhaps under the circumstances he can stop it."

Whittier was gone for a long time. Federal pickets were advancing, and a soldier with a flag of truce entered Confederate lines to warn that the men must fall back or take the consequences. Lee sat in his place as if he had decided to hold that post at all costs.

After a wait of almost an hour Lee sent off to Grant a second note:

General,
　　I ask a suspension of hostilities pending the adjustment
of the terms of the surrender of this army, in the interview
requested in my former communication today.

Only when advancing bluecoats were within a hundred
yards of him did Lee ride toward Longstreet's lines. On the way
he had a second message from Fitz Lee, reporting that the information carried by Jack Haskell was false; the way to freedom
was firmly closed. Lee accepted this without a trace of surprise.
He sent a courier to Gordon, telling him that hostilities were
suspended, pending further word from Grant.

Lee soon had a note from General Meade, assuring him that
a brief truce would be honored—but that an hour must be the
limit. The Federal proposed that Lee send still another message
to Grant in an effort to hurry communication. Lee halted in an
apple orchard and dictated a fresh dispatch, ending:

　　I therefore request an interview at such time and place
as you may designate, to discuss the terms of the surrender
of this army in accord with your offer to have such an interview contained in your letter of yesterday.

E. P. Alexander was again with the commander; he took
blankets from his saddle, spread them across fence rails beneath
an apple tree, and persuaded Lee to lie down. Soldiers began to
crowd about, and Colonel T. M. R. Talcott of the engineers, who
had come up, strung a cordon of men around the tree.

Longstreet joined Lee, and the commander talked in slow,
brief sentences of the note from Grant, which concerned him
because it made no specific proposal. He feared that Grant might
demand "harsh terms."

"I know Grant well enough to say that the terms will be
about what you would demand under the circumstances," Longstreet said.

Lee watched glumly as a Federal officer rode up under a
white flag. Longstreet tried to cheer the commander. "If he
won't give you honorable terms, break it off, and tell him to do
his worst."

Lee straightened, and Longstreet concluded that the "thought of another round seemed to brace him."

The Federal rider introduced himself as Colonel Orville Babcock of Grant's staff. He brought a letter from Grant:

General R. E. Lee,
Commanding C.S. Army:

Your note of this date is but this moment (11:50 A.M.) received. In consequence of my having passed from the Richmond and Lynchburg road to the Farmville and Lynchburg road. I am writing this about four miles west of Walker's church and will push forward to the front for the purpose of meeting you. Notice sent on this road where you wish the interview to take place will meet me.

Very respectfully, your obedient servant,
U. S. Grant
Lieutenant-General.

Lee prepared to meet Grant. He handed Venable the worn map of photographic linen he had used for months. "Burn it, Colonel," he said. Before this could be done E. P. Alexander cut off a strip for a souvenir. It read: "South Side James River, R. E. Lee."

Lee asked Taylor and Marshall to ride with him. Taylor shook his head. "I have ridden twice through the lines this morning, General," he said. Lee excused him, and Taylor was grateful. The bridegroom wrote: "I shrank from this interview."

Marshall was in "a dilapidated state." He borrowed a fresh shirt and collar, and exchanged his plain sword for a more presentable one.

The group went up the hill toward Appomattox Court House. Sergeant Tucker led, but had to pause at the stream, where Traveller drank. They were well up the hillside before infantry caught sight of them. Cheers broke out, but faded as the troops saw the white flag. Silence fell.

There was another wait for the party on the outskirts of the village, when Lee sent Marshall ahead to find a place for the meeting. Marshall stopped a man, a Major Wilmer McLean, who had evacuated his family to this quiet spot from the field of Manassas, where war had twice overrun his farm.

McLean showed Marshall a vacant brick building, a disheveled house empty of furniture. Marshall shook his head. "Isn't there another place?"

McLean led him toward his house, a thin-shanked brick two-story dwelling at the roadside near the courthouse, its lawn shaded by young locusts. Marshall approved, and Lee soon arrived. He led the way into the house. They passed to a room at the left. Marshall wrote: "So General Lee, Babcock and myself sat down in McLean's parlour and talked in the most friendly and affable way."

Lee sat by a small table, where he could look through a south window across the valley of the Appomattox. He placed hat and gauntlets on the table, and sat with crossed legs. He wore new boots embroidered in red silk. His handsome sword glittered. Its handle was white, crowned with the head of a lion, its guard and wire wrapping of gilt. The scabbard was blue steel, trimmed in gilt. One side of the blade was engraved: "General Robert E. Lee, from a Marylander, 1863." On the reverse side was written: "Aide toi et Dieu t'aidera."

At the front John Gordon's troops were still fighting, "furiously fighting in nearly every direction," the general said, when a courier handed him Lee's note about the flag of truce. Gordon summoned Colonel Green Peyton of his staff.

"Get a flag of truce and take a message to General Ord for me. I want you to say this to him: 'General Gordon has received notice from General Lee of a flag of truce, stopping the battle.' Tell him that and nothing more."

Peyton nodded. "But we have no flag of truce, General," he said.

"Well, take your handkerchief, and tie that on a stick."

"General, I have no handkerchief."

"Then tear your shirt, sir, and tie that to a stick."

Peyton said, "I have on a flannel shirt, and I see you have. I don't believe there's a white shirt in the army."

"Get something, sir. Get something and go."

Peyton at last rode out with a dingy rag. He could not find Ord, but did find Sheridan and returned with a colorful visitor. Gordon wrote:

"He returned to me accompanied by an officer of strikingly picturesque appearance. This Union officer was slender and graceful, and a superb rider. He wore his hair very long, falling almost to his shoulders. . . . He saluted me with his saber and said, 'I am General Custer, and bear a message to you from General Sheridan. The General desires me to present to you his compliments, and to demand the immediate and unconditional surrender of all the troops under your command.' "

"You will please, General, return my compliments to General Sheridan, and say to him that I shall not surrender my command."

"He directs me to say to you, General, that if there is any hesitation about your surrender, that he has you surrounded, and can annihilate your command in an hour."

"I'm probably as well aware of my situation as General Sheridan. I have nothing to add to my message from General Lee. If General Sheridan decides to continue fighting in the face of a flag of truce the responsibility for the blood shed will be his, and not mine."

Custer rode away.

Hundreds of men in the village took note of Custer. Lieutenant J. F. J. Caldwell was leading some of his South Carolina infantry when the Federal cavalryman galloped by: "The men saw the stars on his shoulder straps and congratulated themselves that there had been another of the enemy's generals captured. We had left General Gregg behind us . . . this one, with him, would make a fine pair of birds to have in our net, they thought."

Other men noticed that Custer "bore himself in the manner of a conqueror," and also waved a white flag. Caldwell said, "Why should there be truce in such a time as this? Then the sickening thought of surrender first entered my mind."

One of the men moved Caldwell deeply, a veteran who came up and put his arms around the neck of the lieutenant's horse. He was crying. "Is it true? Is it true General Lee has surrendered?"

"I fear there's no reason to doubt it."

"My God, that I should have lived to see this day! Caldwell,

I didn't think I'd live to see this day. I hoped I should die before this day."

I. G. Bradwell, the Georgia private in Gordon's ranks, saw a Federal rider come in from the left, waving a red bandanna, shouting:

"Who's in command here?"

"Gordon!"

The Federal was now in easy range, and Private John Thursby of the 31st Georgia raised his musket, "I'll get that scoundrel!"

A companion knocked the barrel aside, "Don't, John. It may be already surrender, and might cause trouble."

"That's not a white flag, and I'm not bound to respect it."

The men about Thursby held him until the officer passed from sight.

Thomas Devereux and his companion, Tuck Badger, had feasted in the morning: "In the road where the wagon train had passed we picked up some corn which had been spilled, about a bushel, I suppose. Tuck and I fed our horses, built a fresh fire, divided our corn with the rest of the staff, and parched a belly full."

After sunrise, when he had taken a short nap, Devereux was roused and sent forward with his troops; they had charged about a mile in the direction of Lynchburg, driving Yankees within sight of the Appomattox railroad station, when two officers, one of them a bluecoat, rode down the lines with white flags. Someone said the Federal was Custer. Devereux and his men recrossed the Appomattox:

"Without orders the men began to throw up extemporized breastworks of logs, fence rails and so forth. In a very few minutes General Grimes rode up and told us to stop working, that there would be no more fighting."

"The Army has surrendered," Grimes said.

Devereux would never forget the moment: "Some burst

into tears, some threw down their guns, others broke them against trees, and I saw one man thrust his musket between a forked sapling, bend the barrel and say, 'No Yankee will ever shoot at us with you.' A crowd surrounded General Grimes, who in a few words explained the situation, and said we would receive rations during the day. Then we went into camp, and the war was over."

A. C. Jones, in Gordon's ranks, thought there was "something ominous" in the air as he watched General Lee ride toward the village.

"He looked about as usual except that he wore a bright, new uniform. A few minutes afterwards I was standing in the road directing the moving of a rail fence to be used in building works when, to my astonishment, a squad of Yankee cavalry appeared, led by an officer carrying a white flag. In passing I distinctly heard him say, 'Those men had as well quit work.'"

There was soon an order to stop. Jones was half expecting word of surrender, but even so it "was a mental shock that I am unable to describe, just as if the world had suddenly come to an end. Lying flat upon the ground with my face to the earth, I went almost into a state of unconsciousness. Aroused from this condition by the excited voices of the men, I found that a number of them, led by Dick McDonald, a boy of eighteen, were insisting upon destroying the guns, swearing that the Yankees should not have them. With some difficulty I prevented this, and soon we all calmed down to a realization of the situation."

Almost instantly, Jones noticed, the generals of the army disappeared, and only regimental officers were left to handle the men.

Captain Fred Colston and Lieutenant Joseph Packard walked from their camp to the courthouse and on the way were passed by Robert Lee and his small party.

Since Colston had never seen him with a sword except at a review, he halted. "Packard, that means surrender."

Colston then saw Custer in the street: "Recognized . . . by

his long, yellow hair, and the red neckerchief of his command."

Custer talked with General Longstreet as Colston listened, and the two had an angry exchange.

Captain Sommers, a Confederate quartermaster who had been captured, paroled and recaptured during cavalry attacks on the wagons in retreat, confronted Custer:

"General Custer, I'd like to ask just what my status is. You see, I got captured, and then——"

Custer snapped, "Oh, I've no time to attend to that now."

William Owen, the artilleryman, met Robert Lee and Colonels Marshall and Taylor as the commander made his first ride to the outer lines. Owen saluted and Lee halted:

"Good morning, Colonel. How are your horses this morning? Do you think you can keep up with the infantry today?"

"I think I can. They had a pretty good feed of shucks. But, General, I have no orders."

Lee pointed to a hill. "You will find General Longstreet there. He will give you orders." He touched his hat and rode off. Owen wrote:

"I noted particularly his dress. He was in full uniform, with a handsome embroidered belt and dress sword, tall hat, and buff gauntlets. His horse, 'Old Traveller', was finely groomed, and his equipment, bridle, bit and so forth, were polished until they shone. All this seemed peculiar. I had never seen him before in full rig, and began to think something strange was to happen. He always wore during the campaigns a gray sack coat with side pockets, quite like the costume of a business man in cities."

Owen took his men and guns toward the sound of firing, and met Generals Alexander and Longstreet, who were seated on a log. Alexander rose and greeted Owen.

"General Lee sent me here for orders," Owen said. "What do you want me to do?"

"Turn into the field on your right and park the guns," Alexander said. He then lowered his voice. "We are going to surrender today."

Owen wrote: "We had been thinking it might come to that, sooner or later; but when the shock came it was terrible. And was this to be the end of all our marching and fighting for the past four years? I could not keep back the tears that came to my eyes."

Alexander warned him to keep the news from his men, and Owen took the guns into the field. He saw a flag of truce. The gunner was one of many who saw Custer as he tried for a second time to entice a Confederate commander to surrender, this time Longstreet. He sketched Custer's approach:

"He wore his hair very long, and it was of a light or reddish color. In his hand he carried a white handkerchief, which he constantly waved up and down. He inquired for General Lee, and was directed to General Longstreet upon the hill. Upon approaching he dismounted and said, 'General Longstreet, in the name of General Sheridan and myself I demand the surrender of this army. I am General Custer.'"

"I'm not in command," Longstreet said. "General Lee is, and he's gone back to meet General Grant in regard to our surrender."

"Well," Custer said, "no matter about Grant. We demand the surrender be made to us. If you do not do so we will renew hostilities, and any blood shed will be upon your head."

"Oh, well," Longstreet said. "If you do that I'll do my best to meet you." Old Pete turned to his staff.

Colonel Manning," he said, "please order General Johnson to move his division to the front, to the right of General Gordon. Colonel Latrobe, please order General Pickett forward, to General Gordon's left. Do it at once!"

There was surprise on Custer's face as these orders were passed. Owen said:

"He, cooling off immediately, said, 'General, probably we had better wait until we hear from Grant and Lee. I will speak to General Sheridan about it; don't move your troops yet.' And he mounted and withdrew in a much more quiet style than in his approach."

When Custer had gone, Longstreet chuckled. "Ha! That young man has never learned to play the game of 'Brag.'"

Owen joined the laughter; he knew that the divisions of Johnson and Pickett had disappeared after Sayler's Creek.

W. C. Powell marched with Company I of the 1st Engineers, carrying a Mississippi rifle in awkward, unaccustomed fashion, and was in Gordon's front when Custer rode into the Confederate lines:

"We thought they were prisoners and gave them a hearty cheer."

Custer passed, and yells came from the woods ahead, where the enemy lay. Colonel Talcott yelled to the Engineers, "Ready! They're coming."

A solitary horseman came from the woods. Powell and his companions thought he was a captured Confederate making his escape, and cheered for him. But when he came within hailing distance the rider shouted, "Lay down your arms, you damned Rebels! Surrender!"

"He's a Yankee," someone said. "Shoot him."

Without an officer's command, thirty-five or forty rifles fired. Powell wrote: "The man and the horse went down, the man rolling like a ball over the head of the horse with enough momentum to bring him up to and through our line, and when he straightened out he was dead."

Soon afterward a Federal walked from the woods with a white flag. Colonel Talcott sent a Sergeant Delacy, of Company I, to interview the bluecoat. Delacy returned. "He says Lee's surrendered."

W. L. Moffett, a private of Company D, 14th Virginia Cavalry, helped capture one of the enemy cannon, a final prize of the Army of Northern Virginia. He rode down a hill after Poague's big guns had cleared the field and was one of the riders who herded back part of a Philadelphia battery. He recalled it:

"I was ordered to guard them fellows, and when I got rid of them, the regiment had gone somewhere, I did not know where. But I did know I was left with some Yankees, and could only see the dust . . . to my right and to the Yankees' left.

"General W. H. F. Lee came along my way as I stood with the prisoners, and I asked him where the command was. He answered: 'It has gone. You turn them fellows aloose and come with me.' And I came. As I looked over my shoulder, as I rode down the hill we had charged up, I saw a regiment of Yanks riding by with their carbines slung, and carrying a white flag in the middle of the regiment and gradually expanding around our camp."

The Federal battery Moffett had helped to capture passed him, going back toward the enemy lines. One bluecoat shouted, "Guess you didn't keep us very long, did you, Johnny?"

E. M. Boykin rode into the open on the east side of the village with General Gary and the 7th South Carolina Cavalry, by now wide awake. In the distance a number of Federals clustered about a big white house; a bluecoat officer was studying Appomattox Court House with field glasses.

"Let's charge 'em," Gary said.

"It looks like a flag of truce party, General," someone said.

Gary swore explosively and urged them on; the riders drove the few Federals from the house and into woods. Boykin took a prisoner, a good-humored little man with his head bound heavily in bandages who behaved as if he knew his capture would be brief indeed. Boykin wrote:

"We were having it, as we thought, all our own way—when, stretched along behind the brown oaks, and moving with a close and steady tramp, was a long line of cavalry, some thousands strong—Custer's division, our friends of last night. This altered the complexion of things entirely."

Gary ordered a retreat by the flank, and Custer's line came after the South Carolinians, slowly, firing no volleys, but dropping shots from a skirmisher here and there, herding the Confederates. Boykin later surmised that the Federals knew of the truce, and were aware that Gary's men did not. The shots ceased when a courier, Tribble of the 7th South Carolina, rode past with a white flag, yelling news of the surrender.

A Federal captain rode to General Gary and shouted, "What do you mean by keeping up the fight after surrender?"

Gary bellowed, "Surrender! I've heard of no surrender. We're South Carolinians, sir, and we don't surrender. Besides, sir, I take commands from no officers but my own, and I don't recognize you or any of your cloth as such."

Boykin expected a duel, but other Federal officers intervened, and one assured Gary that a flag of truce was out, and that Grant and Lee were to confer. Only then did Gary sheathe his sword and lower his voice:

"Don't suppose, sir, that I have any doubt of the truth of your statement. But you know I can take orders only from my own officers. I'm perfectly willing to accept your statement and wait for those orders."

Captain W. W. Blackford of the Engineers came to Gary with orders to cease fighting, and the fragments of the cavalry were gathered in a field to wait.

Boykin kept an eye on Gary; the general turned his horse away, and with a captain and two others rode from the village.

Blackford's memory of the scene was more vivid. He was sent to Gary's field with a Federal officer who had come under a flag of truce, Lieutenant Vanderbilt Allen of Sheridan's staff. Allen rode ahead of Blackford, and gave Gary the first news of surrender. The General was apoplectic:

"And you expect me to believe any such damned tale as that? Where is the officer who brought you here? No sir, you shall go to the rear with the rest of the prisoners."

"I'm the officer, General," Blackford said. Gary rode aside with Blackford.

"What does this mean?"

"It means the army is surrendered, sir." Blackford had a long memory of Gary's reaction:

"He quivered as if he had been shot, and sat still in his saddle a moment, and then, returning his saber, which he held still drawn in his hand, he said, 'Then I'll be damned if I surrender.' And that night he passed out of the lines to join Johnston's army, I heard."

John Gordon had more guests at the western front of the army. He remembered:

"In a short time a white flag was seen approaching. Under it was Philip Sheridan, accompanied by a mounted escort almost as large as one of Fitz Lee's regiments. Sheridan was mounted on an enormous horse, a very handsome animal. He rode in front of the escort, and an orderly carrying the flag rode beside him."

Gordon's sharpshooters were still close about him. As Sheridan's riders came within range, Gordon said, "a half-witted fellow" raised his rifle.

"No," the general said. "You can't fire on a truce flag."

The man lowered the barrel sullenly, keeping it in position, and was raising it once more when Gordon seized the barrel.

"Well, General," the marksman said, "let him stay on his own side."

Gordon went to meet Sheridan. The Federal said that Grant had not notified him of suspension of hostilities, but when he read Gordon's note from Lee, he sent officers to halt firing. He was sitting on the ground with Gordon when a burst of firing rolled from the left. Gordon wrote:

"General Sheridan sprang to his feet and fiercely asked: 'What does that mean, sir?' I replied: 'It's my fault, General, I had forgotten that brigade. But let me stop the firing first, and then I'll explain.'"

Men went to stop the shots on the flank—Captain Blackford and Lieutenant Allen.

Gordon sized up Sheridan:

"His style of conversation and general bearing, while never discourteous, were far less agreeable and pleasing than those of any other officer of the Union army whom it was my fortune to meet . . . there was an absence of that delicacy and consideration which was exhibited by other Union officers."

Sheridan's insults were thinly veiled, Gordon thought. The Federal opened by saying "with a slight tinge of exultation," "We have met before, I believe, at Winchester and Cedar Creek, in the Valley." Gordon acknowledged his role in the Confederate defeats. Sheridan added:

"I had the pleasure of receiving some artillery consigned to me through your commander, General Early."

"Yes," Gordon said. "And this morning I received from your government artillery consigned to me through General Sheridan."

The little cavalryman was incredulous. He could not believe that some of his guns had been taken during the day.

The generals parted, Gordon noted, "without the slightest breach of military courtesy."

★ PURSUIT ★

THE HOURS after midnight near the settlement of Curdsville were quiet. Sleepy sentries lounged at the two houses occupied by Meade and Grant. At 4 A.M. a figure emerged from the Clifton house and stumbled into the yard. It was Grant.

Upstairs, General Horace Porter stirred:

"I rose and crossed the hall to ascertain how the General was feeling. I found the room empty, and upon going out the front door found him pacing up and down in the yard holding both hands to his head."

"How do you feel, General?"

"The pain is terrible. I had very little sleep."

"Well, there's one consolation in all this," Porter said. "I never knew you to be ill that you did not get some good news. I've become a little superstitious."

Grant smiled wanly. "The best thing that can happen to me today is to get rid of this pain."

Other men of the staff were now up, and persuaded Grant to go to Meade's headquarters for coffee. Porter thought the commander already felt better. Grant paused when he had reached Meade's house and wrote his first dispatch of the day to Robert Lee; it went out while the staff was at breakfast.

When full daylight came Grant was anxious to be off. Porter urged him to ride in an ambulance, so that he would be protected from the hot sun later in the day. Grant refused. He mounted Cincinnati and led his staff on a wide detour of the Rebel army, seeking Sheridan's front. They left Meade behind.

Porter and the newspaperman, Cadwallader, found it a hard ride across country and along little-used trails. Their route was to the village of New Store, thence south, across the Appomattox, into a wagon road leading from Farmville to Appomattox Court House. They were eight or nine miles east of the courthouse village when a rider overtook them. It was about 11 A.M.

The party had stopped in a newly cleared field to rest the horses, and several officers had lighted cigars from one of the burning piles of logs and brush. Someone looked rearward. Cadwallader wrote:

"A horseman was coming at full speed, waving his hat above his head, and shouting at every jump of his steed. As he neared us we recognized him as Major Pease, of General Meade's staff, mounted on a coal black stallion, white with foam from his long and rapid pursuit of us."

The rider was Lieutenant Charles E. Pease; he had brought a dispatch from Robert Lee, sent forward by Meade.

Pease saluted Aaron Rawlins and handed him the envelope, which the officer opened with agonizing deliberation. Rawlings passed the letter to Grant with no comment.

Cadwallader studied Grant's face: "There was no exultation manifested—no sign of joy—and instead of flushing from excitement, he clenched his teeth, compressed his lips, and became very pale."

Grant read the letter with care and gave it back to Rawlins. "You had better read it aloud, General," he said. Cadwallader thought Grant's face no more expressive than "last year's bird's nest."

Rawlins breathed deeply. His voice was deep, but tremulous, as he read the note from Lee, beginning:

> General:—I received your note of this morning on the picket line . . .

He came quickly to the final words:

> I now ask an interview, in accordance with the offer contained in your letter of yesterday, for that purpose.

There was a long moment of silence. Cadwallader was aware that the moment was historic:

"No one looked his comrade in the face. Finally Colonel

Duff, chief of Artillery, sprang upon a log, waved his hat, and proposed three cheers. A feeble hurrah came from a few throats, when all broke down in tears, and but little was said for several minutes."

Grant spoke of the dispatch at last: "How will that do, Rawlins?"

"I think *that* will do," Rawlins said.

Grant summoned his military secretary, Colonel Ely Parker, a huge brown-skinned man known to the army simply as "The Indian." The commander dictated his reply to Robert Lee, noting the time as 11:50 A.M. Parker scratched industriously; he was the best penman in Grant's headquarters entourage.

Parker was the most striking of the men around Grant, a quiet, round-faced giant who was the last Grand Sachem of the Iroquois; he had already carved a notable career. In his youth he had known Webster, Clay and Calhoun, and been befriended by the widow of President Polk. A law graduate, he had belatedly discovered that, since he was not an American citizen, he was barred from practice; he then graduated from Rensselaer Polytechnic Institute as a civil engineer, worked on the Erie Canal, and was chief engineer for the Chesapeake and Albemarle Canal.

Parker had become Grant's friend before the war, when he helped build the Marine Hospital in Galena, Illinois; ex-Captain Grant was a clerk in a harness shop, and had been rescued from trouble in a drunken episode by Parker.

The War Department rejected Parker as an engineer early in the war, but he somehow appeared at Vicksburg as a captain, impressed Grant with his work and joined the staff. Everyone seemed to know him. Horace Porter liked to tell of a man who came to headquarters to see Grant:

"Where's the old man?"

Aaron Rawlins, who was busy, jerked a thumb toward Grant's tent. The visitor got a glimpse of Parker.

"That's him, all right, but he's got all-fired sunburnt since I saw him last."

Grant had joshed Parker about the incident for months. The Indian had been the commander's private secretary, with rank of Lieutenant Colonel, since August, 1864.

This morning Parker quickly finished his work, and at noon the message went off to Lee under a white flag, accompanied by Lieutenant Colonel Orville Babcock and a lieutenant.

Pease had also brought Grant a note from Meade, explaining that he had opened the dispatch, and as a result had arranged a brief truce. Grant's officers noted the effect of this as they resumed their ride. Heavy firing of the morning faded, and they rode for some miles in silence. They trotted.

Horace Porter was still concerned about Grant. Over and over he had asked, "How do you feel, General?"

Now Grant grinned. "The pain in my head seemed to leave me the minute I got Lee's letter."

They came into a road near the village which was filled with men, horses and wagons, and turned across fields. A rider overtook them—Colonel Newhall of Sheridan's staff, who had one of the duplicate dispatches from Lee, sent off to insure delivery. There was a brief halt to read this, and Grant led them on. They drew near lines of troops, and when they saw these men were Confederates, the headquarters party turned back. Porter wrote:

"A short ride further would take us into his lines. It looked for a moment as if a very awkward condition of things might arise, and Grant become a prisoner in Lee's lines, instead of Lee in his. Such a circumstance would have given rise to an important cross entry in the system of campaign bookkeeping."

Cadwallader saw both armies as he trotted into the open valley about Appomattox Court House: "Officers were galloping in all directions, colors were flying, and it had more the appearance of a grand review of troops, than of two contending hosts."

At closer range, however, he saw "dirty, tattered, ranks of soldiers, none of them well clad, and nearly all officers in fatigue dress."

They crossed the upper end of the main street of the village and moved toward the courthouse. The landscape was sketched by the observant Morris Schaff:

Lee's campfires were along the Lynchburg road, which runs southwest to Appomattox. Along here lone and bushy ravine-scored fields tilt for a mile, at least, to a timbered

ridge circling southwestward around the birthplace of the
river. . . .

This ridge, where it is crossed by the old road, is flat-
tish, crowned with woods, and about half a mile wide,
breaking down sharply on its northern side into the bed of
Rocky Run, a pleasant brook that goes gurgling around the
ridge's base and falls into the Appomattox about a mile
below the courthouse.

Beyond the run the ground begins to rise at once in
a long commanding incline to the top of a higher ridge. . . .
On each side are beautiful leaning and dipping fields. . . .
At the top of the second ridge the road enters woods and
then sweeps directly to the east by New Hope Church on
toward New Store and Farmville. The prevailing timber
through which it bears is oak . . . roamed by wild turkeys.

The Appomattox, whose murmur can almost be heard
at the courthouse, is nothing more than a good-sized willow-
fringed run that a country boy can jump. The rivers' [Ap-
pomattox and James] birthplace is at the feet of shouldering
knobs, covered with monarch oak, and from any one of
them you can overlook the old courthouse village, and all
the scene of the last struggle.

Grant's party met Sheridan and Ord and their staffs at
the edge of the village.

"How are you, Sheridan?" Grant said.

"First-rate, thank you. How are you?"

Horace Porter detected exultation in the cavalryman's voice.
Grant's memory of the moment was different:

"I was conducted at once to where Sheridan was . . . with
his troops. . . . They were very much excited, and expressed
their view that this was all a ruse employed to enable the Confederates to get away. They said they believed that Johnston
was marching up from North Carolina now, and Lee was moving
to join him; and they would whip the rebels where they were now
in five minutes if I would only let them go in. But I had not a
doubt about the good faith of Lee."

Grant turned to Sheridan. "Is Lee over there?"

"Yes. He's in that brick house."

"Well, then, we'll go over."

George Meade was better this morning, but stuck to his ambulance. Soon after Grant left Curdsville, the commander of the Army of the Potomac was carried into the covered vehicle. Colonel Lyman heard a Federal band playing "Dixie" to mock the almost-surrounded Confederates, and thought the enemy must be seized by despair at the sound. At 6:30 A.M. Meade's wagon got away "at a round trot."

Lyman complained, "Ninety miles have I trotted and galloped after that Lee, and worn holes in pantaloons, before I could get him to surrender!"

After an hour the ambulance and staff met 6th Corps infantry streaming into the main road and Meade's party halted to talk with General Horatio Wright.

At ten thirty, two Negroes came with news: Federals had entered Lynchburg yesterday, far to the west, and Lee was now cut off at Appomattox Court House. Lyman wrote:

"This gave us new wings!"

An aide went off to hurry General Humphreys and the infantry, all wagons were ordered out of the road, and the 6th Corps regiments passed at a trot. Lyman sketched a lively scene:

"Away went the General again, full tilt, along the road crowded by infantry, every man of whom was footing it as if a lottery prize lay just ahead! A bugler trotted ahead, blowing to call the attention of the troops, while General Webb followed, crying, 'Give way to the right! Give way to the right!'

"Thus we ingeniously worked our way, amid much pleasantry.

" 'Fish for sale!' roared one doughboy.

" 'Yes,' joined in a pithy comrade, 'and a tarnation big one, too!'

"The comments on the General were endless.

" 'That's Meade.'

" 'Yes, that's him.'

" 'Is he sick?'

" 'I expect he is. He looks kinder wild.'

" 'Guess the old man hain't had much sleep lately.' "

When the party came near the Rebel lines Lyman overheard some of the confusion of the truce. General Humphreys got a request to suspend an attack until Grant and Lee had met, but shouted, "They shan't stop *me!* Receive the message, but push on the skirmishers!"

An officer came through the lines with a dispatch from Lee saying that General Ord had ceased firing on the far end of the line, and asking for extension of the arrangement to this sector. The flurry over this brought Meade to the rear of his wagon.

"Hey! What! I have no sort of authority to grant such suspension. Lee has already refused Grant's terms. Advance your skirmishers, Humphreys, and bring up your troops. We will pitch into them at once!"

Lyman thought his voice "harsh and suspicious." Before orders could be passed General James W. Forsyth came through the Rebel lines from Sheridan. He urged a suspension of fighting, and Meade reluctantly agreed.

"Well, I'll wait till two o'clock, to let you get back to Sheridan. And then, if I get no communication from Lee, I'll attack."

Forsyth left with a satchel full of notes and orders, and Meade's staff waited impatiently for almost two hours. More Negroes came in with reports: Rebel pickets had thrown away their guns and fallen back. One of them said, "The Rebs have done give up."

Meade pulled out his watch. "Two o'clock," he said. "No answer. Go forward." The pickets met a Federal and a Confederate officer, who had an order from Grant to halt the troops. Lyman sketched the Rebel:

"Major Wingate, of General Lee's staff, was a military-looking man, dressed in a handsome gray suit with gold lace, and a gold star upon the collar. He was courageous, but plainly mortified to the heart. 'We had done better to have burnt our whole train three days ago,' he said bitterly. And there he struck the pith of the thing."

Meade and his officers settled down to wait.

The bluecoat cavalry between Appomattox Station and the courthouse was late in settling for the night. When General Crook came up, Sheridan sent him to anchor Devin's line and block the road to the Rebels. Across the dark road, Custer's men tried to clear the field of captured guns, men and horses, to reform broken squadrons, and find their wounded.

George Custer was out until almost dawn, and before he went to his campfire visited the makeshift hospital of his division for a look at the wounded troopers. One of his men wrote: "Had it been daylight he would have seen green saplings about which his men . . . fought, bent and split by canister, the trees and artillery carriages perforated by bullet holes; horses wallowed in the bloody mud. . . . Surgeons of wide experience in the cavalry said they had never treated so many extreme cases in so short a fight."

In the front line lay the veterans of the 1st Maine Cavalry, commanded by Colonel Jonathan P. Cilley, of Crook's Division.

It was 1 A.M. when they were led into position across the Bent Creek Road, no more than three quarters of a mile from the courthouse. Cilley posted the videttes himself and had hardly finished when there were sounds from below. The colonel listened intently: Confederate artillery, he decided, making camp. Cilley walked through his lines and crept near enough to hear shouts of Rebel drivers to their horses. He returned to his men and made his headquarters simply by sitting at the foot of a chestnut tree and sat, drowsing, idly listening to the noises of the enemy camp. Overhead, through an occasional break in the clouds, he saw stars.

Half a mile behind him, running across this road, but with its center on the Lynchburg Road, was the full division, Crook's main line, where troopers had dug in behind piles of rails and logs.

The front on the Lynchburg Road was held by the 3rd Brigade of Crook's Division, under Colonel Charles H. Smith. It had pushed forward after midnight, until Smith found himself on a slight ridge, where he had men pull rails from fences and block the road. He dismounted his men and placed a couple of guns. The horses were taken to the rear, to be out of sight in case of Rebel attack.

Long before dawn orderlies had roused Sheridan in his cottage at Appomattox Station. General Ord arrived. The head of his Army of The James was in, having marched all night. The lead division was Robert Foster's, of Gibbon's 24th Corps. Sheridan wrote of Ord's arrival:

"As he ranked me, of course I could give him no orders, so after a hasty consultation as to where his troops should be placed we separated."

Sheridan rode to a hill near his front lines and Ord directed Foster's men into a woodland behind the cavalry. Behind them was another division of the corps, followed by the entire 5th Corps; Negro troops were among them. Sheridan made a move of the cavalry, as well, sending MacKenzie to Crook's left flank.

The fog lying against hillsides did not prevent Sheridan's accurate diagnosis of firing in his front—waves of Rebel infantry were pushing back his videttes, and on a flank a cavalry attack was breaking the line. He had so close a look at John Gordon's infantry in the field that he sensed danger. Morrris Schaff wrote:

> They were now advancing firmly with colors, and there were so many standards crimsoning each body of troops—to their glory Confederate color bearers stuck by Lee to the last—that they looked like marching gardens blooming with cockscombs, red roses and poppies. One glance told Sheridan that Crook and MacKenzie could not possibly hold their ground.

Sheridan ordered the two officers to pull back their lines before the Rebels, and sent another aide to wake Custer and Devin, who were asleep in a field near the headquarters cottage.

Colonel Cilley's men were pushed back hurriedly, and Confederates poured toward the main line of cavalry. On Colonel Smith's front, action was slower, for the Rebels halted, uncertain whether they faced infantry or dismounted cavalry, and while they waited to bring up artillery, Ord's infantry came up from the station, literally running into position.

On one flank MacKenzie's little cavalry brigade was smashed by a Rebel charge, and, at the height of this, Confederate infantry broke Crook's line. While the most determined troopers fought the graybacks, a fresh cavalry charge struck their flank, led by Rooney Lee. Schaff wrote of it: "Back through old fields and heavy copses of young pine and shaggy jack oaks Crook and MacKenzie were driven, their lead horses and batteries retreating in great confusion, leaving a gun—and perhaps two of them, for the number is in doubt—in the enemy's hands. . . . Crook and MacKenzie out of their way, Grimes wheeled his line of battle . . . and the Lynchburg road was cleared. . . . The tattered forces that had cleared it burst into cheers."

The Rebel yells were cut short, for through the broken ranks of fleeing cavalry came Foster's division, with the 39th Illinois, and the 62nd and 69th Ohio in front. On one flank Negro troops fought their way into the open. Artillery fire halted these lines for a moment, but the 8th Maine and 199th Pennsylvania charged and silenced the guns. Fighting spread to other parts of the field.

General Joshua Chamberlain, of the Maine troops, got an order from an excited rider, "General Sheridan wants you to break from your column and come now. The Rebels are pressing him hard. Don't wait for orders through regular channels. Act at once."

Chamberlain took his men into a pine woods, running. Sheridan had a quick greeting: "Now smash 'em!" Once, after Chamberlain had the men charging over a field, he got an order to halt. He wrote:

"But in the impetuosity of youth and the heat of conflict I pushed on. . . . We fought like demons across that field and up that bristling hill. They told us we would expose ourselves to the full fire of the Confederate artillery once we gained the crest, but push on we did."

A number of men fell, dropped by the last volley of Cox's Rebel brigade. As the echoes died Chamberlain saw from his hill: "On the opposite ridge a full mile across the valley the dark blotches of the Confederate infantry drawn up in line of battle; the blocks of cavalry further to our right. . . .

"In the valley, where flowed the now narrow Appomattox . . . was a perfect swarm of moving men, animals, and wagons, wandering apparently aimlessly."

Sheridan had one glimpse of this: "I decided to attack at once, and formations were ordered at a trot for a charge by Custer's and Devin's divisions down the slope."

Custer was ready, but there was a delay with Devin's men,

and in the wait an aide brought Sheridan word: "Lee has surrendered. Don't charge. The white flag is up."

Sheridan sent word of this to Ord, but could not find Custer, and supposing that he had gone toward the courthouse, rode in that direction. He was in front of his staff when Confederate infantry fired at him. He halted, waved his hat, and yelled, "There's a truce. Stop firing!"

Bullets sang about his head and Sheridan took cover behind a ridge. He rode into the village with a sergeant who carried a battle flag on a staff, and was forced to turn back and save the colors:

"I heard a Confederate soldier demanding my battle flag from the color bearer, thinking, no doubt, that we were coming in as prisoners. The sergeant had drawn his saber and was about to cut the man down, but at a word from me he desisted."

Sheridan found General Gordon in command of the front, and was speaking to him when firing broke out.

Gordon seemed embarrassed by this. Sheridan said: "General, your men fired on me as I was coming over here, and undoubtedly they are treating Merritt and Custer the same way. We might as well let them fight it out."

"There must be some mistake," Gordon said.

"Why not send a staff officer and have your people cease firing? They are violating the flag."

Lieutenant Vanderbilt Allen and a Confederate officer rode off to the flank.

Sheridan's version of the last moments of this meeting:

"When quiet was restored Gordon remarked: 'General Lee asks for a suspension of hostilities pending the negotiations which he is having with General Grant.'

"I rejoined: 'I have been constantly informed of the progress of the negotiations, and think it singular that while such discussions are going on, General Lee should have continued his march and attempted to break through my lines this morning. I will entertain no terms except that General Lee shall surrender to General Grant on his arrival here. If these terms are not accepted we will renew hostilities.'

"Gordon replied: 'General Lee's army is exhausted. There is no doubt of his surrender to General Grant.'"

A Confederate rider with a scrap of a white towel on the tip of his saber came into the Federal lines, and met the 7th Michigan Cavalry of Devin's Division.

"I'm Captain Sims from General Gordon," he said. "Where's your commanding officer, Sheridan? I have a message for him."

"He's not here, but Custer is. You'd better see him."

"Can you take me to him?"

The captain went with Custer's chief of staff, Colonel E. W. Whitaker, and found Custer riding with his squadrons toward the front.

"Who are you and what do you want?" Custer asked.

"I'm from Longstreet's staff, with a message from Gordon to Sheridan to ask suspension of hostilities until General Lee can be heard from."

"We'll listen to no terms but unconditional surrender. We're behind your army and it's at our mercy."

"Will you let me take this message back?"

"Yes, go on."

"Do you want to send an officer with me?"

Custer hesitated, but sent Colonel Whitaker and Major George Briggs of the 7th Michigan with the Confederate. A moment later the waiting ranks saw Whitaker galloping along the front with two grayback officers, yelling to the Federal infantry.

In front of Joshua Chamberlain's line Whitaker called, "This is unconditional surrender. This is the end."

A Confederate also yelled, "I'm just from Gordon and Longstreet, and Gordon says for God's sake stop that infantry or hell will be to pay."

"I've no authority to stop the movement," Chamberlain said. "Sheridan's in command."

"Then I'll go to him," the Confederate said. Chamberlain stopped his men. About this time, Morris Schaff noted, the last shots were fired, from a Confederate battery. The last men killed, so far as he could tell, were a Lieutenant Clark of the 185th New York, and William Montgomery, of the 155th Pennsylvania, the latter fifteen years old, the victim of a Rebel Minié ball.

The Federals pushed forward until they were in the edge of the village, overlooking Confederate lines on every hand. Colors were planted and guns were parked. A quiet celebration spread in the ranks.

A gray-haired officer shouted, "Glory be to God, Chamberlain. Yes, and on earth, peace, goodwill toward men."

★ WILMER McLEAN'S HOUSE ★

THE McLEAN house sat back from the country road on the east side, behind a sagging fence and a carriage gate. Blue grass sprouted in the yard under the locusts. A wooden porch ran the length of the building, and near the north end, by the porch, a Confederate orderly grazed three horses.

Grant approached with a dozen or more officers, with others trailing tentatively behind. Sylvanus Cadwallader was along, as watchful as ever.

A staff officer put his horse over the fallen fence into the yard near the Rebel. "Whose horses are they?"

The graycoat orderly was Sergeant G. M. Tucker: "General Lee's," he said. "He's in there."

Cadwallader inspected the horses, one of them "a dapple gray" with a Grimsley saddle, a plain single-reined bridle, and none of the trappings of rank.

Grant turned into the yard. Except for the soiled shoulder straps of a lieutenant general—gold-bordered rectangles of black velvet each bearing one large and two small stars—he might have been a private of cavalry. His companions noted nothing remarkable in his manner, but he wrote as if strangely distracted in these moments:

"I had known General Lee in the old army, and had served with him in the Mexican War; but did not suppose, owing to the difference in our age and rank, that he would remember me; while I would more naturally remember him distinctly, because he was the chief of staff of General Scott in the Mexican War."

Grant also had a thought of his appearance as he mounted the broad steps of the country house:

"When I had left camp that morning I had not expected so soon the result that was then taking place, and consequently was in rough garb. I was without a sword, as I usually was when on horseback on the field, and wore a soldier's blouse for a coat, with the shoulder straps of my rank to indicate to the army who I was."

Orville Babcock came from the house onto the porch as Grant climbed the steps. Horace Porter sketched the commander:

"Then nearly forty-three years of age, five feet eight inches in height, with shoulders slightly stooped. His hair and full beard were a nut-brown, without a trace of gray in them. He had on a single-breasted blouse, made of dark blue flannel, unbuttoned in front, and showing a waistcoat beneath. He wore an ordinary pair of top boots, with his trousers inside, and was without spurs. The boots and portions of his clothes were spattered with mud. He had on a pair of thread gloves, of a dark yellow color."

Grant entered the house. Officers thronged on the porch and in the yard, draping themselves over two wooden benches flanking the doorway.

Charles Marshall wrote: "In about half an hour we heard horses, and the first thing I knew General Grant walked into the room. . . . He looked as though he had had a pretty hard time . . . dusty and a little soiled."

A few officers had entered with Grant, but witnesses did not take careful note of them. The two commanders passed remarkable greetings. Horace Porter remembered it:

Grant: "I met you once before, General Lee, while we were serving in Mexico, when you came over from General Scott's headquarters to visit Garland's brigade. I have always remembered your appearance, and I think I should have recognized you anywhere."

Lee: "Yes, I know I met you on that occasion, and I have often tried to recollect how you looked, but I have never been able to recall a single feature."

There was a wandering conversation, marked by occasional pauses. Babcock went to the door and summoned other officers,

Sheridan, Seth Williams, Rawlins, Horace Porter, Ely Parker and half a dozen others including Cadwallader. Babcock called for two more by name: Robert Lincoln, the President's son, and Grant's military secretary, Adam Badeau. The room on the left filled with men. Porter said:

"We walked in softly and ranged ourselves quietly about the sides of the room, very much as people enter a sick chamber when they expect to find the patient dangerously ill."

Some Federals sat on the sofa but most of them stood. Grant sat near the center of the room, facing Lee, who was by the front window with Marshall, a tiny oval table at his side.

Porter noted that it was about 1:30 P.M.

Marshall's memory of the conversation of the commanders was sparse:

"General Grant greeted General Lee very civilly, and they engaged for a short time in a conversation about their former acquaintance. . . . Some other Federal officers took part in the conversation, which was terminated by General Lee saying to General Grant that he had come to discuss the terms of the surrender of his army, as indicated in his note of that morning, and he suggested to General Grant to reduce his proposition to writing."

Porter remembered more:

"I suppose, General Grant," Lee said, "that the object of our meeting is fully understood. I asked to see you to ascertain upon what terms you would receive the surrender of my army."

"The terms I propose," Grant said, "are those stated substantially in my letter of yesterday—that is, the officers and men surrendered to be paroled and disqualified from taking up arms again until properly exchanged, and all arms, ammunition, and supplies to be delivered up as captured property."

"Those are about the conditions I expected," Lee said.

"Yes, I think our correspondence indicated pretty clearly the action that would be taken," Grant said. "I hope it will lead to a cessation of hostilities . . . preventing any further loss of life."

"I presume we have both carefully considered the proper steps to be taken, and I suggest that you commit to writing the terms you have proposed, so that they may be formally acted upon."

"Very well," Grant said, "I will write them out."

Ely Parker brought a little marble-topped table to Grant's side, and the commander scratched for a few minutes with a pencil in his orderbook. Porter took special note of Grant's hesitation at the end, when the general raised his head, glanced at Lee's glittering dress sword, and wrote a sentence: "This will not embrace the side arms of the officers, nor their private horses or baggage."

Babcock had gone to the door when Grant began writing. General George Forsyth, who was outside, saw him:

"Babcock came to the door again, opened it, and glanced out. As he did so he placed his forage cap on one finger, twirled it around, and nodded to us all, as much as to say, 'It's all settled.'"

Another onlooker was Henry Wing, an enterprising young New York reporter who had arranged such a signal. Inexplicably, he turned his horse from the yard and dashed through the lounging men in great haste.

Cadwallader was impressed by Grant's poise, but thought Lee magnificent.

"He wore his hair and whiskers cut short, both of which were iron gray in color. He was rather stout and fleshy than otherwise; with bronzed face from exposure . . . but showing a remarkably fine white skin above the line of his hatband. . . . His manners and bearing were perfect, and stamped him a thoroughbred gentleman in the estimation of all who saw him . . . that happy blending of dignity and courtesy so difficult to describe . . . no haughtiness or ill-humor betrayed on the one hand; nor affected cheerfulness, forced politeness nor flippancy on the other. He was a gentleman—which fully and wholly expresses his behavior."

Sheridan saw less when he glimpsed Lee: "When I entered McLean's house General Lee was standing . . . dressed in a new uniform and wore a handsome sword. His tall, commanding form thus set off contrasted strongly with the short figure of General Grant."

Grant wrote:

"What General Lee's feelings were I do not know. As he was a man of much dignity, with an impassable face, it was impossible to say whether he felt inwardly glad that the end had finally come, or felt sad over the result, and was too manly to show it. Whatever his feelings, they were entirely concealed from my observation; but my own feelings, which had been quite jubilant on the receipt of his letters, were sad and depressed . . .

"Our conversation grew so pleasant that I almost forgot the object of our meeting. . . . General Lee called my attention to the object."

The writing of surrender terms was explained by the Union commander: "When I put my pen to the paper I did not know the first word that I should make use of in writing the terms. I only knew what was in my mind, and I wished to express it clearly, so that there could be no mistaking it."

When Grant finished his letter he beckoned his senior adjutant, Lieutenant Colonel T. S. Bowers, but this officer said he was "too nervous" to copy the document. Grant called Parker. Porter wrote:

"When he had finished the letter he called Colonel Parker . . . to his side and looked it over with him and directed him as they went along to interline six or seven words and to strike the word 'their' which had been repeated . . . he handed the book to General Lee and asked him to read over the letter."

Lee's deliberate movements fascinated the Federal staff. He placed Grant's book on the table and took from a pocket a pair of steel-rimmed spectacles, wiping the lenses carefully with a handkerchief. He crossed his legs with a squeaking of the new boots, and read slowly:

> General R. E. Lee, Commanding C.S.A.
> Appomattox Ct.H., Va., April 9, 1865
> General: In accordance with the substance of my letter to you of the 8th inst., I propose to receive the surrender of the Army of Northern Virginia on the following terms, to wit: Rolls of all the officers and men to be made in duplicate, one copy to be given to an officer designated by me, the other to be retained by such officer or officers as you may designate. The officers to give their individual paroles not to take up arms against the Government of the United States until properly, and each company or regimental commander to sign a like parole for the men of their commands. The arms, artillery, and public property to be parked, and

stacked, and turned over to the officers appointed by me to receive them. This will not embrace the side arms of the officers, nor their private horses or baggage. This done, each officer and man will be allowed to return to his home, not to be disturbed by the United States authorities so long as they observe their paroles, and the laws in force where they may reside. Very respectfully,

U. S. Grant, Lieutenant-General

Lee looked up when he had read the first of the two pages: "After the words, 'until properly,' the word 'exchanged' seems to be omitted. You doubtless intended to use that word."

"Why yes," Grant said. "I thought I had put it in."

"With your permission I will mark where it should be inserted."

"Certainly."

Lee fished in a pocket for a pencil, but found none, and Horace Porter passed one to him. Lee continued to read, and all the while twisted the pencil nervously, or tapped delicately at the table with its point.

As Lee read Grant's sentence allowing Confederate officers to keep their arms, horses and baggage, Porter noticed "a slight change of countenance . . . evidently touched by this act of generosity."

"This will have a very happy effect upon my army," Lee said.

"Unless you have some suggestions to make in regard to the form," Grant said, "I will have a copy made in ink and sign it."

Lee hesitated. "There is one thing I would like to mention. The cavalrymen and artillerymen in our army own their own horses. Our organization differs from yours. I would like to understand whether these men will be permitted to retain their horses."

"You will find that the terms as written do not allow it," Grant said. "Only the officers are allowed to take their private property."

"No," Lee said, "I see the terms do not allow it. That is clear."

There was a subtle eloquence in Lee's silence. Porter wrote: "His face showed plainly that he was quite anxious to have this concession made."

Grant hurried as if he were embarrassed to have Lee make the request: "Well, the subject is quite new to me. Of course I did not know that any private soldiers owned their animals, but I think this will be the last battle of the war—I sincerely hope so—and . . . I take it that most of the men in the ranks are small farmers, and it is doubtful whether they will be able to put in a crop and carry themselves and their families through next winter without their horses.

"I will arrange it in this way: I will not change the terms as they are written, but I will instruct the officers to let all the men who claim to own a horse or mule take the animals home with them to work their little farms."

"This will have the best possible effect upon my men," Lee said. "It will be very gratifying and will do much toward conciliating our people."

Lee handed the book to Grant, who passed it to Parker. The Indian went to the rear of the room to write, but discovered that he was out of ink. He borrowed a small boxwood inkwell from Charles Marshall.

Marshall wrote a brief letter of acceptance of the terms for Lee, but was forced to change his draft when Lee read it.

"Don't say, 'I have the honor,'" Lee told the aide. "He is here. Just say, 'I accept the terms.'"

When Marshall began to make a copy in ink, he found himself out of paper, and borrowed a few sheets from one of the Federal officers.

Quiet conversations began in the room. Grant introduced his officers to Lee. Porter said:

"He did not exhibit the slightest change of features during this ceremony until Parker was introduced to him. . . . When Lee saw Parker's swarthy features he looked at him with evident surprise, and his eyes rested on him for several seconds. What was passing in his mind probably no one ever knew, but the natural surmise was that at first he mistook Parker for a Negro, and was struck with astonishment to find that the commander of the Union armies had one of that race on his personal staff."

Porter's surmise was in error, or he did not hear what passed between Lee and the Indian, for Parker recorded:

"After Lee had stared at me for a moment, he extended his hand and said, 'I am glad to see one real American here.' I shook his hand and said, 'We are all Americans.'"

Lee spoke to General Seth Williams, whom he had known intimately since his days as commandant at West Point; he thanked Williams for having sent word of the safety of Custis. Williams responded with an attempt at jollity. Porter caught Lee's reaction: "He did not unbend, or even relax the sternness of his features."

Marshall sat beside Sheridan on the sofa, and provoked brief laughter.

"This is very pretty country," the Federal said.

"General, I haven't seen it by daylight. All my observations have been made at night, and I haven't seen the country at all myself."

Grant interrupted the chuckling Sheridan:

"General Lee has about a thousand or fifteen-hundred of our people prisoners and they are faring the same as his men, but he tells me his haven't anything. Can you send them some rations?"

"Yes."

"How many can you send?"

"Twenty-five thousand."

There was more of this discussion, in the memory of Michael R. Morgan, Grant's assistant Commissary General. Grant asked Morgan:

"Colonel, feed the Confederate army."

"How many men are there?"

Grant turned to Lee. "How many men have you, General Lee?"

"Our books are lost," Lee said. "Our organizations are broken up. The companies are mostly commanded by noncommissioned officers. We have nothing but what we have on our backs. . . ."

Morgan interrupted, "Say twenty-five thousand men?"

"Yes," Lee said, "say twenty-five thousand."

Morgan left the room, and outside found Colonel M. P. Small, Ord's commissary general:

"Can you feed the Rebs?"

"I guess so," Small said. Morgan thought his reply was given with confidence.

"All right. Send them three days' rations. Fresh beef, salt, hard bread, coffee and sugar." Small rode away.

Grant seemed unable to forget his dress, and looked at Lee's sword again. "I started out from my camp several days ago without my sword," he said. "And I have not seen my headquarters baggage since. I have been riding without side arms. I have generally worn a sword as little as possible. . . . I thought you would rather receive me as I was, than be detained."

"I'm much obliged to you, " Lee said. "I'm very glad you did it in that way."

There was a little more scattered conversation, some of it provided by Sheridan, who protested to Lee about the Confederate cavalry's violation of the truce in the morning. Lee had in his hand two copies of Sheridan's earlier note of complaint, and Sheridan asked for one of them.

Lee replied patiently, "I'm sorry. It is probable that my cavalry at that point of the line did not fully understand the agreement."

Lee shook hands with Grant and left the room, followed by Marshall. It was 4 P.M.

Adam Badeau was at Grant's elbow.

"This will live in history," he said. Grant did not reply, but his expression gave Badeau an impression: "I am sure the idea had not occurred to him until I uttered it. The effect upon his fame, upon history, was not what he was considering."

Sergeant Tucker had loosed Traveller's bridle, sensibly, the watching General Forsyth thought. Traveller seemed to Forsyth "a fairly well-bred-looking gray in good heart though thin in flesh." All three of the Confederate horses ate hungrily.

Forsyth was awaiting the end of the surrender conference with a ready pencil:

"I became aware from the movement of chairs within that it

was about to break up. I had been sitting on the top step of the porch writing in my notebook, but I closed it at once, and stepping back on the porch leaned against the railing nearly opposite and to the left of the door, and expectantly waited.

"As I did so the inner door slowly opened and General Lee stood before me. As he paused for a few seconds . . . I took my first and last look at the great Confederate chieftain . . . a clear, ruddy complexion—just then suffused by a deep crimson flush, that rising from his neck overspread his face and even tinged his broad forehead . . . deep brown eyes, a firm but well-shaped Roman nose . . . an exquisitely mounted sword, attached to a gold-embroidered Russian leather belt, trailed loosely on the floor at his side, and in his right hand he carried a broad-brimmed soft gray felt hat, encircled by a golden cord, while in his left he held a pair of buckskin gauntlets. Booted and spurred, still vigorous and erect, he stood, bare-headed, looking out of the open doorway, sad-faced and weary."

All the Federal officers snapped to salute as Lee crossed the porch. He returned this "mechanically but courteously," Forsyth thought, and went to the head of the steps, all the while staring beyond the yard into the valley where the army waited. Forsyth wrote:

"Here he paused, and slowly drew on his gauntlets, smiting his gloved hands into each other several times after doing so, evidently utterly oblivious of his surroundings.

"Then, apparently recalling his thoughts, he glanced deliberately right and left, and not seeing his horse, he called in a hoarse, half-choked voice: 'Orderly! Orderly!' "

Tucker called from below, "Here, General, here!" The sergeant slipped the bridle over Traveller's neck, and Lee descended the steps to stand beside the animal until Tucker had finished. Forsyth still watched from the porch:

"As the orderly was buckling the throat latch the General reached up and drew the forelock out from under the browband, parted and smoothed it, and then gently patted the gray charger's forehead in an absent-minded way, as one who loves horses, but whose thoughts are far away, might all unwittingly do. Then, as the orderly stepped aside, he caught up the bridle reins in his left hand, and seizing the pommel of the saddle with the same hand, he caught up the slack of the reins in his right hand, and placing it on the cantle he put his foot in the stirrup, and swung himself slowly and wearily, but nevertheless firmly, into the saddle (the old dragoon mount) . . . and as he did so there broke unguardedly from his lips a long, low, deep sigh, almost a groan in its intensity, while the flush on his neck seemed, if possible, to take on a still deeper hue."

Marshall came down the steps behind Lee, slight and erect in his worn gray uniform, with his heavy spectacles giving him an expression of thoughtful anxiety. Forsyth surmised that, though Marshall looked rigidly before him, he missed nothing within range of his vision.

When Marshall had mounted, Lee urged Traveller through the yard. The orderly followed them at a slow walk.

In the crowded yard was a New York *Tribune* correspondent, Thaddeus S. Seybold. The reporter turned to a Confederate, a young aide of General Armistead Long, and, pointing to Lee, asked:

"Who's that distinguished-looking officer?"

"That is the greatest man the country ever produced, General Robert E. Lee."

Grant came down the steps, hurriedly, head down, and halted when he found Lee riding across his path. Grant looked up, and the two raised their hands in farewell. Grant mounted Cincinnati.

The Federal commander moved to the gate, then turned back, speaking to Sheridan, "Where will you make your headquarters tonight?"

"Here, or near here," Sheridan said. "Right here in the yard, probably."

"Very well, then. I'll know where to find you. Good day."

Sheridan was surrounded by officers on the porch, but he noted the departure of Lee:

"He mounted his chunky gray horse, and lifting his hat as he passed out of the yard, rode off toward his army, his arrival there being announced to us by cheering, which, as it progressed, varying in loudness, told he was riding through the bivouac of the Army of Northern Virginia."

Joshua Chamberlain was almost in front of the McLean House with some of his Maine men:

"And just then the glad news came that General Lee had surrendered. Shortly after that we saw pass before us that sturdy Rebel leader. . . . He was dressed in the brilliant trappings of a Confederate army officer, and looked every inch the soldier that he was. A few moments after that our own beloved leader, General Grant . . . came riding by. How different he was in appearance from the conquered hero."

Cadwallader did not leave the house with the departure of the commanders. He watched the brisk auction and looting of Wilmer McLean's furnishings:

Custer bought one of the tables used in the conference for $25; Ord bought another for $50. Somehow Sheridan obtained another.

Officers besieged McLean on his porch, offering ever-higher prices for chairs which had been used by officers in the surrender room. McLean stubbornly refused.

Officers forced greenbacks into his hands, but McLean threw them on the porch. Officers hurried away in the crowd, carrying chairs and other pieces. When the confusion had subsided, a cavalryman rode up, handed McLean a ten-dollar bill. "This is for the Major's chair," he said, and galloped away. No one knew where the furniture had gone. Cadwallader wrote:

"Cane bottomed chairs were ruthlessly cut to pieces; the cane splits broken into pieces a few inches long, and parceled out among those who swarmed around. Haircloth upholstery was cut from chairs, and sofas was also cut into strips and patches and carried away."

★ GRAY ★

GENERALS of both armies had occupied the courthouse village and posted cordons of sentries to keep common soldiers from the streets and buildings. Bottles were produced, and conviviality spread.

Robert Lee rode through the street as if it were empty, downhill toward the apple orchard where he had rested in the morning.

His troops were quick to guess what had been done. Regiments began destroying their flags, burning or burying them.

The 11th North Carolina officers, led by Captains E. R. Outlaw and M. R. Young, went into a roadside thicket, built a fire and made ready to burn their flag. Several officers tore strips from each of its color fields before throwing it into the flames. Outlaw saw his men squatting there, shedding "bitter and sorrowful tears."

Some officers, expecting harsh treatment from the Federals, ripped off all insignia of rank, but in the 5th Alabama were rebuked by Colonel Edwin L. Hobson, who was commanding a brigade, but had been promoted so recently as to have only one star on each shoulder.

Hobson set an example by clipping the star from one shoulder and pinning it to the other, saying to his men, "I'm ready for the consequences, whatever they are."

The 75th North Carolina was near the village as Lee passed. One of its officers said, "We drove our guns into the hard earth to tie our horses to, made a fire, burned our flag to keep the Yankees from getting it, and waited for further orders and something to eat."

Thomas Devereux, the young North Carolinian, first thought of his slave, George. He went back to camp, gave the Negro boy one of the five remaining five-dollar gold pieces he had sewn in his uniform jacket, told him to take his horse, Trumps, and to go home, a free man. Devereux wrote:

"The poor fellow looked at me a moment in silence as if hardly understanding and then blubbered out, 'Mars Thomas, I can't do it. Ise gwine to stay with you. If you can stand a Yankee prison, I can too.' I told him he'd not be allowed to go with me, and that he had better lose no time in doing as I said, but all to no avail. He took my hand and with the big tears running down his face said, 'No, Mars Thomas, I dassent face Mammy without you. When I left home with you to join the army the last words Mammy said was, "Now George, you have the care of that child, and don't you ever show your face to me without you bring him

back with you, dead or alive." Mars Thomas, I've got to mind
Mammy and stay with you.'"

Fletcher Massie of Lamkin's Battery had a guest, an irate
young Federal officer "hot as pepper" because of the last-minute
capture of his cannon that morning. When his anger had cooled,
Massie returned the artillery to him.

Federal gunners hitched it and the caisson and took it out of
the Confederate lines.

"You fooled us this morning," the Federal lieutenant said.
"They told us the way was open, and we came on. Your cavalry
got all around us, and we didn't get off a shot before they took
the gun."

Massie had also appropriated the fine horses the enemy had
pulling the gun and caisson, but he had quickly traded them to
friends, and replaced them with some of the bony, worn-out
horses straying about the village. The enemy lieutenant saw he
had been tricked, Massie said, "But he never said a word about
it."

Massie saw Lee passing, and joined a group of chattering
officers:

"A group of us . . . agreed together that we would not go
to prison, would cut our way through the lines some way or other,
but we would not surrender to be captured and carried off."

They heard the gossip from other men that all troops were
to be paroled, and abandoned their scheme to escape.

Lee rode a few hundred yards into the orchard below, amid
a swarm of Federal officers who looked curiously about. Colonel
Talcott soon had a picket of the engineers to keep them out, and,
in the words of Captain W. W. Blackford:

"General Lee occupied the shade of a tree . . . where he
paced backwards and forwards all day long looking like a caged
lion. . . .

"General Lee seemed to be in one of his savage moods . . .
So his staff kept to their tree except when it was necessary to in-
troduce the visitors. Quite a number came . . . some came from

curiosity, or to see General Lee as friends in the old army. But General Lee shook hands with none of them. It was rather amusing to see the extreme deference shown by them to General Lee. When he would see Colonel Taylor coming with a party towards his tree he would halt in his pacing and stand at 'attention' and glare at them with a look which few men but he could assume. They would remove their hats entirely and stand bareheaded during the interview while General Lee sometimes gave a scant touch to his hat in return and sometimes did not even do that . . . the interviews were short."

Dispatches went in and out of the orchard; rations were promised by the Federals, for immediate delivery. Men of the army were to be formally paroled, and Lee and his staff were the first to sign one of the little documents:

> We, the undersigned prisoners of war belonging to the Army of Northern Virginia, having been this day surrendered by General Robert E. Lee, C.S. Army, commanding said army, to Lieutenant General U. S. Grant, commanding Armies of the United States, do hereby give our solemn parole of honor that we will not hereafter serve in the armies of the Confederate States, or in any military capacity whatever, against the United States of America, or render aid to the enemies of the latter, until properly exchanged, in such manner as shall be mutually approved by the respective authorities.
>
> Done at Appomattox Courthouse, Va., this 9th day of April, 1865
>
> R. E. Lee, General. W. H. Taylor, Lt. Col. and Asst. Adjt. Genl. . . .
>
> The within named officers will not be disturbed by the United States authorities so long as they observe their parole and the laws in force where they may reside.

Near sunset Lee left the orchard and rode to his headquarters. His army seized the passage for an impromptu demonstration.

Among the first to catch sight of him was E. M. Boykin: "As soon as it was seen it acted like an electric flash upon our men; they sprang to their feet, and, running to the roadside, commenced a wild cheering that roused our troops. As far as we could see they came running down the hillsides, and joining in, along the ground and through the woods and up into the sky, there went a tribute that has seldom been paid to mortal man."

Tom Devereux had a glimpse:

"As he approached we could see the reins hanging loose on his horse's neck and his head was sunk low on his breast. As the men began to cheer, he raised his head and hat in hand he passed by, his face flushed and his eyes ablaze. I was on the road side nearest to the Courthouse, and so did not know what passed at the other side of the line. Some said he halted and spoke a few words. . . . I saw none of it."

Longstreet wrote:

"From force of habit a burst of salutations greeted him, but it quieted as suddenly as it arose. The road was packed by standing troops as he approached, the men with hats off, heads and hearts bowed down. As he passed they raised their heads and looked upon him with swimming eyes. Those who could find voice said good-bye, those who could not speak and were near, passed their hands gently over the sides of Traveller.

"He rode with his hat off, and had sufficient control to fix his eyes on a line between the ears of Traveller and look neither to right nor left until he reached a large white oak tree, where he dismounted to make his last headquarters, and finally talked a little."

The commander passed a body of South Carolina infantry, among them a young private, Frank M. Mixson:

"We commenced yelling for Lee. The old man pulled off his hat, and with tears streaming down his cheeks, without a word, he rode through us . . . all were bowing heads with tears."

John Gordon came in front of Lee before the end, to prepare the men. An Alabama private remembered:

"Soon Gordon came galloping down the road from the direction of the Federal lines and announced the terms of surrender as he passed, and asked the men to give General Lee 'a hearty cheer, for he was feeling greatly depressed.' "

Captain Blackford followed Lee down the route, through the closely packed lines of men. He noted that Lee began to weep as soon as the cheers began, and rode with tears dropping into his beard, hat in hand, bowing his acknowledgment to the men:

"This exhibition of feeling on his part found quick response from the men, whose cheers changed to choking sobs as with streaming eyes and many cries of affection they waved their hats as he passed. Each group began in the same way with cheers and ended in the same way with sobs, all the way to his quarters. Grim bearded men threw themselves on the ground, covered their faces with their hands and wept like children. Officers . . . sat on their horses and cried aloud."

One of the officers, Blackford saw, was the commander's son, Rooney.

Blackford thought that Traveller enjoyed the attention; the horse acknowledged it by tossing his head, to the cheers of the men.

One soldier held out his arms to Lee. "I love you just as well as ever, General Lee!"

The commander soon reached his tent, and though Blackford knew that he said a few words to those crowding around him, he could not hear what was said.

Lieutenant George Mills of the 16th North Carolina was close by, and heard Lee's brief speech:

"Boys, I have done the best I could for you. Go home now, and if you make as good citizens as you have soldiers, you will do well, and I shall always be proud of you. Goodbye, and God bless you all."

Mills thought: "He seemed so full that he could say no more."

Lee disappeared into his tent.

When the troops had quieted, General Armistead Long went into Federal lines with Colonel Thomas Carter of the artillery and two couriers, one of them young Percy Hawes. The boys were in a playful mood. Hawes wrote:

"On our way Owen and I concluded we would play a trick on the Yankee orderlies and make them hold our horses as well as our officers' horses and that we would stand around in a quiet, dignified way as if we were officers. . . .

"As we approached General Ord's headquarters the orderlies ran to hold our horses as eagerly as the average street gamin does during a holiday parade. We galloped up to the quarters and dismounted with all the dignity and style of men who knew they had done their duty."

Long was in search of his brother-in-law, General E. V. Sumner, but did not find him. Sheridan appeared, and Long talked with Ord and the cavalryman.

"What's become of Sumner?" Long asked.

"You fellows gave him such a drubbing this morning that Grant sent for him to know what was the matter with him," Ord said.

Sheridan straightened and spoke in what Hawes thought an "indelicate" manner: "Ah, damn it, he ought to have been with me!"

General C. W. Field, the infantryman, was with his men when positive news of the surrender came. He had a brief memory of it: "I saw the tears streaming down the face of the chivalrous Colonel Coward of South Carolina. Some proposed that if I thought it honorable and would lead them, that they would try to cut their way out. Some few did leave, but I had their names surrendered as though they were present. I did not see Pickett's Division at all, nor Kershaw's but once."

Federals flocked into the lines, and the army received them without animosity. E. M. Boykin wrote:

"Success had made them good-natured. Some came up and said:

" 'We've been fighting one another for four years. Give me a Confederate five dollar bill to remember you by.' "

Boykin found "nothing offensive" in their manner.

An officer of the 33rd North Carolina hung about the newly established tent of a Federal commissary officer:

"Give me some bread for my men, old fellow. They've had nothing for three days."

"I can't do it," the bluecoat said. "But you walk around the tent carelessly and fill your haversack with crackers and loaf sugar and your canteen with whisky, and I won't see you."

The officer went out, laden, to cheer his men.

The private, I. G. Bradwell, found himself near the village in the late afternoon:

"We formed in line, so weak that we could hardly stand, in rags, facing the Yankees. . . . The silence was finally broken by someone in their ranks, and the whole line began to curse and use the most opprobrious language. This continued for some time, when an officer, riding to and fro in the rear of their line, spoke:

" 'These Confederate soldiers are brave men. If you were half as brave as they are, you'd have conquered them long ago. If I hear another cowardly scoundrel curse these men again, I'll break my sword over his head.' "

The Rebels gave a shout for the Federal major, who disappeared.

Lieutenant Joseph Packard, late of Reserve Ordnance, was well dressed for the army's final day. He had followed Captain Fred Colston's example and put on the best of his uniform coats— one he had been issued at the opening of the war. And in the morning he had exchanged his sword, with its old Richmond-made scabbard, for a finer one captured from a Federal artillery-man.

Packard's hat, alone, was disreputable, but he refused to part with it; he had worn it since just after Gettysburg, holes and all. In the afternoon he bought a spare cap from an enemy artilleryman, paying him, after a desperate scramble for negotiable values, "A five-cent piece, a three-cent piece, and a three-cent postage stamp."

At night Packard made camp under a wagon cover on a hillside. It was not long before help came: "Our friends, the enemy, sent us some beef and crackers and to each officer a quart of whisky, which helped to pass the time."

Many escaped. Fitz Lee, Colonel Elijah White and others had led remnants of the cavalry west, beyond the enemy screen, and W. P. Roberts, the boy cavalry general from North Carolina, had urged his staff to scatter; they were not included in the surrender.

Fitz Lee had an encounter with a Confederate infantryman on his road of escape, a veteran who was hurrying in the direction of the courthouse.

"Never mind, old man," Fitz said. "You're too late now. Lee has surrendered. You'd better go home."

"What's that, Lee surrendered?"

"Yes, that's right."

The soldier stared, tears filling his eyes, then blurted, "You can't make me believe Uncle Robert has surrendered. It must've been that goddam Fitzhugh Lee!"

Among the fugitives in the Lynchburg road west of Appomattox, was young James W. Albright, who had, the night before, burned his letters and diary. After an all-night march, he somehow resumed the diary entries:

> We halted in a complete trap. Saw the situation, and Captain Gregory and myself and *one* wagon—all that was left of the 12th Virginia Battalion that we could muster— marched for Lynchburg. . . . Lynchburg at 5 P.M. Heard the troops had surrendered. Told by officers to leave the guns, fill up with rations and go, if I didn't want to be caught.

William Graham, the Georgia private who had wandered from the army with his companions, ate breakfast with a family named Jimerson in the back country, and made an attempt to dispense justice:

"Mrs. J. tells us that we are welcome to anything she has but after we are finished eating she just wants the whole party to go back to the next house, the one just passed, Mixon's, and help ourselves to some of his flour and lard and meat—that he has a smoke house full of such things—and refuses to feed a single soldier—but pleads poverty and sends all comers to Mr. Jimerson's, a really poor man.

"Forbes and three others determine to go back and make the rascal disgorge. When they get there and make known their intention Mixon talks pretty independently at first and rather dares them to help themselves.

"Kelly, one of the men, thereupon gets a rail and very deliberately proceeds to batter open his smoke house door. When Mixon sees his determination he offers to open the door—but the lock had been injured by the blows from the rail and refused to be opened and to make a long story short Forbes relents and returns to us sans meat, sans flour, sans everything he went after. A more wishy washy enterprise never had a more ignominious end."

They were several miles on the main road west when these men were overtaken by Confederate cavalry, who hailed them, "Throw away your guns, boys. You'll not need 'em now. Lee's surrendered the army."

Graham wrote: "Of course we consider it a hoax at first, but when party after party pass us unarmed repeating the same story—we are bound to believe it. Presently a general comes along and corroborates the statements of the others."

The party of four separated, two of them going toward Petersburg, and Graham with one companion turning south. They heard one final sound from the armies back at the courthouse village:

"This evening we hear the booming of the cannon, the Yankees are firing a salute."

John L. G. Woods, the drummerboy of the 53rd Georgia, had slept in a camp of strange cavalrymen on the Lynchburg road:

"I never slept more soundly in my life and didn't wake up next morning until the sun was about two hours high. To my utter surprise not a soul did I see anywhere. The cavalry, my horse, and all were gone.

"I had tied my horse securely and as close to me as possible, yet he was gone. I felt cheap, sad and lonely. Resuming my tramp on to Lynchburg, I entered the city about noon."

There were few final details to be attended at Robert Lee's headquarters in the evening. The ordnance department reported that it had a large amount of U. S. currency, and asked what should be done with it. Lee sent the problem to Longstreet, who wrote:

"As it was not known or included in the conditions of capitulation, and was due (ten times more) to the faithful troops, I suggested a pro rata distribution of it. The officer afterwards brought $300 as my part. I took $100 and asked to have the balance distributed among Field's division—the troops most distant from their homes."

Colonel Charles Marshall saw Lee once more this night:

"General Lee sat with several of us at a fire in front of his tent, and after some conversation about the army and the events of the day in which his feelings towards his men were strongly expressed, he told me to prepare an order to his troops."

Private Frank Mixson and others of his regiment were ordered to camp:

"That evening we were taken into the oak grove and put in the Bull Pen, as we called it. This was only going into bivouac with a guard around us, but not a Yankee guard . . . our own men for guards."

They were not allowed out of their lines, nor were the curious Federals permitted to enter: "But they hung around and seemed surprised that they had such a hard time in overwhelming such a crowd of ragamuffins."

These South Carolinians stumbled upon a treasure—a barn filled with corn inside their prison pen. "We were soon scrambling for this and men could be seen going in all directions with

an armful of this corn. It looked exactly like each man was going
to feed a horse. . . . We now filled up on our parched corn, and
by good dark everybody seemed to be asleep. The first sleep we
had had for seven days and nights, since we left Richmond."

Somewhere nearby a North Carolina soldier mourned:
"Damn me if I ever love another country."

From Danville to the west, Jefferson Davis hopefully sent
Robert Lee a telegraph message during the day:

> . . . I had hoped to have seen you at an earlier period,
> and trust soon to meet you. The Secretary of War, Quarter-
> master General, Commissary General and Chief Engineer
> have not arrived. Their absence is embarrassing. We have
> here provisions and clothing for your army and they are
> held for its use.
>
> You will realize the reluctance I feel to leave the soil
> of Virginia and appreciate my anxiety to win success North
> of the Roanoke. The few stragglers who came from your
> army are stopped here and at Staunton Bridge. They are,
> generally, however, without arms. . . . I hope soon to hear
> from you at this point, where offices have been opened to
> keep up the current business until more definite knowledge
> would enable us to form more permanent plans. May God
> preserve, sustain and guide you.

★ **BLUE** ★

OLD GEORGE MEADE's ailment was miraculously cured.
His headquarters party lounged about his ambulance until
almost 5 P.M., with a few rumors circulating among them, but uncertainty still in the air. General Humphreys amused the younger
officers; he had found a barrel of Confederate money in some

captured wagons, and passed it about. Colonel Lyman wrote:

"It was a strange spectacle, to see the officers laughing and giving each other $500 notes of a government that has been considered as firmly established by our English friends!"

The news came soon thereafter. Charles Pease rode in shouting, "He's surrendered!"

Generals led the staff in cheers, three for the army, and then three for Meade. One general dashed off to take the news to the 2nd and 6th Corps, in adjoining camps. Lyman sketched the scene:

"The soldiers rushed, perfectly crazy, to the roadside, and there crowding in dense masses, shouted, screamed, yelled, threw up their hats and hopped madly up and down! The batteries were run out and began firing, the bands played, the flags waved. The noise of the cheering was such that my very ears rang. And there was General Meade galloping about and waving his cap with the best of them!

"Poor old Robert Lee! His punishment is too heavy—to hear those cheers, and to remember what he once was! God willing, before many weeks, or even days, I shall be at home, to campaign no more!"

U. S. Grant lost none of his calm, but he forgot himself, and was well along the road toward his camp before an officer jogged his memory:

"General, hadn't you better notify Washington of the surrender?"

Grant dismounted and on a roadside bank wrote a telegram:

Headquarters Appomattox C.H. Va.
April 9th, 1865, 4:30 P.M.
Hon. E. M. Stanton, Secretary of War,
Washington

General Lee surrendered the Army of Northern Virginia this afternoon on terms proposed by myself. The accompanying additional correspondence will show the conditions fully.

U. S. Grant,
Lieut.-General.

When the party reached the commander's tent, officers took chairs nearby, anxious to hear his comments on Lee, the South and the end of the war. Grant settled in comfort and turned to Rufus Ingalls, asking him if he remembered an old white mule one of their friends had ridden in the Mexican War.

"Why, perfectly," Ingalls said, and Grant was off on a long reminiscence about army life in Mexico, and said nothing of the war he had ended during the day. It was after supper before he mentioned Lee or the Confederacy, and then was disappointing to Horace Porter and his companions. Grant said merely that he thought other Rebels would follow Lee's example, and quit fighting. He surprised all of them with an announcement:

"I'm going on to Washington tomorrow."

When the others had gone, and Grant was alone in his tent with Adam Badeau, he became talkative. Badeau wrote:

"I had been used to sit up with him late into the night, to write his letters or keep him company, for he could not sleep early. Then he always talked with greater freedom than at any other time. This night we spoke of the terms he had granted Lee. There were some of his officers who disliked the idea of paroles, and thought at least the highest of the rebels should have been differently dealt with—held for trial.

"This was not my feeling, and I spoke of the effect his magnanimity was sure to have upon the country and the world. He was not averse to listen."

At the end Grant said quietly, "I'll keep the terms, no matter who's opposed. But Lincoln is sure to be on my side."

Grant had shown one sign of firmness with his troops in the evening: When the guns began firing salutes amid wild cheering, he had them stopped. "The Confederates were now our prisoners, and we did not want to exult over their downfall."

Cadwallader played a final joke on Orville Babcock in the evening. The reporter found Babcock pompous in his flourishing of a pencil he had from Robert Lee as a souvenir in the morning; the colonel showed it to everyone who came along, announcing it as his only trophy of four years of war. Cadwallader wrote:

"The staff were badgering him about it till night, wanting to buy it, to trade for it, and making him all manner of extravagant offers for it, and proposing every ludicrous exchange for it their waggish propensities could think of, ranging from broken jack knives to a fine-tooth comb."

The reporter at last persuaded Babcock to let him cut off a small piece of the pencil for himself.

"Just one inch, now. Promise you won't take a whit more, or you can't have it."

Cadwallader made a solemn promise, and then took off his inch from the point, returning to Babcock the butt end of his ruined souvenir. The staff howled with laughter.

Rain began in the night, softly at first, then drumming hard on the ancient tavern and courthouse of the village, and the tents and wagons and thickets where the armies lay.

★ RICHMOND ★

Judith Brockenbrough McGuire wanted to pay another visit to Mrs. Robert E. Lee in the Franklin Street house, but "had no heart to go."

She heard from friends of the invalid Mary's incredible persistence, even when she had been told of the surrender at Appomattox:

"General Lee is not the Confederacy. There is life in the old land yet."

John Beauchamp Jones went to church this Palm Sunday, where he noted that the prayer for the President of the United States was omitted, as had been agreed with the Federal authorities. In the afternoon his pastor, The Rev. Mr. Dashiell, called on Jones.

The weather was bright and beautiful in the city and many people were in the streets. Jones wrote:

> Confederate money is valueless, and we have no Federal money. To such extremity are some of the best and wealthiest families reduced, that the ladies are daily engaged in making pies and cakes for the Yankee soldiers of all colors, that they may obtain enough greenbacks to purchase such articles as are daily required in their housekeeping.

At 10 P.M. big guns from forts across the James jarred the city. The Federals fired one hundred guns before it was over—a gigantic salute. Bands seemed to spring from everywhere, blaring over the water when the echoes of the artillery died. Jones was mystified until he asked the guard patrolling before his house:

"A dispatch from Grant," the soldier said, "announcing the surrender of Lee."

Phoebe Pember saw growing distress among the city's people on her forays from the hospital:

"Strange exchanges were made on the streets of tea, coffee, flour, and bacon. Those who were fortunate in having a stock of household necessaries were generous in the extreme to their less wealthy neighbors, but the destitution was terrible. The Sanitary Commission shops were opened, and commissioners were appointed by the Federals to visit the people and . . . draw rations, but to effect this after receiving tickets required so many appeals to different officials, that decent people soon gave up the effort.

"Besides, the musty cornmeal and strong codfish were not appreciated by fastidious stomachs—few gentle natures could relish such unfamiliar food."

The Federal surgeons overcame Phoebe at last; they moved her Confederate patients to a smaller hospital and took over Chimborazo for the Union army. The ladies of her new neighborhood helped by bringing meager supplies from their homes. Within a few days Phoebe had worked herself out of a job, for the last of her invalids was well enough to walk—or had died.

She had no way to draw rations, and found herself with

nothing but a box of useless Confederate money and a silver ten-cent piece. She made a final purchase: A box of matches and five cocoanut cakes. In the morning she discovered that kind neighbors had left some food at her door.

Sallie Brock Putnam, like many women of the city, had overcome her fears since the start of occupation, and could now speak with asperity of Richmond businessmen who had fleeced the public.

She had seen a woman friend on Franklin Street on last Monday, when the Yankees came in. The woman had carried a tiny vial of paregoric.

"I just bought this on Main Street at my old friend's drug-store," the indignant woman said. "The town is burning, and yet for this spoonful of medicine for a sick servant, I had to pay five dollars."

Sallie Putnam now took satisfaction in noting that the drug-store had been gutted by the fire. She wrote piously; "This incident points a moral which all can apply."

Sallie kept a close eye on the lone newspaper, the Yankee-toned *Whig,* and noticed that within a week civilians in the city had drawn almost 18,000 ration tickets from Federal headquarters. At least a third of Richmond's people, she calculated, "were driven to the humiliation of subsisting alone on supplies of food furnished them by the conquerors."

This food, "of the coarsest and most substantial kind," was taken gratefully by most of Richmond's hungry, but the loyal Sallie concluded that most of them ate with "sickened hearts."

Cornelia Hancock, a Federal nurse, entered the city during the day. She left her hospital at City Point during idle hours, since patients had been shipped to Washington to prepare for an expected tide of casualties after Lee's surrender.

They took horses on the river steamer and cruised in the sunshine:

"The lower part of the city was smoldering with the fire started by the rebels. The white people were all hidden in their houses, but the colored people were jubilant and on the streets in gay attire. We visited Libby Prison that was at this time filled with rebel prisoners. Flowers were blooming . . . beauty was apparent even in the desolate and dejected city."

Cornelia visited many places in the city, but was most impressed with the fact that General Weitzel actually had made quarters in the mansion of Jefferson Davis, and that "perfect order prevails."

After dark she was back at the hospital, and felt a strange loneliness: "After nightfall I walk up and down my long deserted stockade. I see the great change from war to no war, and brace myself for a new order of things."

★ MR. LINCOLN ★

THE *River Queen* entered the Potomac estuary in the early morning, beginning to labor as she fought the tide; for several hours her deck was swept with spray. Later, between narrowing banks, the steamer pushed smoothly upstream.

Stewards passed among the passengers, but refrained from offering champagne to Mr. Lincoln, as they had on the rough downward voyage. He had amused them with his reply:

"No, my young friend. I have seen many a man in my time, seasick ashore from drinking that very article."

Lincoln entertained his guests in the salon, and Senator Sumner, his cultivated adversary, was surprised by a Lincoln he had never seen.

Lincoln read to them for an hour or more from Shakespeare, especially from *Macbeth*. Count de Chambrun thought the speech of Macbeth after the murder of Duncan especially dramatic in Lincoln's quiet reading. The Frenchman wrote:

"Now and then he paused to expatiate on how exact a picture Shakespeare here gives of a murderer's mind when, the dark deed achieved, its perpetrator already envies his victim's calm sleep. He read the scene over twice."

The President left an indelible memory with de Chambrun and Sumner in particular as he repeated the lines with an obvious familiarity:

> "Duncan is in his grave;
>   After life's fitful fever he sleeps well;
>   Treason has done his worst: nor steel, nor poison,
>   Malice domestic, foreign levy, nothing
>   Can touch him further."

Lincoln recited from other works—poetry, too. He droned a few verses of Longfellow's *Resignation:*

> ". . . The air is full of farewells to the dying,
>   And mournings for the dead . . .
>   We see but dimly through the mists and vapors;
>   Amid these earthly damps
>   What seem to us but sad funeral tapers
>   May be heaven's distant lamps."

As the afternoon wore on and the boat made a great turn of the river, Mount Vernon came into sight. Adolphe de Chambrun was stirred. He turned to Lincoln.

"Mount Vernon, with all its memories of Washington, will be no more honored in America than your own home in Springfield."

Lincoln broke his gaze at Mount Vernon's hill "as though awakened from a trance" and said, "Springfield! How glad I'll be to get back there—peace and tranquillity."

The party was soon at the dock in Washington. Sumner, de Chambrun and the Lincoln party rode in the Presidential carriage.

As they rolled toward Washington, Mrs. Lincoln broke her silence, looking ahead:

"That city is full of enemies!"

Lincoln turned with what de Chambrun thought "an impatient gesture" and spoke to her:

"Enemies! Never again must we repeat that word."

William Crook, the bodyguard, wrote of the approach to the city:

"When the carriage left the wharf the streets were alive with people, all very much excited. There were bonfires everywhere. . . . We halted the carriage and asked a bystander, 'What has happened?'

"He looked at us in amazement, not recognizing Mr. Lincoln.

" 'Why, where have you been? Lee has surrendered.' "

★ ACKNOWLEDGMENTS ★

I am indebted to Scott Hart of Washington, D.C., who proposed this book; to Ralph Newman of Chicago, who gave it a title; and to Richard B. Harwell of Chicago, who so expertly advised me on sources.

Among many others who aided and to whom I owe much:

Irene Hester of the Greensboro Public Library, who patiently conducted a year-long, nationwide search for source books; Ray D. Smith of Chicago, whose index to *Confederate Veteran* magazine brought to light many personal narratives; Philip Van Doren Stern and Ishbel Ross of New York, for generous assistance; North Callahan of New York and Colonel John M. Virden of Washington for stimulation, support and advice.

To researchers and typists, Mrs. Ruth Laughlin, Mary Anne Bass, and Mrs. Martha Montague, of Greensboro, and to Mrs. Minnie Ransom Norris of Raleigh, North Carolina.

To Jay Monaghan of Santa Barbara, California; Mrs. Margaret B. Price of the North Carolina State Library; Mrs. Marjorie Memory and Miss Marjorie Hood of the Woman's College Library, University of North Carolina; the libraries of Duke University and the University of North Carolina at Chapel Hill, and William Howell of Greensboro, for a variety of kindnesses.

To Joseph M. Hunt, Jr., Emily and Richardson Preyer, Earl Causey, Eve and Floyd Craft, George and Martha Moore, for indispensable friendship.

And to Carl O. Jeffress and Miles H. Wolff of the Greensboro *Daily News*, and to my wife and children.

Greensboro, North Carolina
September 25, 1958   BURKE DAVIS

★ BIBLIOGRAPHY ★

This informal history of the Appomattox campaign is woven from more than two hundred eyewitness accounts. Though bolstered by documents, the stories of the men and women, chiefly from journals, reports and memoirs, are paramount. This is less a military history than a tale of human beings under stress. The narrative does not halt to examine minor conflicts in testimony, nor to explore points of controversy.

The accounts are chosen from many hundreds, chiefly from published sources, though many are obscure. No previous attempt has been made to collect and compress these into a narrative.

Since most of the eyewitness accounts come from a single source in each individual case, and since most of them run in tiny threads throughout this book, the work has not been burdened with footnotes, which would have been unavoidably repetitious.

This unorthodox bibliography lists the chief characters of the book alphabetically, in two groups—Confederate and Federal—and cites major sources. Page references are used only in the case of magazines and other periodicals.

CONFEDERATE

Albright, J. A.: *Diary.* Southern Historical Collection, Louis R. Wilson Library, University of North Carolina, Chapel Hill, N. C.

Alexander, E. P.: *Military Memoirs of a Confederate,* by E. P. Alexander. New York, 1907.

Banister, Anne (Anne Banister Pryor): *Confederate Veteran,* 1931, p. 54.

Blackford, W. W.: *War Years with Jeb Stuart.* New York, 1945.

Blakey, C. G.: *Confederate Veteran,* 1931, p. 198.

Bouldin, John E.: *Confederate Veteran,* 1914, p. 557; *Southern Historical Society Papers* (hereafter *SHSP*), Vol. 36, p. 13.

Boykin, Edward M.: *The Falling Flag,* by E. M. Boykin. New York, 1874.

Bradwell, I. G.: *Confederate Veteran*, 1915, p. 21.

Breckinridge, John C.: *Recollections of a Naval Officer*, by W. H. Parker. New York, 1883.

Brunson, William: *Lee's Sharpshooters*, by W. S. Dunlop. Little Rock, 1899.

Caldwell, J. F. J.: *History of a Brigade of South Carolinians Known First as "Gregg's" and Subsequently as "McGowan's Brigade."* Philadelphia, 1866.

Campbell, John A.: *Recollections of the Evacuation of Richmond*, by J. A. Campbell. Baltimore, 1880.

Cary, Constance: *Recollections Grave and Gay*, by Constance Cary Harrison. Richmond, 1911.

Claiborne, Dr. John H.: *War Talks of Confederate Veterans*, by G. S. Bernard. Petersburg, Va., 1892; *Seventy-Five Years in Old Virginia*, by J. H. Claiborne. New York, 1904.

Collier, Charles F.: *SHSP*, Vol. 22, p. 69.

Colston, Fred M.: *Confederate Veteran*, 1908, p. 227; *SHSP*, Vol. 38, p. 1.

Conerly, Buxton: *Confederate Veteran*, 1907, p. 505.

Cooke, John Esten: *Life of General Robert E. Lee*, by J. E. Cooke. New York, 1871.

Cumming, J. D.: *SHSP*, Vol. 36, p. 262.

Davis, Jefferson: *Jefferson Davis, a Memoir by His Wife*, Vol. 2. New York, 1890; *Century Magazine*, Nov., 1893, p. 130; *Flight into Oblivion*, by A. J. Hanna. Richmond, 1938; *The Rise and Fall of the Confederate Government*, Vol. 2, by Jefferson Davis. New York, 1881; *Jefferson Davis, Constitutionalist*, edited by Dunbar Rowland. Jackson, Miss., 1923.

Davis, Varina H.: *Recollections of a Rebel Reefer*, by James M. Morgan. Boston, 1917; *Belles, Beaux and Brains of the Sixties*, by T. C. DeLeon. New York, 1907; *First Lady of The South*, by Ishbel Ross. New York, 1958.

Dearing, James: *History of the Laurel Brigade*, by W. N. McDonald. Baltimore, 1907.

DeLeon, T. C.: *Four Years in Rebel Capitals*. Mobile, 1890; and *Belles, Beaux and Brains of the Sixties*, by T. C. DeLeon. New York, 1907.

Devereux, Thomas P.: *T. P. Devereux Papers*. Southern Historical Collection, Louis R. Wilson Library, University of North Carolina, Chapel Hill, N. C.

Doswell, R. M.: *Confederate Veteran*, 1915, p. 404.

Douglas, Henry K.: *I Rode with Stonewall*, by H. K. Douglas. Chapel Hill, N. C., 1940.

Duke, R. T. W.: *SHSP*, Vol. 25, p. 136.

Dunlop, W. S.: *Lee's Sharpshooters*, by W. S. Dunlop. Little Rock, 1899.

Dwight, Charles S.: *A South Carolina Rebel's Recollections*. Columbia, S. C., 1917.

Ewell, Richard S.: *SHSP*, Vol. 12, p. 247; *Battles and Leaders of the Civil War* (hereafter *B&L*), Vol. 4, p. 721.

Field, Charles W.: *SHSP*, Vol. 14, p. 560.

French, Marcellus: *Confederate Veteran*, Vol. 8, p. 258.

Garrison, A. A., *Confederate Veteran*, 1908, p. 514.

Gary, Martin: *The Falling Flag*, by E. M. Boykin. New York, 1874; *War Years with Jeb Stuart*, by W. W. Blackford. New York, 1945.

Gerald, S. S.: *Confederate Veteran*, 1910, p. 432.

The "girl in the Arlington": *A Virginia Girl in the Civil War*, by M. L. Avary. New York, 1903.

Gordon, John B.: *Reminiscences of the Civil War*, by J. B. Gordon. New York, 1903; *Campfires of the Confederacy*, by Benjamin LaBree. Louisville, 1899.

Gorgas, Amelia: *Confederate Veteran*, 1917, p. 110.

Gorgas, Josiah: *The Civil War Diary of General Josiah Gorgas*. University of Alabama, 1947.

Gorman, J. C.: *Lee's Last Campaign*, by J. C. Gorman. Raleigh, N. C., 1866.

Graham, William: *A Confederate Diary of the Retreat from Petersburg*, edited by R. B. Harwell. Emory University Library, 1953.

Grimes, Bryan: *SHSP*, Vol. 27, p. 93.

Harris, John: *Confederate Veteran*, 1904, p. 170.

Haskell, Alexander Cheves: *Alexander C. Haskell*, by Louise Haskell Daly. Norwood, Mass., 1934.

Haw, Joseph: *Confederate Veteran*, 1926, p. 450.

Hawes, Percy: *Confederate Veteran*, 1919, p. 341.

Hill, Ambrose P.: *SHSP*, Vol. 11, p. 564 (Sergeant G. W. Tucker); *SHSP*, Vol. 19, p. 183 (G. P. Hill); *SHSP*, Vol. 12, p. 184 (Percy Hawes); *SHSP*, Vol. 20, p. 349 (John W. Mauk); *A. P. Hill*, by W. W. Hassler. Richmond, 1957.

Howard, McHenry: *SHSP*, Vol. 31, p. 131.

Irvine, H. R.: *Confederate Veteran*, 1926, p. 383.

Jefferson, George: *Confederate Veteran*, 1931, p. 206.

Jones, A. C.: *Confederate Veteran*, 1915, p. 314.

Jones, A. K.: *SHSP*, Vol. 31, p. 56.

Jones, J. B.: *A Rebel War Clerk's Diary*, Vol. 2. Philadelphia, 1866.

Jones, Thomas G.: *SHSP*, Vol. 21, p. 96.

Kershaw, Joseph B.: *SHSP*, Vol. 12, p. 252.

Lamkin, James N.: *Confederate Veteran*, 1926, p. 383.

Lee, Fitzhugh: *General Lee*, by Fitzhugh Lee. New York, 1894 (*See also* Munford, T. T.).

Lee, George T.: *South Atlantic Quarterly*, July, 1927, p. 238.

Lee, G. W. Custis: *SHSP*, Vol. 31, p. 131; *SHSP*, Vol. 12, p. 254.

Lee, Mary: *General Lee*, by Fitzhugh Lee. New York, 1894; *Confederate Veteran*, 1919, p. 341; *Diary of a Southern Refugee*, by Judith B. McGuire. New York, 1868.

Lee, Robert E.: *Military Memoirs of a Confederate*, by E. P. Alexander. New York, 1907; *A Life of General R. E. Lee*, by J. E. Cooke. New York, 1871; *The End of an Era*, by John S. Wise. Boston, 1899; *Memoirs of R. E. Lee*, by A. L. Long. New York, 1886; *My Confederate Girlhood*, by Kate C. Logan. Richmond, 1932; *From Manassas to Appomattox*, by James Longstreet. New York, 1898; *Reminiscences*, by John B. Gordon. New York, 1903; *Personal Memoirs*, by U. S. Grant. New York, 1886; *An Aide-de-Camp of Lee*, by Charles Marshall, edited by Frederick Maurice. Boston, 1927; *General Lee*, by Walter Taylor. Norfolk, Va., 1906; *Four Years with General Lee*, by Walter Taylor. New York, 1877; *Reminiscences of a Private*, by Frank M. Mixson. Columbia, S. C., 1910; *General Lee*, by Fitzhugh Lee. New York, 1894; *Recollections and Letters of Robert E. Lee*, by R. E. Lee, Jr. New York, 1904.

Lee, W. H. F. (Rooney): *The Education of Henry Adams*, by Henry Adams. Boston, 1918.

Long, Armistead L.: *Memoirs of Robert E. Lee*, by A. L. Long. New York, 1886.

Longstreet, James: *From Manassas to Appomattox*, by James Longstreet. New York, 1898.

McCabe, Gordon: *Memories and Memorials of William Gordon McCabe*, by Armistead C. Gordon, Vol. 1. Richmond, 1925.

McGuire, Judith Brockenbrough: *Diary of a Southern Refugee*, by J. B. McGuire. New York, 1868.

Mahone, William: *From Manassas to Appomattox*, by James Longstreet; *War Talks of Confederate Veterans*, by George S. Bernard.

Mallory, Stephen: *Recollections of a Naval Officer*, by W. H. Parker. New York, 1883.

Marshall, Charles: *SHSP*, Vol. 21, p. 353; *An Aide-de-Camp of Lee*, by Chares Marshall, edited by Frederick Maurice. Boston, 1927.

Massie, Fletcher: *SHSP*, Vol. 13, p. 247.

Mayo, Joseph: *The Capture and Occupation of Richmond*, by George A. Bruce, n.d., n.p.; *A Southern Woman's Story*, by Phoebe Yates Pember. New York, 1879.

Mixson, Frank M.: *Reminiscences of a Private,* by F. M. Mixson. Columbia, S. C., 1910.

Morgan, James Morris: *Recollections of a Rebel Reefer,* by James M. Morgan. Boston, 1917.

Munford, Thomas T.: Manuscript, *History of The Battle of Five Forks,* by T. T. Munford, in Duke University Library, Manuscripts Division (details of the celebrated "shad bake" at Five Forks involve Fitz Lee, Thomas Rosser, and Munford); *Life of Lt. Gen. Richard Heron Anderson,* by C. Irvine Walker. Charleston, S. C., 1917.

Myers, Frank M.: *The Comanches,* by F. M. Myers. Baltimore, 1871.

Osborne, Hampden: *Confederate Veteran,* 1917, p. 226.

Owen, William: *In Camp and Battle with the Washington Artillery of New Orleans,* by W. Owen. Boston, 1885.

Packard, Joseph: *Confederate Veteran,* 1908, p. 227.

Parker, William H.: *Recollections of a Naval Officer,* by W. H. Parker. New York, 1883.

Pegram, William: *Memories and Memorials of William Gordon Mc-Cabe,* Vol. 1, by A. C. Gordon. Richmond, 1925; *Ham Chamberlayne, Virginian,* edited by C. G. Chamberlayne. Richmond, 1933; *SHSP,* Vol. 14, p. 18.

Pember, Phoebe Yates: *A Southern Woman's Story.* New York, 1879.

Pendleton, William N.: *Memoirs of William Nelson Pendleton,* by Susan P. Lee. Philadelphia, 1893.

Peyton, Henry: *War Talks of Confederate Veterans,* by George S. Bernard. Petersburg, Va., 1892.

Pickett, George E.: *Pickett's Men,* by Walter Harrison. New York, 1870 (*See also* Munford, T. T.).

Powell, W. C.: *Confederate Veteran,* 1904, p. 592; 1906, p. 383.

Putnam, Sallie Brock: *Richmond During the War,* by Sallie B. Putnam. New York, 1867.

Ransom, Matt: *Histories of the Several Regiments and Battalions from North Carolina in the Great War,* edited by Walter Clark, Vol. 2, p. 289. Raleigh, N. C., 1901.

Reagan, John: *Memoirs.* New York, 1906.

Robinson, W. F.: *Confederate Veteran,* 1924, p. 470.

Rosser, Thomas: Letters. *Philadelphia Weekly Times,* April 5, 1885, and April 29, 1902 (*See also* Munford, T. T.).

Semmes, Raphael: *Memoirs of Service Afloat During the War Between the States,* by R. Semmes. Baltimore, 1869.

Stiles, Robert: *Four Years Under Marse Robert,* by R. Stiles. Washington, 1903.

Sulivane, Clement: *B&L,* Vol. 4, p. 725.

Talcott, T. M. R.: *SHSP*, Vol. 32, p. 67.

Taylor, Walter: *Four Years with General Lee*. New York, 1877; *General Lee*. Norfolk, Va., 1906. Both by W. Taylor.

Thompson, Magnus: *Confederate Veteran*, 1921, p. 302.

Timberlake, W. S.: *Confederate Veteran*, 1912, p. 119.

Tomlinson, A. R.: Confederate Veteran, 1922, p. 141.

Tucker, G. W.: *SHSP*, Vol. 11, p. 564.

Tucker, Commodore John R.: *Four Years Under Marse Robert*, by Robert Stiles; *Confederate Veteran*, 1912, p. 119.

Venable, M. W.: *Confederate Veteran*, 1924, p. 303.

Walker, Fannie: *Confederate Veteran*, 1905, p. 305.

Watehall, E. T.: *Confederate Veteran*, 1909, p. 215.

Wharton, H. M.: *War Songs & Poems of the Confederacy*, by H. M. Wharton. 1904. N.P.

White, Elijah: *Confederate Veteran*, 1921, p. 302; *History of the Laurel Brigade*, by W. N. McDonald. Baltimore, 1907.

White, W. S.: *SHSP*, Vol. 11, p. 552.

Wilcox, Cadmus M.: *SHSP*, Vol. 4, p. 30.

Wise, Henry A.: *SHSP*, p. 18.

Wise, John: *End of an Era*. Boston, 1899.

Wood, H. E.: *Confederate Veteran*, 1908, p. 397.

Woods, John L. G.: *Confederate Veteran*, 1919, p. 140.

Wood, John Taylor: *Diary*, p. 1, Section 3. Southern Historical Collection, Louis R. Wilson Library, University of North Carolina, Chapel Hill, N. C.

FEDERAL

Adams, Charles Francis: *A Cycle of Adams Letters*, Vol. 2, edited by W. C. Ford. Boston, 1920; *Autobiography*, by C. F. Adams. Boston, 1916.

Badeau, Adam: *Grant in Peace*, by A. Badeau. Dayton, O., 1887.

Bruce, George: *The Capture and Occupation of Richmond*, by G. Bruce. n.d.; n.p.

Cadwallader, Sylvanus: *Three Years with Grant*, by S. Cadwallader. New York, 1955.

Chamberlain, Joshua: *SHSP*, Vol. 32, p. 355; *Passing of the Armies*, by J. Chamberlain. New York, 1915.

Coffin, Charles C.: *The Boys of '61*, by C. C. Coffin. Boston, 1896.

Crook, W. H.: *Harper's Magazine*, Sept., 1909, p. 532.

Custer, George A.: *From Manassas to Appomattox*, by James Longstreet. New York, 1898; *Reminiscences of the Civil War*, by J. B.

Gordon. New York, 1903; *Confederate Veteran*, 1908, p. 227; *Military Memoirs of a Confederate*, by E. P. Alexander. New York, 1907; *In Camp and Battle with the Washington Artillery of New Orleans*, by William Owen. Boston, 1885.

de Chambrun, Adolphe: *Impressions of Lincoln and the Civil War*, by A. de Chambrun. New York, 1952.

Edwards, Oliver: *SHSP*, Vol. 25, p. 136.

Forsyth, George A.: *Harper's Magazine*, April, 1898, p. 704.

Grant, U. S.: *Personal Memoirs of U. S. Grant*, Vol. 2. New York, 1887; *Grant in Peace*, by Adam Badeau. Dayton, O., 1887; *Three Years with Grant*, by Sylvanus Cadwallader. New York, 1955; *Campaigning with Grant*, by Horace Porter. New York, 1907; *Sunset of the Confederacy*, by Morris Schaff. Boston, 1912; *The Passing of the Armies*, by J. L. Chamberlain (*See also SHSP*, Vol. 32, p. 355); *B&L*, Vol. 4, p. 708.

Graves, T. Thatcher: *B&L*, Vol. 4, p. 726.

Hancock, Cornelia: *The South after Gettysburg*, by C. Hancock. Edited by Henrietta Jaquette. Philadelphia, 1937.

Humphreys, A. A.: *The Virginia Campaign of 1864 and 1865*, by A. A. Humphreys. New York, 1883.

Keckley, Elizabeth: *Behind the Scenes*, by E. Keckley. New York, 1868.

Keifer, Warren, *B&L*, Vol. 4, p. 721.

Lincoln, Abraham: *The Death of Lincoln*, by Clara E. Laughlin. New York, 1909; *Behind the Scenes*, by Elizabeth Keckley. New York, 1868; *Impressions of Lincoln and the Civil War*, by Adolphe de Chambrun. New York, 1952; *Charles Sumner*, by George H. Haynes. Philadelphia, 1909; *The Collected Works of Abraham Lincoln*, edited by Roy P. Basler. New Brunswick, N. J., 1953; *Lincoln and the Doctors*, by M. H. Shute. New York, 1933; *Campaigning with Grant*, by Horace Porter. New York, 1907; *Memoires of the White House*, by W. H. Crook. Boston, 1911; *Incidents and Anecdotes of the Civil War*. New York, 1885; and *Naval History of the Civil War*, by David D. Porter.

Lincoln, Mary: *Life of Lincoln*, by Ida M. Tarbell, Vol. 2. New York, 1924; *Mary Lincoln, Biography of a Marriage*, by Ruth P. Randall. Boston, 1953; *Behind the Scenes*, by Elizabeth Keckley. New York, 1868.

Lyman, Theodore: *Meade's Headquarters*, edited by George R. Agassiz. Boston, 1922.

Mauk, John W.: *See* A. P. Hill.

Meade, George Gordon: *Meade's Headquarters*, edited by George R. Agassiz. Boston, 1922.

Parker, Ely S.: *The Life of General Ely S. Parker*, by Arthur C. Parker. Buffalo, N. Y., 1919.

Porter, David D.: *Incidents and Anecdotes of the Civil War*. New York, 1885; and *Naval History of the Civil War*, by D. D. Porter.

Porter, Horace: *B&L*, Vol. 4, p. 708; *Campaigning with Grant*, by H. Porter. New York, 1907.

Ripley, E. H.: *SHSP*, Vol. 32, p. 73.

Schaff, Morris: *Sunset of the Confederacy*, by M. Schaff. Boston, 1912.

Sheridan, Philip H.: *Personal Memoirs of Philip Henry Sheridan*, by Michael V. Sheridan. New York, 1902; *Sheridan: A Military Narrative*, by Joseph Hergesheimer. Boston, 1931; *Harper's Magazine*, April, 1898, p. 700.

Townsend, George A.: *Rustics in Rebellion*, by G. A. Townsend. Chapel Hill, N. C., 1950.

Warren, Gouverneur K.: *B&L*, Vol. 4, p. 722.

Williams, Seth: *SHSP*, Vol. 20, p. 56; *Confederate Veteran*, Vol. 8, p. 258.

Other Sources Consulted:

GENERAL

Divided We Fought: a Pictorial History of the War, 1861-1865, edited by David Donald. New York, 1952.

The Life of Johnny Reb, by Bell I. Wiley. New York, 1943.

The Long Arm of Lee, Vol. 2, by Jennings C. Wise. Lynchburg, Va., 1915.

Mathew Brady: Historian with a Camera, by James D. Horan. New York, 1955.

The Negro in the Civil War, by Benjamin Quarles. Boston, 1953.

The North Reports the Civil War, by J. Cutler Andrews. Pittsburgh, 1955.

Numbers and Losses in the Civil War, by Thomas L. Livermore. Boston, 1900.

Photographic History of the Civil War, edited by F. T. Miller. 10 Vols. New York, 1911.

The Rebellion Record: a Diary of American Events, edited by Frank Moore. 12 Vols. New York, 1868.

The Sable Arm: Negro Troops in the Union Army, 1861-1865, by Dudley T. Cornish. New York, 1956.

War of the Rebellion: A Compilation of the Official Records of the Union and Confederate Armies. Washington, 1902.

BIOGRAPHY, MEMOIR, ETC.

Abraham Lincoln, by Benjamin Thomas. New York, 1952.

Abraham Lincoln, the Last Full Measure, by J. G. Randall and Richard N. Current. New York, 1956.

Abraham Lincoln: The War Years, by Carl Sandburg. New York, 1939.

The Beleaguered City, by Alfred Hoyt Bill. New York, 1946.

A Belle of the Fifties, by Virginia Clay-Clopton. New York, 1904.

Campfires of the Confederacy, by Benjamin LaBree. Louisville, 1898.

The Collapse of the Confederacy, by Lawrence H. Gipson. Cedar Rapids, 1918.

The Collapse of the Confederacy, by Charles S. Wesley. Washington, 1937.

The Coming of the Civil War, by Avery Craven. Chicago, 1942.

A Confederate Surgeon's Letters to His Wife, by Spencer G. Welch. Washington, 1911.

Gouverneur Kemble Warren: the Life and Letters of an American Soldier, by Emerson G. Taylor. Boston, 1932.

The Harrisons of Skimino, by Burton Harrison. New York, 1910.

In the Days of My Father, General Grant, by Jesse Grant. New York, 1925.

Inside the Confederate Government, edited by Edward Younger. New York, 1957.

James Longstreet, by H. J. Eckenrode and Bryan Conrad. Chapel Hill, N. C., 1936.

John A. Campbell, by Henry G. Connor. Boston, 1920.

The Last Four Weeks of the War, by E. N. Hatcher. Columbia, S. C., 1891.

The Last Hours of Sheridan's Cavalry, by H. E. Tremain. New York, 1904.

The Last Year of the War, by E. A. Pollard. New York, 1866.

Lee and His Lieutenants, by E. A. Pollard. New York, 1867.

Lee's Confidential Dispatches to Davis, edited by D. S. Freeman. New York, 1919.

Lee's Lieutenants, Vol. 3, by D. S. Freeman. New York, 1944.

Letters of a War Correspondent, by Charles A. Page. Boston, 1897.

The Life and Letters of George Gordon Meade, by George Meade. 2 vols. New York, 1913.

The Life of John A. Rawlins, by J. H. Wilson. New York, 1916.

A Memoir of the Last Year of the War for Independence in the Confederate States of America, by Jubal A. Early. Augusta, Ga., 1867.

A Memoir of Robert M. T. Hunter, by Martha T. Hunter. Washington, 1903.

Music on the March, by Frank Rauscher. Philadelphia, 1892.

A Rebel's Recollections, by George C. Eggleston. New York, 1875.

Recollections of a Confederate Staff Officer, by G. Moxley. Washington, 1917.

Recollections of a Varied Life, by George C. Eggleston. New York, 1910.

Reminiscences, by Basil W. Duke. New York, 1911.

Reminiscences and Documents Relating to the Civil War During 1865, by John A. Campbell. Baltimore, 1887.

Reminiscences of a Rebel, by Wayland F. Dunaway. Washington, 1913.

A Reporter for Lincoln, by Ida Tarbell. New York, 1927.

St. Pauls Church, Vol. 1, by Elisabeth Weddell. Richmond, 1931.

The South to Posterity, by D. S. Freeman. New York, 1939.

Wearing of the Gray, by John E. Cooke. New York, 1867.

Women of the South in War Times, by Matthew P. Andrews. Baltimore, 1920.

NEWSPAPERS

Boston *Journal*
New York *Herald*
New York *Times*
New York *Tribune*
New York *World*
Petersburg *Index*
Richmond *Examiner*
Richmond *Times*
Richmond *Whig*

MAGAZINES

American Historical Review
Century
DeBow's Review
Harper's
Journal of Southern History
The Land We Love
McClure's
Mississippi Valley Historical Review
Scribner's
South Atlantic Quarterly

★ INDEX ★

2006-/1